PUBLIC SPEAKING
AS A
Liberal Art

PUBLIC SPEAKING
AS A
Liberal Art

FOURTH EDITION

John F. Wilson

*Herbert H. Lehman College of the
City University of New York*

Carroll C. Arnold

The Pennsylvania State University

ALLYN AND BACON, INC.
Boston · London · Sydney · Toronto

Copyright © 1978 by Allyn and Bacon, Inc.
Copyright © 1974, 1968, 1964 by Allyn and Bacon, Inc.
470 Atlantic Avenue, Boston, Massachusetts 02210

Library of Congress Cataloging in Publication Data

Wilson, John Fletcher, 1923–
    Public speaking as a liberal art.

    Includes bibliographical references and indexes.
    1. Public speaking.   I. Arnold, Carroll C., joint
author. II. Title.

PN4121.W46   1978   808.85′1   77-16508

ISBN 0-205-06108-7

CONTENTS

Preface

The fourth edition of *Public Speaking as a Liberal Art* is a substantial revision of the third. In response to questions and suggestions from users of the third edition we have extensively revised chapters 1, 3, 5, 9, and 11. All other chapters have been fully reconsidered and revised as research findings or the characteristics of illustrations required.

We continue to conceive of *public speech* as any continuing utterance that occurs in a rhetorical situation specially dependent on a single communicator. However, in this edition we have given additional attention to those situations in which individual speakers speak publicly in collaboration with colleagues, as when committees report and symposia are presented. Appendix B is offered as a realistic illustration of such classroom presentations. We hope it will also suggest ways in which practice in public speaking, speech criticism, and group problem solving can be combined to reinforce rhetorical training.

As we have held in previous editions of this book, we hold here to the view that understanding and reflection must precede informed practice in public speech. Such understanding undergirds all liberal education. In our view intelligent choice in speaking, which is an exercise of freedom, arises only from such liberal study. Hence, we prescribe minimally, considering the general problems of rhetorical invention, disposition, style, delivery, and memoria, as we lay before the student his or her options for resolving those problems in day-to-day situations. Our own experiences in classrooms have convinced us that Lloyd F. Bitzer's concept of "the rhetorical situation" furnishes the best conceptual base from which students can reason out and practice their best adaptations to the varying requirements of effective public speaking. In this edition we have accordingly given extra emphasis to this concept and its use from first to final chapters. Appendix A, "Rhetorical Theory: A Heritage," remains substantially as in the third edition. We hope it will serve teachers who wish their students to understand the cultural context out of which the textbook's counsels have grown. Perhaps, it can also serve as a personal resource for inexperienced teachers who are not familiar with the historical background of modern study of public communication.

For assistance in preparing this edition we express our thanks to our students in basic courses and to: Bie Arnold; Professor Joseph Aurbach, Herbert H. Lehman College, The City University of New York; Mary A. De Vries, Editorial Services; Professor Stephen E. Lucas, University of Wisconsin-Madison; Professor Michael M. Osborn, Memphis State University; Janice E. Peterson, University of California-Santa Barbara; Frank Ruggirello, Editor, Allyn and Bacon, Inc.; and Susan May Wilson.

John F. Wilson
Carroll C. Arnold

PUBLIC SPEAKING
AS A
Liberal Art

The Art of Public Speaking

We ought, therefore, to think of the art of discourse just as we think of the other arts, and not to form opposite judgments about similar things, nor show ourselves intolerant toward that power, which, of all the faculties which belong to the nature of man, is the source of most of our blessings. For in the other powers which we possess . . . we are in no respect superior to other living creatures; nay, we are inferior to many in swiftness and in strength and in other resources; but, because there has been implanted in us the power to persuade each other and to make clear to each other whatever we desire, not only have we escaped the life of the wild beasts, but we have come together and founded cities and made laws and invented arts; and generally speaking, there is no institution devised by man which the power of speech has not helped us to establish.

Isocrates, "Antidosis"[1]

For many centuries citizens of Western countries have thought of *public speaking* as oratory, as a kind of formal, stylized, inflated eloquence. You probably know from your own experience that this idea is still with us. Upon opening this book you may have expected to read about oratory. You may have thought we would provide you with recipes for eloquence or with formulas to help you pronounce words more clearly. If you want those things you can stop reading. If, on the other hand, you expect us to tell you some ways you may become a more confident, more influential, practical speaker before audiences, you should read on for we have some preliminary explanations and arguments you need to know.

In these pages we will be dealing with an art. This *art*, as a British author rightly said in discussing the famous Greek speaker Demosthenes, is "a development of the relation between [the speaker] . . . and his hearers."[2] A famous French writer put the matter of what an art is in substantially the same way when he said, "By 'art' I mean . . . the expression of significant relations between human beings, or between minds and things."[3] That is what this book is about: developing relations between yourself and others and between yourself and

1. From Isocrates, "Antidosis," trans. by George Norlin in *Isocrates* (Cambridge, Mass.: Harvard University Press, 1956), II, p. 327.

2. J. A. K. Thomson, *The Art of the Logos* (London: George Allen & Unwin, Ltd., 1935), p. 180.

3. André Malraux, "Sketch for a Psychology of the Moving Pictures," first published in the journal *Verve* 8 (1940): 69–73, and reprinted in Susanne K.

things outside yourself—through your capacity to speak. Formulas do not accomplish this kind of artistic relationship any more than playing music or painting by-the-numbers yields fine musicianship or quality works of art. What this book tells you is how to think about yourself in relation to ideas and other people. It tries to show you the *choices* you can make as you try to compose artistic, influential speech.

Do not let our talk about art dismay you. Speakers, writers, basketball players, chefs, engineers, journalists, parents, and virtually every other kind of person you can think of are in some sense artists, or they manage their tasks less expertly than they could. Their arts are often not thought of as arts because they are practical and useful and other arts such as music, painting, and dance are aesthetic. Public speaking is a utilitarian art. Its purpose is to achieve practical responses rather than to elicit admiration or vicarious pleasure.

To be an artist of any kind is to know yourself, other people, and especially the possibilities of the materials with which you work. Accordingly, we are going to consider the possibilities open to you in speaking publicly. Speaking publicly may or may not involve speaking to large audiences.

SPEECH AS A LIBERAL STUDY

Why do we call the art of speaking publicly a *liberal* art? Consider first the liberal or general or distribution elements of the curriculum you are following. From our point of view they are there to make you a freer, more adaptable person, through studying writing and literature, science and mathematics, history and sociology, and other general or liberal subjects. Of course, those subjects may give you immediately useful skills, too, but such studies also equip you to become your best self because they help you understand the entire world you live in. Still more important, such studies, commonly called the *liberal arts and sciences*, ought to help you to think as a free, whole human being, not just as someone equipped to fill some tiny niche in society.

The so-called liberal studies, at their best, teach you how to make inferences, how to think, concerning more matters than you consider your specialty. To take a very simple case: you could plan a house, solid and roomy, and that's all; or you could plan a solid, roomy house that would suit the real estate market (economics), would conform to the ordinances of the community in which it was to be built (politics and sociology), and would be attractive on the lot on which

Langer, ed., *Reflections on Art* (Baltimore: The Johns Hopkins Press, 1958), p. 326.

you hoped to place it (aesthetics). In the second case you would see house planning as more than a single specialty unassociated with social and aesthetic knowledge. If rightly studied, social and artistic knowledge gives backgrounds for, and guidelines to, specialized knowledge, *so decisions can be made to fit life as we live it*. This is what any study does if it liberalizes our ways of thinking and living, and it is precisely what an understanding of public communication does for anyone.

Making Decisions

We could enumerate a number of ways in which the art of public speech is a liberal art in the senses we have just described. But we will focus on only two, one general and one specific. There are two tasks no healthy, social person can avoid: making decisions and explaining or defending decisions.

How does studying the art of public speech help anyone learn decision making? How do decisions come about? We draw upon all the knowledge we have with respect to the issue we must decide. We weigh the choices we could make according to our knowledge. Finally, we choose a course of action, or a belief, or a position relative to the issue. Either before we make the final decision, or after making it, or sometimes at both points, we build a case that will justify our final choice. This process occurs everywhere. Whatever our tasks, we review information, consider options, choose, and argue with ourselves or others in defense of our choices.

The art of public speech is an art that invariably and inevitably involves you in choice making (1) on the basis of any kind of information you want to think about, and (2) in respect to what can and cannot work as communication. Every time you practice speaking in public you will practice and gain experience in surveying information, weighing options, making choices, and explaining or defending them (at least to yourself). The process of decision making is an integral part of the art of public speaking, as we will show you again and again in this book.

Public speech is also exercised in communicative argument and explanation—processes no social person can avoid using constantly. This is the specific way in which study and practice of public speaking is liberalizing and liberating. Every stage of creating and presenting public speech is an exercise in choice making of a specific sort: choosing among communicative options. Some years ago in a speech about speaking, Dean Everett Lee Hunt said,

An enlightened choice is a choice based upon a wide knowledge of all the alternatives, but knowledge about the alternatives is not enough.

> There must be imagination to envisage all the possibilities, and sympathy to make some of the options appeal to the emotions and powers of the will. Such dignity as man may have is achieved by the exercise of free choice through the qualities of learning, imagination, and sympathy; and we should add to these qualities as a fitting accompaniment, what may be called civility.[4]

Notice the words "imagination to envisage all the possibilities," "sympathy to make some of the options appeal," and "exercise of free choice through the qualities of learning." They emphasize the importance of choosing from among the ways one *might* say something. Hunt sees the best choices in speaking as those that will evoke some favorable feeling in the listener and as choices made in a knowing, learned way.

Your public-speaking course will offer you continual opportunities to accumulate wide knowledge about whatever subjects interest you and to try out ideas and various methods of communicating this knowledge. The course also offers an opportunity for you to increase your powers of imagination and of sympathy with the interests of other people. The knowledge you accumulate and the imagination and sympathy you acquire must guide you in choosing what, and by what means, you communicate thoughts and decisions that are important to you.

Choices and decisions about what to communicate and how to communicate it confront every public speaker over and over. In studying public speaking you ought to learn how to make such choices in an enlightened way, ever mindful of the principles of human, oral communication that have been developed over the past twenty-five centuries. You will choose subjects to talk about and ideas and evidence with which to develop them. The principles of what we call *invention* must guide you here. You will choose from among optional ways of structuring ideas, using principles of what we label *disposition*. You will decide what language to use, paying attention to its grammatical soundness and its potential for arousing images. There you will need principles of *style*. You will make decisions as to what bodily actions and vocal patterns are appropriate in a given situation, considering principles of *delivery*. You will make decisions about how to manage and control yourself and your total plan for presenting what you will say during the moments of utterance. Here you will need principles of *memoria,* a Latin term having the special sense of "command of the total speech" rather than the literal meaning "memory." Principles of memoria will be suggested to you especially in connection with principles of disposition and delivery.

---

4. Everett Lee Hunt, "Rhetoric as a Humane Study," *Quarterly Journal of Speech* XLI (April 1955): 114. Used by permission of the author and the Speech Communication Association.

So, we hope to show you that your experiences in studying public speaking as a liberal art also teach you how to practice the inescapable human activity of decision making. Further, these experiences provide an understanding of the principles to be observed if you are to transform private ideas imaginatively and sympathetically into public speech meant for particular audiences in particular places.

WHEN SPEECH BECOMES PUBLIC

What do we mean by *public speech*? We mean any speech where someone is given responsibility for maintaining communication over a certain period, while someone else or some group assumes the role of a relatively quiet listener. That is a loose definition, and it may at first seem strange to you. But what is it that the term *public* really means? It means "open to the view of all." We talk of public business and private business, of the public papers of a president and his private correspondence, of public showings and private showings. Using "public" in that sense, we want in this book to discuss all speech that is open to and addressed to those present, whether one or many. "Open to all" implies that as speech occurs someone has assumed a responsibility to others. Someone is in charge of maintaining communicative relationships with those present. There is a speaker, and there is a public to whom the speaker's behavior is open and to whom the speaker ought to direct attention. What would *private speech* be by contrast? It would be talk to and for one's self or talk with others in circumstances where there is no particular public and where responsibility for maintaining communicative relations has not become fixed on anyone in particular. This seems to us to be the only reasonable way to distinguish public speech from speech that is not public.

No one would say, "Speech is public if seven people hear it but private when six or fewer hear." So, it is not the *numbers* of people involved that make us all feel some of our speaking is public and some is not. Yet no one would deny that he or she *believes* "conversation is different from public speaking." Then, where is the difference, if not in numbers? We think it is in the key fact that in conversational settings *no one in particular bears responsibility* for creating and maintaining interpersonal relations through speech. In conversation, in private speech, the location of responsibility is unpredictable, and assumption of it is on the whole voluntary. Also, the questions of who shall be talked with and whether there shall be any talk at all are unpredictable in some settings. In other settings a tacit understanding has somehow evolved that Mr. X or Ms. Y *will* talk. Such a situation could even occur during an interview. It is in that moment of obligation that Mr. X or

Ms. Y *feels* differently. He or she is "on" now. The situation has become *public*. It is on speaking in all such moments of responsibility or obligation that we choose to focus as we treat public speaking. The audience may be one or many persons. The public is simply those people who are in a position to listen. The public speaker is the person who is assigned or who assumes responsibility for addressing them.

Is there much of this kind of public speaking? It goes on all about us. We all participate in it, sometimes well and sometimes not so well. One study of clerks, secretaries, technicians, and engineers in a large research and development laboratory found the staff spending 35 percent of all working time in face-to-face talk. The observers did not examine whether the face-to-face talk was public or private in the senses we are using these terms, but in a working place much of it must have been reporting or otherwise functioning in a public way.[5] A secretary tells a supervisor what supplies are in the office inventory and what must be bought. A lab assistant reports data to the supervising chemist, or the chemist gives directions to his assistants. Thousands of small public speeches take place in every business organization—and not only there. An athletic scout returns from scouting a future opponent and tells its game strategies to the head coach, or to two or three coaches, or to the coaches and the entire team. A committee member tells the committee the facts he was asked to collect. You summarize a research report for your professor or for your classmates. A teacher talks briefly or at length to a class. It is all public speaking, for someone has responsibility for maintaining mutually rewarding communicative experience with an audience that acquiesces in the arrangement for some, not always predictable, period.

To do its work well, all of this speaking needs rightly chosen information, cogent organization, clear and evocative language, and direct, expressive delivery. Therefore, this book is about minispeeches as well as about extended speaking.

MISCONCEPTIONS ABOUT SPEAKING

Just as there are misconceptions about how speech becomes public, there are misconceptions of what speaking and developing skill in speaking involve. Some of the misconceptions are understandable because the very ways we learn speech discourage us from thinking systematically about it. This unique ability, which only human beings seem to have, is learned from those around us: parents, friends, teach-

---

5. E. T. Klemmer and F. W. Snyder, "Measurement of Time Spent Communicating," *The Journal of Communication* XXII (June 1972): 142–58.

ers, social and religious leaders, movie and television personalities. The learning is largely unself-conscious. So naturally enough, we take our speech habits for granted until something happens that makes us see our talk is not producing the effects we want it to. Then comes the sense that "communication has broken down," and that sense is not rare. A Louis Harris poll has indicated that 32 percent of a cross section of 26 million Americans between the ages of fifteen and twenty-one had trouble communicating with parents, and 74 percent of these people thought the communicative problems stemmed from both sides.[6]

Without suggesting that they account for all or even most breakdowns in speech communication, we want to point to some common misconceptions about how oral communication works. Some of them account for an unknown number of failures in social and family situations. Any one of them can prevent you from becoming as effective as possible in public speech.

First, there is the idea that effectiveness in oral communication cannot be learned, that it is inherited or just rubs off on you, or fails to. Unquestionably a good environment encourages good speech behavior. But it is equally true that few people who seriously study and practice speech as an art fail to improve whatever skills they began with. Educators and corporation executives have tested for the effects of speech training as rigorously as they have known how and have concluded that able people become abler communicators after studying the nature and methods of speaking.[7] The testimony of those who have studied speech seriously, along with improvement evinced in speech classes, confirms that whatever may have been inherited or rubbed off can be refined by thoughtful, informed study and practice.

A second and long held misconception is that if you have something to say, you need not worry about how to say it. Good content assures its effective presentation. This idea dies hard, yet everyone knows from experience that good subject matter does not guarantee interesting communication. You have probably had a teacher or friend who knew his stuff, yet was constantly unclear or boring. You have heard and watched well-qualified speakers talk to their shoes rather than their listeners. Such experiences amply refute the content-is-enough notion. Being fully informed about, say, the public welfare system in your state does not at all guarantee you will explain the system clearly and effectively to a welfare client or an audience of your

---

6. Anon., "Change, Yes—Upheaval, No," *Life* LXX (January 8, 1971): 22.

7. There is relatively little published research on this point, but our product has never been more rigorously tested than when we taught public speaking for industrial firms and other private organizations. One of our universities has for several years maintained a flourishing in-service training program in speech communication for school systems and their teachers, which supervisors and teachers agree enhances the work of even experienced teachers.

classmates.   You must also know how to adapt ideas to different kinds of people.

Equally unfounded is a third misconception that content is *not* important.   The folk saying, "It's not what you say, it's how you say it," contains a grain of truth in a bushel of falsehood.   Experiments have shown clearly that so-called dynamic speakers are greeted with suspicion rather than conviction.   You probably know someone you have considered a windbag or too smooth because he talked glibly but did not know very much.   You can sense the difference between showmen and real teachers.   The playwright Arthur Miller wrote *Death of a Salesman*, often called an American tragedy, in part to dramatize the sad insufficiency of the doctrine that a good shoe shine and a smile can sustain either a reputation or a life.   "How you say it" is important, but manner alone does not protect the absence of matter in talk.

Closely related to this third misconception is a fourth.   Some hold that instruction in public speaking is instruction in sophistry, in dishonesty.   They find it distasteful or dishonest to tamper with what comes naturally in talk; they view the adaptation of thoughts for different situations as somehow hypocritical.   They say, in effect, "Let my speech alone.   Let me be me.   I won't be myself if I change my spontaneous impulses, even though I might be a better speaker in other people's eyes."   But there is nothing dishonest about improving the likelihood that other people will understand you as you wish to be understood.   That's what working to improve your public speech is, as we mean to teach it.   Listeners have rights as well as speakers. Listeners have the right not to be bored unnecessarily; they have the right to learn from you as easily and interestingly as possible; they have the right to have their feelings and knowledge taken into account whenever you occupy their time and attention.   Principles of fitting your best thoughts to listeners' best understandings are not principles of trickery or self-sacrifice; they are principles of respectful, decent, human relationship.   They are principles that allow you to reveal your best, humanly sympathetic self.   This book is about ways to become a fuller, more regardful human being in public situations.   It is about how you can be *you* more fully.

A fifth misconception has particularly to do with what courses in public speaking are really about.   It is the view of many that a course in speech is primarily concerned with management of body and voice, with how to move about a lectern and speak in seductive tones.   Specialists in communication do teach effective vocal behavior and devote considerable attention to nonverbal communication.   But study of the *whole act of speaking* effectively to others is primarily concerned with preparing ideas for public reception.   Ideas need to be reinforced by voice and gesture, but the best vocal and gestural acts are incidental, not central, matters in creating effective communication for any public.

This point is obvious to all who have explored the nature of public communication; still, the idea that a speech course is a course in delivery is found whenever college and university students are interviewed before they have taken any speech courses. As you begin the course of study developed in this book, you should expect to give attention to your delivery but more attention to discovering ideas and feelings and adapting them for public communication.

A sixth misconception is that speaking to an audience, especially a large one, is something like acting. A number of students enter public-speaking courses thinking that public speakers learn to play roles, learn how to become someone other than themselves. Actually, speakers rarely dare project personalities other than their own. Why? Because listeners in our culture normally expect their speakers to talk as themselves and for themselves. Tomorrow an audience will hold a speaker responsible for what he said yesterday, so he had better be himself on both days. If a speaker tries to establish one kind of relationship with an audience on one occasion and a wholly different relationship on another occasion, he will be found perplexing at best and hypocritical at worst. Acting, in the sense of trying to play roles that are not your own, is one of the very best ways to make listeners disbelieve. In chapter 5 we consider this matter more carefully when we take up how speakers use themselves as proofs of what they say.

Seventh, there is a widespread notion that reading aloud and speaking extemporaneously to an audience require substantially the same kind of attitude toward what one is doing. *Extemporaneous speaking* is speaking with preparation but without memorizing or using a text. As is so evident when public speakers quote others in their speeches, *reading* to an audience is not in fact like *talking* to it. The instant you begin reading someone else's words you get into a special relationship with that person's material. If you are to read well, you must have discovered the *author's* intellectual and emotional meanings, and you must transmit *these* meanings to the audience. This requires a different imaginative capacity from that required when you speak your *own* thoughts. When another's material is to be read, the ideas and words have been chosen by someone else. As a reader you must now select speech behaviors that will convey the *other* person's meanings. You must find ways to *interpret*. When you speak extemporaneously, you speak for yourself according to your own feelings *now*. But even to quote an authority in a speech is to assume the obligations of speaking on behalf of someone else's thoughts and feelings experienced at the time the quotation was composed.

Consider other possibilities. People sometimes read to audiences for special purposes. For example, you might want to read from a news story to provide information, or from a textbook to instruct, or from an editorial to persuade. Your purposes in these instances would be largely practical, that is, utilitarian. But elsewhere your purpose might be aesthetic for the most part. In reading from a play you might be seeking response to the beauty of a passage from, say, Shakespeare's *Romeo and Juliet*. This is response that the ordinary content of practical, rhetorical speaking does not try to evoke. "How beautifully said!" is not the usual response sought in speaking, but it is what you want if you read aesthetic material for others' appreciation. Our point here is that reading the words of others can involve you in goals different from those that occupy you primarily when presenting your own words.

Even when you read your own material, you face problems different from those you face when you speak extemporaneously. Those who read their own speeches usually do so because they have not had time, or taken time, to gain full command of their ideas, because they lack confidence, or because any deviation from plan or wording could have serious consequences, for example, in diplomacy. Before the coming of voice recording, able speakers sometimes memorized or read for a reason that no longer applies: to insure accurate printed reproduction of what was said. Today, however, there is really only one good reason for reading one's own words: to guarantee that nothing will be different from what was planned. That is not likely to be a reason you will have in your speech class or even on very many occasions outside it. So the nub of the matter is that reading your own speeches can never be more than a second-best choice. The reason is that reading requires you to *reinterpret* words you composed at some other time. Now you are back in the reader's bind. You cannot *quite* be your total, believable self in the moments of speaking. The inescapable fact is that you can get closest to an audience by speaking extemporaneously; whatever you read will draw *you* away from that audience in some degree.

The final misconception is the idea that a classroom is such an artificial place that meaningful public communication cannot occur there. Those who take this view have said things such as, "An instructor is always there. The audience is a captive one. Time limits are arbitrary. Rhetorical purposes and, sometimes, subjects are assigned. The atmosphere is unreal!" We have two answers.

First, a speech classroom is, indeed, a kind of laboratory. That is an advantage, although there are some disadvantages. A laboratory is a place where people can experiment under conditions created to *represent* the real world. A football team scrimmaging on the field in its stadium has created such a laboratory, but no one would say all that goes on in the scrimmage is wholly unreal. *Real* plays are developed. Part of the squad *really* represents Saturday's opponent, and so on. But not until Saturday will the *real* game take place. A speech classroom can be turned into just that kind of realistic *representation* of the real world of human communication.

Second, despite its constraints and sometimes because of them, *real* communication occurs in classrooms. In our own classrooms we constantly hear real speeches that are made because other real things have happened.[8] We have heard other speeches that produce real results: a petition signed and sent, a canister passed for contributions to research on leukemia, pledge cards signed promising donations of blood and of organs after death. In some instances there have been conversations that showed real learning had taken place or that some real decisions had been made on the basis of what had been said by classroom speakers.

In one of our classes a group of students invited a university administrator to visit the class to hear and respond to their carefully worked-out critique of a speech he had given. He came, listened to the series of speeches about his speech, and responded—happily confessing that the students had rightly divined his original purposes. Here was reality, and *in a classroom!* (See appendix B. Since we will refer to Dr. Upcraft's speech often in the pages that follow we suggest you take a few minutes to read it now.)

Only students and teachers can drive reality from classrooms!

RHETORICAL SITUATIONS

We never talk to one another without having to adjust, without having to build some sort of relationship between speaker and listener. This necessity for adaptation may be the single most important fact about speech as a way of communicating. To speak is to make an adjustment to our own and someone else's presence together in time, under specific circumstances. Not all communication is of this sort. If someone writes a poem or some class notes in a notebook or composes a bit of music, that author does not have to worry about who is present or where he or she happens to be at the moment the poem or note or music is created. Speaking is different. There is little sense in talking at all unless you take into account who is listening, in what way, and under what circumstances. Even if you talk to yourself, you do it for the sake of helping yourself, entertaining yourself, or otherwise affecting yourself, *now*, in the moments of the talk.

This central fact about speaking, publicly or privately, is what has led a number of modern thinkers about human communication to try to describe in detail the various features of what they commonly call "rhetorical situations." Lloyd F. Bitzer is one of these thinkers who has helpfully clarified the elements of rhetorical situations.

---

8. See the examples of the biology student's speech discussed on pp. 57–58 and Bob Barth's speech discussed on pp. 113–14.

Bitzer depicts events in which speakers face audiences. But, he points out, not all situations with a speaker and an audience are rhetorical. For a situation to be *rhetorical* there must be a potential, a possibility, for change as a result of the speaker's communication. The event must be ripe for action, at least of mind, and perhaps of body. Some set of forces in the setting and in the relationship of speaker to listeners must have created a possibility of change. If there is no possibility of change, of action within the situation, you have a situation that is *nonrhetorical*. Consider a pair of examples.

Imagine yourself having something of some importance to say to a friend or several friends. The question that ought to come before everything else is: will they listen to you seriously enough to act at least to the extent of taking your idea as something worth considering? If your friend or friends are engrossed in watching a favorite television program, the situation may be nonrhetorical. This may *not* be a time or place in which you can reasonably hope to influence your friends through speaking of the idea you have in mind. But it is also possible that you could change this situation into a rhetorical one by urging your friends to attend to you, right now, rather than to the television program. If you succeed the situation becomes rhetorical. Or you might choose to wait until the program is finished and the situation becomes a rhetorical one for you in a natural way.

Professor Bitzer says that a *rhetorical situation* is "a complex of persons, events, objects, and relations presenting an actual or potential exigence" that can be modified by "creation of discourse which changes reality through the mediation of thought and action."[9] Another way of putting this might be: a rhetorical situation is made up of people, conditions, physical features, and human relations within which there exists some need or possibility that practical communication can cause to be changed in some degree. In any situation, then, anyone who wants to make practical talk needs, first, to ask what possibilities there *are* for change, given the people (audience), the conditions and physical features (the occasion), the speaker, and his or her subject matter.

Consider another example: your speech class. Is it a rhetorical situation? Yes. The people, the fact that it is a class, the meeting place and all of its physical features make it so. In addition previous relations with your classmates and theirs with you and each other create a situation in which changes are possible. Talk can make those changes. Things said during a class period, speeches made there, can generate new ideas and actions or modify existing ideas or ways of acting. But, of course, there will be times when the content of what is said, its organization, its style, or the way it is said (delivered) will turn off the audience because in one way or another the speaking is not

---

9. Lloyd F. Bitzer, "The Rhetorical Situation," *Philosophy and Rhetoric* I (January 1968): 1–14.

what Bitzer calls a "fitting response" to the exigences (needs, readinesses, potentialities) the classroom provides.   When this happens it does not mean that the class was *not* a rhetorical situation; most speech classes are rhetorical situations all of the time.   What the turn-off probably means is that the potential for change was present, but the communication or some aspect of it missed drawing upon the possibilities that were there.

The important implication of the concept of rhetorical situation is that all practical speakers must learn to analyze situations because until they can do so, they can have little assurance that what they have in mind to say and do can make differences of the sorts they hope for.

Is there a method for analyzing situations to discover whether they are actually rhetorical and what is likely to fit them?   Figure 1-1 is a diagram that suggests the kinds of questions you need to ask to discover the rhetorical possibilities that exist in any situation.

The *audience* in the diagram represents all who comprise the speaker's immediate public.   The *occasion* is the specific set of circumstances (psychological as well as physical) under which speaker and audience meet.   *Material* is whatever the speaker knows about himself, the audience, his subject, and the occasion.   When you, as speaker, enter a situation, all of the relationships suggested by the double-headed arrows in the diagram are yours to use and alter in the interests of eliciting responses from the audience that shares this situation with you.   If you are related to the audience as chairman to group members, you can use your position as something authorizing you to speak now, *unless* the relation of audience to occasion is one that decrees that this is a time for conversation, not public speaking.   Even so, it is possible that your *idea* (material) is *so* important to the audience that it can overwhelm the preconceptions of what the occasion calls for and, upon attention being called to your thought, dominate the situation as an idea that authorizes consecutive discourse from you, just now.   Different balances of the forces within a situation could, of course, produce quite the opposite conclusion: that this is *not* a rhetorical situation for *you* at all.   You might have to conclude that the occasion so authorizes conversation just now that you must not try to engage in public rhetorical speech.

The diagram gives you compass points of a situation—by which you can calculate whether the situation is a rhetorical one inviting public speech.   If it is, it tells you what factors you must use to succeed in creating the changes you want.   The diagram suggests the following questions, which you ought to review in your mind as a preliminary to giving final shape to any message you decide to release into the intellectual-psychological system.

1. What is my relationship to the audience?
2. What is the audience's relationship to me?

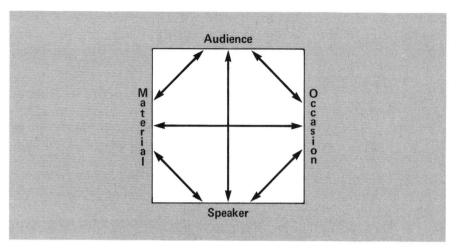

FIGURE 1-1

3. What is the relationship between the audience and the occasion?
4. What effect does the occasion, the particular circumstances in which the speech is to be delivered, have upon the audience?
5. What influence does the audience exert upon my material, upon what I have to say?
6. What is the relationship of my speech content, my material, to the audience?
7. What is my relationship to my material? What do I as a person bring to my material to determine its final substance and form?
8. What effect does my material (my subject choice, the facts, opinions, and illustrations) have upon me as a person?
9. What is my connection with the occasion?
10. What is the effect of the occasion upon me as a speaker?
11. What influence does the occasion have upon my materials, upon what I intend to say?
12. What will the content of my speech do to modify the nature of the occasion?

Depending on your circumstances, some answers to these questions will prove more informative than others. Often the best answers you can give will be merely educated guesses, as our example below indicates. But in every speech situation you will need to calculate as best you can the answers to as many of these questions as possible. If you do not, you will not understand your relation to the situation you hope is rhetorical and that you plan to enter.

Here is a summary of the thoughts of a student who wanted to speak in praise of B. F. Skinner and George Orwell for their illustrations of controlled societies that people may face in the future.[10]   It was the beginning of the course, and this student was about to give her first speech to her classmates.   This is the substance of her situational analysis, as she reported it to her instructor.

The student concluded that since these were the first speeches given in her class and since she had so far had little direct contact with anyone in the class, she had no other relationship to the class than that of another class member.   Neither, she thought, would the audience relate to her in any particular way, since she had so far said little in the classroom.   She and the audience would meet as relative strangers, sharing only the fact that all had to speak publicly to all others.   What would be required of her, she concluded, was that she make her ideas about Skinner and Orwell seem significant and interesting.

The student thought the occasion for her speech would have no special significance either, except for the fact that she would be one of the later speakers.   She was a trifle worried lest her audience be tired of hearing speeches before her turn came; but since she had noticed no restlessness so far (the second day of speaking), she assumed that she would face no special problems in this respect.

It was by asking herself questions 5 and 6 (above) that this student discovered the special *exigence* (readiness) she must address if she were to turn the classroom situation into a genuine rhetorical situation for herself and her subject.   She realized that few listeners would have read Skinner's and Orwell's books.   On the other hand, she was convinced that virtually everyone in the classroom would feel somewhat fearful of controlled societies.   Here was the exigence on which she could seize, the readiness through which she could generate change out there.   She decided she must first remind the listeners of their distaste for controlled societies and then point to the fact that Skinner and Orwell had both set out the dangers of governmental control over people's thoughts.   "They already have a certain relationship to my material," she wrote.   "I hope to broaden it."   In response to question 7 she wrote, "I am concerned about . . . a controlled society and the significance of humans as individuals. . . . If I am able to communicate effectively, I will at least bring [about] a sense of concern. . . ."   Now, she knew she had a true rhetorical situation before her.   Rightly managed, her talk *could* bring about change in the classroom situation because there were needs and concerns out there that *she* could work with to bring about change.

The student speaker decided she knew enough about Skinner's and Orwell's books to justify talking with her classmates about the

---

10. This paper was prepared by Lisa Roberts of the University of California, Santa Barbara, for a public speaking course taught by Janice E. Peterson.

significance of these books; and what she had read, she said, "makes me realize how extensive a control over others people could gain." Answering questions 7 and 8 assured her that she was an appropriate person to try to work the changes in the situation for which she hoped.

On the other hand, trying to answer questions 9, 10, and 11 led this student to believe that when it came her turn to speak to the class she would have no special advantages from the occasion: "I will be in a situation where my only real alternative is to try to do well," she wrote, and she added that the prospect was a little unnerving since she had not made a speech for a year and a half. Her only option was to plan carefully to touch as effectively as possible the readiness to believe that she had found in the situation. She added, wisely, "I could say quite a bit more than I will," because the assignment was to speak in praise of someone's views, not to expand on those views.

In answering question 12 she capped her survey of the situation she would enter. It was, in fact, a *rhetorical* situation for *her*. She, as a person, could confidently bring her material to this audience on this occasion with a genuine hope of inducing change, *provided* she remembered to work from the listeners' distaste for social control toward admiration for Skinner and Orwell. The audience and occasion would be open to her, and she knew both how to sift the available material and how to focus on exigences already existing in the situation.

The above is a true summary of one student speaker's first analysis of a classroom situation that, as it turned out, invited what Bitzer calls "a *fitting* response," not "just any response." It is the kind of survey of possibilities you need to make of every situation you anticipate entering with public speech.

To summarize, this is a book about *public speech,* speech that is relatively uninterrupted and in which a communicator *recreates* his or her own ideas and *symbolizes* them to elicit *practical responses* from an audience having somewhat changeable conceptions of its relations to the world, the specific situation, and the speaker who addresses them briefly or at some length. To carry out such communication is to practice an art, a practical, liberalizing, and therefore liberating art. Pursuing this art is to practice the universally human task of decision making, choosing from among alternatives and defending one's choice either to one's self or to others. We conceive of public speech as sustained social interaction in which one accepts responsibility for maintaining communication and communicative human relations. What is at issue for you, as a student of the liberal art of public speaking, is to develop your capacities to discover what is possible in rhetorical situations and to discover the resources available to you for taking advantage of what the situations allow.

Commanding public speaking as a liberal art is not a matter of thoughtlessly doing what comes naturally, of being simply glib, of pretending to be what you are not, of concentrating on delivery to the neglect of ideas and situations, or of becoming a good reader of your own or someone else's words. Commanding this art requires that you, first, understand human situations, discover whether they invite or allow rhetorical public speech, and, if they do, understand and apply the principles of adaptive speaking in responses you make in genuinely rhetorical situations.

In the remainder of this book we invite you to look at speaking in public as a process of satisfying the demands of audience, content, self, and occasion, to alter rhetorical situations. After a brief survey of matters particularly important to your first experiments with public speech, we examine successively five constellations of problems all speakers must solve in designing communications that will fit rhetorical situations. We first examine the problems associated with rhetorical *invention,* considering the nature of audiences and the means by which ideas for speeches may be discovered and sifted. Next we consider the *disposition* of materials selected for inclusion in a speech —the principles according to which they may be assembled and structured. Our third and fourth considerations concern the symbolization of ideas—*style,* and *delivery* of the finished speech. What ancient writers called *memoria* or command of the entire speech as planned is discussed at various points in the chapters that follow, since many of the decisions that speakers make during discovery, disposition, and symbolization of ideas have direct bearing on ability to retain command over plans until delivery is completed. In considering each of these five major aspects of public speaking we seek to determine what demands you must meet and the reasons they must be met if you are to be understood as you intend in the situations you enter.

In our final chapter we consider how a critic of the art looks at public speech. There, we treat speech as a critical object and explore practical methods of general and classroom speech criticism.

EXERCISES

Written

1. Keep a diary on two or three hours of your normal activities, noting all the occasions on which you found people, including yourself, speaking to others in relatively uninterrupted fashion and with the aim of altering listeners' perceptions of their relationships to people, ideas, and things having significance for them.
2. Write a criticism of the definition of public speech given in this chapter on page 19.   Support, expand, refute, or delete elements of the definition, but give reasons for each change you make.

3. After viewing a movie, television, or live theatre performance, list the major things you observed the actors doing that were (a) similar to and (b) different from the things you have observed in the practices of public speakers you consider superior.

4. In anticipation of your first speech in your class, choose a subject you hope to speak on and analyze the class as a rhetorical situation for your speech, answering the twelve questions posed on pages 16–17 as far as is possible. (Or form a group with four or five other members of the class and construct a general analysis of the class as a situation in which rhetoric is going to occur.) Write a paragraph or two explaining what advantages and disadvantages you (or each member of your discussion group) will have in speaking in this rhetorical situation. Or present your conclusions to your class orally.

Oral

1. Make a short talk in which you describe a specific rhetorical situation and point out aspects of it to which you might have been insensitive had you not attended this class and read this chapter.

2. Report to your classmates how many public speeches (as defined in this chapter) you have given in the last twenty-four hours. Indicate where you were most and least successful and why.

3. Observe a public speaker (student, teacher, television personality, or any other) and report on his or her strengths and weaknesses in adapting to the rhetorical situation.

First Considerations

One day in your class a speech will be assigned to you. A time for the speech will be set. You will know when you are expected to appear and make a talk. When the announcement is made, questions will begin to crowd your brain: What shall I talk about? What must I do to carry off the assignment successfully? How can I avoid saying things that have been said a dozen times before? How shall I start to prepare? How can I avoid being too nervous to talk at all?

Ideally, you should know all the theoretical and practical knowledge in this book before making a speech; but to have ample opportunity to learn from experience, your experiments in speaking must begin early. There is more to be gained than lost from this. Each opportunity to speak will allow you to explore your own nature and capacities as a communicator and to study others as they listen and react to what you say. You can learn enough quickly to make useful *experiments* in public speech, as we try to show in this chapter.

Your development as a fully informed speaker will be gradual. As your study, understanding, and control develop, you will become increasingly able to meet high standards and solve difficult problems in communication. But first experiences can be profitable ones, too. So this can be true, we ask you to study the elemental observations in this chapter before your first classroom speech. These first considerations have special value at the beginning of a course in public speech.

In the following pages we deal with six topics you need to think about before addressing any audience. The topics are listening, basic procedures in speech preparation, readying a first speech assignment, kinds of delivery, stage fright, and oral rehearsal.

LISTENING

Whenever we talk there are listeners. They are a part of every communication situation. So some basic facts about listening to public speech are significant first considerations.

There are at least three ways in which listening especially concerns you as a developing public speaker: (1) You need to adapt what you say and how you say it to the basic ways people listen; (2) if you are to help your colleagues develop as public speakers, you will need to listen to them in ways that will allow you to give other speakers clear reports on the reasons for their achievement or lack of achievement; (3) you must have opportunities to refine your own listening habits so you can listen more effectively outside your speech class—in lecture halls, before television sets, and among friends.

What are the basic facts about how people listen? One of the best-informed students of human listening has said: "How well a person *can* listen and how well he does listen are not the same thing. Furthermore, how well he does listen depends on two factors: his listening habits and his willingness to listen."[1] There is also a third factor of great importance—the natural capacity to listen. What is *capacity*? The quality that correlates most highly with capacity or ability to listen is intelligence.

Listeners' habits, their intelligence, and their willingness to listen, then, are the basic factors that determine what they take in and how. Isn't it obvious that you, as a speaker, must concentrate on making listeners *willing* to hear you? You cannot do much about the habits they already have or their intelligence, but you can do a great deal to make what you say interesting, attractive, and worth their attention.

It would be too simple to say that making listeners interested in what you say is the basis of the art of public speech. But it is not simplistic to say that no speaking is artistic unless every effort has been made to make the listeners *want* to hear what you say. This is the only direct control you have over how well your audience will listen.

Another thing we know about listening is that people listen in different ways under different circumstances. Experiments and common sense tell us that listeners listen for what they *expect* to hear.[2] The foremost guideline this implies is that if you want your listeners to hear you as you mean to be heard, you must help them see what's coming and let them know what they can expect from you in the situa-

---

1. Carl H. Weaver, *Human Listening: Processes and Behavior* (Indianapolis: The Bobbs-Merrill Company, 1972), p. 7.
2. See Charles T. Brown, "Studies in Listening Comprehension," *Speech Monographs* XXVI (November 1959): 288–94; Charles M. Kelly, "Listening: Complex of Activities—and a Unitary Skill?" *Speech Monographs* XXXIV (November 1967): 455–66; Weaver, *Human Listening*, pp. 34–42.

tion you share with them. The importance of guiding expectations is the basis for what we say in this chapter and later about making goals clearly understood, providing clear and motivating introductions and transitions, and building proofs toward clear conclusions. A basic principle of the art of public speech is: help listeners anticipate your goals and the patterns of your talk. The justification for the principle is simply that listeners listen according to their anticipations.

The fact that listeners listen according to their expectations is important to you as a listener, too. What we listen *for* influences the *way* we listen. When we listen to weigh arguments we tend to pay less attention to style than to other aspects, unless the language begins to confuse us or is exceptionally striking. When we listen to be entertained we pay minimal attention to arguments and a good deal of attention to language because we expect much of the amusement to arise from quick turns of language. Such shifts in what is attended to in speech mean, again, that as a speaker you need to give listeners cues about *how* to listen to what you say. When *you* are the listener, however, you ought to recognize that you can listen in a number of ways *if you want to.* Knowing this, you can inspect your listening habits to see whether you are listening according to what your speaker's intentions require. If not, you can change the focus of your attention.

This leads to some steps you can take to improve your listening habits. A speech class is an excellent place to do this. A classic program of research some years ago identified ten components or necessities of effective listening:

1. Previous experience with difficult material
2. Interest in the topic at hand
3. Ability and willingness to adjust to the speaker
4. Good physical condition and adequate energy level
5. Ability and willingness to adjust to abnormalities in the situation
6. Ability to adjust to emotion-laden words
7. Ability to adjust to emotion-rousing points (as contrasted to words)
8. Ability and willingness to focus on central ideas rather than non-essential details
9. Ability to take notes judiciously
10. Ability to supplement and reinforce what is heard while hearing it.[3]

What this description of listening says is that you will be wise to broaden your experience by listening to difficult material, to try not to be carried into irrelevant thoughts by emotional content, and to

---

3. These components of listening were originally presented in Ralph G. Nichols, "Factors in Listening Comprehension," *Speech Monographs* XV, no. 2 (1948): 154–63, and were later discussed at length in Nichols and Thomas R. Lewis, *Listening and Speaking* (Dubuque, Ia.: Wm. C. Brown Company, 1965).

practice directing your thoughts toward expanding and interpreting what you are hearing. The description also suggests that you need as much tolerance as possible for things such as eccentricities in speakers and distractions in listening situations. All of these counsels imply that listening effectively is largely a matter of teaching yourself to focus on ideas rather than on extraneous matters. But the list of necessities in listening further suggests that focusing on *central* ideas is better than concentrating on details and that if it is necessary to make notes, the notes should record the main elements of a speaker's content. In short, one needs to *work* at listening to get what is there. We need to energize ourselves for listening just as we must for speaking. Finally, the second item in the list we have given brings us back to the topic with which we began this section: a listener's *interest* in what he hears is a key determinant of what he gets from listening.

As a speaker, you cannot safely suppose listeners will be interested in what you say. You have to exert yourself to try to interest them. But as a listener, you can help yourself by making conscious efforts to *be* interested. You will hear speeches on many topics in your classroom. You may not be avidly interested in some of them. Why not try to find something interesting in them? You will not be bored, and you will learn things you otherwise would miss.

Your speech classroom is a listening laboratory if you choose to make it so. You can direct your own listening behavior along all the lines suggested by the list we have just given. You will have the opportunity to do so day after day. Research has shown that people do improve in the abilities and adjustments enumerated above.

Developing listening abilities may or may not be a part of the formal syllabus used in your class; if it is not, you can still create your own laboratory learning program. But whether or not you train yourself as a listener, what you cannot avoid as a speaker is the absolute necessity of *rousing listeners' interests* and *guiding their expectations*. In your first talk and in all later ones you will confront these two, inescapable necessities—because we all listen selectively and according to our anticipations.

BASIC PROCEDURES IN SPEECH PREPARATION

Preparing any speech is a matter of exercising judgment. In judging what to do and what not to do, your intellect needs to be specially guided by what you know of the nature and frailties of human thought, the conventions of communication, and the nature of listening. In later chapters we consider these factors more fully, but we need to mention certain procedures at this point.

Subjects and Goals

Before you can make an effective speech you must know your goal and what needs to be said to accomplish it.   Goals and what to say are interrelated.   In classroom speaking it does not matter whether you first decide to talk about drug abuse and then decide to try for the goal of making the extent of the problem clear, or settle first that you will try to make a problem clear and then choose drug abuse as the problem.   Outside the classroom, however, subjects are often *assigned,* in the sense that people are invited to speak on specified topics or they decide they *must* speak to a specific topic.   In general, then, setting your goal is an early task when a speech is to be made, although it may not always be your first task in classroom speaking.

Determining the Response

Given a subject, your job is to decide what sort of response you may reasonably seek from your particular audience.   For example, you must determine whether to inform, inquire, reinforce, persuade, or entertain.   This decision made, you must next determine what central idea is to dominate as you seek the response you have envisioned.   Let us briefly examine how each of these decisions is made.

As we pointed out in chapter 1 (see pp. 13–14), you should think of classroom speaking as real communication rather than as an unrealistic exercise.   Suppose you decide to speak to your colleagues about the drama club to which you belong.   As soon as you decide this, you have to decide what sort of response you want to elicit from the class.   Should you inform them of something they do not know about the club's purposes and activities and seek the response, "Yes, I understand"?   Should you want to review and amplify some club project they have heard of, you will still be giving information but seeking the response, "Yes, I understand *better* (or more fully)."   Or should you persuade the group to attend a coming production by the club, thus trying for the response, "Yes, we ought to go" or "Yes, that seems worthwhile"?   If you decide to inquire with the class, raising some question about the proper function of groups like the drama club, your goal will be to excite the response, "We ought to think more about that" or "We ought to discuss this issue."   If you reinforce something your audience already believes and try to get them to strengthen their affirmations, you will seek a response such as, "Yes, drama *is* an important cultural influence on this campus."   Or should you simply entertain the audience with satire or irony or amusing things you have experienced with the club?   If the last is your goal you will be seeking smiles, laughter, and "That's funny" as responses.   These are your normal options in deciding the response you seek in preparing any speech. A subject may be treated in several ways; how you should treat it depends on how you want your listeners to react.

The five purposes we have just identified need not be mutually exclusive in your speech. You may inform to persuade or reinforce. You may persuade to get a group to inquire. You may entertain as you inform. But even though the five primary purposes can be intermixed, one purpose must dominate and the others must be subordinate, existing only as substructures upon which the dominant purpose rests. The reason for this is as simple as it is inexorable; neither you nor your listeners can think clearly about any subject unless you plainly understand the *chief* reason for thinking about it at all.

Choosing Your Subject

As we said earlier, the group that asks you to speak may specify your subject and purpose. But a class assignment may simply say, "Talk to us about anything you want to." When you must choose a subject, there are several guidelines you should follow.

1. First is your own experience. It is unwise to choose a subject about which you know absolutely nothing. Experience, however, is not the whole answer. We think of the student who had much experience with turtles—he was a turtle expert. He spoke first on diamond-back turtles. The class was fascinated with his breadth of knowledge, enthusiasm, and thoroughness. Experience served him well. The second time, he chose to talk about snapping turtles. He was still interested in turtles and he was still experienced, but the audience had heard enough of turtles and turned its attention elsewhere. In this case, experience and personal interest did not serve.

We also think of the students who, told to consider their personal experiences in choosing subjects, gave speeches on "my summer job as a milkman" and "my days as a lifeguard." Their subjects were not well received, although they had experience and enthusiasm. What they had to say was trite and familiar, incapable of stimulating their audiences to think.

2. Prior knowledge is a second factor to be considered. If you do not know your subject, you must learn before you have earned the right to take your listeners' time. Remember, 5 minutes spent before an audience of twenty people consumes 100 minutes of the world's time. Therefore, you will need to decide upon a subject you already know a great deal about or about which you can know a great deal before your speaking engagement.

3. The availability of material becomes a third determinant in

choosing a subject. Do not choose speech subjects without making a preliminary survey of the resources for obtaining the information you will need. We mention possible sources of speech materials on page 33 and discuss them further in chapter 4. Unless you make a preliminary inventory you may find there is just not enough material to warrant a speech.

4. The audience will also have a bearing upon your choice. Age, sex, expectations, and knowledge may rule out some subjects that otherwise seem excellent. We treat these matters more fully in chapter 3.

5. A fifth determinant in your choice ought to be the speech situation with its inherent limitations: what will have gone on before, the time of day, the setting, and so on. In the classroom some subjects will be inappropriate because of the assignment, the time allowed, and listeners' special expectations.

6. Time, just mentioned, makes it important for you to consider the complexity of subjects and whether each possibility can be narrowed or broadened to suit the agreed-upon time. You may find some subjects too simple to occupy the minutes profitably and others incapable of being cut down and remaining meaningful.

7. Finally, subjects ought to challenge the audience and the speaker. Something ought to be gained by both. There ought to be news. Brain stretching and creative cogitation ought to be products of good subjects. Puerile and parochial subjects do not encourage that kind of thinking.

Sometimes it is not the subject that is responsible for a poor choice but your selection of the aspect to be treated. The merit of a speech often has to do with how you treat it rather than with the subject itself.

Given the general topic of drama for your first speech, your real business in finding a subject begins with deciding what kind of response you want from your audience and with determining how you can narrow down this topic to a specific subject for a particular talk with a clear purpose that can be accomplished in the time you will have. If you can reduce the topic of drama to a subject such as "Off-Broadway Theatre during the Late 1970s," you can turn at once to deciding whether you want to inform, inquire, persuade, or amuse your listeners. On the other hand, if you have come no farther than "Recent Off-Broadway Drama," you still have decisions to make concerning what period "recent" covers. That decision, again, is going to be significantly guided by what kind of *response* you want to seek. If you want to inform about recent history, you must decide *how much* history you want to inform about. If you want to persuade listeners that recent Off-Broadway drama has certain characteristics, you must decide *which parts* of *what* recent history support your persuasive goal. You will have the same experience with any speech subject. As you shape it to manageable *and purposeful* dimensions, the crucial, defining question is: what response do you want from your listeners?

Locating Your Central Idea

If you are assigned a report, or choose to give one, your task becomes to inform. If the assignment, or your choice, brings you one step farther so you can say what specific subject it is you will report on, your purpose and your subject are decided. When you have arrived at this stage, your next task is to locate a central idea, a proposition or thesis or subject sentence upon which to structure what you will say. In framing this core idea it is helpful to think of it as the hub of a wheel from which supporting spokes extend, or the roof of a pavilion supported by pillars, or the apex of a pyramid supported by blocks of specific information that substantiate the epitomizing statement.

Any praiseworthy speech has a central idea or proposition to which the audience's attention is directed and for which a specific response is sought. Detailed ideas, reasons, or assertions may form points in the general framework of your speech, but you must subordinate such details to a central subject sentence that your listeners can focus upon. Once your subject and purpose are known, your task becomes one of deciding upon that statement which will express pointedly the encompassing thought that embraces all you will say. Once this statement is determined, you are ready to search for the lesser ideas that will amplify, substantiate, and vivify the central thought in ways that will evoke the response you want.

To sum up: sometimes you must choose your own subjects; sometimes it is assigned; sometimes you must locate a narrower, more specific subject within a topic or subject area. Always you must define the responses you seek from listeners; always you must formulate a central idea that epitomizes the content of what you say; always you must locate the subordinate ideas that give meaning to your central thought. We emphasize conscious identification of desired responses and conscious and precise formulation of central ideas because of the nature of listening. Listeners look for "the point of it all" in what they hear. Their demand must be met.

Phrasing Your Subject Sentence

Listeners welcome some ingenuity in the framing of central ideas and statements of purpose. "I shall inform you this morning. . . ." or "Let me instruct you. . . ." or "It is my purpose tonight to persuade you that. . . ." can suggest lack of regard for the mentality of an audience. If your intentions are stated so bluntly your listeners may also back away, feeling you have come to manipulate them. To say, "This morning I will explain the four ways pulp is processed," fulfills the formal requirements of a good subject sentence, but it is rather bald. The purpose stands out obtrusively and is tritely phrased. It is an excellent, clear statement for you to carry *in your head,* but your intention can be *communicated* more deftly and more interestingly. It would be better to say, "The paper in my hand is the product of one of four ways that pulp is produced." Without being flashy or at all unclear, a subject sentence that is baldly put to guide the speaker can usually be altered in actual communication to catch the listener's interest.

A listener not only wants to be interested by a speaker's purpose; he wants to be able to detect a rhetorical purpose in the words of a subject sentence. He can get a clue to purpose from both the contents and the grammatical form of a subject sentence if you will observe the following conventions. Assertions are usually used for speeches of information and entertainment. Questions usually indicate that the purpose is inquiry. Propositions suggesting an "ought" or a preference indicate that persuasion is intended. Suppose a speaker's subject is advertising on television. For each of the usual rhetorical purposes his or her subject sentence might be worded in the following way:

INFORMING: The history of televised advertising clearly reveals its purpose and nature.

PERSUADING: The federal government ought to regulate televised advertising.

INQUIRY: To what extent, if at all, should the federal government regulate televised advertising?

REINFORCING: Advertising provides us the service of showing what products are available to us.

ENTERTAINING: Advertising presents the comedy of human life.

Notice that each of these sentences does three things: (1) reveals the subject of the speech, (2) states the central idea clearly, and (3) plainly implies the kind of response sought.

Good subject sentences are phrased so a single idea emerges clearly and unambiguously. They are framed in uncomplicated and uncluttered fashion. They do not focus thought on only *part* of what is to be said, and they express but a single idea. Beware of compound statements—sentences containing *and* or *but*. Conjunctions are often signals that two main ideas are present. Avoid sentences such as "The Bessemer steel process is important, because planes are made of steel" and "The Scottish poets ought to be studied, and the poems of Sir

Walter Scott ought to be analyzed by all who study British literature."
The first narrows to a specific heading. The second contains more
than a single idea.

Supporting the Central Idea

Let us suppose you have completed the initial steps of finding a
subject, determining your purpose, narrowing your subject, and framing your subject sentence. Now you must find materials to clarify, to
add detail to, or to prove your subject sentence. What you need are
things such as (1) facts; (2) quotations; (3) examples, whether long
or short, real or hypothetical; (4) anecdotes; (5) statistics; (6) comparisons, contrasts, and analogies; (7) definitions; (8) descriptions;
(9) repetition and restatement; and (10) audiovisual aids. You will
hardly use all of these in a first speech, but you will need some mixture
of these kinds of supporting materials. We discuss these materials in
detail later (pages 147–61), but for now it is enough to point out that
you need such materials. When you have found what you need, the
details will have to be structured as simply as possible into a coordinated, unified whole that becomes a speech. In your first attempts,
try for clear, simple arrangements. It will also be wise to select only a
few pieces of support for perhaps only one or two main points. Once
you have prepared and given one or two short, simple speeches, you
will see that longer speeches are but a series of such simple units as
you have already worked with.

The easiest and most practical first speech is one that consists
of only a single point that might well be a segment of a longer speech.
To prepare such a speech you ought to proceed as follows:

PREPARING A FIRST ASSIGNMENT

1. First, select from a subject area interesting to you and your
audience a relatively simple, single idea. This idea should be one you
can clarify for your audience or that you want them to accept. Sometimes you can arrive at such an idea by making a rough plan for a
longer speech and then selecting one main point from it.

2. Once this idea has been selected, phrase it accurately in a
single subject sentence.

3. Concentrate on a single, simple method of development—a
structural pattern. Explain or persuade, for example, by arranging
your materials in chronological, spatial, effect-to-cause, or problem-
solution order.

4. Draw upon several sources other than personal experience for material to amplify or support your idea.

5. Carefully plan even this short speech; prepare an outline, although it may consist of only five or six items.

6. Make each of the items bear upon your subject sentence. Be ready to show the audience that each item does clarify or support your subject sentence.

7. A final test of the speech will be an affirmative answer to one of two questions: Does my audience understand the subject better now that I have spoken? or Does my audience more nearly accept the idea I have been proposing?

A simple outline will serve in planning this first speech. To illustrate how you might locate and outline a single point for a brief talk, let us imagine that you think a major speech might be given on the subject sentence: "Alcoholism is a problem that should be given immediate attention in public education." If you ask yourself what would be the main headings of such a speech, the following might occur to you:

I. Alcoholism is a serious problem.
II. Alcoholism in our public schools has become a problem of major concern.
III. How to treat alcoholism is a perplexing question.
IV. We should give support to educational agencies attempting to deal with the problem.

Any of these four points could be used as a central idea for a shorter speech, although the fourth is least promising because it depends for support on the other three. If you chose the first of these points for a one-point speech, you would need to prepare a simple outline or plan of its development. It might look like this:

SUBJECT SENTENCE: Alcoholism is a serious problem.[4]

SUPPORTING MATERIAL:

Statistics	1.	Between 1960 and 1970 United States consumption of alcohol increased 26 percent.
Example	2.	A friend of mine, a teacher in high school, finds parents relieved at being told their children are heavy drinkers not drug addicts.
Statistics	3.	The National Institute on Alcohol Abuse and Alcoholism reports:

---

4. This sample outline and the speech text as delivered are by Eloise Paige. Used by permission.

        a. About one in ten Americans who drink is either an alcoholic or a problem drinker.

        b. After heart disease and cancer, alcoholism is our biggest health problem.

        c. Half of all murders, a quarter of all suicides, and at least half of all auto deaths are alcohol related.

Definition   4. An alcoholic is one who is unable consistently to choose whether or not to drink, and who, if he drinks, is unable consistently to choose whether or not he will stop.

Fact   5. Alcoholics Anonymous is the oldest, biggest, and most successful treatment agency.

Quotation   6. An Atlanta business executive explains why Alcoholics Anonymous works: "Doctors cannot cure alcoholism because it is not simply a sickness of the body. Psychiatrists cannot do it because it is not simply a sickness of the mind. And ministers cannot do it because it is not a sickness of the spirit alone. You must treat all three areas, and that's what AA does."

    To show you what a complete one-point speech is, as delivered from this outline, we furnish its text, taken from a tape recording.

    Alcoholism is a serious problem. In the past few years this has been especially so among teenagers and women. Between 1960 and 1970, U.S. per capita consumption of alcohol had increased 26 percent. This is the equivalent of 2.6 gallons of straight alcohol per person per year. Alcohol consumption is presently at an all time high.

    A friend of mine, who is an instructor in high school, has had to confront parents to inform them that their children were heavy drinkers. And she's been surprised that the parents were actually relieved upon hearing this. They would usually say, "Thank God, I thought he was on drugs."

    Too few people seem to realize the serious problems that can be attributed to alcohol abuse. According to the National Institute on Alcohol Abuse and Alcoholism, about one in ten of the Americans who drink is either an alcoholic or a problem drinker. After heart disease and cancer, alcoholism is the biggest health problem. It shortens the life span by ten to twelve years. In one-half of all murders in this country, either the killer or the victim, or both, had been drinking. One-fourth of all suicides show alcohol in the bloodstream. And at least one-half of each year's auto deaths and injuries can be traced to a driver or a pedestrian who is "under the influence."

    An alcoholic can be defined as one who is unable consistently to choose whether he should or should not drink, and, who, if he does drink, is unable to decide whether or not he should stop.

There are many treatment centers available to the alcoholic. There is no miracle cure, but there is at least one treatment or a combination of treatments that will offer him a good chance of recovery.

Alcoholics Anonymous is the oldest, the biggest, and the most successful in treating the alcoholic. Here the treatment is nothing more than the gathering together of alcoholics. They discuss their problems with each other. But they can do so only if they will admit to one another that they are powerless to control their drinking problem. An Atlanta business executive who has been an AA member for over twenty-five years has been quoted as saying, "Doctors cannot cure alcoholism because it is not simply a sickness of the body. Psychiatrists cannot cure it because it is not simply a sickness of the mind. Ministers cannot do it because it is not a sickness of the spirit alone. You must treat all three areas, and that's what AA does."

The above illustration deals with a current problem. A comparable plan for a one-point speech amplifying a proverb might look like this:

SUBJECT SENTENCE: "There is nothing new under the sun" is a saying worth contemplating.

SUPPORTING MATERIAL:

Fact, Example	1. If we think we have new inventions, we have only to look at the ancient collections in the Egyptian Museum in Cairo where we will find such supposedly modern items as comic books, fly swatters, and jockey underwear.
Anecdote *Example, extended*	2. A friend of mine invented what he thought was a new kind of cigarette holder, but the U.S. Patent Office turned it down because they had already registered one just like it. (Tell story.)
Example, brief	3. My married sister told my Mother she had found a new recipe for chocolate cake calling for coffee, but my Mother said, "That's nothing new. I've been putting coffee in my chocolate cakes for years!"
Fact	4. Time and again, students have discovered that their thoughts were the same as those of others who lived long ago but whom they have never read or studied.
Restatement	5. We can put it another way by saying, "History repeats itself."

Restatement   6. Whether we are dealing with human experiences, ideas, or physical objects, we continually find that what we think is new is really "old hat."

Our present concern is chiefly with how one amplifies or proves a main point, hence the illustrative outlines printed here are not developed in full detail as are the outlines in chapter 8. (See pp. 235–41.) But here the bits of supporting material are labeled to show the kinds of support these speakers used. Notice the variety of those types of support; variety enlivens communication.

MODES OF DELIVERY

There are four general ways people deliver consecutive talk: *impromptu, extemporaneously,* by *reading* it, and from *memory.* Your first classroom talks are most likely to be presented extemporaneously; possibly some will be given impromptu. These methods of delivery are the ones that best promote development of conversational quality in speaking—the quality preferred far above others in our society. We discuss *impromptu* and *extemporaneous* delivery briefly here and then return to the general subject of delivery in chapter 10.

You may be among the many who confuse impromptu speaking with extemporaneous speaking. As the terms are used in the study of communication, they do not refer to the same processes. The *impromptu* manner of presentation is one in which you make no formal preparation until a few minutes (at most) before you begin to talk. The most preparation you do is jot down a few words. Impromptu speaking is spur-of-the-moment activity. It is not a way of speaking from which you will *learn* much about the art of public speech, but it is a kind of speaking that demands you *put quickly to use* all you know about speaking in public. Except as an exercise in self-command and in emergencies, speaking impromptu is almost never a satisfactory way of speaking if one has had any forewarning at all. On the other hand, it is the way you must speak if you are a member of a committee and find it important to make moderately extensive remarks on points of discussion as they arise.

In *extemporaneous* speaking, as we use the term, you will have had time to think out what to say and will have planned with considerable care. You will probably have outlined your plan and also rehearsed orally. Finally, you will present your thoughts publicly with or without notes to guide you. In this kind of delivery you can be at your best, as a person and as a communicator. You have freedom to adjust to the speech situation, you can be spontaneous in language, and most important, you can deal with your listeners directly—*converse* with them.

You may or may not be allowed to use notes for classroom extemporaneous speeches. If you use notes, they should be unobtrusive and kept to a minimum. Do not call attention to them. On the other hand, it is best not to try to hide them in the palm of your hand or under your sleeve. Few in the audience will expect you to memorize troublesome sets of statistics or long quotations. It is natural to read them. But few listeners will feel you are direct and in control of your ideas if your eyes are constantly on your notes. Whether you do or do not take notes with you when you are going to talk continuously for a bit of time, the less you have to refer to them the better. The reason? Listeners want to be shown you are thinking of *them*, not of pieces of paper.

Wherever you speak in public, and especially in the classroom, you ought to keep yourself free of preset wordings and mechanical physical movement. If you freeze fast your ideas and words during preparation, you may finally talk with precision but you are apt to be rigid in ideas, language, and action. Then, you simply cannot *interact* with those who listen; and yet, oral communication never is fully communicative unless speakers show their alertness to the listeners and listeners respond openly to speakers. This is what a famous teacher of speech, J. A. Winans, meant when he coined the phrase, "vivid realization of the idea at the moment of utterance" and made it the key idea in his educational revolt against elocutionary speaking. His point is crucial. No listener—including you—enjoys listening unless there is clear evidence that whoever he is listening to is thinking, realizing, his ideas *as he says them*. Speaking extemporaneously allows speakers their best compromise between the cold mashed potatoes of a rigidly learned talk and the haphazard mix of thoughts impromptu speaking so commonly produces. For classroom speaking and for much outside speaking you *can* prepare, rehearse to set your line of thought firmly in mind, and still *re-create* those thoughts as real talk vividly, spontaneously, and directly, realized *for listeners* as the thoughts are uttered. This kind of directness is entirely possible for you in public speech, and your speech class is precisely the place to develop your particular extemporaneous style. Not all extemporaneous speaking sounds exactly the same.

Many lecturers and some legislators and lawyers appear to their audiences to speak impromptu when in reality they have made extensive preparation during years of authoritative investigation, experience, and practice. Those who seem to speak impromptu when they are really speaking extemporaneously are commonly people who engage in formal speaking almost daily, so practice sessions are not a necessity for them. If you lack such experience and practice, you must conduct a specific investigation to enrich each utterance and must gain command over each particular set of ideas by rehearsing them in special, oral practice sessions. But you need not be less spontaneous in public speech because of that.

By urging you to practice and develop skill in extemporaneous presentation of public speech we are not disparaging all reading and memorizing in public settings. Some people read aloud very well, and some can memorize material and recite it so their listeners never know that it is memorized. In chapter 10 we discuss reading in some detail. (See pages 304–11.) We are saying that the beginner is more likely to achieve conversationality in his speaking if he speaks extemporaneously. This mode allows not only careful, thorough preparation but audience adaptation and spontaneous regeneration of ideas when the speech is given. We discuss oral rehearsal for extemporaneous speaking in a later section of this chapter. (See pages 42–44.)

STAGE FRIGHT

Although not everyone will admit it, most beginning (and very many experienced) speakers are apprehensive about facing audiences. If you are worried about how your audience will react, rest assured that your concern is normal.[5] After all, in facing even classmates you are taking a risk. You hope they will respond favorably or at least sympathetically. Chances are that they will, but you are not quite sure. This doubt, felt by most good speakers in some degree, results in fear and anxiety, producing conflict. How to resolve such conflict, how to ease the feelings accompanying it and still adjust optimally to an audience, becomes a special problem.[6]

At the outset, you ought to remind yourself that the real causes of stage fright are psychological. For the most part *attitude* is at the bottom of the matter. Lack of self-confidence results in fear. Insecurity stems from the uncertainties of the situation. Literally, you become afraid if you feel you may lose control of the audience. Or you may be apprehensive about your mastery of what you are going to say. Then you are apt to experience fear because you feel unprepared or that you are not perfect. Or you may experience fear because you are anxious about how well your voice and body will function, or whether

---

5. According to one study, 77 percent of experienced speakers experienced stage fright when beginning to speak. Elma Dean Orr Wrenchy, "A Study of Stage Fright in a Selected Group of Experienced Speakers," unpublished M.A. thesis (University of Denver, 1948), p. 37.

6. Otis M. Walter treats the matter of resolving such conflict in an excellent article entitled, "Developing Confidence," *Today's Speech* II (September 1954): 1–7.

you will choose the right words. The mere fact that you are separated from the listeners in a formal situation may be responsible for feelings of insecurity and aloneness. For some people, wishes to avoid such situations, to flee from them, have caused them to make such serious excuses that they have not had to speak at all. Thus they have reinforced their fears by preserving the causes.

The fear that causes anxiety about speaking results in physiological changes. Some who undergo these changes think they are organically ill, that they may have some sort of secretion imbalance or other fundamental disorder. What actually happens is that the flow of epinephrine (adrenaline) accompanying anxiety and fear sets off additional changes. Blood pressure, rate of respiration, and nerve conductivity increase. More blood sugar, furnishing energy, enters the system. More thyroxine may be secreted, speeding the burning of blood sugar. More oxygen is taken into the blood. More poisons are removed from your system. As a result of these changes fatigue probably lessens, and you may experience the kind of increase in strength that frequently accompanies the release of tensions during anger. These bodily changes may interest you, but they are not the *causes* of fear.

How can you reduce fear and, subsequently, the tensions that afflict you? The solution to this problem can be discovered only by going back to the causes to see what can be done to remove them.

First, realize that everyone else at some time experiences the same apprehensions you do. The most any speaker can do is guess how an audience will react, then calmly calculate how best to promote the responses he or she seeks and to meet the demands an audience makes. Insights to human behavior come with experience, but they are always less than perfect. Realize this fact, but make educated guesses on how you can best adapt to your particular audience to get the people to react as you want them to. They are human beings like you. They may vary in age, interest, and creed, but they are similar to you in more ways than you probably realize. We know it is easy to say, "Feel at one with the audience," "Know that they will be more uncomfortable than you are if you don't succeed," "Remember that they are faced with the same problems, the same fears, and the same reactions to fear as you are." All of this is to say, "Get yourself in the right frame of mind." But determining to adopt an attitude conducive to a feeling does not necessarily guarantee that you will have the feeling you seek. Yet you must make first tries; you can gain composure by repeatedly making speeches in the face of varying conditions. One of the functions of a speech class is to give you these kinds of experiences. Striving for realistic attitudes, coupled with such practice as you gain in classrooms and elsewhere, can teach you how to make natural insecurity a positive asset.

A second way to cope with stage fright is to be thoroughly prepared. If you are not well prepared and think you are not worth listening to, you will certainly be fearful of the reception you will receive. But such doubts will have no foundation if you prepare wisely. Pay close, careful attention to your pattern of organization, to your supporting and amplifying materials, to phrases of greatest importance, and to potentially troublesome spots in your plan. If fear of speaking can cause you to prepare more carefully, it has provided its own best antidote.

Wise preparation inevitably involves oral rehearsal and practice. Through rehearsal you learn that you can, indeed, succeed. Rehearse well and thoroughly. (See pp. 42–44.) Practice in a second sense: seek repeated, real experience. Take every opportunity you can to practice speaking in public situations. This activity will contribute to habituating yourself to specific aspects of rhetorical situations. Certain things about speaking in public will become so familiar to you that you will feel more at ease each time you experiment.

In addition to taking advantage of opportunities to speak, take advantage of opportunities to use bodily action. Walk about and make gestures. Use facial expression and head movement. But do these things meaningfully, not randomly. The point is that by using bodily activity you will release tensions. Some students have found that using some sort of audiovisual aid puts them at ease because it gives them something to do with their hands and other parts of the body. This is a good idea, but be cautious in trying it (see pp. 157–61). Channeling some of your excess energy, which results from your physical state, into meaningful bodily activity helps alleviate tension and usually proves to be a desirable method of ridding yourself of stage fright.

Proper attitudes, preparation, practice, and movement ought to be any sensible person's response to the risks we all sense in formal communication. But the wish to communicate is a still more powerful protection against unease. If you *want* to speak, you have won half the battle in most instances. If you have more than enough to say and are determined to make the audience understand or accept your point of view, you will have come a long way toward releasing your tensions into meaningful, constructive actions that will contribute to the accomplishment of your goals.

Setting goals before speaking has been found to be the most important step toward gaining confidence for reticent speakers. If you have a clear, specific goal, you will have a desire to communicate. If your desire to communicate is strong enough, you will forget to worry about your hands or feet or what they are doing. This is not to say that you will forget you have a voice and body you must control. It is to say that if you bend all efforts toward gaining specific audience responses, you will have your best opportunity to accomplish what you set out to do. You will be like a swimmer in a race who, once he has hit the water, lets nothing divert his attention until he reaches the finish line. All distractions will be swept aside or ignored. With proper practice, you can substitute controlled gestures for wasted motion. Wordings will become economical, because your mind will be filled with the business of communicating that which you know securely. You will say just enough and no more to elicit the reactions you seek. Losing yourself in your speech without losing your self-control will cause you to forget fears.

Natural insecurity about formal speaking can also be countered by being sure that what you will say is worthy of you, of the time spent in preparation, and of your audience's time. Confidence on these matters allays fear; misgivings about them generate fear. Only by choosing wisely and carefully what you will say can you hope to approach a speech situation with confidence. If you believe what you are going to say is not worth much to you or your audience, if you believe your ideas are shabby, that you have settled for words that are dull or imprecise or that your speech is just something to get over, of course you will be afraid, and you deserve to be!

REHEARSAL AND ATTITUDES TOWARD SPEAKING

Oral rehearsal for extemporaneous delivery can insure mastery of your plan, remembrance of the succession of points in it, and confidence in your skills in delivery. The problem in extemporaneous speaking is to transfer your plan to your mind and become thoroughly familiar with its sequence of ideas. Specific choices of words will, and ought to, vary from one rehearsal to another. This will give you a large stock of verbal resources from which you can choose at will as you present your structured ideas in your meeting with listeners. But *how* you rehearse makes a difference. If you rehearse for extemporaneous speaking wisely, rehearsal becomes a route to confidence. The suggestions outlined below will help you. Following them can give you considerable reassurance, clarity of mind, and even serenity when you go to talk to your audience.[7]

1. Read through your written plan, fixing your mind on the succession of main points. Reread it, this time concentrating not only on the main points but on the details supporting each point.

---

7. The material that follows is adapted from *Manual for Public Speaking,* I, p. 22, by H. A. Wichelns and others (1932) and *Manual for an Elementary Course,* by H. A. Wichelns, G. B. Muchmore, and others, p. 19.

2. Still referring to your outline, speak through the speech in whatever words happen to come. Talk out loud, not under your breath. You will find it helps to stand up and face an imaginary audience. Try out gestures as your verbalize. Get through the whole speech. If you bungle a part, go right on to the end without stopping to straighten out the troublesome section. Come back to that when you have finished running through the entire speech.

3. Without using your outline or any memoranda except those notes you will use on the platform, stand up and speak through the speech as before. If you can find a patient listener or group of listeners, so much the better.

4. When you can get through your total speech fairly well, time yourself and adjust the speech to the time allotted for your actual presentation. Such an adjustment may call for omissions or condensations, or it may call for additions or expansions of points. It is important to acquire a sense of time on the platform and develop the habit of keeping within time limits.

5. In the moments before speaking keep the plan of your speech uppermost in your mind; review it. This is the most constructive outlet for tensions.

6. During preparation and just before speaking renew your desire to share a worthwhile message with others. Remind yourself that the experience before you is not a "performance" but an opportunity. You have earned that opportunity through the knowledge you have acquired and your position as a respected human being in a communicating society.

7. Recall that your auditors are persons not very different from yourself, that they want you to succeed.

8. Do not expect to avoid all tension. Some tension is good for you. Properly channeled, tension can serve you positively by increasing your alertness and your available supply of energy.

9. As a general rule, avoid last-minute changes in your speech, especially during your maiden efforts. Do not add to uneasiness by entertaining misgivings about choices already made. Adapt to the moment and to other speakers but do not make changes that undermine the overall plan you established in your mind by systematic rehearsal.

Oral rehearsal is insurance. Fluent discourse demands it. Speakers are often tempted to omit this important stage of speech preparation because of self-consciousness or because they are unwilling to take time for it. It is significant, however, that from ancient times to the present even the busiest of public figures who became known for effective speech have found the time to rehearse for major speeches. They have known what you should learn if you do not already know it:

control over self and control over content are imperative when what you say is important, and both kinds of control are established through such oral rehearsal as we have described.

AN OVERVIEW OF PREPARATION

In the foregoing pages we have emphasized the things a speaker ought to consider in preparing for a simple assignment requiring that he or she speak publicly. In concluding we summarize the sequence of preparatory steps serious speakers have found it important to follow. Ordinarily you will need to do the following things in getting ready to speak to an audience:

1. Considering the nature of your audience and the occasion, decide what response you seek concerning the topic you have decided or been assigned to talk about.
2. Narrow or expand your topic until you have located the specific subject that will fit your capacities, your goal, and the requirements of the situation.
3. Wed your rhetorical purpose and your central idea in a clear-cut statement expressing unambiguously the coverage of what you will say and your reason for saying it.
4. Gather the variety of materials that will most strongly and interestingly amplify or support what is expressed in your subject sentence.
5. Organize these materials into a structure that can be shown clearly and systematically in outline form.
6. Consider what kinds of language will best interrelate your materials to form a *whole* that interestingly asserts the basic message contained in your subject sentence.
7. If it is at all possible, prepare yourself to present your talk extemporaneously, so you can speak in an organized, informed way, yet spontaneously and adaptively.
8. As insurance for your plan and against stage fright, rehearse your speech orally to gain full control of the pattern of your ideas, alternative wordings, and timing.

By listing preparatory steps as we have, we do not mean you must invariably proceed in exactly the way our summary suggests. For example, a speaker asked to talk about his recent experiences as a member of a rehabilitation project in Peru need not pause very long over step 4, but he may have more trouble than some others with the narrowing and focusing processes of steps 1 and 2. A speaker assigned to make a report on the budget has step 1 settled for him, as is most of the work of steps 2 and 4.   The speaker who has been in Peru may find his most difficult problem is to sift out irrelevant knowledge to accomplish step 5.   The speaker giving the budget report may find that there are standard forms for budget reports that accomplish most of step 5 for him.   On the other hand, when you decide to talk to your colleagues on a topic you have only recently learned about, you will probably need to devote about the same amount of attention to each of the eight steps listed.   But if a committee in your class should ask you to report on the history of the National Association for the Advancement of Colored People, you would find that most of the considerations implied by steps 1, 2, and 3 were suggested in the way the assignment was given.   However, to be sure you understand the assignment clearly, it would still be useful to run through the first three steps quickly in your mind.

We have tried to summarize the normal preparatory procedures for *any* speaking in which you will bear special responsibility for creating and sustaining human interaction through speech.   What needs to be done at each stage may vary from speaking assignment to speaking assignment, but *each of these speech problems must be settled somehow*.   Whether some have been taken care of by an assignment or by your own experience or by your listeners' expectations is something *you* must decide.   That is your freedom and burden as a communicator.

In this chapter we have touched on matters you need to consider before speaking in a speech class (or elsewhere).   We hope to have suggested that getting ready to present a short talk involves more than following some set of routine prescriptions.   A good deal of thinking about what you are doing, why, and where is required if your talk is to fit well the rhetorical situation you will enter.   We have tried to imply that planning a talk is a matter of adjusting your private knowledge and impulses to accommodate listeners who will be present in a particular kind of setting.   We have argued that you will learn most in a speech class if you treat the classroom as a laboratory for experimenting with your own capacities for speaking and listening.   Treating the classroom in this way gives you opportunities to observe listening habits and improve your own and, through growing understanding of how oral communication works, to refine your ability to be conversationally direct and flexible in relating to audiences.   If the prospect of speaking extemporaneously troubles you, remember that stage fright is not to be overcome without recognizing that fear of oral communication is a matter of attitudes, not of nature.

The thesis of this chapter has been that careful preparation— neither too rigid nor too casual—is the best available antidote for uncertainty about and fear of speaking and the best way of responding to the nature of humans' listening.   What careful preparation involves we have summarized in hope of helping you in your first experiments.

EXERCISES

Written

1. Write five simple, single ideas you think would be good ones for development in a speech of two to three minutes.
2. Select a subject area. Frame a subject sentence for each of the rhetorical purposes: informing, persuading, inquiring, reinforcing and entertaining.
3. Listen carefully to a speech by one of your classmates. Take notes in outline form on what he or she is saying. Following the speech, compare your outline with the one the speaker used. Check to see (a) how accurately you noted what was said and (b) how much you missed noting.

Oral

1. Deliver a three-minute speech in which you develop a single point that could be one of several main points in a longer speech. In developing your point use at least three kinds of supporting material. In preparation, prepare a simple outline like that found on pages 34–35.
2. Prepare and deliver a brief speech on a proverb of your own choosing. Select at least five items to support its truth or falsity. In preparation devise a simple outline like that on pages 36–37.

3

Understanding Audiences

When he can thus give a satisfactory account of the kind of man that is amenable to any particular kind of argument, and is further able to recognize in practice the kind of thing he was discussing when it occurs before his eyes, and can fit his speech and method of persuasion to it, when he has learned all this he must learn when to speak and when to be silent, when is the moment for brevity, when for an appeal to pity or fear and all the things he has learned. Then, and not until then, has the art of speaking been well and fully acquired. But whenever any one who falls short of this in speaking, teaching or writing, boasts that he is an expert, we shall be right not to believe him.[1]

Plato, Phaedrus

No one will achieve the knowledge Plato demands in the quotation above. Plato did not attain it. No psychologist or psychiatrist has it. No one is completely able "to handle arguments according to the rules of art, as far as their nature allows them to be subjected to art." There are no philosopher kings of whom Plato dreamed, for the reason that we all remain more than a little mysterious to ourselves and to each other. We think that fact is a happy one, but it seems that trying to understand and deal with one another considerately and acceptingly is a worthy ideal. We will never know all—either about the things of which we speak or the people to whom we speak. But that should not depress us or discourage us from being as understanding as we can be. Plato's challenge can be useful if it pushes us toward trying to know as much as we can about ourselves, the people we talk to, and what we tell them. By trying, we can hope to win understanding from others more often than we lose it. This act of trying requires us to *think* our ways through the complexities of human communication. Impulse will not carry us through.

This chapter will not teach you *the nature of the soul* (human psychology, we would say, today). That is a matter of heated debate among psychologists and philosophers and theologians. We are none of these. What we hope to do here is move you a little closer toward understanding yourself and your future listeners as communicating

---

1. Plato, *Phaedrus*, pp. 271–72. As translated by G. M. A. Grube, *Plato's Thought* (Boston: Beacon Press, 1958), p. 214.

beings.   We will remind you of many things you already know but too seldom remember.   Perhaps we will be able to bring you a few new thoughts.

When we speak seriously with someone, we normally watch for responses.   We speak because we want to be heard, understood, and reacted to.   We watch our listeners and try to "read" what they feed back to us.   Everyone knows we do this, but we all have some tendency to forget the importance of doing it as the situations in which we speak become more and more formalized.   Then, college students, at least, have a tendency to "talk writing" at their listeners.   But if speaking is to be effective, the human relationships of speakers and listeners have to be more intimate than those of writers with readers.   Poets, novelists, composers of epigrams, many scientists, and others can sometimes concentrate on the timelessness, the universal significance, or the beauty of what they compose.   Instead of having to monitor immediate responses, they can try to reach beyond their immediate surroundings, even to other cultures and times.   But when any of us communicates through speech, we must relate to our immediate listeners, *now*.   If it is not for them that we speak, we should be speaking somewhere else or should be using some other medium of communication.   If we are really speaking seriously and respectfully to listeners, we will pay careful attention to their responses.   Their responses tell us how to continue. We need whatever signals they give us to understand how to communicate.   Watch an experienced comedian work with an audience and you will see how fully he or she understands this fact of oral communication, even though many political and educational speakers seem ignorant of it.

Speaking to listeners is a process, yes.   Everyone recognizes that.   But what many students and others forget is that speech is also a *personal relationship* attempted by someone with someone else. Speaking is always relationship building—effectively or ineffectively. This is so even when we are only thinking about speaking to someone. Then we are *thinking about relating* to someone and about that someone's probable responses, or we are talking only to ourselves.   Do not be fooled by the fact that when you speak on the telephone, over radio, or on television you cannot see and fully interact with all of your listeners.   They are out there, and you know it.   If you are alert to what you are doing, you will imagine them as real people with whom you are trying to establish personal bonds.   Experimental evidence and the testimony of broadcasters and other speakers agree that speech communication deteriorates when speakers have no *live* (real or imagined) audiences to whom they can adjust what they say.   All evidence reinforces two propositions:

1. As humans we need human feedback, if we are normal.
2. Speakers who know how to "read" listeners and adapt to them find that visible listeners enhance communicative effectiveness.

Egocentrism as an Influence

What we have just said about audience adaptation is true, but it is equally true that all of us tend to ignore it.   We are all rather egocentric, although we are also social beings.   Self-love tells us that listeners *ought* to attend to what we say, or that "just being myself" ought to be enough.   Or we tell ourselves, "They *ought* to listen and understand because I'm telling them how I thought it out."   Sometimes the thought runs: "I'll tell them what they *need* to know."   Then, if they do not listen as we hope, we complete the self-delusion by saying, "Well, that's their loss; the stuff was there.   They should have tried harder to understand."   What we overlook in such moments is that we are thinking about *ourselves* and not about communicating with and for other people.   We are shutting out thought about and communication from the people out there.   We cannot in that way be clear or fully interesting to others because for communication to work where more than one person is present *all* must be interacting participants.

Egocentrism is not necessarily a destroyer of communication. We would speak to one another very little if our desires to express and to influence did not impel us.   The problem in relation to oral communication is: how are we to balance egoism and social concern to create orally effective messages?   The answer is to take *both* ourselves and our listeners into account at every moment of preparing to speak and of speaking.   The task is to adjust to both our own and our listeners preferences.   It can be done.

Adjusting to Listeners' Preferences

What effective conversationalists and formal speakers seem to accomplish is to act on the premise that not even their own egos can be well served unless *listeners'* preferences and expectations are accommodated.   To do this takes conscious, careful thinking—in advance of and during speaking.   But anyone can make the adjustment *if* he will think seriously about what communicating with a particular group of listeners does and does not require of him.   Here is an example of one student's efforts in this direction.

A student of landscape architecture whom we will call Dick Barnes was in a basic course in speech taught by one of us. Barnes was not especially effective orally, but he recognized that in his chosen profession he had to be able to reduce abstract and often technical concepts of landscape architecture to terms and images nonspecialists could understand and think with. He, his instructor, and the class struck a bargain. It was that Dick would talk regularly about landscape architecture, another student of architecture in the class would report on whether what Dick said was professionally sound, and the class would write down anything that confused or bored them as Dick talked. In conferences the instructor tried to help Dick think of ways to get around obscurities and causes of apathy among listeners. Twice Dick tried to explain architectural concepts; both times his colleague said he was sound, but his other listeners said things such as, "I couldn't get it," or "You told me more than I wanted to hear about that." Dick and the instructor tried to rethink his strategies, and they concluded that Dick had not translated his concepts into images his listeners could see and he had not associated his ideas with values about which they had feelings. Dick decided that next time he would concentrate on the visuals. His third try worked. He was sound, but he turned his subject, "The Values in Open Spaces," into seeable, feelable realities. Here is a bit of what he said:

> Consider the area behind the Dairy Building. It's small, but it's a pleasing area to walk through. You can walk through it and have different experiences each time because of the very different kinds of plantings—shrubbery, flowers, trees. It's an enjoyable place to be. But so is the Mall. It has a canopy. You see it walking through. Half way up, ahead of you, the trees arch together. You are "inside," yet you're out-of-doors. And there at the center of the arch's end you see Pattee Library, with its straight columns. It completes the enclosing of the area. You feel "inside," but you know you're outside and free. These are things a landscape architect means when he says outdoor spaces have "value" or can be given "values." He's saying he tries to put things into outdoor space in such ways that you will say it's interesting to be there or that you like to be there. The value he's talking about is your good feeling; that's what he tries to create with his shapings and plantings.

There was no weakening of the architectural concepts of space and value. Barnes simply illustrated their reality by transporting his listeners to campus spots they all knew well enough to picture in their minds. Then he made them feel the values he spoke of as his words directed their eyes and movements—in imagination. In these ways the speaker's and listeners' egocentric inclinations were balanced. Barnes *willed* that listeners *should* sense what values are to an architect, but he transformed the professional concept into experienced sensations. That is what his listeners had been demanding of him. Without in any degree becoming a sycophant, he accommodated his own *and* the listeners' wishes. There was communication!

Of course, listeners do not always make it easy for speakers to adjust to their demands. They are not always as open in their demands as Dick Barnes's classmates were. We have all played the role of polite but evasive listener, signalling some kind of acceptance but actually engrossed in our private thoughts. An astute speaker will not take signs of quiet acquiescence as enough. He or she will not presume that listeners will or even can give unbroken attention to what is said. An astute speaker will plan adaptations to the ways listeners behave—to their tendencies to drift in and out, to their fascination with tangential details, to the necessity of pressing them to focus on what is important.

Here is a fair representation of how listeners listen. Notice the partly pertinent, partly irrelevant thoughts a juror recalls having had as a prosecuting attorney began to speak:

> As he faced us head-on, I noticed how weary he seemed and how arched his eyebrows were behind his glasses. His dogged determination had kept the case moving against the defendants for almost four months; this morning he suffered from laryngitis. I recalled my hostility toward him during the long days of jury selection. Now I listened intently.[2]

No doubt the juror "listened intently," but he was not thinking of the prosecutor's *ideas* in those seconds when he was reflecting on the lawyer's health, eyebrows, apparent weariness, and earlier behavior. But let every speaker take note and remember: this juror was listening as people really do listen. His attention was drifting in and out of the flow of ideas the speaker was *steadily* creating through words and action.

The paragraphs above have said little you did not know. But have you applied this knowledge in getting ready to speak formally or informally, and in the act of speaking? We hope to have pulled to the forefront of your mind the importance of watching for and using whatever feedback listeners give you. We hope to have reminded you that egocentrism is always a danger to your effective speaking but need not blind you to ways you can adapt to equally egocentric listeners. Listening is an errant process; if you are to control it in the interests of your purposes you will need the full resources of rhetorical art, which, in turn, requires that you give special forethought to the kinds of situations you enter as speaker.

---

2. Giraud Chester, *The Ninth Juror* (New York: Random House, 1970), p. 104. Mr. Chester, once a teacher of speech and broadcasting and now a broadcasting executive, wrote this interesting book to recount his experience as a juror in a criminal case in New York City.

SPEECHES AND SITUATIONS

For a great many years it was customary to say that in formal and informal speaking a speaker must analyze his subject, his audience, the occasion, and his own relation to all of these.   That was not mistaken, but we now have a better, more comprehensive way of putting the matter.   As we indicated in chapter 1, in 1968 Lloyd F. Bitzer published an award-winning essay in which he suggested that we think of speakers as entering *situations* in which allowing and restraining forces interact with one another and upon the speaker and his or her message.   Bitzer's way of thinking is so useful that we will continue to borrow heavily from his "Rhetorical Situation"[3] here and in later discussions.

Here is a practical explanation of Mr. Bitzer's concept.[4]   Suppose you are to speak to a group of people.   The situation may be formal or informal.   There will, of course, be people—an audience—but something will have brought them into the relationship of being an audience and not just an aggregation.   Whatever it is that caused them to be an audience is part of what you or any potential speaker must take into account.   This audience will have both individual and collective histories.   Those histories will affect what can be accomplished through talk—if anything at all can be accomplished.   Similarly, objects and events this audience is aware of will have an effect.   Add to all of the forces just mentioned the fact that the audience will also respond to all of their past relationships to you and what you represent and to all circumstances they know of concerning objects and persons related to you and the conditions under which they come into contact with you.   These, too, will be part of the situation in which you meet your listeners.

Professor Bitzer's point is that rhetorical speech happens within a complex of conditioning forces; it is wiser to think of speaking as bringing a message into a set of conditions than to think of it merely as making statements to specific persons.   Those persons, Bitzer insists, are parts of a "complex of persons, objects, events, and relations" that generate certain *exigences* or needs or readinesses.   These needs or readinesses may or may not be alterable through talk, and they may or may not invite talk from a particular speaker.   As an obvious example of his way of thinking, Bitzer calls attention to the days immediately after a president has been assassinated.   Somehow, the entire nation feels certain people must *say* something about the shocking event and about the dead president.   One cannot imagine this

---

3. Lloyd F. Bitzer, "The Rhetorical Situation," *Philosophy and Rhetoric* I (January 1968): 1–14.   The essay received the James A. Winans Award for Distinguished Scholarship in Rhetoric and Public Address in 1968.
4. It may be useful to refer to pp. 15–17 in chapter 1 when you have completed reading the present paragraph.

national situation being properly handled without several kinds of public talk from several kinds of speakers. It isn't just *who* the audience is that determines who needs to talk and what things need saying, it is the whole complex of events *and* people *and* human relations that defines what remedy-through-talk fits the public need. As in all other rhetorical situations, potential listeners need, or at least will allow, special human relationships with speakers within conditions that envelope everyone and impose opportunities and restrictions on what may be *fittingly* said and done.

Entering a Rhetorical Situation

If you think about speaking publicly in this way, you will not think of yourself as "addressing an audience" as much as you will think of yourself as "entering a situation" in which other people and you are conditioned by time, place, occasion, past history, and expectations that certain kinds of changes are supposed to take place as the result of your coming together. Bitzer stresses another important point: influenced by all these forces, the people in the situation may or may *not* think their situation needs some *talk*. There are situations in which money or clothes or something else, but not *talk,* can solve the exigence or urgent needs. But if the forces that created the situation have created an exigence or urgency that can be helped by talk of some sort, then obviously *you* can enter the situation with some prospects of making it change. There will also be situations in which the need is for some talk from *you* and not from someone else. On the other hand, there will be situations within which you will first have to create a need for *talk* from *you*—make room for yourself within the conditions that constitute the speech situation. For example, a political speaker at a non-political picnic will need to give those attending some reasons for becoming serious and political before he or she can safely launch a discussion of political issues.

How do you diagnose a situation to discover whether there is any exigence or readiness that talk from *you* can fill? You do it by asking yourself questions such as those we presented in our first chapter, pp. 16–17. When you have done that, a few other questions and their answers can tell you what you, as speaker, can do. Ask yourself: if the situation does not already invite *me* to change it by talk, can I reconstruct it so it *will* accept me and the main ideas I want to bring to it? If the ideas I want to talk about do not fit the allowances of the situation exactly, can I modify them or add to them to make them fitting? Will I need to qualify myself in special ways so *I* can fit the allowances of the situation fully? Answering such questions will tell you whether you have two tasks or one: to change the situation first and *then* present the talk you have in mind, or simply to enter a situation that is already set to receive your influence through talk.

We have been rather theoretical in the preceding paragraphs; let us now come down to the practical level of classroom speaking. If your class has been studying how information can best be given orally, and if an assignment has been made for a series of five-minute explanations, everyone in the class will have been conditioned by study and the assignment. Informative speech by anyone in the class will fit the rhetorical situation that previous study and the assignment have created. What will happen in these circumstances if you give a talk that entertains more than it explains? Certainly some listeners will be perplexed and some may begin to feel embarrassment for you. Some will wonder: "Doesn't she know she was to inform us?" "How's our instructor going to react to this?" Why such questions? Everyone likes to be entertained. Yet you could present the most hilarious speech anyone ever heard and still there would be some perplexity and uneasiness in your audience. The reason is best explained through Bitzer's notion of rhetorical situations: "a natural context of persons, [previous] events, objects, relations, and an exigence" has defined what kind of speaking fits and does not fit the circumstances just now. Thinking only about the audience as people will not explain why entertainment misfires in the set of circumstances we are imagining. A good way to put the matter is that situations make assignments that can only sometimes be altered by speakers.

When an Assignment Is Imposed

Some incidents will illustrate when rhetorical situations can be altered and when they cannot.

One of us taught a speech class where there occurred a group discussion in which several students expressed great concern about preserving wildlife in the United States. A few days after, there was a series of speeches, several of which also dealt with ecology. Discussions following those speeches produced many remarks sweepingly critical of disturbers of nature. Criticism was showered on various groups from industries to hunters. At this point a biology major decided privately that the climate of opinion was becoming too one-sided and, since wildlife management was one of his special interests, he decided to straighten things out by making a speech in favor of regulated hunting of female deer. It happened that doe hunting was then being criticized by some conservationists. What had happened in the class and what was being printed in newspapers and being broadcast all generated a situation in which another speech on ecology could have influence. But a speech endorsing hunting would have to be worked out with care for a bias against hunting had developed in the class and was being fed from outside it. The biology major adapted so skillfully to this situation that he changed some attitudes.

He began his speech by recalling earlier talk about "management," "protecting the balance," "caring about nature," and the like. Then he said:

> I want you to think some more about "balance." I want you to think about how we are to keep the deer of this state in balance with the space and food we are willing to allow them. I'd like you to think whether you want to protect healthy deer or sick and scrawny ones, whether you want more deer killed on highways, and whether you have any sympathy for the human beings who run the farms of our rural areas. Let me tell you about the balancing problems that affect the lives of deer.

He went on to show that natural reproductive processes would cause deer in his state to overpopulate available wild land every two years unless a certain number of does were regularly eliminated. Fewer than the required number had been killed in past years, he said. The present imbalance was justification for extending the annual doe season. Several listeners' reactions were well expressed by one student who said, afterward: "Now you've got me almost embarrassed. I don't hunt; I don't even like the idea. But the way you put it, it seems like I *ought* to take up hunting deer if not enough other people do. Really, I don't feel too comfortable!"

The incident illustrates that where the forces creating a speech situation have only shaped *opinions,* an astute speaker can usually change the constraints or restrictions of the situation by taking time to discover what there is in the opinion-making background that can be used to justify *other* directions of thought. The biology major seized upon the ways in which "balance" had been installed in his listeners' minds as a proper concept, and he artistically made his thoughts about doe hunting suitable for the situation by linking all of his potentially unacceptable or irrelevant ideas to that agreed-upon, positive value.

You will find another instance in which a speaker was able to change an opinion-dominated situation in the speech discussed by students in appendix B.

Violating Assignments

Although speakers can alter the allowances of rhetorical situations, situations can also be so exacting that they dictate *assignments* to speakers. Assignments are much harder to change than the opinions of listeners—as we saw in our example of the classroom on p. 57.   To take another kind of example, academic ceremonies tend to dictate that education be talked about.   Few can escape that kind of assignment, although sometimes a speaker may be so important that he can deviate without apology.   Sir Winston Churchill was once invited to speak at a convocation at Westminster College in Missouri.   The situation would normally prescribe a talk about education, but Sir Winston gave his famous "Iron Curtain" speech describing Cold War tensions. In 1977 President Carter spoke at a convocation honoring the president of Notre Dame University in Indiana.   Mr. Carter observed the exigences of the immediate situation by praising the university's president, but he also discussed American foreign policy.   Apparently no one worried about these speakers' evasions of some normal dictates of academic ceremonies, but not many speakers have the prestige or status to recreate situations at will.

A far more representative event happened at a national conference of officers of college and university women's associations.   This conference's planning committee invited a well-known newswoman to be the conference's keynote speaker.   With student affairs predominantly coeducational, the women's associations needed to redefine their functions on campuses.   Accordingly the conference was to be devoted to exploring new areas of service for women's groups.   We do not know exactly what the conference's planners told their keynote speaker, but the call for the conference and the published titles of the workshops were so written as to make clear what the conference's problem was.   The planners had scheduled things in hopes that the keynote speech would contain starting-off ideas about what the women's associations ought to be doing.

The keynote speaker spoke interestingly of problems and gratifications experienced by professional women, especially journalists. Nothing was said about college and university women's associations or specific problems they faced.   The conference leaders were deeply upset, and audible murmurs developed during the speech—apparently indicating that listeners were perplexed or losing interest.   The speech was an excellent one for this speaker to make, but this was not the situation for it.   The publicity and planning had announced something different would happen.   Moreover, the conference itself got off to a very slow start according to one of the planners, for the program's success depended on the keynote speaker to provide the workshops with starting points.   She had not done this.   Perhaps the planners had created a speech situation the speaker could not fill or had failed to brief her on the created situation, or perhaps the speaker had not investigated the situation as she should have.   In any case, the assignment was violated; the speaker suffered, the audience became uneasy, and conference plans went awry. The assignments of situations cannot be ignored with safety.[5]

What we have been saying about analyzing rhetorical situations from a practical standpoint is this: Although it is essential to adapt to listeners and to settings, one must also look beyond listeners and settings to discover the whole set of forces requiring attention on any occasion. Remember that not every situation involving people calls for *talk*. Some situations not initially calling for rhetorical talk can be altered—perhaps by talk itself—so as to be receptive to your message. The whole situation must be studied in advance. Plans must be made to make the situation ready for whatever speech you judge will fit.

CONCEPTUALIZING AUDITORS AS POTENTIAL LISTENERS

Audience is a common term, but we often think unclearly or too sweepingly about what an audience for ordinary public communication is. You have probably read or heard discussions about "the mass audience" that leave the impression that any large audience is a mass of faceless beings who present an impressionable surface on which speakers may make imprints at will. Even in more sophisticated discussions it seems often implied that people, because they are together with others in an audience, can be made to lose or abandon their individualities.

We know that in what we are going to say next we are making assertions about matters that since the 1890s have been highly debatable for social psychologists. Nonetheless, we think you will make very serious mistakes if you approach any audience you are likely to meet as though the people in it are anything but highly individualistic, self-controlled beings chiefly interested in their private interests and the interests of the groups and individuals they value. Even if there is such a thing as *crowd psychology* or *deindividuation* or some other psychological process of stripping away individuality and imposing group or mob feeling, we do not think you are going to encounter or use it very often. We think most of the audiences you will talk to will be small and large groups of people who need to be treated as though they had these qualities:

---

5. During the next year one of the disappointed planners was wise enough to invite the newswoman to give the *same* speech to a campus gathering of women students. This time the occasion was announced as a speech and discussion on "Women in Professional Life." This time the same speaker, with substantially the same speech, was eminently successful. So was the entire meeting.

1. They have standards of judgment they feel can be relied on in interpreting what you say and do.
2. They have developed a readiness to *question* what other people give them as interpretations of the ways things are or of what they, the listeners, ought to do or think.
3. Even when they do not have precise standards for evaluating what you say and do, they will feel they have other, related standards by which to judge the worth of what you say.

Those are the conditions of mind of people exercising *critical ability*.[6] We think the vast majority of your listeners, certainly in the classroom and probably throughout your life, will in fact hear you critically in these senses.

Conformity in Audiences

There is, of course, a large literature in psychology and theory of communication that emphasizes the ways in which group pressure, the behaviors of other people, can influence members of small and large groups.[7] The practical problem is that very little of this research deals with normal rhetorical communication in ordinary settings.

In the absence of clear evidence concerning how crowd pressures work in ordinary rhetorical settings, we think the safe thing to do is to think about listeners as *individuals* and as subgroups of individuals whose special patterns of experience have generated attitudes dis-

---

6. These statements are adapted from Hadley Cantril, *The Psychology of Social Movements*, originally published in 1941, reissued and cited here (New York: John Wiley and Sons, 1963), pp. 76–77.

7. The classic experiments on group pressure and individual judgments were conducted by S. E. Asch. They showed that college students regularly gave wrong judgments about the lengths of lines when a majority of the group of eight took what were in fact wrong positions. When these experiments are cited as evidence that people overwhelmingly conform to the behaviors of those around them, it is usually forgotten that *if just one other group member agreed on a judgment,* most of Asch's subjects held out for their own *right* judgments about the lines. See Bernard Berelson and Gary A. Steiner, *Human Behavior: An Inventory of Scientific Findings* (New York: Harcourt, Brace and World, 1964), pp. 335–36. Furthermore, more recently it has been argued that at least 32 percent of the conformity Asch claimed to have found was actually "adoption of a new public position, while the private position remains unchanged from what it was before." See Lawrence S. Wrightsman et al., *Social Psychology for the Seventies* (Monterey, Calif.: Brooks/Cole Publishing Co., 1972), p. 481. Wrightson and his colleagues list among the "unresolved issues in the study of conformity and nonconformity" the facts that the natures of *non*conformity have been far less studied than the presence of conforming *overt* behavior, and that psychological research has generally not distinguished overt compliance with unchanged private opinion from compliance in consequence of conformingly changed opinion.

tinguishable from the attitudes of other subgroups. But there will also be the fact that all your listeners will share their humanity and behave generally in moderately predictable human ways. In addressing audiences thought of in these ways, you will need to take account of how people in general and in commonly present subgroups give attention to speech and form attitudes toward what they hear.

First, how do people in general attend to speech?

GETTING ATTENTION

A great German zoologist wrote, "The outside world—the world perceived by the senses—is the source of all that a form of life is and does, thinks and feels."[8] One way to describe listeners is to say that they "form themselves" by what they hear and see. But what *will* they choose to hear and see? Generally, that will be determined by (1) the stimuli that impinge upon them, (2) what previous experience has led them to expect, and (3) what they want and need just now.[9] Out of these generalizations about how people respond we can build some rules of thumb for adapting communication to audiences of any size. One of these rules is: what will allow a listener a strong sense experience (actual or vicarious) is apt to be attended to and responded to. This means that actions and words that allow listeners to see, hear, feel, taste, or smell draw attention. They are strong speech stimuli. It means vivid words that *suggest* sensory experience are special resources for getting and sustaining attention. A listener may sense once more the blue-grey glint of a desert sky if someone reminds him or her of it with words. Or the word *lightning* may trigger a reliving of the zigzag outline of a lightning bolt seen at some other time. The point is that actions and language that draw on listeners' previous sensory experiences are a major resource any speaker can use to get and hold attention.

Experience, and either innate or learned needs, seem to make listeners search for intelligible *relationships* among stimuli. They try to relate likenesses and dissimilarities among things heard with what they have experienced before. So here we can find another rule of thumb for securing and holding attention: Keep relationships— comparative and contrastive—clearly before those who hear you. You will be logically clear and be gratifying a need or wish of your listeners.

---

8. Wolfgang von Buddenbrock, *The Senses,* trans. Frank Gaynor (Ann Arbor: The University of Michigan Press, 1958), p. 12.
9. Berelson and Steiner, *Human Behavior,* p. 100.

The Task of Control

Speakers often misjudge their task in controlling attention. They suppose *securing* attention is the important thing. But getting attention is easy. Usually you have only to move about in some way— generate any kind of change—and you will draw attention. This is why introductory gimmicks, so beloved by exhibitionists, always seem to work. They were not needed in the first place! Anyone can get attention at the beginning of speaking; it is *directing* and *holding* attention that is the real, artistic task. We have just mentioned two rules of thumb for controlling listeners' attention. The rest of this chapter deals with additional ways by which you can sustain attention to what you say and at the same time increase the prospects of invoking the changes you want in the rhetorical situations you enter.

LISTENERS' READINESS TO BELIEVE OR CHANGE

Many experiments and other inquiries have been made to determine just what controls people's willingness to change beliefs and attitudes or alter their perspectives on things. Some findings are uniform enough to yield generalizations that speakers can use. For other possibilities systematic research has given no clear answers. We therefore have to draw on both scientific evidence and common sense in presenting a practical image of members of audiences as attentive, changeable beings.

Gratifying Biological Needs

We can begin with the basic fact that everyone in your audiences will be biologically mammilian and have the bodily and organic needs generally found among mammals. All of us want gratifications for hunger, for thirst, for our need for oxygen, for sexual drives, and for security from injury, punishment, and other kinds of painful or depriving experience. But being human we also exercise preferences in many of these matters. We seek gratifications for our physical needs, but we are also capable of deferring or even suppressing some of these needs when we want something else still more. For example, audiences are often willing to undergo a certain amount of physical discomfort—undue heat or hard seats—if they believe that what they will hear and see will protect them from some later harm or pay off in long-range satisfactions.

So if you want to hold and direct listeners' attention, one rough rule is to show them that you can help them toward gratification of some biological needs. They are likely to listen to you at least until they begin to doubt your promise or suspect that following what you urge will force them to give up still more important goals. Modern advertising constitutes a veritable textbook in how appeals to biological needs can secure and direct attention and motivate human choices.

Here are some examples taken from recent magazine advertisements: "Stouffers knows that there's nothing like a great meal to make business a pleasure. American Express knows that at Stouffer's fine dining is more than fine food." "Macho. It's b-a-a-a-d. The powerful scent for men by Faberge. Macho is b-a-a-d. And that's good." "How early we must learn to be respectful of fire. And how grateful we are throughout life that science and industry continually improve the technology of fire prevention to protect us. FMC Corporation." Some of these appeals you will find too crude or blatant for listeners' tastes, but the fact remains that when you can link your thoughts even indirectly to physical needs of your listeners, you ought to do so. It will almost surely increase the prospect of your being heard and heard with favor.

Sex

Sex is both a biological and a social condition that makes differences in listeners' readiness to attend, believe, and change. As a speaker you ought to try to accommodate what you say to these differences. Today, there is much argument about what interests, motivations, and degrees of persuasibility differentiate women from men, but scientific and other evidence makes it plain that men and women do not react precisely alike to all communicated material. Why should it be otherwise? Female and male roles and experiences are not always identical; so where male and female experiences are apt to have differed, any sensible speaker ought to take that into account in what he or she says to a mixed audience or an audience of one sex only. There is also some evidence that women are more critical of female speakers than men are, and vice versa. So if you are a woman you ought to expect more difficulties in securing and directing the attention and attitudes of women than men. If you are male it will be wise to assume that the other males in your audiences will be a bit harder to persuade than the women. Finally, as the last decade has shown very plainly, the roles and relationships of women and men have been and are changing continually. You will be wise, then, to take into serious consideration, as you prepare any speech, just what sex roles and relationships are conventional and accepted by the particular audience you address.

Age, too, affects listeners' attitudes and their general responses to communication. This is another biological and social difference among people to which society has become especially sensitive in the past decade.

To generalize across situations about any age group is precarious, and there is not much research on the relation of age to judgments, except in relation to specific subjects. What we do know, however, tends to confirm the suppositions of traditional lore in rhetoric and literature: The young are more persuasible than their elders and the elderly are cautious; the young, middle-aged, and old tend to give closest attention to different aspects of ideas and issues. What is scientifically known suggests that in speaking you can safely follow the implicit guidelines of Aristotle, unless you know something special about a situation or audience that indicates otherwise. None of the observations we are about to paraphrase from Aristotle has been disproved as a generalization about our own society, and many have been confirmed sociologically.

Aristotle tried to address himself, as few modern psychological studies have, to "the proper means of adapting both speech and speaker to a given audience." He sought rhetorically applicable generalizations about the young, men in their prime, and the elderly. Below is a quick summary of his observations, and if you take the trouble to compare them to the results of public opinion polls that report opinions by age groupings, you will be struck by the modernity of what he said, except for his neglect of women's views.

In youth "men have strong desires, and whatever they desire they are prone to do. Of the bodily desires the one they let govern them most is the sexual; here they lack self-control. They are shifting and unsteady in their desires. . . ." They are "quick to anger, and apt to give way to it," and they are "fond of honor" and even "fonder of victory." Money means relatively little to them "for they have not yet learned what the want of it means." They are not cynical; rather, they are trustful "for as yet they have not been often deceived." Being quick to hope and living much in anticipation, "they are easily deceived." Although brave and spirited, they are also shy. Being idealistic, "in their actions they prefer honor to expediency" and are dogmatic. "All their mistakes are on the side of intensity and excess. . . ."

In middle life, Aristotle thought, people "will be neither excessively confident . . . nor yet too timid; they will be both confident and cautious. They will neither trust everyone nor distrust everyone; rather they will judge the case by the facts. Their rule of life will be neither honor alone, nor expediency alone. . . ." They will temper valor with self-control, and they will be neither parsimonious nor prodigal with their possessions. Generally, "all the valuable qualities which youth and age divide between them are joined in the prime of life." Is it not so of both men and women?

The aged have characteristics opposed to those of the young. Thus, "they err by an extreme moderation" and are "positive about nothing" for they have lived long and been disappointed much. They tend to be cynical and "put the worst construction on everything"; they are suspicious, and sometimes small-minded. They "aspire to nothing great or exalted, but crave the mere necessities and comforts of existence." They are constantly apprehensive and "live their lives with too much regard for the expedient and too little for honor." What other people think means little to them, for they "live in memory rather than in anticipation."

Aristotle concluded: "Now the hearer is always receptive when a speech is adapted to his own character and reflects it. Thus we can readily see the proper means of adapting both speech and speaker to a given audience."[10]

A speaker cannot, of course, always gratify the idealism of youth and the caution of age with the same argument; nor can he or she depend on it that there are *no* cautious youths and *no* radical elders in an audience. But more often than most speakers realize, ideas are at once *right* and *fair* (satisfying idealists) and *practical* (satisfying the cautious). If you look at Dr. M. Lee Upcraft's speech in appendix B, you will see that he addressed both the issue of fairness and the issue of practicality. His immediate audience was relatively young, but what he said would be publicly reported and must make sense to people of all ages associated with his university. It is well, then, that he spoke as he did. His appeals to "right" certainly struck home with his young audience, but his emphasis on the practicalities of the university's legal position and the students' future prospects seem to have made *some* impression on the immediate audience and also could stand as a strong justification of the university's position for *everyone*.

Our main point here is that as a speaker you can and ought to include something for each prominent age group in any audience. Almost any subject is open to treatment in relation to ideals and also practicalities. Although age groups may differ in the intensity of their

---

10. From *The Rhetoric of Aristotle*, translated and edited by Lane Cooper, pp. 132–37, bk. II, chaps. 12–14. © 1932, renewed 1960 by Lane Cooper. Reprinted by permission of Prentice-Hall, Inc., Englewood Cliffs, New Jersey.

interest in one or another line of thought, their differing interests are seldom in total conflict. Adapting to age groups' special interests is largely a matter of *emphasis* and *manner* of development, not of subject matter itself.

Intelligence

Intelligence is another attribute everyone has in some degree. But levels of what is usually measured as intelligence differ, and those differences suggest very important guidelines for speakers.

What is it that our society generally measures when a measure of intelligence is wanted? Although testing programs are changing, estimates of intelligence still tend to be estimates of ability in a specific set of skills. These are verbal comprehension, handling numbers, spatial perception, remembering, reasoning, fluency with words, and perceptual speed.[11] Notice how important language skills are in this set of abilities! This suggests that the higher your listeners' intelligence, the better they will be able to understand speech; the lower their intelligence, the more help you must give.

At first glance, what we know about relations between general intelligence and responses to communication seems confusing. Summarizing the evidence as of 1967, one pair of authors said:

> . . . it is as plausible to assert that the factor of intelligence is positively correlated with persuasibility as it is to assert a negative correlation, or even no correlation. On the one hand, the more intelligent a person, the better able he is to comprehend the issues. The less intelligent person, because of his limited comprehension, is less susceptible to persuasion on complex issues. On the other hand, the more intelligent a person, the greater his critical ability, and the less he is influenced by persuasion. There is literature in support of the null, the positive, and the negative relationship.[12]

Understanding of these relationships has not changed much in the last decade. For a practical speaker the uncertainties these authors express seem discouraging; but if you study the statements carefully, you can extract some good advice. The *higher* the intelligence of your listeners, the more readily you can expect them to understand what you say, *but* the quicker they will be to criticize you if you make what they take to be mistakes. Your safe course with highly intelligent listeners, then, is to be careful to justify and qualify your data and your claims. However, if there are people of limited intelligence among your listeners,

---

11. Berelson and Steiner, *Human Behavior*, pp. 212–15.

12. Ralph L. Rosnow and Edward J. Robinson, *Experiments in Persuasion* (New York: Academic Press, 1967), p. 198.

you will need to worry about being especially clear and explicit to help them comprehend what you say.

To these generalizations another can be added: regardless of intelligence levels, people who have little or no initial knowledge of what is said to them are likely to accept what they hear *first* about that subject. Accordingly you will need to consider what your listeners already know about your subject. If they know the subject well, be careful to leave no doubt that you are in full command of the relevant material—and be doubly careful if you believe your listeners are highly intelligent. On the other hand, if you are clear, plainly well informed, and unpretentious, you can expect both the gifted and the ungifted to pay attention to you, comprehend you, and find you believable. Never make the mistake of supposing that clarity and the greatest simplicity a subject will allow are viewed as weakness by listeners of any intelligence level.

Strength of Attitudes

Strength of attitudes already held by listeners is another quality to try to estimate in audiences. All listeners have *some* attitudes toward most things you can speak of, and you need to think about what those attitudes will be in each rhetorical situation. R. E. Lane and D. O. Sears have made a succinct statement of what you will be up against in this connection:

> People who differ from you will tend to distort your views. When you differ slightly from your friends, they will think you agreed with them. Your enemies will think you disagree with them more than you actually do. Both tendencies will weaken your capacity to influence them in the way you wish to.[13]

This kind of predictable situation implies that speakers ought to reflect carefully on whether the various segments of their audiences will be friendly, indifferent, or hostile to ideas that need to be present. If you can discover which attitudes prevail strongly among your hearers, Lane and Sears's statement suggests what kind of *misunderstandings* you need to guard against. You can then gauge more closely what you can reasonably expect to accomplish. A careful student of human communication has said,

> One of the best established findings in social psychology is that individuals who have well-established attitudes and beliefs act so as to

---

13. R. E. Lane and D. O. Sears, *Public Opinion* (Englewood Cliffs, N.J.: Prentice-Hall, 1964), p. 51.

maintain them; the more extreme the attitudes, the more difficult they are to change.[14]

From the data about the roles strong attitudes play in regulating responses at least two clear guidelines for speaking can be inferred. One is: the more firmly your listeners hold a view, the easier it will be for you to strengthen or vitalize that view; but the *less* change *from* that view you should ask for. Even hostile listeners' opinions can be changed a *little* if you proceed cautiously and with respect for attitudes already held; but if you ask for immediate, major changes, you are apt to be rejected. On the other hand, if what you need to say confirms attitudes your listeners hold, merely to restate those views somewhat freshly can intensify the opinions already held. Another useful guideline is: if you believe certain attitudes are *lightly* held by your listeners, you are safe in asking for large changes and for full acceptance of your ideas on those points. When attitudes are lightly held, accepting new views is often easier for a listener than splitting hairs about the matter.

Commitment

People may be committed to positions about ideas in varying degrees, as we have just implied. Three aspects of *commitment* or involvement will deserve your attention when you analyze any rhetorical situation.

First, listeners' involvement with ideas—their commitments to them—can be deep even though the attitudes toward those ideas are moderate. *Moderation* in outlook should not be confused with holding views lightly, for listeners can be strongly committed to their moderate stands.[15] Suppose you were to advocate federal regulation of water resources. If your audience were a general one, there would doubtless be some people almost automatically favorable to federal planning; some would be as automatically unfavorable to federal planning; and there would probably be some who held the view that the best planning is that in which federal, state, and local governments all participate. This last view might be thought of as a moderate view relative to your position, but you would err if you thought (without investigating the

14. Gary Cronkhite, *Persuasion: Speech and Behavioral Change* (Indianapolis: The Bobbs-Merrill Company, 1969), p. 139.

15. For general discussion see Carolyn Sherif, Muzafer Sherif, and Roger Nebergall, *Attitude and Attitude Change: The Social Judgment-Involvement Approach* (Philadelphia: W. B. Sanders Company, 1965). A particularly inclusive experiment generally confirming the points made here is C. David Mortensen and Kenneth Sereno, "The Influence of Ego-Involvement and Discrepancy on Perceptions of Communication," *Speech Monographs* XXXVII (June 1970): 127–34.

matter) that these moderates were any more *indifferent* to questions of planning than the other two groups. Our point is simply that whenever you prepare to speak to an audience, you ought to find out (if you can) how committed the neutrals or moderates are to their already held positions. You must be prepared to treat neutrals and moderates just as you would people with firmly held positive and negative attitudes; there can be deep commitment to neutrality and moderation or, perhaps, even to compromise.

A second aspect of commitment or involvement also deserves your thought. Simply put, the question is: have any listeners already *done* things that have deepened their commitments to a view or feeling you must touch upon? Put differently, have they committed themselves by previous *actions*? There has been a good deal of research on how actions commit people, for the future, to whatever was involved in their acts. But we still do not know how much or under what circumstances particular kinds of acts produce commitment. It does appear, though, that just making a speech or writing an essay in support of a view can fix that view more firmly in people's minds—even if they formerly disagreed with the view. Certainly, if this is true, any speaker ought to check whether prospective listeners have joined organizations, given money, marched, or done other major acts relative to a topic or position the speaker wants to treat. If any have, the speaker has nothing to lose by assuming the acts are evidence of firm, fixed views. If he can use those views in support of his own he ought to. If he cannot use them he ought to avoid arousing those acted-on beliefs. If he must alter those views he must ask only for minimal changes in any one speech.

Another kind or degree of commitment is often disregarded by inexperienced speakers simply because it is not very important in classrooms but is so commonplace everywhere else that it is overlooked. This is the commitment expressed toward a speaker by a listener's simply *coming* to hear. In your classroom your listeners are there as much because they have to be as because they are breathlessly waiting to hear you speak. In a class the presence of an audience expresses no special commitment to you or any other speaker, but in most out-of-class speech situations things are different. Consider yourself. It takes at least curiosity to get you out of your apartment or dormitory and into a meeting where someone talks publicly. It expresses some kind of commitment to some set of ideas for you to be in the meeting at all. It even expresses a kind of commitment in favor of a speaker when you turn your head on campus to listen more closely to someone else. The basic point is that when listeners listen *voluntarily*, their effort is an expression of a favorable commitment to the person who speaks—unless we know that the listener's real purpose in listening or attending a meeting is to scoff or oppose. There are, of course, speech situations in which desire for information or desire for reasons to be-lieve is what brings listeners into the situation. Very many rallies, seminars, lecture-discussions, caucus meetings, testimonials, teach-ins, and the like are meetings where listeners come for the very purpose of committing themselves toward speakers and their subjects. Wherever this occurs, the speaker has a great advantage, for he or she has clear signs that there are favorable attitudes to work with. But the speaker also has great responsibilities. *Not* to be informative, convincing, im-pressive, or inspiring according to the listeners' expectations will violate their commitments and make them strongly negative toward the offend-ing speaker.

What we have just said emphasizes the challenge of classroom speaking. The presence of listeners in a class is not a sign of commit-ment in favor of those who speak. But it could *become* so. The acid test of classroom speaking is: can you establish a climate of opinion in which your colleagues actually try to make class just to hear you? We have seen this achieved. It is the ultimate compliment to a speaker who is serious about his or her communication.

In this section we have been pointing to generally predictable conditions that exist within all rhetorical audiences whether large or small. *All* audiences will have certain biological needs, will be male or female, will be of some age or range of ages, will be of some level or range of intelligence, and will have attitudes held with some degrees of confidence and commitment. You can be sure of these things about every audience, and if you have even general acquaintance with a par-ticular rhetorical situation you can make valuable estimates of how ready the audience will be for what you have to say. As an illustration, here is a true account of how one of us used such minimal knowledge in preparing a speech.

I had accepted an invitation to talk with an audience on the subject, "On Listening: What Does Rhetoric Have to Say to Cognitive Psychology?" The audience would be anyone who chose to attend a conference on "Cognition and the Symbolic Processes." The conference was held on a university campus. The conditions of the invitation to speak were that a formal essay on the assigned subject should be sub-mitted in advance of the conference to be distributed at the opening of the conference. The speaker would then, at his designated hour, talk his message to the audience. This was only the second time in my life I had ever made a speech to professional psychologists and those who join with them in their conferences. So what could be estimated about this prospective audience to guide me in preparing the talk version of an already distributed paper?

BIOLOGICAL NEEDS. The time for the speech was 1:30 p.m., follow-ing the conference's luncheon period. Everyone would be sluggish, perhaps wanting a nap as much as anything else. I decided to build in some specific examples that would actively involve the listeners in what I had to say about listening.

SEX.   The audience would be male and female, but a common interest in psychology would be far more significant than any sex-grounded differences of interests. Sex could be ignored as a feature of this audience.

AGE.   According to the program some people present would be in their sixties and seventies, but I also learned that both undergraduate and graduate students would be present. It would be an audience of all ages; so I inserted into my talk some allusions to the state of knowledge forty years before, some data from the 1950s, and I expanded a reference to a brand-new book cited only briefly in my formal paper.

INTELLIGENCE.   Almost by definition this audience would be highly intelligent. Accordingly I inserted some assurances that I was not trying to make sweeping generalizations from the limited data I had to offer. (In fact, a succeeding speaker criticized me for not having claimed enough in the paper, which was more assertive than the talk!)

STRENGTHS OF ATTITUDES AND COMMITMENTS.   This being a conference on cognition and symbolic processes, I could predict that my listeners would believe behaviorism, as a way of studying psychology, can never answer the most fundamental questions about human nature. This is almost a tenet of faith among those who call themselves "cognitive psychologists." With relief, then, I expanded a section of the paper saying that philosophical and phenomenological research have enlarged understanding of what it is to *be* in communication with one another. Of course, since no one had to attend the conference, and some would have crossed the entire United States to get there, I could be confident that everyone was committed to learning and discussing how we think and use symbols. I had no need to offer pleas for a hearing on this subject.

This, in fact, was almost all I had to think about in readjusting the content of an already written paper for a talk with this audience. Without at least this much knowledge of the audience—which any speaker can almost always secure—I simply would not have known anything to do other than bore the audience with a rehash of exactly the material the listeners already had received.

Our point is that ordinary review of the broad characteristics of any audience does, indeed, provide strategies for maintaining attention and for influencing any specific audience.

AUDIENCES' READINESS FOR SPECIAL RHETORICAL FEATURES

There are certain rhetorical patterns—ways of saying things—that all audiences in all circumstances are specially receptive to. When ideas can be said in the ways we are now going to discuss, you can be confident that their likelihood of being attended to will be heightened. They make speech engaging and interesting, no matter who the listener is. They can be *built into* thoughts and language. They are sometimes called *factors of attention,* but we think it is clearer to say they are special rhetorical features for which audiences are always ready— apparently just by virtue of being human beings who have the unique ability to think and speak symbolically.

There are at least nine of these special rhetorical features: activity, proximity, realism, familiarity and novelty, conflict and suspense, vitality, specificity, intensity, and humor. Below is a brief statement of what each of these features is, accompanied by the general reason that the feature is likely to control or direct attention. Brief examples of the features are also given.

RESOURCE

BASIS OF INFLUENCE

1. *Activity.* Actual movement suggested by the idea itself or by verbal imagery or by activity displayed in speaking. You refer to racing cars, draw a sweeping curve on the blackboard, or you say, "He *scurried* out of his hiding place."

The presence of change or movement always tends to attract attention; real or imagistic movement creates the sense of change; a speaker's movement *is* change.

2. *Proximity.* Showing that things are near in time or space to the listener, or near to one another (actually or figuratively). You draw two shapes close to one another, or you say, "Such a person could be sitting *next to you* on the bus," or "The planet, Mars, is now our *neighbor.*"

Adjacency is among the simplest relationships to perceive, and real or imagined adjacency to a listener implies the listener is or could be directly involved in experiencing whatever you are speaking of.

3. *Realism* or *vividness.* Pictorial or other sensory qualities introduced by imagistic language or by action or by physical illustration. You say, "I was covered

Learning through the senses, directly or vicariously, is the basic experience by which knowledge is gained, survival defended, and many of our with *black sticky mud*," or you point to where the mud covered you, or you bring some mud and show what it is really like.

4. *Familiarity and novelty.* Association of ideas with what listeners know, or presentation of what was either unknown or never perceived in the way proposed. You compare governmental budgeting to family budgeting, or the family budget to regulating the international balance of payments.

All humans prize and attend to what they have experienced before; they also enjoy or are curious about experience that is new.

5. *Conflict and suspense.* Showing either animate or inanimate things in opposition to one another or in competition with one another, the details or the outcome being in either case uncertain in some degree. You create an image of a contest between science and the environment, or you say, "This is a race between ideas and fear," or you inject a "fight image" or illustration when amplifying.

Opposition is the most obvious of differences, hence easily perceived. When active clash or competition is present, *change* and the *unknown* are both present to draw human attention.

6. *Vitality.* Associating ideas or objects with matters that directly affect the lives of listeners. You relate the cost-of-living index to listeners' food budgets and breakfast tables, or you make listeners see *their* future lives depend on the science-environment contest.

Personal interests and purposes are prime reasons for granting attention; what seems to touch life itself has special significance for all.

7. *Specificity.* Presentation of precise detail. You say "spreading oak" instead of "tree," or you show a model or mock-up instead of just describing, or you give descriptions for which listeners can fill in details, as Dick Barnes did with campus scenes (see pages 53–54).

The more concrete or specific any concept, the more easily it is acquired by humans—provided the detail does not obscure the nature or meaning of the *whole*.

greatest pleasures experienced.

8. *Intensity.* The force of any aspect of communication—of voice, movement, or energy of language. Wide variations in intensity levels are possible in speech: of sound, of physical energy, of vividness or color in language. You increase loudness for emphasis, move to lean toward listeners, or point, or you say with deliberateness, "This next point is the most important one," or you say, "The floor was littered with garbage," instead of "covered with debris," thus getting greater intensity through greater specificity.

Within certain limits (too complicated to explain here), the strength of impact of any stimulus tends to vary with the intensity of the stimulus; also, noticeable *changes* in stimuli and *contrasts* between intensities of stimuli draw attention to the *dissimilarities* and to *change.*

9. *Humor.* Introduction of exaggeration, incongruity, irony, word play, unexpected turns of thought or phrase. Left-handed people have been discussed as an oppressed minority denied "equal rights." You might talk of football as "agitation of a bag of wind," or of jogging as "running with no place to go."

The nature of response to humor is not fully understood. But the attractions of the *novel* or unexpected and satisfactions from safely regaining reality—*the familiar*—after having expectations built up, then reversed, appear to be involved.

What the columns above show is that all listeners are psychologically attuned to certain kinds of speech content. If you are to take advantage of these kinds of readiness, you need to be sensitive to the kinds of ideas and language that respond to those human interests. To search for such ideas and language is to be rhetorically sensitive, to be a person who:

1. Tries to accept role taking as part of the human condition
2. Attempts to avoid stylized [routine] verbal behavior
3. Is characteristically willing to undergo the strain of adaptation
4. Seeks to distinguish between all information and information acceptable for communication
5. Tries to understand that an idea can be rendered in multiform ways.[16]

---

16. Roderick P. Hart and Don M. Burks, "Rhetorical Sensitivity and Social Interaction," *Speech Monographs* XXXIX (June 1972): 75–91. This significant essay deserves to be read in full by everyone interested in the nature of communicative adaptation.

Points 2, 3, 4, and 5 in this statement by Roderick Hart and Don Burks bear especially on our present point. Skillful use of the rhetorical features we have just enumerated *is* avoidance of the routine, *is* adaptation to the natures of listeners, *is* selection of the most communicable aspects of information, and *is* recognition that some ways of saying things are rhetorically better than others.

This chapter has been about what one must recognize in situations and human beings if one is to be rhetorically sensitive. Some who have studied previous editions of this book have complained that we have not been explicit enough, have not shown the rights and wrongs of effective public speech. One of our hopes is that from having read this chapter about audiences you will see that there can be no such thing as formal rules for adapting to them. They and the situations you will share with them are too variable. The only way to effective, artistic speech in rhetorical situations is through reflective analysis of each specific situation and audience as you meet it. But that analysis must raise the questions and find the answers that allow a "fit" to each situation to be "built" in speech preparation and presentation. The authors we just quoted have put the task especially well:

> The rhetorically sensitive person is . . . always unsure, always guessing, continually weighing. The rhetorically sensitive person deals with the most slippery of intellectual stuff, the values, attitudes, and philosophical predispositions of others. But once the rhetor understands that he must cope with the contingent, that he necessarily swims in a sea of probabilities when engaging another in discourse, once he appreciates that the complexities and inconsistencies of men are given in the interpersonal equation, then social cohesion becomes possible. [Then] . . . we can begin to grapple optimistically with the problems of rhetorical creation and adaptation that social interactions simply demand of us.[17]

In other words, neither you nor we will ever create the science of audience analysis of which Plato dreamed in the quotation at the head of this chapter. We will not be truly adaptive speakers (or writers!) until we accept that condition. It is only then that we will really understand the communicative world as it really is: one in which the human relationships through speech, which *we* need, can be created only by adjusting ourselves to the discernible expectations of people listening; the special dimensions of specific situations; the broad principles of human attention; the variable conditions of age, sex, intelligence, and attitudinal commitment; and the universal preference of humans for particular kinds of communicative expression. This is slippery in-

---

17. Ibid., p. 91.

tellectual stuff indeed.   But it is with these general understandings that a speaker must approach each rhetorical situation if he or she is to deal with it sensitively.   These are the features—the major topics for consideration—that need to be *thought about* relative to each specific situation of speaking.   Rhetorical sensitivity and creation of influential speech have their beginnings exactly here—in *thought* about what a rhetorical situation is and what people are like when they are listeners. We have tried to give you the topics and some guidelines for such thinking.   What conclusions are right for the situation you will enter, we cannot say.   Only you know the specific data about that situation and the particular people in it.

When you have formed your judgments concerning the situation you will enter rhetorically, the next step to effective, artistic public speech is to work over goals and ideas to create content that will fit both you and the rhetorical situation.   Traditionally this stage of speaking has been called *invention*.   The term suggests what must go on at this stage: discovery, sorting, research, forming proofs and clarifications, and humanizing.   The goal is to invent, to create, the substance of a message that will fit the listeners in a particular situation. Our next three chapters explore the problems and options that arise at this stage of creative activity.

EXERCISES

Written

1. Write a careful analysis of some rhetorical situation with which you are familiar (involving a fraternal group, club, religious congregation, or some specific occasion for speaking) giving special consideration to the following:
   a. The special allowances and requirements of the situation
   b. Chief biological wants and needs, if any, that affect the audience
   c. Special social wants and needs, if any, that affect the audience
   d. Any special characteristics of age, sex, expectation, knowledge, and attitudinal commitment that all speakers should take into account
   When you have completed the analysis, indicate what *special* adaptations any speaker entering this situation will have to make.
2. You are to prepare a short speech using the central idea: "Television should be used as a major resource in general education."   Outline the major points you might make in such a speech if it were to be given to audience *a* below; then outline the major points you might try to make if the speech were for audience *b* below.   Justify any differences there may be in the two outlines.
   a. An audience of twenty college students aged seventeen to twenty-two, made up of ten men and ten women, assembled for an informal class

on study habits organized for students whose academic records do not "meet the potentialities indicated by standardized aptitude-test results."

    b. An audience of twenty college students aged nineteen to twenty-two, all cadet teachers in an elementary school attending one of a series of weekly seminars. The seminar topic for this meeting is "Motivation." There are eighteen women and two men in the group.

3. Using the text or a recording of any speech, identify the points at which the speaker seems to have adapted content for the specific purpose of suiting it to one or another of the audience characteristics discussed in this chapter. Identify and evaluate the effectiveness with which he took advantage of special resources to make the speech fit the particular situation.

Oral

1. With four or five classmates work out through discussion an outlined description of your class as a rhetorical situation for the next group of talks to be given in your class. The subpoints of Written Exercise 1 above may serve as starting points for your descriptive outline.
   OPTIONAL. As an exercise in group reporting, assign parts of your completed outline to each member of your group and, together, make a joint presentation to your class of your group's conclusions.

2. Do the necessary research and then report orally to your class on one of the following subjects: the psychological process called reinforcement; the psychological process called suggestion; the social (or ethical or other) values of college students today; the expectations of ceremonial audiences; the unique expectations of audiences that have power to make policy or legislate; authority (or evidence) as a source of persuasion; theories of crowd behavior; Sherif and Sherif's concepts of "latitudes of acceptance and rejection" (see reference in footnote 15 of this chapter).

3. Prepare and deliver an oral report on the methods of audience analysis and adaptation used by a trial lawyer, preacher, or political speaker you have observed or read about.

4. Prepare and deliver a talk on some aspect of audience research, advertising or market research, or the relation of market research to industrial design.

4

INVENTION: BASIC PROCESSES

. . . even in the field of sensation, our minds exert a certain arbitrary choice. By our inclusions and omissions we trace the field's extent; by our emphasis we mark its foreground and its background; by our order we read it in this direction or in that. We receive in short the block of marble, but we carve the statue ourselves.

William James, "Pragmatism and Humanism"[1]

Every speaker ultimately faces five sets of problems. They are the problems of *inventing* what to say in a rhetorical situation, of *shaping* what is to be said into some communicable form, of *choosing and refining* the language to be used in communicating, of *presenting* or delivering what has been planned, and of *commanding* the message while presenting it. With this chapter we begin an exploration of inventing what to say, but first you must recognize that your problems of invention for classroom speaking are slightly different from those you will usually face in other places.

Outside the classroom most of us speak because someone invites us to say something about a subject we are well acquainted with. The example of a professor's invitation to address a conference of psychologists, cited in chapter 3, is typical of everyday professional experience. Another ordinary experience is finding ourselves in a situation where we want to talk about a subject that comes up in a meeting or in conversation. Still another common circumstance is that as members of committees, research teams, or other groups with special responsibilities we must report to those to whom we are responsible. In general, subjects and speaking responsibilities *choose us* more often than we freely choose subjects. Few people outside classrooms are asked to talk publicly about "anything you want to."

---

1. "Pragmatism and Humanism" is Lecture Seven of James's *Pragmatism* as originally published in 1907. See William James, *Pragmatism* (Cleveland: World Publishing Co., Meridian Books, 1955), p. 161.

But in speech classes you will almost surely be asked to speak sometimes on subjects of your own choosing. This will give you both opportunities and difficulties. Your first rhetorical problem will be to invent a subject appropriate to the classroom as a rhetorical situation. Accordingly, we focus in the next few paragraphs on choosing subjects for practice speeches. What we say will also be practical advice for any other occasion on which you have to select your own subject for public speech.

CHOOSING SUBJECTS

A good speech subject—for a class or anywhere else—ought to be timely and significant for the listeners who will share their rhetorical situation with you. This means it must also be appropriate for you as a person who will try to create a purposeful human relationship in that situation. Of course, you should be able to say what you need to say about the subject within the time and other restraints the situation will impose.

To list requirements for a speech subject in this way gives the tests of a suitable subject, but it does not help you to *locate* satisfying subjects. There is a better way of discovering inviting, suitable subjects for discussion in public places.

To find a subject that can interest you and also have significance for your listeners, let your mind run freely over all kinds of subject matter. Suspend your doubts and critical inclinations temporarily. Just try to see what is interesting in the world about you and within you. The next paragraph illustrates how the process sometimes called *brainstorming* can work. The subjects and subject areas discovered are printed in brackets following the stimulus that brought them to mind.

It happens that this paragraph was originally written in the spring, in a motel apartment. That fact will affect the thoughts that come to mind [the power of suggestion; hotel-motel-hostelry operations]. The highway is visible from the window [mass transportation problems, highway construction, auto and truck licensing, highway safety, scenic routes]. Across the highway is a row of shrubs [horticulture, landscaping, plant breeding, land use, plant pathology]. The storm windows are still on the motel [insulating materials and properties, maintenance industries, glass making, fabricating for the construction industries, custom building vs. prefabrication]. A school bus passes [the topic of education calls up too many possibilities to enumerate]. The typewriter is before me [mechanisms of communication, the publishing industry, business machines, automation]. A bookshelf is at my side. On it stands *The Ugly American* [foreign policy, diplomacy, the responsibility of the press], a murder mystery [escapist reading, paperbacks, censorship], and Chaim Perelman's *Traité de L'Argumentation* [foreign language study, foreign travel, methods of persuasion, the study of philosophy, the relative merits of different academic subjects].

Twelve minutes passed while this little brainstorming experiment took place and the results were typed out. By the most conservative count thirty-two discussable subjects and general speech topics were discovered and typed. If this had been your brainstorming, you could almost surely locate something to talk interestingly about within these thirty-two topics. If there is no prospect here—and we doubt it —do your own brainstorming for ideas, wherever you happen to be right now. Look up from this page and let your thoughts run freely, jotting down each idea that occurs to you. Or think about the classroom in which you will speak and the people who will be there. Look forward to pp. 235–38 where Alma Lajara's outline appears. She must have come to her so closely adaptive subject by meditating on her class and classroom as sources of speech subjects.

A different tack using the same general practice of brainstorming is to walk along library shelves noting book titles. Or watch closely any group of people, animals, machines, or plants. Or take any class of things as your starting point and begin enumerating members of that class. Try "vehicles," "buildings," "clothing," "inventions," or "authors" as a start. At the moment of writing that last sentence "vehicles" suggested "hang-gliding" to us because from a restaurant window we both watched some hang-gilders soaring last evening. Do you know any odd, interesting, or specially important things about vehicles?

The fund of potential speech subjects is virtually inexhaustible if you let your mind run freely in one direction after another. But keep some record of the often strange, often familiar ideas free-wheeling thought grinds out. If you do not use anything from these notes this time, keep them anyway. Some idea there could help you decide on a subject for some future occasion—even as an idea with which to start a conversation.

Once you have a list of *available* subjects, reactivate your critical powers and judge the results. Cull the list for timely, significant themes that interest *you*. Do not ask, yet, whether a subject is manageable, and do not worry about whether your audience will be interested. If a subject is timely and interests you, there may be a way to trim or expand it to make it manageable. Your immediate problem is to draw from random lists of ideas those that are potentially timely and potentially *significant for you*. In this and succeeding chapters we try to help you fit such ideas to specific kinds of speech situations.

To be a live option, a subject need not be patently within your present knowledge and preparation. It need only be one you can and want to learn more about than your audience already knows. Given that much, it is probable that you can learn enough about some phase of the subject to make it vital for your listeners. What you need is *a* subject or subject area to begin working on *now*. You can perfect it as you work with it. From whatever list you have created choose *something* you are willing to try to do as a communicator. This is important because dawdling and choosing overworked subjects are the two most frequent, enfeebling faults of students when choosing speech subjects.

A colleague of ours who studied diaries of more than a thousand college students in speech classes found that a consistent difference between good speakers and poor speakers was that the good speakers chose subjects for speeches carefully but swiftly and then stuck with their choices. Most of their available time went into preparation. Poor speakers consistently reported that they spent days trying to settle on acceptable subjects. We do not know just how indecisiveness is related to poor speaking, but the evidence is clear that good speakers choose subjects promptly and stick with them; poor speakers do not. If indecisiveness is your problem, it could be useful to keep a simple chart of the hours you spend on each phase of speech preparation: choosing a subject, locating your specific purpose, searching for further ideas, outlining, rehearsing. Perhaps if you see in graphic form where you actually spend your time, you will be able to use time more efficiently by setting deadlines for the various tasks.

A second practice that endangers success in speaking is choosing overworked subjects. This comes about in two ways. Some students find *an* article on an unusual (to them) subject and without any further investigation adopt that subject. Then if the subject happens to be very popular in the press, the speakers unknowingly bring to their listeners something everyone already knew—having read about it somewhere else. We think of a period when it seemed every magazine and newspaper feature section was carrying articles on child abuse. One of our students read one such article, based a classroom speech on it, and in the discussion period found that a half-dozen of her classmates knew more about the subject than she did because they had run across better articles than hers. Just a little research in current periodicals would have enabled this speaker to bring some *news* about child abuse because she would then have known her subject more broadly than her peers. It was the narrowness of her research that confined this speaker to the aspects of her subject that were commonplace; there was plenty to be learned about the subject that was not commonplace or overworked.

The other, more obvious kind of overworked subject is the one about which there is little or nothing new to say *if the subject is treated conventionally*. Who doubts that "Advertising Is Big Business" or "Christmas Is too Commercial" or "Travel Is Broadening" or that "We Need to Keep Physically Fit"? Conceived in the ways we have phrased the subjects here, these are trite subjects that promise no significant news for anyone. However, the *consequences* of massive advertising, what to *do about* the commercialization of Christmas, how to *get the most out of* travel, and how to *evaluate* physical fitness programs are all matters about which almost anyone could profitably use some information and counsel. Our point is simply that to avoid shopworn subjects you need to discriminate needed, interesting, useful aspects of topics from aspects of the same topics about which your listeners have no need to know or already do know. There is probably no overworked subject if you make this discrimination. To make it is actually to begin to fit your subject to the situation you will enter.

CLASSROOMS AS SPEECH SITUATIONS

There is a cliché in modern education that classroom life is necessarily artificial. To the contrary, we contend that a speech class can be an ideal life situation in which to *practice* human communication. You are unlikely ever to find another situation so generous to people seeking communicative contact with others. First, you can learn about your audience rather easily. Naturally, your listeners change, grow in understanding, and develop special needs and yearnings as the result of their shared experiences, but they also learn more about you as a speaker. They alter their expectations accordingly, and that makes communication easier for you. Everyone, including you, shares in all these developments; so there can be rare, mutual understanding between speaker and audience in a classroom. But most fundamentally, a speech class is filled with live *people* jointly bent on exercising their humanness fully. All alike, they seek encouragement to make the class a real community—a vibrant communicative, learning system.

An inhumane way to view the rhetorical situation in a speech class is to see it as a communicative system populated by captives to be talked at. A humane view would show a speech class as a place where people are eager to be informed and interested and eager to see one another grow as communicators. They are not, of course, receptive to mere self-expression in speaking; like anyone else, they want their needs and preferences considerately treated. If they get that much, the audience in a speech class will be the most generous and helpful group of listeners you will encounter. The issue for you, your colleagues, and your instructor is: are you going to treat your classroom as a haven for soliloquies, or will you all contribute toward creating a situation where "communication presupposes other minds"?[2]   This is partly your instructor's choice, of course, but it is especially yours. Every time you choose a subject to talk about, every time you choose an idea for inclusion in a talk, every time you arrange thoughts for communication, you will extend communication *toward* your colleagues or take a step backward *from* them.

What are your listeners really like generally?   An eminent psychologist described them.   He was writing about all of us:

> ... people want a good opinion of themselves both in their own eyes and in those of others.   Self-respect and popular esteem are active needs.   If a man is deprived of them he becomes anxious, tense, and restless. ...   Abilities are rarely useless, and to be able to exercise one's wits may be a means of self-respect and general esteem.[3]

Mr. Thomson's observations imply this question for you as a speaker: Will you consider *others'* opinions of themselves, *their* self-respect, and allow *them* the exercise of wits they want and need to exercise?   Your answer determines whether you will make your classroom a real or an artificial communicative setting.

DISCOVERING LINES OF THOUGHT

When you have found a subject about which you can say something significant for both you and your colleagues, your next problems in invention will be to find out what you *might* say, then to choose what you *ought* to say to this audience in its particular situation.   A systematic search for ideas is preferable to an impulsive one.   So the question becomes: how shall I work my mind when searching for ideas worth talking about?

In the first edition of this book, in 1964, we proposed a systematic way of inventing ideas for communication.   The method was actually centuries old.   It was recommended and used by historic figures such as Aristotle, Cicero, Francis Bacon, and hundreds of other speakers and scholars of the past; then it was somehow lost to Western culture.   We found it useful and consistent with modern research on learning and concept formation, so we proposed it anew without scientific research to support it as a method of communicative

---

2. Henry W. Johnstone, Jr., *The Problem of the Self* (University Park, Pa.: The Pennsylvania State University Press, 1970), p. 131.
3. Robert Thomson, *The Psychology of Thinking* (Baltimore: Penguin Books, 1959), p. 155.

invention. It was and is a method of generating ideas for speaking (or writing) by stimulating one's mind through reviewing a set of *topics* or cue words.

Happily, a series of experiments has now shown that this method of rhetorical invention does help speakers and problem solvers to think up more and better ideas for use in the tasks they confront. Even when thinking about what they considered uninteresting topics, students who had brief training in the method we are about to present produced 10 percent more ideas about subjects than their peers who were not using any systematic way of thinking about the same subjects. When the students used subjects they thought were interesting, those using the topics or cue-words produced an *average* of 17 percent more ideas in a given time.[4] In a later experiment using groups of students assigned to solve a social problem, the groups using the self-cuing system produced significantly more ideas about their problem, and they developed solutions considered to be superior to solutions developed [for the same problems] by free recall [untrained] groups."[5] Additional experimental research has shown that a number of different cuing systems can be helpful to students and others who want to generate ideas for use in discussing topics of almost any sort.[6] In short, if you want to think systematically and especially productively about a subject for public speech, here is a way to do it that has demonstrated advantages. It is not the only way, but history, everyday experience, and experimental evidence show that it works well.

Classifying Your Rhetorical Situation

Speaking very broadly, rhetorical situations tend to invite one or more of three kinds of ideas from speakers. Some call predominantly for *advice;* some call predominantly for talk that shows how facts ought to be *judged* in the light of specific standards or rules; some call for *reinforcement* of beliefs already held by the audience. We can say there are these three classes of *exigences* or needs you will face in speaking. So if you can decide which of these

---

4. William F. Nelson, "Topoi: Function in Recall," *Speech Monographs* XXXVII (June 1970): 121–26.

5. This experiment was conducted by William F. Nelson and John L. Petelle and was reported as "Topoi: Functional in Group Problem Solving," a paper read at the International Communication Association convention, Montreal, Canada, 1973. The findings are also summarized in John L. Petelle and Richard Maybee, "Items of Information Retrieved as a Function of Cue System and Topical Area," *Central States Speech Journal* XXV (Fall 1974): 191.

6. For a good summary of the findings and their implications for a theory of how we store and retrieve information see Petelle and Maybee, "Items of Information," pp. 190–97.

types of situations yours will be, you immediately discover what general sort of information you will need most in developing a subject to fit that situation. Here are some illustrations.

When an audience will have to decide on a course of action, or ought to decide on such a course, it is *advice* that is needed. For this kind of situation the basic question for both speaker and listener is: what will be done or left undone? In the language we will be using later in this book, this kind of situation invites *persuasion about a proposition of policy.* It is a situation in which any alert speaker's central idea is almost certain to contain the words "should" or "ought to" or their equivalents. Central ideas will run: "Nurses' aides ought to be used more widely in hospital care," or "Students should be represented by voting members on the promotion and tenure committees of our school," or "You should vote in the coming election."

If you see that you will be entering a situation that calls for or allows advice of this sort, you can immediately narrow your field of research and thinking. Ideas having to do with the expediency of different courses of action will be the ones you will especially need. These are ideas that have to do with rewards and costs in the future and with the prospects of happiness for those who are going to support or take the action, or who will refuse to support it.

So a useful shortcut in research and thinking has been discovered. When your situation invites a speech on a central idea concerning the *future behavior* of your listeners, most of your initial preparation time ought to be spent finding facts and lines of thought that say something about the consequences of the actions (and inactions) among which your listeners are to choose. Simply by recognizing that you are going to talk about "should's" and "ought's," you isolate a particular type of material your speech must include.

A second class of situations in which we speak are those in which audiences function as judges rather than as deciders of future action. In discussing these circumstances Aristotle talked almost entirely of judgments at law, but we require a broader view. Audiences have to or want to render judgments about facts and events in many different situations. Every speech to inform is such a case. Most of what one says in a speech of inquiry deals with what the facts are, although when solutions are being considered, the situation becomes concerned with policies and future actions. All persuasion about propositions of fact succeeds or fails *in some degree* according to the judgments of fact finally rendered by the listeners, although this does not mean that judgments of fact will be the *main* things you seek.

When your central idea focuses on what something is or on whether it exists, you will know you will have chiefly to get your listeners to interpret facts or events in light of some code or set of standards. The code may be the law of the land, the theory of probabilities, the standards of historical research, the canons of artistic excellence, personal standards for distinguishing truth from error, or something else. Whatever the code, your judging listeners will especially need two kinds of knowledge: (1) knowledge about the facts or events they are to judge, and (2) knowledge about the codes or standards they are to use in weighing the facts or events. Once more, simply thinking about what your listeners will be asked to *do* quickly reveals the main kinds of ideas you will need to give them.

To restate this guide: If in informing, inquiring, or persuading you are going to ask for judgments, you will need ideas that define and clarify whatever is to be judged and the standards to be used in judging. You may need other information too, but these two kinds of content are certain to be crucial.

Ancient Romans had a special interest in legal argument. This led them to notice that three subordinate kinds of information about facts have special usefulness when listeners make judgments of the sort we are now considering. These kinds of information are (1) information about whether there really *are* relevant facts to talk about; (2) information about *what* facts are worth talking about; and (3) information about how acknowledged facts are to be *interpreted* in the light of whatever criteria apply to them. Knowing that these are the kinds of information you will need further narrows your hunt for ideas. If you understand this, you will know what it is most important to find out: What facts must you supply so your audience will know *enough* to make the judgments you will ask for? What, if anything, will you need to say about what should count or not count when they make the judgments? Will you have to *supply* the rules for judging, or will the audience already know those rules? Your answers to these questions narrow the list of ideas you have to find— in your own mind or elsewhere.

There are also speaking situations in which the main exigence or need is to have old beliefs strengthened, to have familiar beliefs made more firm, to have convictions deepened, or to have old knowledge rendered amusing or diverting. In such situations *new* judgments and *new* courses of action are usually neither sought nor very much wanted. Commencement exercises are such situations. So are many worship services, service club meetings, fellowship meetings, banquets, and political rallies. Those who attend commencements accept the worth of education; worshippers accept the greatness of their deity; fellowship groups accept the worth of being together and wish their association to be strengthened by being made more enjoyable. Whoever prepares to speak to such audiences must locate the kinds of ideas that deepen, enrich, magnify, or even exaggerate the listeners' current knowledge. The chief end of the worship service may be to strengthen faith that already exists; the chief end of the club dinner may be not calorie intake but some magnification of the joys of friendship.

This kind of situation invites you to look especially for ways to connect your subject with well-known virtues such as justice, courage, moderation, liberality, gentleness, power, and similar *goods* honored by your audience. Of course, if you are to speak against those who differ severely from your hearers, you will want to find ways of connecting those persons and their actions with the *opposites* of the values your listeners regard highly: cowardice, excess, meanness, ignorance, and so on.

When you are going to enter a situation of this sort, your preparation ought to begin with a hunt for the virtues possessed by whatever it is that you and your audience are committed to.

If you prepare speeches in the way we are proposing, you will (1) get an understanding of the rhetorical situation you will enter, (2) decide on what subject you will speak, (3) classify your situation as one of the three types we have just described, and (4) begin your invention of the speech by exploring your own mind and other sources for the kinds of subject matter your type of situation *specially* requires. To proceed in this way does not suppose that you will need no other kinds of material for the final speech. What the procedure does is send your mind after the *most important* types of material *first*. That saves time and effort. You do not run around in your thinking or in a library gathering speech material that will not fit the rhetorical situation and your purpose. You can gather miscellaneous material later, when you *know* you need it.

Here is an illustration of beginning the process of invention as we have proposed. The situation we will imagine occurs annually in most colleges and universities. At some time in an academic year there is an orientation program or a careers day on which students who have chosen their major subjects of study talk to incoming or lowerclass students about what it's like to be a major in this or that subject or academic program. Almost anyone might be invited to make such a talk on what is special about chemical or environmental engineering, journalism, Hispanic studies, speech communication, or any of the hundreds of other concentrations college students can choose. Let us suppose you have been asked to make such a talk to a group of students who have not chosen their majors.

So we can be realistic in our example, we will suppose that you are majoring in environmental engineering—a rather new field in engineering. As you come out of your chemistry lab, a friend hails you. He says, "I just came from Professor James's class in ecology and water resources, and he says there's a meeting of freshmen engineers on Friday in the Forum Building. Each of the branches of engineering is to have an upperclass major talk about the work in his or her department. Professor James is in charge of eco engineering's schedule, and he wants you to speak for eco engineering. So, get to James's office and get the crib sheets on dirty water and foul air!" Since you are reading this book we piously hope you will know better than to take your friend's last bit of advice. There are better ways to think than to contemplate rushing to a professor for help upon such a notice.

As someone who has been around your school for a while, you can diagnose the prospective rhetorical situation rather easily. The audience will be a mixture of still-bewildered and clear-eyed underclassmen and underclasswomen. They will all be interested in engineering careers. Some will have chosen their majors; most will not. Yours being a relatively new kind of program, many will be vague about environmental engineering as a major and as a career. You know, but many listeners will not know, that your program begins with the usual series of basic courses in the general engineering curriculum, and at the junior year you shift into general courses in ecology and then into a concentration on the relation of engineering to problems of (a) air pollution, (b) water pollution, or (c) sound pollution.[7] But your immediate inventional problem is to decide what portions of what you know about this major deserve to be presented in the situation Professor James is going to ask you to enter.

As soon as you know this much about your prospective assignment, you can begin to sort out what you will need to think up for your talk. You will be entering a situation in which the listeners' most urgent need will be for *facts* about environmental engineering as a curriculum and as a career. But you will want to make your major look good, too; so you will be asking your listeners to *judge* the program a *desirable* one, whether or not they elect to enter it. This is a general meeting where all majors will be discussed; it is not a place to sell or advise people on any one major. It is certainly not a situation in which just reinforcing existing knowledge will meet the exigences. This puts you in a position to begin creating appropriate speech material.

Because you will be asking for judgments on facts you will need to supply, you will need to know and be able to explain and adapt two sorts of information: (1) the details about the environmental engineering program as it is organized at your school, and (2) how the underclassmen and underclasswomen distinguish "good" from "not-so-good" in thinking about academic majors in engineering. The

7. These are the options in one program we know about. There are, of course, many other ways in which concentrations in this kind of program are divided.

first kind of information you can get from reviewing your college catalogue and from talking with Professor James and others who direct the program.   The second kind of information you can probably find out best by talking with representative underclass and upperclass students about how and why they chose their majors.

There you are.   You know what information to pursue immediately.   You also begin to see where you are apt to find it, if you do not already have it.   Merely deciding that your "rhetorical situation" will be a "judgment situation" focuses you on what it will be most important to invent as material for a speech.   If you had been invited to talk at a Parents' Day gathering, you might decide that *advising* parents on whether they ought to encourage their sons and daughters to investigate environmental engineering as a career would be the best way of responding to their expectations and needs.   Then, the *future prospects* of engineering in general and environmental engineering in particular and the demands of these career choices would become the kinds of material to search out in detail.   Had you been invited to talk to the organization of environmental engineering majors, you would choose to search for ideas about the *worth* and the exciting prospects of careers in that field.

You do not need to know anything about engineering or the relatively new field of environmental engineering to see the point of our illustration.   In any circumstance you can point your search for speech material in useful, not wasteful, directions if you decide promptly *what you will be asking of your listeners and they of you.* What will you want them to *do:* decide about courses of action, make judgments about facts or events, or develop stronger or less strong attitudes toward what they already know or think?   Make that decision, and you will know where to go for information.

Making the Detailed Search

Once you know the general kinds of information your rhetorical situation is likely to require, the natural thing to do is go and get it if you do not already have it.   But what is *it*?   Our environmental engineer could get the university catalogue and read its description of the environmental engineering major to his audience. Anyone ought to know this would be a mistake.   Why would it be a mistake, beside the fact that this is not a situation in which reading is appropriate?   If he regurgitated the catalogue's information he would be (1) depending solely on the editor of the catalogue for what needed to be said, and (2) failing to ask whether *this* situation and *this* speech purpose call for any special kinds of information. Our example is extreme but, in principle, it illustrates the mistake many student speakers make in invention.   They let writers who were addressing quite different audiences determine what they, as speakers in special rhetorical situations, will say.

A way of thinking that we call *topical review* prevents this difficulty. It is the ancient yet new system of rhetorical invention of which we spoke early in this discussion. From the time of Aristotle to the days of Francis Bacon, this general method of invention was proposed as the only feasible way a speaker could gain any assurance that he or she had properly reviewed even his or her own knowledge about a subject to be discussed with a specific audience. Bacon wrote:

> . . . a faculty of wise interrogating is half of knowledge. For Plato says well, "whosoever seeks a thing, knows that which he seeks for in a general notion; else how shall he know it when he has found it?" . . . The same places [topics] therefore which will help us to shake out the folds of the intellect within us, and to draw forth the knowledge stored within, will also help us to gain knowledge from without; so that if a man of learning and experience were before us, we should know how to question him wisely and to the purpose; and in like manner how to peruse with advantage . . . books and parts of books which may best instruct us concerning what we seek.[8]

The places or topics Bacon was writing about were simply a set of headings or cues that formed a checklist of the kinds of things one *might* want to know and talk about in communicating. By running through such a list, asking, "Will I need to say anything of that sort?" a researcher can uncover from memory or from any other set of sources all of the material *pertinent* to a speech or a point in a speech being prepared for a particular audience. This method of topical review has been little used in the past 200 years, but as we pointed out on p. 88, recent research shows it helps students get more ideas, even out of their own memories.

Fortunately a self-cuing method of invention for speaking does not have to be long or complex. The reason is that we talk about a limited number of themes. Treatments of these themes vary, but not the basic ideas themselves. We discuss the same types of ideas over and over. This is not a sign of laziness. It is the natural result of our shared ways of thinking about human affairs. Here is a tolerably complete list of topics we constantly think about and discuss with each other, *no matter what the subject*.

A. Attributes commonly discussed
　　1. *Existence* or nonexistence of things
　　2. *Degree* or quantity of things, forces, etc.
　　3. *Spatial* attributes, including adjacency, distribution, place

---

8. Francis Bacon, *De augmentis scientiarum*, V, p. 3, *Works*, IV, p. 423.

4. Attributes of *time*
5. *Motion* or activity
6. *Form,* either physical or abstract
7. *Substance:* physical, abstract, or psychophysical
8. *Capacity to change,* including predictability
9. *Potency:* power or energy, including capacity to further or hinder anything
10. *Desirability* in terms of rewards or punishments
11. *Feasibility:* workability or practicability

B. Basic relationships commonly asserted or argued
1. *Causality:* the relation of causes to effects, effects to causes, effects to effects, adequacy of causes, etc.
2. *Correlation:* coexistence or coordination of things, forces, etc.
3. *Genus-species* relationships
4. *Similarity* or dissimilarity
5. *Possibility* or impossibility

As a speaker you seldom need information on all of these topics for any particular rhetorical situation. Neither is every imaginable thought suggested as soon as you ask whether you need to talk about one of these attributes or relationships. However, if you form the habit of reviewing these headings each time you plan a speech or search for ways to develop a point, you will discover your mind and your books and other people have more help for you than you thought. Simply ask about each cue: Will I need any information about *that?* Or, Have I overlooked anything that's important about *that?* Here is an illustration of how you can use the sixteen topics listed above.

Suppose you have decided to speak to your class on the subject of voting. You have decided you want to get more of your listeners to vote in local and national elections. Obviously this is going to be a situation in which you will be *advising* them to vote more regularly. This situation tells you that ideas about future behavior and the rewards and costs of voting or not voting are what you will need most. With that in mind what might happen if you ran through the sixteen topics in the list above?

First try *existence.* Will you need any facts or ideas about the existence of anything? The right to vote exists for every citizen over age eighteen. Your listeners will know that, but it won't hurt to mention it. *Nonexistence* might remind you that this is a *new* right. *We* have it; our parents did not. There's a theme that might be useful, so jot it down. That is all I get out of this topic in two minutes of thought, so we will suppose you move on, too.

Will there be anything important to say about *degree*—the quantity of anything? Absolutely. You must get the figures on how many eighteen- to twenty-four-year-olds there are, what proportion of them voted in recent local and national elections, and whether those are high or low turnouts. If you do not have these data, you will have to try to find them somewhere, so jot down reminders. Perhaps *degree* will also suggest that you ought to have comparable data on voting for people older than those you will talk to. Jot that down. *Degree* might also suggest that the *amount* of political knowledge and interest eighteen- to twenty-four-year-olds have in politics might be useful. If you could find some polls on this it would perhaps be helpful. Make a reminder to yourself to look for this kind of information. Notice that this topic of *degree* has suggested several *specific* kinds of statistical information you will need; now you will not have to think vaguely about *whether* to use statistics or *what* statistics to search for. You know, and a lot of wasted motion is going to be saved.

Now try *spatial attributes*. What pops into my mind at this point is: how *far* will it be to a polling place? If you could find out that none of your listeners would have far to go to cast a vote in the next election, that would be a good argument for a claim of: "See how easy it is!" Make a note to investigate that line of information further: Where do your classmates live? Where are their polling places? (If yours is a residential school, getting this information is going to be easy; if you are all commuters, it will be very difficult and perhaps impossible. In that case, you will need some other way of showing that getting out to vote does not cost too much.) *Spatial attributes* also suggests that you might look into whether voting by young people is higher or lower than average in the *areas* from which your listeners come. There might be a basis for arguing that, "We ought to top the competitors in voting," or "In our area the record is shameful." Make a note to see if you can find these figures.

Try *time* as a topic now. Most elections are held at the *time* that colleges and universities are in session. Make a note of that. It may mean you can or ought to argue for a get-out-the-vote drive on your campus and on others. Whether you should include such a unit will need to be decided later, but a possibility has been turned up.

Does *motion* or *activity* suggest anything sayable or any information you will need? It suggests nothing at all that is pertinent to me as I type these pages. Maybe you will see something here. Good luck, but one should not worry if a cue does not trigger useful ideas. The thing to do is just go on to another cue.

Form, either physical or abstract, can suggest *registration forms*. If one of your listeners is not registered to vote, how does he or she get registered? What forms must be filled out? Sent to whom? By what times? This is going to be crucial information to include in this speech, for your goal is to get an action. Then you must be prepared to show your listeners *how* to act in the way you are advising. Make a note to get all of this kind of information and, if possible, a sample of the registration forms (if there are any) your listeners must have completed if they are to be eligible to vote.

Now, *substance:* physical, abstract, or psychophysical. That can suggest that voting is a *right* and perhaps you will want to argue that it is an *obligation* of citizenship. Jot down that possibility. You may or may not want to use it, but keep it for future consideration. Nothing else comes to mind as this paragraph is being written. So, we move on.

Capacity to change seems rich as a topic. What changes can a higher voting level bring about—particularly in the areas where your listeners would vote? What changes have been brought about by students' votes? A number of mayors have been elected by the votes of eighteen- to twenty-four-year-olds. This is a line of research you should surely follow. Write down the reminder. *Change* also suggests one of the mental obstacles you are going to have to overcome: the notion that "one vote can't change anything." You must find material to refute that. Remind yourself to see if you can find instances of close votes on bond issues, ordinances of concern to college students—housing codes, regulation of entertainment, law enforcement, and the like.

Potency or capacity to further or hinder anything may suggest that a high level of voting by eighteen- to twenty-four-year-olds could prevent something they would prefer to prevent in their areas. Graft? Overrepresentation of one party or a clique? Some ecological danger? If anything like that is suggested to you, jot it down for future consideration. Would you have any use for a slogan like "youth power"? Make note of that; you may want it.

Desirability in terms of rewards or punishments can remind you that no ideas about the costs of *not* voting have cropped up yet. Any of the desirable features of voting could be turned around into losses if that seems wise when the speech is finally shaped, but that can wait. The loss of your voice in public affairs might make a theme worth developing briefly, so that ought to be jotted down. In the specific areas where your listeners would vote, there may be special losses if the young do not vote. You ought to remind yourself to check into that when you have found out about their voting areas.

Feasibility brings up the old problem of being in one place and being registered to vote in another—voting is not feasible because it is so awkward for some people. If your audience is mainly living away from their permanent homes, you must be ready with precise information about two things: how to change one's voting registration and how to secure and vote by absentee ballot. If you do not know about these procedures in your state or the political units that make the rules for most of your audience, you must find out about

them.   Also make a note, if it occurs to you, of who or what would
be the best source to consult about this.   The *feasibility* of having
everyone in your audience vote is a major hurdle you will have to find
ways of getting over.

Now we can turn to the relationships in the list.   For any
given subject certain of these relationships are likely to be very
fruitful cues and others of little use.   How well will these relationships work in treating the matter of eighteen- to twenty-four-year-olds'
voting?

Causal relations: is there anything important to be known
and said about them?   Yes.   Does a low turnout of young voters *cause*
anything?   It at least causes a considerable part of the population
to go unrepresented in public affairs.   It could cause any of the
losses we have already turned up, of course, and a high turnout
could cause any of the benefits already thought of.   All that seems
to be suggested here is that you could argue there is a *direct,* causal
relation between voting and public consequences.   That will make
your case stronger logically.

Correlation or the co-existence of things does not suggest much
to me.   All I think of is that listeners might reasonably be told that
a satisfying sense of having done a worthy, responsible thing goes
with voting.   Is anything else suggested to you?

Genus-species relationships are especially important when you
are defining things or differentiating things from each other.   If
your speech were about civil rights in general instead of voting it
would be important to talk about what specific *rights* (species)
properly fall under the *class* (genus) of *civil* rights, and *civil rights*
would need to be differentiated from *civil privileges.*   But for a
speech advising a class to exercise their rights to vote, no such differentiations seem important.   Everyone will know what voting is.
It might be important to make some differentiations between voting
regularly and voting as an absentee, but that will depend on whether
you find out your listeners are or are not familiar with the voting
laws of their areas.

Similarity-dissimilarity as a topic ought to remind you that
you must investigate whether most of your listeners come under the
same voting regulations or fall under different ones.   If most are
from the same state, you will have little trouble; if considerable
numbers come from different states with different voting regulations,
you will have to find out what those differences are and decide later
how important it will be to talk about their similarities and dissimilarities.   This topic could also suggest looking into the ways in
which the rights and the voting records of your listeners are like
and unlike the rights and records of other groups of young people

in other parts of the country, among young people not attending college, and of young people in other countries. Maybe there will be ways of making your listeners feel proud or ashamed or responsible if you have such comparisons and contrasts to use.

Finally *possibility or impossibility* can suggest at least one very important idea for your speech: it is very seldom impossible for a citizen of the United States to vote. Only a very recent change of residence, conviction of crime, or total physical incapacitation prevents voting in most places. You could build an impressive point from this: Every listener, virtually everyone, *can* vote; the only issue is whether each one cares enough and wants to vote. A fairly persuasive case for "obligation" could be made, as we have seen; if you were to connect it with the theme that there are very few real excuses for not voting, the argument could be still stronger.

These are examples of the directions in which thought and research can be guided by reviewing sixteen familiar topics in the earliest stages of speech preparation. The whole step can be completed thoughtfully in twenty minutes to a half-hour once you know your subject and the kind of situation you are going to enter. What does our example show you can get from such a review? At least these things:

1. Recovery of some bits of fact and other information about your subject and the nature of your audience
2. Some specific *ways* of presenting data and ideas that will have to be covered
3. A list of specific information you ought to gather now that the review is finished
4. A list of some problems of audience adaptation you will need to consider at a later time in your speech preparation
5. Perhaps, as in the case of the ballots, some notion of what would be desirable visual aids and other materials for demonstration
6. A list of some things it will be very important to find out about your specific audience
7. Recognition of where some of the problems are going to arise in composing this speech—eradication of indifference and one-vote-can't-change-anything will be a major task in achieving persuasion

From such a review you gain much more than simply a retrieval of data from your memory bank. You get a preview of the research you must do and a preview of some promising ways of building units of the final speech. What you will gain more than repays you for the short time it takes to make a topical review as an early move in rhetorical invention.

RESEARCH

With the kinds of notes you will have after a topical search for potentially useful data, ideas, questions, and kinds of material to be drawn from other sources, you are ready to begin collecting material from sources other than yourself. Concerning this kind of research we will repeat some advice familiar to you, because we all need reminding that some ways of digging for information are more practical than others. We will also mention some sources you need to know about, but nothing short of personally investigating the research facilities of the library available to you can equip you to prepare speeches adequately.

Books are among the very best places to go for information, but they are not the only wells of knowledge. We have already pointed out that *you* are a valuable source of information. Perhaps instead of talking about research for speeches, we ought to speak of "recovery, inquiry, and research for speeches." In preparing to speak, ask yourself: what have I already read about this subject, or this point? What have I heard in conversation, in lectures, on radio or television? What have I seen firsthand or in photographs? Such questions often stir the memory. Any expectant speaker ought to explore his memory and check his notebooks as an early step in research.

Other people are excellent resources. What photographer is not happy to answer questions about photography? What traveller is not all too pleased to reminisce about what he or she has seen? What professional person is unwilling to talk about the problems and accomplishments of his or her profession? We all know people who would be happy to supply information; yet, just as we often forget to probe our own minds, we neglect convenient, willing resource persons.

Public officials, teachers, businessmen and businesswomen, and others are often overlooked as sources of valuable information. One must be careful about seeking assistance from such persons because of the heavy demands on their time, but even the busiest people are frequently willing to grant limited aid to those who know what they want and are able to draw out needed information efficiently. The busier these people are, the more likely they are to have responsible aides and researchers who can provide you with factual information even more readily than their principals. We recall a speech student who wanted to cite a statement the president of her university had made in an unpublished address. She went to the president's personal aide, hoping to see the president. She did not need to see him. The aide was able to produce within minutes a mimeographed copy of the speech the student needed; he was also able to give her a quick review of the occasion and audience for the speech. She had the key information needed for her speech— and at no trouble to the president. Congressmen and other officers have staff members specifically assigned to care for requests for service from their constituents—and this includes supplying documentary information. Many major corporations maintain public-information departments whose business it is to supply data to people interested in their operations. To draw on such resources you need chiefly a very clear idea of what it is you want and knowledge— from prior research—of who is most likely to know what you want to know. Carefully planned, prearranged interviews or clear and precise letters are the usual ways of securing help from busy people. Such interviewing and correspondence ought to be a normal part of an effective speaker's preparation.

Personal investigation is another neglected avenue of research. We would think ill of a person who, after urging us to read Kurt Vonnegut's *Slaughter House Five,* turned out to have only seen the movie. What then of speakers who deplore the low level of television programming without having checked the full program listings and explored the viewing options open to their particular listeners? To take other examples, you are fortunate if you have never been subjected to speeches on juvenile delinquency by speakers who had never visited a youth court, a settlement house, or even talked with young people of the kinds they discuss. One need not be an ex-convict to speak of prisons or a parent to discuss children, but to neglect obvious and convenient opportunities for firsthand inquiry is to miss vital and immediately relevant information.

Do not overlook your friends as resources. Discuss with them ideas you think of presenting to an audience. At the least you will have a test of how these thoughts go over; at best you may come away from such conversation with new information or new directions in which to look for information.

Unless you already know your subject very well, it is best to begin research on a specific topic by looking at general books, survey articles, and encyclopedia articles. These will give you background material into which you can later fit specialized data. If your subject deals with as familiar a topic as the speech about voting we just imagined, you will probably have no need to begin with general works of this sort, but suppose you wished to speak about the classical Greek theatre or Greek scientific theories or Greek politics? Your topical review of possible ideas and lines of thought would doubtless remind you that you would need to have background on the ancient Greek world in which these institutions and ideas were set. Then you ought to begin with some brief, general, authoritative essay or book on ancient Greek society. Edith Hamilton's *The Greek Way* is a readily available, short book of this sort.   Or an encyclopedia article on Greek art (or science, or politics) might suit.   Remember, too, that there are excellent specialized encyclopedias.   On any topic concerning social psychology, the *Handbook of Social Psychology,* edited by Gardner Lindzey and Elliot Aronson, is almost sure to have an excellent essay.   Many other fields have similar encyclopedias and handbooks; philosophy, biological sciences, theology, and social work are just a few.   Your object in reading such works should be twofold: (1) to get an overview of the topic, and (2) to secure leads to other, more detailed information.   Of course, a third possibility is that you will discover nothing useful under the heading you check; in that case you have probably saved much time you might otherwise have spent combing individual books and essays on a useless topic that at first seemed promising.

General source materials usually do not contain the detailed information you will ultimately need if you want to establish, say, the precise *degree* or the *desirability* of something.   But when you search general works you hope you will be led toward specific kinds of information that will complete your understanding.   Let us illustrate with examples.

At best, your general work—an encyclopedia article or general book—will tell you where to go next for specialized information.   If your speech subject concerned advertising in the United States, you might consult a source such as the *Columbia Encyclopedia,* 4th edition. There, under "advertising," you would learn that advertising is thought of in reference to who buys most advertising (food marketers, drug companies, etc.), the medium of communication used (newspapers, radio, TV, etc.), and the business of advertising agencies—thought of as "Madison Avenue" business.   Notice that this breakdown of the subject suggests some ways you could narrow your focus for a single speech.   This short article will also give you the names of the leading trade associations (sources of further research materials).   You will also find the names and authors of four major, general books on advertising, published between 1958 and 1970.   These are sources you can go to for more specific information on advertising today.   You should know, too, however, that such standard indexes as *The Readers' Guide to Periodical Literature* and the *International Index to Periodicals* will give you additional leads to articles on advertising in *general* journals.   The point is that for most topics there is a general, survey essay *that you can understand* in some encyclopedia or book for general readers.   Find it, and you will have a good start on your research and, often, the same general source will give you guidance on where to turn next.

But research does not always go as smoothly as our first example suggests.   Here is an actual experience I had just before writing these sentences.   I entered my university's main library, saying, "I'll pretend I want to make a talk on some aspect of *libel*." Going directly to the reference section of the library, I chose the first encyclopedia that met my eye: *The Encyclopedia Americana, International Edition.* Under "libel" I found a well-written, clear article that defined "libel," distinguished it from "slander," discussed what constitutes publishing a libel, and explained exceptions to the general rule. An excellent, understandable essay—but no directions at all as to where to turn next! So, I tried the most famed of encyclopedias, *The Encyclopaedia Britannica.* There I found a longer, more technical essay. It covered substantially the same topics that were treated in the *Encyclopedia Americana,* but some of the technicalities were beyond my understanding. To the *Britannica* article was appended a bibliography telling where to go to find the most authoritative histories of libel law in the United States, Great Britain, and Scotland. All titles sounded too technical for anyone but an expert to consult. Thinking one might become discouraged at this point, I decided to change my attack and consult the other invaluable resource every library has—the card catalogue of books held. Under the heading "libel" were cards for almost sixty full-length books. Their publication dates ranged from 1906 to 1976. Legal interpretations change, so obviously only the more recent books would have information suitable to an up-to-date talk; hence all books published before 1950 were ignored. We cite the titles of some of the post-1950 books because we want to make an important point about choosing *what* to read in getting information for a speech. Some post-1950 titles were:

- Clark Gavin, *Foul, False, and Infamous: Famous Libel and Slander Cases of History* (1950).
- Charles Angoff, *The Book of Libel* (1966).
- Paul P. Ashley, *Say It Safely* (1976), 5th edition.
- Clifton C. Lawhorne, *Defamation and Public Officials: The Evolving Law of Libel* (1971).
- Robert H. Phelps, *Libel: Rights, Risks, and Responsibilities* (1966).
- George P. Rice, *Law for the Public Speaker* (1958).

Confronted by titles such as these, the practical question for a speaker doing research for a speech is, "What book is most likely to give me the comprehensive material I need at the start of my research?"

Anyone who reflected for even one minute on the information printed on the catalogue cards for the above six books should choose Ashley's *Say It Safely.* These are the reasons. The book was in its fifth edition in 1976, although it was first published in 1956. Someone thinks it's worth buying! It is published by The University of Washington Press, Seattle, Washington. University presses are careful about their reputations and would be unlikely to publish a book that discussed laws carelessly. Such a press might, however, publish a very technical book. But this title is casual, communicating that it may be a book a layman could read understandingly. For the other books there are reasonable grounds for not making them *first* reading materials: Gavin's, Lawhorne's, and Rice's books are obviously specialized; they might be useful later but not just now. The titles of Angoff's and Phelps's books are ambiguous; they may or may not be useful just now. Of the six books, *Say It Safely* seems most likely to give modern information in layman's terms. I decided to ask for *Say It Safely* first. My reasoning, and some luck, paid off. The book turned out to be written by an attorney for broadcasters, journalists, and students, "for the day-to-day use by all who write or process copy." Its chapter headings promised history of libel legislation, legal definitions of libel, discussion of libel in relation to public figures, and special treatments of libelous broadcasts and pictures. The book contained examples of kinds of statements, pictures, and the like that would or would not be libelous; best of all, it *interpreted* all the legal decisions it cited. Clearly this was an ideal special source to read if one were working up a speech for a general audience on the subject of libel.

As a talk takes shape there will be times when exact bits of information will be needed. Our experiment with a topical review of possibilities for a speech on voting by college students illustrated this. You would need statistics, authoritative estimates, dates, and other facts about when the Constitutional amendment lowering the voting age to eighteen was ratified, the total number of people in the eighteen-to twenty-four age group, their voting records in recent elections, laws about the distribution of voting places, laws about the registration of voters, influence of young voters on outcomes of elections, voting records of other countries and areas of the United States, and the like. Such specific data would be needed to fill small gaps in what you would finally say in your talk. On a different occasion you might need unexpected information such as the area of some battlefield, the probable authorship of the "letters of 'Junius,'" the date of President John Kennedy's assassination, or something similar. When you need this kind of information it is time to explore some of the many volumes of classified data: *The World Almanac; The Statistical Abstract; Facts on File;* the specialized encyclopedias; compendiums of statements like *Bartlett's Quotations;* and other specialized sources like Gavin's *Foul, False, and Infamous: Famous Libel and Slander Cases in History,* and Jane's *Ships of the World* or *Aircraft of the World.* These are sources of isolated, classified facts. Your reading in them will, of course, be far more selective than in any of the general works.

There is another resource in almost every college and public library that students and faculty members too seldom use. On the library staff is probably someone designated "reference librarian," often with a staff of assistants.   These people are hired to help *you* solve re-search problems, find useful information, and conquer the many in-dexes and other research facilities of the library.   Overwhelmingly they *want* to help you, but they have to be asked—asked clearly so they can understand your needs precisely.   Appeal to these people when the routines we have described do not work; they are experts on aids to research.

In all exploratory activities connected with preparing speeches, you should never forget that the purpose of it all is to extract what is necessary to create a *communication that will serve as your person-alized way of getting a particular set of responses* from a specific audi-ence that is going to meet with you on a specific occasion at a specific time.   One does not assemble a speech; one collects specific kinds of raw materials out of which one can mold a personal message—a unique composition.   Research for speaking properly ends whenever you have collected most of the raw materials for weaving together an original, informed communication that will serve a specific purpose with the audience that will hear it.

In all research an important but somewhat technical matter is: how should you *record* information you find by reflecting, conversing with others, and reading?   Speaker after speaker compounds his difficulties by jotting research information randomly on page after page of notebook paper.   If he paused to think how he was going to use that information, he would adopt very different methods of note taking.

Whoever does research for speaking will ultimately have to weave together the materials discovered.   Doing this is clumsy busi-ness if you have to turn notebook pages back and forth to rediscover what you have collected.   Suppose you are going to talk about cancer and you wonder whether you should discuss *types* of cancer.   If all your notes are scattered through a notebook or on sheets of paper and are ordered as you found them in thought, interviews, and reading, your information about types of cancer will be thoroughly mixed in with other kinds of information—about causes, methods of control, tests for, and so on.   Your recovery task would be simple if all your notes were on individual slips of paper or cards, each labeled according to the subject covered.   You could then in a few moments shuffle the cards marked "Cancer—Kinds" out of your full pack of notes, examine what you have, and decide clearly what to do with that set of information.

There are many satisfactory ways of recording information for convenient use during speech composition.   Figure 4-1 illustrates one way.

What you need from any record of information is very clear: The record should be complete enough so you need not make a second trip to the original source; it must give you an accurate representation of

---

Rhetorical Situations—Kinds

Don Ihde, *Listening and Voice: A Phenomenology of Sound* (Athens, Ohio: Ohio University Press, 1976), p. 181.

"In the face-to-face meeting . . . the shock generated by the other gives way to an invitation to word. This is so even if the word is perfunctory. Face to face meeting without any word results in awkward silence, because in the meeting there is issued a call to speak."

(Ihde is professor of philosophy at State University of New York, Stony Brook. Judging from the book he isn't thinking of *rhetorical* situations at all. He may not even know of them, but the idea expressed here adds something to the description Lloyd Bitzer gives and to the discussion in *Public Speaking as a Liberal Art.*)

FIGURE 4-1. Note Card.

what you found; it must allow items of information to be separated, sorted, and compared in any conceivably useful way. As far as we know, only recording individual units of information on individual slips of paper meets the last requirement. So we say: note separate bits of information on separate slips and put the complete reference to your sources on all slips, or work out some code system for identifying exact sources. Also, note on each slip the qualifications of the source, if you know them, and what it was that made you interested in the item when you took it down. Doing all of this can become tedious, but it saves steps and the bother of wondering later why you wrote something down in the first place. We know from experience the extra steps we have taken in consequence of sloppy note taking, and we have wondered too often why in the world we took down a note. Be forewarned!

Thus far in this chapter we have been dealing with stages of preparation that precede the actual composition of a message to be spoken. We have suggested a simple series of topics and questions that can direct thought toward the types of information you need. These topics and questions can efficiently guide explorations of your own mind and your explorations of the minds of others and of the world of print. We have pointed out that different kinds of source materials are needed at different stages of preparation and that they must be studied in ways appropriate to their natures and to what you need to draw from them. Finally, we have observed that it is laborious and confusing to record the results of research in any way that does not allow you to sort and compare related pieces of information easily. But a speaker is more than a bibliographer or research clerk. He or she investigates to compose and deliver personalized speech that will do what it needs to do in a particular rhetorical situation.

HUMANIZING IDEAS

Too many speakers believe the task of composing is finished when research is finished. They forget that what *they* now know must still be reshaped for a particular audience in a particular situation. To press you on to complete the basic processes of invention, we are going to close this chapter by returning to themes we discussed in chapter 3. We hope that by doing this we will remind you once more that in public speech all raw materials need to be psychologically adjusted to the readiness of the human beings who will listen.

Accommodating to Audiences

No matter what seems compelling to you, you dare not use *only* your own personal judgments of adequacy, clarity, or persuasiveness in rhetorical communication. No communicator is completely free, but because speakers always face particular listeners in specific situations, they are less free than essayists, poets, or writers of imaginative prose literature. An essay, a poem, a novel, or a scientific paper can be composed as an expression of private feelings and can be published on a take-it-or-leave-it basis. But no speaker dares treat his listeners thus. He must meet and deal with listeners in a particular time, place, and set of circumstances. If the listeners are unready for him and his ideas he must create readiness. No speaker can retire to the bookshelf to wait until his audience falls into a mood to seek out what he had to say. As Lloyd Bitzer's conception of rhetorical situations and Don Ihde's conception of simply meeting someone (see figure 4-1) suggest, to bring a message into someone else's presence implies that a *sharing* is going to take place.

Moreover, there is almost never only *one* way of communicating anything, as Don Burks and Roderick Hart point out in the passages we quoted from their essay on "Rhetorical Sensitivity" in chapter 3 (75–76). To be rhetorically sensitive in research and in composing public speech is to find the best material in support of your views or purposes and to treat it in ways that will appeal to your listeners in the situation that will be theirs and yours.

Subtle Adaptive Decisions

Adaptation is not, of course, always just a matter of simplification and partition. There are more subtle adaptive decisions that speakers have to make. One of the most famous examples in literature is found in the story of St. Paul's sermon on Mars Hill in Athens. As it is told in the book of Acts in the Bible, Paul came on a missionary journey to Athens, Greece. There he became upset at the many idols he saw in the city, and he argued strongly in synagogues and on the streets against idol worship. However, there was in Athens a group of philosophers and religious thinkers who held regular discussions in an open meeting place called the Areopagus at the top of Mars Hill, overlooking the city. One day these men invited Paul to come to speak with them. The rest of the account, including a summary of what Paul said, runs this way in the Revised Standard Version:

And they took hold of him and brought him to the Areopagus, saying, "May we know what this new teaching is which you present? For you bring some strange things to our ears; we wish to know therefore what these things mean." Now all the Athenians and the foreigners who lived there spent their time in nothing except telling or hearing something new.

So Paul, standing in the middle of the Areopagus, said: "Men of Athens, I perceive that in every way you are very religious. For as I passed along, and observed the objects of your worship, I found also an altar with this inscription, 'To an unknown god.' What therefore you worship as unknown, this I proclaim to you. The God who made the world and everything in it, being Lord of heaven and earth, does not live in shrines made by man, nor is he served by human hands, as though he needed anything, since he himself gives to all men life and breath and everything. And he made from one every nation of men to live on all the face of the earth, having determined allotted periods and the boundaries of their habitation, that they should seek God, in the hope that they might feel after him and find him. Yet he is not far from each one of us, for

'In him we live and move and have our being';

as even some of your poets have said, 'For we are indeed his offspring.'

"Being then God's offspring, we ought not to think that the Deity is like gold, or silver, or stone, a representation by the art and imagination of man. The times of ignorance God overlooked, but now he commands all men everywhere to repent, because he has fixed a day on which he will judge the world in righteousness by a man whom he has appointed, and of this he has given assurance to all men by raising him from the dead."[9]

The story of this speech closes with these words:

> Now when they heard of the resurrection of the dead, some mocked; but others said, "We will hear you again about this." So Paul went out from among them. But some men joined him and believed. . . .[10]

This account of a missionary's speech carefully designed to win a hearing within Greek culture poses most of the harder questions speakers must solve in talking to audiences that do not agree from the beginning. Would Paul's personal, religious convictions have been better honored had he *not* suppressed, for this speech, his strong distaste for the Greek religion? This was his first opportunity to talk to some of the most important religious and philosophical thinkers in Athens. He deplored their religion, but to get a hearing he chose not to say so directly (as he had apparently been doing in the streets). He actually used a facet of his listeners' paganism as a means of getting to his own central idea. His choices were rhetorically wise; had he not moderated his criticism of paganism and had he not used the entire situation delicately to assure that he would be heard out, he would have undermined his whole reason for going to the hilltop to talk. If he wanted to convince any leading thinkers in Athens, he had to treat them as we have said in chapter 3 doubters must always be treated. They must be moved from their strongly held positions and commitments by slow degrees. Generally, although not at every point, that was how Paul approached his task. The account says some listeners rejected the message because Paul still went too far for them when he talked of resurrection. But we are told others were moved far enough to be willing to hear more. Later, it appears, some who heard more came to believe Paul.

There are few records of persuasion that illustrate so clearly the delicacy of judgment you and all speakers have to exercise to get even *some* acceptance from those who doubt your truth. No matter how convinced *you* are, a doubter simply will not see the merits of your ideas if you only proclaim them. Doubts and counteropinions are truths, too. Real communication occurs only when "speakers' truths" and "listeners' truths" are accommodated to one another—in the best way rhetorical art allows.

---

9. From the Revised Standard Version of the Bible (New York: Thomas Nelson, 1959), Acts, 17. 19–34. Copyrighted 1946, 1952 © 1971, 1973 by the Division of Christian Education and the National Council of Churches of Christ in the U.S.A. Reprinted by permission.

10. Ibid., 32–34.

Talk as the Medium

For reasons we will state shortly, *talk* was an entirely suitable medium for St. Paul's religious message. But talk is not the ideal medium for every kind of material. This means that as a speaker you have further need to adapt your views. You need to present them in the ways that communicate them best. Our courts recognize that some content is better communicated in print than in speech, so an attorney normally prepares a written brief as well as an oral plea. The judge studies the brief at leisure. If an engineer or any other speaker must deal with highly technical details, he is likely to reinforce what he says with visual or other more efficient communication. An architect prepares floor plans, sketches, sectional drawings, and models, recognizing that building plans are never adequately communicated by speech or writing. Likewise, each speaker must discriminate between what can be told through speech and what is better conveyed in some other way.

The balance of effectiveness is not always against speech as a communicative medium. A person's attitude toward a proposition or toward another person is exceedingly difficult to picture and more difficult to convey through writing than through speech. Feeling or emphasis is better conveyed in person than in print. Speech best communicates the relationships between ideas and human experience. Aspects of an idea or event that have strong human significance are naturals for oral communication, and ideas that lack human significance must either be deliberately associated with other matters of human concern or be consigned to another medium. Given the relationship between religious belief and human feeling, Paul suffered no disadvantage because talk was his only available medium of communication with the philosophers.

As a speaker you have both auditory and visual resources. (Never forget that *you* are your most versatile visual resource.) You will need to choose and emphasize content that lends itself to communication through your media and subordinate or exclude from your speech whatever materials cannot be effectively communicated through speech and action.

When using the medium of speech, you may discover that your ideas have to be given shapes and shadings different from those they had when you first thought them or found them. That you will *speak* may demand accommodation of ideas just as much as the prior beliefs of listeners demand accommodation.

We have been focusing in the last few paragraphs on external forces that hem you in as you plan and compose speech. There are positive forces, too. You can draw on them to compensate for restrictive pressures.

There is seldom only one way of handling an idea. For example, if you find it impossible to demonstrate the existence of life on another planet, you have other options. You can discuss whether conditions on the planet are *potentially* capable of supporting life. Again, many distinctive qualities of a great piece of music are scarcely communicable through words, but this need not prevent you from speaking about the musical work. Although you cannot say all, you can verbally draw attention to some aspects of its structure or *form*. This is precisely the method Leonard Bernstein, laureate conductor of the New York Philharmonic Orchestra, used to make meaningful the verbal portions of his justly famous televised lectures on musical comedy, jazz, rhythm, conducting, and so on. If one attribute or relationship of a subject does not lend itself to oral communication in a given setting, there is probably some other theme or line of thought, almost equal in importance, that *is* orally communicable.

Speakers confronted with ideas that are difficult to communicate or with purposes difficult to accomplish are like scientists confronted by the fact that absolute certainty and rigorously demonstrable answers are not always possible for them:

> There is in the first place the temptation to sloppy thinking—if one knows that rigor can never be attained one is tempted to do less than one's best and let a piece of analysis go that one sees could be improved if one took more time or pains with it. There are situations where a defeatist attitude is too easily adopted instead of pressing the attack to one's utmost.[11]

Very seldom is there no usable analogy, no example, no familiar principle, no easily imagined experience that will create at least an approximate impression of what you want to speak about. St. Paul turned to the methods of philosophical deduction when he wanted to show the superiority of his "Unknown God" to philosophers who were used to this kind of discourse. Thomas Huxley once explained the principles of scientific investigation to an audience of English workingmen by showing how this kind of investigation resembled investigations of crimes. Huxley's speech is still used as a model of exposition; but it would certainly not be had he decided to disregard the limitations of his *audience* (auditors) and proceed by rigorously defining induction, evidence, and generalization.

Some years ago Professor Laura Crowell made a careful study

---

11. P. W. Bridgman, *The Way Things Are* (Cambridge, Mass.: Harvard University Press, 1959), p. 9.

of the complicated changes President Franklin Roosevelt and his team of speech writers made in developing an address to the Congress, delivered on January 6, 1941. The speech went through seven different drafts before it was given, beginning with five pages Roosevelt composed to show his assistants what he wanted. (It is testimony to his art as a composer that 60 percent of this material was appropriate for the final, seventh version of the address.) What Professor Crowell found was that Roosevelt and his staff at first *added* ideas to the initial draft. Then they went through a stage of shifting ideas around in the speech to get the right ones into the important first and last positions. In this process they also began to drop out details and to reduce paragraphs to pithy statements. In the last drafts they seem to have concentrated on sharpening the language—inserting alliteration, parallelism, reconstructing statements to get just the right emphasis, and rearranging statements to achieve climaxes. It was not until the fifth of the seven versions that the final, overall shape of the address began to appear clearly.

As Professor Crowell says, "Often these alterations are not matters of finding appropriate expression for ideas so much as of finding the appropriate ideas for expression." Often only a few words had to be found to add major new dimensions to ideas, as in these instances:

> . . . immediacy of the crisis is not the only time relation developed in the preparation of the manuscript. The claim that before 1914 no foreign war "constituted a real threat against *us* or against *any other American nation*" is changed to read "constituted a real threat against *our future* or against *the future of any other American nation*." . . . The time shadow is lengthened differently in regard to the danger of enforced isolation for future generations: "thinking of our children" is amended to read "thinking of our children *and their children*."[12]

Crowell sums up her tracings by indicating that the process was actually one of fitting "Roosevelt's truths" to "truths of and about American listeners":

> The cumulative effect of these sentences—built to express Roosevelt's concepts of governmental function and relationship, shifted to place the climactic idea in the climactic position, altered and trimmed to add force and effect by the very words chosen—is powerful indeed. Considering that the first wording of the ideas was done by writers with long training on scores of earlier addresses and thus the first sentences embodied much of the style desired, considering that each sentence, each word, underwent severe scrutiny not only in itself but in the

---

12. Laura Crowell, "The Building of the 'Four Freedoms' Speech," *Speech Monographs* XXII (November 1955): 266–83.

light of changes made elsewhere in the address, one begins to understand the power of the final draft.[13]

If experts need to plan and revise in this kind of detail to get it right, the
rest of us should expect to expend considerable planning, adaptation,
accommodation, and revision just to be adequate in communication.

Student speakers can do exceedingly well at finding resources
by which to solve their communicative problems, as this true narrative indicates.

Bob Barth was one of a class of fifteen students, all but four of
whom were college freshmen. Nine were women and six were men.
In conference with his instructor Barth revealed that he would like to
explain the operation of jet aircraft engines in his next speech to the
class but, he said, this probably would be unwise since it was clear that
only two of the fourteen students who would be his audience had even
an elementary knowledge of mechanical and physical principles.
Barth's judgment on his audience was exactly right; most knew nothing
and seemed to care nothing for the world of physics and mechanics.
Nonetheless, Barth's instructor contended that this was a golden opportunity for an experiment with what careful selection of ideas and
methods could accomplish with a difficult audience. Barth reluctantly
agreed to do what he could and set doggedly to work designing a speech
that assumed little interest and no mechanical knowledge on the part
of his hearers.

On the day of his speech Barth began by saying:

> I am going to talk to you today about jet engines. I suspect you think
> you aren't interested. Probably what's in your minds now is some-
> thing like this.

Here Barth uncovered a rough but clear drawing of a jet engine "pod"
covered with words such as "dangerous machine," "complicated," "for
mechanics only," "expensive." He continued:

> The fact is that in principle at least jets aren't complicated. They're
> rather simple. If you've ever blown up a toy balloon and then let it
> out of your hands to watch it shoot through the air as the wind es-
> caped, you not only know something about jet propulsion, you've used
> it. Let's begin right there—with the air escaping out of the balloon.

In this vein Barth covered simply but accurately the elemental
facts about the construction and operation of two types of jet engines.
There was nothing unusual about his delivery, except that it was not
as direct and forceful as it ought to have been. The language of the

---

13. Ibid., p. 282.

speech was simple and the examples were always from everyday life, but there were few other marks of artistry. Even the charts and sketches that communicated things hard to put into words were free-hand crayon drawings on cardboard sheets of different sizes. Yet when Bob Barth ended his talk there was a ripple of applause—the first applause heard in that public-speaking classroom. At the end of the hour two young women who had been in the audience exchanged these observations as they walked from the room. "I learned more today than I do in most class periods," said one. Her companion replied, "Yes. And imagine! I even thought I understood that engine!"

What happened? A speaker accepted his audience as he found it, adjusted to its limitations and its needs, and gave it as much information as its little knowledge, his inventiveness and art, and the time would allow. Without fanfare Barth offered his listeners two always alluring reasons for attending: I can help you understand what's been mysterious to you, and you'll find the whole experience much easier than you expect. Scarcely any subject is unusable in speaking if speaker and audience approach it in this spirit.

ORIGINALITY

It is in the *re*-creation of research materials that you become original, truly an artist. We close this chapter with some observations on originality, for much of which we are indebted to one of our former colleagues, an expert teacher, the late Herbert A. Wichelns.

You may draw information and ideas from printed or oral sources. You may acquire materials from personal knowledge, magazine articles, essays, editorials, or books. You may glean ideas from lectures, plays, movies, television and radio programs, or conversations with fellow students and experts. But once your information is gathered, you must reflect upon it and stamp it with your own personality. Then you must present it in your own words. *To be original you must be able to discover and convey fresh meaning in known matters.* Rarely does even the greatest speaker discuss what was totally unknown before his speech. To realize a truth clearly because you have experienced it in your own mind produces a degree of originality gained in no other way, even though the base for such originality is to be found in readily accepted axioms.

As *you* do when listening, your listeners will be demanding as the price of attention that you have actively thought for yourself, have reached your own point of view, and have reacted as an individual to information you have digested. To be heard with attention and confidence you must exercise judgment in sifting the materials to which you have exposed yourself, and you must test your own reasoning. You must say what you have to say in your *own way,* choosing your *own* words.   Since individualized choices in both matter and struc-ture are involved, you should be extremely wary of constructing speeches based on a single source. If you rely heavily on outlines found in debate manuals or study files or upon ideas expressed in a *single* book or magazine account, you cannot hope for originality even though you actually speak the words conveying the final message. If talk is not a fresh accommodation of yourself and your thoughts to *these* listeners in *their* situation, your human relationship with them will surely be tarnished.

Systematic preparation with full consciousness of your listeners' natures and needs is the key to originality in speaking. You must be-come intimately acquainted with the facts of your subject, and their humanized meanings. You must judge your material with keen aware-ness of the speech situation into which you will bring it.

Sifting the important from the unimportant takes time and reflection and for this reason the likelihood of discovering fresh signifi-cance in a subject will increase if you begin work early. Ideally, a period of several days should elapse between the period of research and final organization and rehearsal of any important speaking—whether delivered in formal or casual settings. During this gestation or cooling-off period you should explore—perhaps using such a topical system as we have provided—the meanings and possibilities of what you know. Ideas about your subject should be forced to grow within you; only thus can they flower into some final form that is right for you, for the speech situation, and for your particular listeners.

It takes imaginative thinking to bring freshness to a subject. You must strive to find the distinct shapes and the potential uses of the materials you use. You must try to see what is unique in your relation to these materials and in their relation to the lives of your hearers. The function of imagination here is not to create the unreal or imaginary but to bring to particular listeners a personalized under-standing of your version of reality. Imagination ought to reinforce and animate fact and probability by revealing what happens *in life* if these facts and probabilities are accepted or rejected.

What are some tests of originality? You should be able to de-fend what you say. You will know more than you have had time—or thought wise—to tell in an initial statement. You will be able and eager to trace ideas to their sources, crediting and evaluating these sources as you talk and afterward. Although you may have borrowed —with acknowledgment—you will always be stating your own ideas, for selection and evaluation of the ideas are *yours*.

If you are original in speaking, you will not rely on others to the extent of repressing your own individuality. You will avoid the hackneyed and be free of clichés because you will say nothing that does not uniquely fit the speech situation.   Like any other work of artistic merit, your work—your talk—well be the product of personal experience, personal insights, and intense awareness of the natures of those with whom you seek to communicate.

EXERCISES

Written

1. Assume you are to speak to a classmate or to your entire class in favor of majoring in the academic subject that interests you most.   Identify three lines of thought (topics) that it would be useful to discuss with the audience you have decided on.   Identify three other lines of thought that are relevant to your subject but that you would *not* choose to discuss with the listeners you have in mind.   Explain the grounds on which you include and exclude each line of thought you cite.
2. Assume you are to give a classroom speech on "Consumers Ought to Educate Themselves."   Which of the sixteen lines of thought (topics) listed in this chapter suggested the most promising lines of research for this speech?   Explain why the remaining cues are not potentially useful as guides to promising information for this speech.
3. Identify the lines of thought (topics) used in some brief, familiar speech such as Lincoln's "Gettysburg Address," Shakespeare's version of Mark Antony's speech over the body of Caesar in *Julius Caesar,* or Dr. Martin Luther King's "I Have a Dream" address.   Defend or criticize the speaker's choice of these lines of thought.   Were there other topics he or she might as wisely have chosen?   If so, illustrate how one of them might have been incorporated into the speech.

Oral

1. Give a short speech in which you explain two ways a proverb or a maxim might be interpreted.   Or choose a specific process and present two ways the process might be effectively explained to an audience.
2. Give a brief report on a speech or editorial you have heard or read and in which you believe the creator made exceptionally inventive use of the lines of thought (topics) available to him—or failed to take advantage of lines of thought open to him.
3. Form a committee with three or four of your colleagues.   Compose an outline or sketch of a speech, editorial, or other practical message intended to accomplish a specific purpose with an audience your committee imagines and describes.   When the committee has settled on purpose and audience, use the cuing terms in this chapter to construct a committee's list of *all* the things it might make sense to include in the message. Then cut this list to the topics that *ought* to be covered, and prepare the committee's sketch or outline of the whole message.

4. To intensify your awareness of the many ways most subjects can be treated in speech, divide your class into groups of three; assign a *noun* to each group (trees, girl, car, Eskimo, etc.); have each group member choose a cue from pp. 94–95 and then prepare and give a two-minute talk on the assigned subject, using chiefly lines of thought (topics) suggested by the chosen cue word. You should discover that there are more interesting things to be said about simple subjects than you supposed.

INVENTION: GENERAL TACTICS

Do you like conversationalists or public speakers who insist on telling you *all* they know about violins or economics or scuba diving? We have heard an audience of students utterly bored by a remarkably informed speaker who tried to tell them how to pick a race horse to bet on. He tried to tell his listeners everything about race horses. He was thoroughly prepared to talk, but did not fit his talk to his situation. He had neglected two basic, tactical activities of planning that any rhetorical situation requires of any informed speaker: to sort and build available materials into *rhetorical proof* that fits the requirements of the situation, and to find the ways of clarifying whatever information deserves to be presented. These two major tasks are the principal concerns of this chapter.

BUILDING PROOF

A simple way of describing *effective talk* is to say it is talk that makes pertinent points and justifies them. As we consider the two processes mentioned above, we will assume you have completed the basic inventional processes of choosing a subject and collecting an appropriate amount of information about it. Now you face the questions: What is my message going to add up to? and Am I sure of exactly what I want to accomplish? It is true that you set goals for yourself before you began investigating your subject, but experienced speakers know only too well that one's sense of purpose changes or may become obscure as general preparation for speaking proceeds.   Most speakers discover that they need to take stock again—to reset goals and to re-express them—following general research.   So with your general prep-aration completed, it is time for you to reconsider your communicative purpose.

Purposiveness

Whether or not you will directly tell your purpose to your lis-teners, *you* must know precisely what you intend to accomplish through speech before you build proofs.   This is true for two reasons.   You cannot prove or support or clarify anything until you are clear about what it is.   Moreover, your talk will need to reflect a sense of purpose on your part if it is to gratify your listeners.   The best way to set your-self to meet these requirements is to formulate a single, concise sen-tence that expresses (1) the kind of experience you intend the hearers to have, and (2) exactly what kind of content will be needed to produce this experience.   We discussed the standards for this kind of sentence on pages 31–33 and will consider purpose sentences further in chapter 6.   Just now we want to develop some thoughts about the values of rethinking purpose statements as one begins to pull together material for speaking.

What is it that hard thought about purpose can do for *you* at this stage?   It will clarify for you which of several kinds of speeches on your subject you really ought to make.   Any subject can be treated in more than one way, so you need to decide which of the possible treat-ments of your subject will be right for your situation and purpose.   You dare not be vague, even to yourself.   "I want to talk about rock forma-tions" does not say which of the dozens of possible talks about rocks you are to frame just now.   By contrast, "I want to help my listeners understand what forces produced each of three rock formations" identifies a *specific* speech about three aspects of geological processes.   "I shall explain the three rock formations that are most common in this area" identifies another speech.   You could make a coherent, influential speech focused on either of the two last statements—as you could never do by using a vague conception such as, "I want to talk about rock formations."

As you move into shaping up any speech, then, you will be wise to review the goals you set for yourself earlier and restate what you *now* want to accomplish.   You will do this best and most efficiently if you formulate a precise sentence that expresses (1) your aim and (2) the range of subject matter to be covered in pursuit of that aim.

We do not mean that your resharpened statement of purpose

cannot be rephrased as you shape the material that will become your speech. You should always feel free to redirect your aims as you think more about your subject and your listeners' readinesses and needs. What is important is that in every moment of building a speech *a* purpose should be utterly clear to you. If it is not, you are apt to ramble in preparation; and when you speak, your listeners are likely to lose their way. Thus, it is for your own guidance and efficiency that you need to pause to rethink your purpose as you begin to construct any public speech.

Rethinking your purpose is also a service to your listeners. As we have said, listening is not a very efficient way of acquiring information and belief. Listeners therefore need what help they can get to extract the right ideas from talk. This is not just a loose opinion. All experiments testing what happens when speakers assert their points and purposes in so many words have demonstrated that this practice helped listeners' understanding and caused them to retain what they heard.[1] This argues that you ought to tell your listeners exactly what your purpose is, but there are times when this tactic is not advisable.

There are times when more will be lost than gained by openly asserting your purpose or stating a point boldly and early in its development. When auditors are doubtful or hostile, it is wiser to develop sensitive ideas, paving the way for acceptance, before you assert directly what conclusions you want drawn. But even in such cases you should not seem to be talking without purpose. When experienced speakers withhold revelation of their purposes, they usually try to indicate that they have some lesser, uncontroversial goals in mind as they move step-by-step to the overall goal they are pursuing.

As always in speaking, one must exercise judgment about what is the tactically sound way of revealing purpose in speaking. There is no formal rule to follow. What we want you to carry away from our discussion at this point is that *you* need a clear sense of purpose all of the time; and your listeners need a continuing sense that you *have* purpose, whether or not you are revealing it completely. Therefore, you ought to pause, following research for speaking, to reset your goal precisely. The way to be sure you have done so is to formulate the kind of purpose statement we have spoken of generally and that we discuss in detail in chapter 6.

---

1. Among experimental studies supporting this proposition are Donald L. Thistlethwaite, Henry deHaan, and Joseph Kamenetzky, "The Effect of 'Directive' and 'Non-Directive' Communication Procedures on Attitudes," *Journal of Abnormal and Social Psychology* LI (July 1955): 107–18; Donald K. Darnell, "The Relation between Sentence Order and Comprehension," *Speech Monographs* XXX (June 1963): 97–100; Ernest Thompson, "Some Effects of Message Structure on Listeners' Comprehension," ibid., XXXIV (March 1967): 51–57; John E. Baird, Jr., "Effects of Speech Summaries upon Audience Comprehension of Expository Speeches of Varying Quality and Complexity," *Central States Speech Journal* XXV (Summer 1974): 119–27.

The purpose governing a well-conceived speech does not accomplish the work it forecasts. Ideas, language, and behavior are deployed to do this work. That is what we mean by *proof*. The somewhat military connotations of the words *tactics* and *deploy*, which we are using, deserve to be taken seriously; it is, indeed, the mix and the placement of forces that will determine the proof-power of any speaking you do.

Your task is always to get someone else to experience something as you would like. You must get people to accept information and use it in special ways if you are to inform them; they must experience heightened desire to investigate if you are to provoke inquiry; they must *re*value their prior knowledge if you are to reinforce their beliefs and attitudes; they must accept *your* interpretations of data and their own interests if you are to persuade them; they must suspend a good many serious concerns if you are to entertain them. Whatever you attempt as a speaker, you ask your listeners to shift their outlooks in some degree. So it is important to think about *why* and *how* people shift their views.

People change views because they think they have found sufficient *reasons* or proofs to indicate that to shift would be a good thing. Of course, what people think of as reasons may or may not involve much private reasoning. What seem to listeners sufficient proofs and goods may have been decided by using much logic or scarcely any at all.

There are three kinds of proof that listeners in any situation demand of communication before allowing it to change their views.

1. They demand that either the communication or their own experiences reveal a *connection* between what is asked from them and their own personal interests, as they understand those interests in the rhetorical situation. (See chapter 3, pages 63–72.)
2. They demand that either the communication or their own experiences provide *rational* justifications for believing what is said to them, now, in the rhetorical situation.
3. They demand that the source of the communication (the speaker and his sources and sponsors) seem *worthy* of confidence—at least on the subject of the communication and in the situation in which they find themselves.

A speech, or any part of it, must in some way satisfy all three of these general demands if there is to be change in the attitudes and beliefs of those who listen. You have often made these demands of speakers, although they may have been expressed in your mind as questions.

Suppose someone is talking to you about a curriculum in business administration. Certain questions constantly pop into your mind: Why should *I* care about business administration? Why bring this up *now*?   Why should I believe the curriculum really *is as you say it is*? Why is what you say to me *wiser* or *truer* than some other version? Why should I listen to *you* on this matter?

Anyone talking about business curricula or any other subject should expect such questions to arise again and again in any listener's mind.   A major part of the job of talking to someone else is to see that all of those questions are answered, unless you know your listener already has clear answers for them within himself.

Notice that some of these questions ask whether the listener's personal interests are going to be satisfied (Why should *I* care?   Why bring this up *now*?); some ask for rational justifications (Why should I believe things *are as you say they are*?   Why is what you urge on me *wiser* or *truer* than an alternative?); and another asks about the speaker's qualifications (Why should I listen to *you* on this matter?).   If you see to it that these five questions are satisfactorily answered either by what you say and do or by something your listeners are already aware of, you will have built into what you say the personal-interest, rational, and source justifications that audiences demand as the price of shifting their attitudes and beliefs.

To explain how one builds these justifications we will have to talk about them separately, but you should bear in mind that these influences never *operate* separately from one another.   You can demonstrate this by examining your own behavior.   When a speaker shows you that something is in your own interest, do you not think better of him for that same reason?   Do you not almost always find your friends more reasonable than people you dislike?   Have you never said, "I see no flaw in your reasoning, but I don't accept your conclusions anyway"? We are dealing with proofs that are almost always intricately interrelated, but to talk about them clearly we must treat them separately.

Developing Personal-Interest Justifications

"Why should *I* care?" and "Why bring this up *now*?" are basic, personal questions.   They spring from our most elementary concerns about ourselves.   We saw in chapter 3 that listeners are anxious about things that affect their private purposes and interests, that people tend to shut out what has no apparent bearing on their immediate affairs, and that all of us behave in this way by virtue of being human.   You, as a speaker, must give your listeners some satisfying answers to why they should care now.

To see *how* listeners may be shown that their own interests justify what you say, it is necessary to review some elemental psychological concepts.   Modern social psychologists argue that we behave as we do in consequence of internal forces, sometimes referred to as needs, drives, tensions, goals, motives, or by other terms. There is general agreement that it is *internal* stimuli that induce us to act as we do. These internal stimuli direct our activity toward simple or complex goals. The *goals* are conditions we feel will satisfy our needs and desires. They may be satisfactions of physiological needs (for food, drink, etc.); some goals are social rewards as well as fulfillment of physiological needs. Thus, the basic need for physical safety and the learned need for social approval may cause us to strive toward the goal of associating with other people in particular ways. As we mature, experience teaches us that certain kinds of behaviors tend to yield satisfactions of certain needs, and thus we acquire predictable patterns of activity to which we rather regularly resort when we experience the tensions of specific needs. For example, we learn that to drink a cup of coffee or a cola at midafternoon picks us up. So under the tension of feeling a bit tired, we go through an activity that also satisfies thirst —even when we are not particularly thirsty. We do not feel any less gratified because the act of drinking is not in and of itself the act that gives us the satisfaction (relaxation) we really seek.

In similar ways we all develop predispositions toward a host of intellectual activities. These learnings are of special importance to speakers. For example, people learn that experienced advisers are more reliable than inexperienced ones. As a result these people become predisposed to accept what, say, a *well-known* scientist or nature guide says. Or people learn that Midwesterners are more friendly than New Englanders. That learning predisposes them to agree if they hear that it is more pleasant to live in Winona, Minnesota, than in Pittsfield, Massachusetts. They may know nothing about either place, but their learning has readied them to believe this kind of statement. Experience has taught everyone thousands of such ready propositions— infrequently verbalized and often contradictory to one another. These learned propositions that lie at the base of our predispositions may or may not be true or informed, but they form our funds of readinesses to respond, and they constitute the forms in which we define within ourselves our personal interests and inclinations. Their intensity—the degree to which we feel it is important to *retain* these formulated predispositions—guides us when we decide what ideas and actions are or are not acceptable to us. But we do not always respond in a simple yes-no fashion. Depending on how strongly we feel concerning what we tend to accept or reject, we may oppose, retreat from, or adhere either more or less strongly to what we hear or to what we felt or believed before.[2]

---

2. For a concise outline of a general theory of attitude change, see Irving L. Janis, Carl I. Hovland, et al., *Personality and Persuasibility* (New Haven: Yale University Press, 1959). Parts of the summary we have presented derive from

The paragraphs above contain some statements on which there is a difference of opinion among scholars. But the summary will serve you as a safe, practical view pending the time when psychologists reach fuller agreement concerning the mechanisms of changing beliefs and attitudes. There is a major point implicit in what we have summarized, and on that point there is general agreement among psychologists: We do not address human needs *directly* with our words. Our words and acts awaken or intensify need-produced attitudes that stand in consciousness as self-committing degrees of adherence or nonadherence to what has been said to us. What speakers do is symbolize that to which they and their listeners respond feelingly. To weave a tapestry of need-justified experience within listeners, a speaker needs to pattern their attitudinal responses in ways that are accepting of what he offers. He does not insert beliefs into other minds; he encourages other minds to evolve their own beliefs and feelings. If he pays too little attention to the attitudinal patterns his hearers possess, he may miss important opportunities to influence or, worse, allow patterns of judgments to evolve in ways that will operate against him rather than for him.

Below are a few lines from a speech by Dr. Daniel J. Boorstin, senior historian at the National Museum of History and Technology in Washington, D.C. Dr. Boorstin was addressing the Associated Press Managing Editors' Association on "Dissent, Dissension and the News." It was important for him to distinguish early in the speech between *debate* and *dissent*. He apparently wanted to bring his listeners quickly to endorse debate and to disapprove of dissent. Notice in the passage below how he attempted to put attitudes into a pattern consistent with his goal. The quotation is broken into thought units, and opposite each unit we have put the kind of response we suppose Dr. Boorstin was working for.

STATEMENTS	POSSIBLE RESPONSES
A debate is an orderly exploration . . .	*Order* and *exploring* are "good." *Debate* has these qualities.
of a common problem that presupposes the debaters are worried by the same question.	*Common interests* and *agreement* make for *order*—debaters have "good" goals.

C. W. Sherif, M. Sherif, and R. E. Nebergall, *Attitude and Attitude Change* (Philadelphia: W. B. Saunders, 1965). We have also drawn upon Ch. Perelman and L. Olbrechts-Tyteca, *The New Rhetoric* (Notre Dame: University of Notre Dame Press, 1969), and Vernon E. Cronen and William K. Price, "Affective Relationship between Speaker and Listener: An Alternative to the Approach-Avoidance Model," *Communication Monographs* XLIII (March 1976): 51–59.

It brings to life new facts . . .	*Facts* and *newness* are also "good"; *debate* has that "goodness" too.
and new arguments that make possible a better solution.	*Newness* and *better solutions* are "good," so *debate* has further merit.
But dissension means discord.	*Discord* is "bad"; *dissension* has this quality.
As the dictionary tells us, dissension is marked by a break in friendly relations.	*Breaking friendship* is a mark of *discord; dissension* has this "bad" quality too.
It is an expression not of common concern . . .	*Dissension* denies the "good" of *common interest,* further rendering it "bad."
but of hostile feelings.	*Hostility* is the opposite of *agreement,* one of the "goods" *debate* develops; another way *dissension* is "bad."
This distinction is crucial.[3]	[No particular attitude is aroused here. Dr. Boorstin missed an opportunity to fix the pattern firmly with something like: "Debate is productive; dissension is discordant, unfriendly, and unproductive."]

Dr. Boorstin offers no formal reasoning, although he does cite the authority of the dictionary. He makes no verbal attempt to show himself uniquely qualified to say what he does (his reputation may already have done this). The thought he wanted endorsed was that debate is valuable but dissent is not. He justified this thought almost entirely by trying to activate a series of favorable and unfavorable attitudes that were already latent within his listeners. Boorstin undertook to evoke attitudes systematically: the favorable ones first and the negative ones afterward. By setting up statements in this way, he arranged matters so every negative response toward dissension could also remind listeners of the contrasting *merits* of debate—to which they had already committed themselves. If the scheme worked within the speech situation, the listeners experienced an increasing intensity of approval of

---

3. The complete text of this speech appears in Wil A. Linkugel, R. R. Allen, and Richard L. Johannesen, *Contemporary American Speeches*, 2nd ed. (Belmont, Calif.: Wadsworth Publishing Company, 1969), pp. 203–11. The excerpt quoted appears on p. 205, as "paragraph" nine.

debate as their estimation of dissension was pushed lower and lower by Boorstin's remarks.   We think Boorstin missed an opportunity to fix his pattern by not adding a final, clinching, summative statement at the end.   Nonetheless, the passage illustrates how ideas-borne-on-language can be managed for the purpose of regulating a mixture of evaluative attitudes favorable to a speaker's purpose.   If Dr. Boorstin succeeded in any degree at all, he supported his own position *through* his listeners' predispositions and self-interests.   With preliminary analysis of your listeners' attitudinal patterns and the situation in which you meet them, you can invent similar, systematic proofs favorable to your purposes.

You will speak on many matters for which the best proofs will be within your hearers, needing only to be awakened and patterned to support what you say.   It would be silly to prove with statistics, quotations, and formal arguments that students need special study spaces in which to work—especially if your audience were made up of students!   The students' experiences and attitudes would supply proofs more potent than any data you could assemble.   They would have learned attitudes such as: you have to be able to spread out your materials when you study; it's hard to study when everyone around you is doing something else; I need protection from interruptions; and having the right atmosphere around you helps you concentrate.   Such beliefs and attitudes would only need to be brought to your listeners' consciousness to become powerful proofs for the proposition that every school must provide special study spaces for students if it is to claim to have adequate educational facilities.

But, of course, few of us are mind readers, so how can we judge when listeners' personal experiences and interests will "prove" for us? To identify all the significant attitudes of even a single audience would require research by a corps of social scientists.   Some political figures and others have the benefit of this kind of research data, but most of us must try to communicate effectively without those scientific advantages.   Even so, we are not without resources.   We can use generalizations about people such as those discussed in chapter 3 to estimate what self-interests reside in our listeners, and we can learn specific facts about specific audiences and situations by general investigation.

You will not need the Gallup polling organization to tell you that young people in your audience will be more disposed than their parents to endorse idealistic and unqualified propositions.   Nor do you need to be a social scientist to predict that people who live in communes are less likely than those who live in fraternities and sororities to have strongly favorable attitudes toward "organization."   You also know that more men than women are apt to admire mechanical ingenuity for itself, and that people having difficulty supporting themselves are likely to be more intensely concerned with personal economics than those who have no economic worries. To compose effective speech you need chiefly to ask what your prospective listeners identify as "good for me and mine" and what they think of as "not so good for me and mine." To ask and answer this is to make a kind of survey of attitudes. Common sense will then reveal that a good many of those attitudes can be called up to sustain attention and to justify your ideas. Your common sense will also tell which of those attitudes you will need to skirt lest they leap into a hearer's consciousness as proofs against you.

The fundamental point to remember about listeners' attitudes is that your listener may call them up himself, spontaneously, or you may call them up by reminding him of things about which he possesses strong attitudes. Whichever way they arise in his consciousness, it is his attitudes that teach him *why* he should or should not (does or does not) care *now*. Your task is to direct his caring toward the conclusions you have in view and not let the caring subside or become associated with things other than those that support you. The biology major, whose classroom speech on hunting female deer was described in chapter 3, and Bob Barth, whose speech on jet propulsion was cited in chapter 4, illustrated how effective ordinary, but thoughtful, analysis of attitudes out there can make speaking. So did Dr. Boorstin's address to the editors. Notice, too, that in these three cases the speakers did not use existing attitudes merely to cause listeners to reaffirm what the listeners already believed; they taught *new* beliefs by connecting old attitudes and new information and thus they caused their hearers to generate thoughts that had not previously existed in their minds. You can do this too.

Developing Rational Justifications

Sometimes "Why should *I* care?" or "Why bring that up *now*?" cannot be sufficiently answered by just triggering and patterning attitudes. When listeners do not understand things and events as you do, and especially when they are doubters, their prime questions are: Why should I believe things really are *as you say they are*? and Why is what you say *wiser* or *truer* than my version? When such questions are in listeners' minds, you have to build proof with reason and evidence. When are people uncertain or doubtful? It is when little or nothing in their experience confirms the views being offered them. Whenever your listeners do not possess knowledge and attitudes that will support what you want to tell them, you must make a *rational case*—which is to say, give them knowledge and reasons they will take seriously. You must give uncertain or doubting listeners new ways of seeing, ways that allow the ideas you offer to make sense and be justified on terms your listeners are familiar with.

Although we often talk as though it were easy, it is not easy to say what a rational ground for accepting a belief is. The trouble is that on most subjects we talk to one another about there is no universal agreement on what makes sense and what does not. What is the most reasonable way to develop nuclear energy? What is the reasonable thing to do if you fall in love? Are you right about the last movie you saw or is the newspaper critic who disagrees with you right? Even in matters of philosophy and of law we cannot say with finality what a reasonable or rational proof is.

How different views can be about "what is reasonable" was illustrated in 1971 when the Supreme Court heard and decided a case in which the federal government sought to prevent the *New York Times* and the *Washington Post* from publishing excerpts from allegedly stolen secret documents that came to be known as "The Pentagon Papers." The Court rejected the government's case by a 6–3 vote. The vote was decisive, but *not one justice agreed totally with any other justice on the proper reasons* for voting on one side or the other. Every justice felt compelled to write and file his own distinct reasons for voting as he did; so six rational justifications were issued for voting as the majority of the Court did and three sets of reasons were issued for voting with the minority. Why? Because the justices, like all of us, used different evaluative standards in determining what was most reasonable. Different perceptions of what was fact, different interpretations of what the law said, different estimates of what could or would happen in the future, and different personal preferences entered into each justice's reasoning. These kinds of differences are always in play when any of us makes judgments. Consequently speakers and all other makers of rhetorical communication need to remember very clearly that almost nothing they ever say will seem certain to everyone who hears them. On most matters what is a reasonable or rational proof depends on who is doing the estimating. The result is that to give another person rational justifications is always to satisfy *his* standards of rationality and sufficiency of evidence. It is to align *his* standards of reasonableness and *his* preferences so he can accept what you offer. It is to fill gaps in his knowledge until his sense of sufficiency is satisfied.

Although we cannot settle here the problem of what the nature of rationality is in a philosophical sense, we can look at a simple case of rational justification going on in actual talk. Below is an excerpt, the ending, of a college student's talk to his class on the state of scientific knowledge concerning marijuana and its effects. His concluding point was that presumably scientific findings about marijuana should be accepted only after examining the methods and purposes of the research. Obviously this kind of proposition could be supported best by reasons and evidence—rational proof.   Steve Mayhew, the speaker, undertook to give his proposition that sort of support.   How, we shall now see.[4]

> *Let me say something finally about some major drawbacks concerning laboratory tests on the effects of marijuana.   There is often a problem with the validity of the tests that are made.*
>
> *Marijuana raises emotional issues and, unfortunately, objective data are sometimes spiced with subjective interpretations.   For example, some tests haven't even had control groups, yet dramatic interpretations have been made.   There was one experiment involving sperm counts where men were locked up for about four weeks in isolated rooms, without seeing any women.   Their sperm counts dropped.   Now, don't you think if there had been a control group without any marijuana, and these poor people were locked up for four weeks, their sperm counts would drop too?*
>
> *Also, hybrid rats have been used in some of the experiments. These are rats that can be bred to be susceptible to almost any disease there is.   They can be bred so as to allow medical examiners to make such reports as that drinking water leads to cancer.   How were the rats used in marijuana experiments bred?*
>
> *So, what I want to say in conclusion is that the public must be wary of medical reports about marijuana and only regard seriously those which have been replicated and which have been done under proper experimental conditions.*

We are going to analyze this segment of Mayhew's remarks in a way that we hope will show you the real nature of rational justification in rhetorical communication: that such justification is seldom *final*, that in popular discussion we seldom prove anything conclusively, and we seldom prove it by reason and evidence *alone*.   What we do is draw upon the principles of logical reasoning that other people have in their minds, and at the same time we motivate them in other ways.

The English logician Stephen E. Toulmin has devised a way of laying out arguments that can help us see the various features of Mr. Mayhew's rational justifications.[5]   Professor Toulmin contends that in rational argument we present some—sometimes all—of six kinds of material.   Among them will be DATA, WARRANT, BACKING FOR WARRANTS, CLAIM.   Sometimes, also, we offer QUALIFICATIONS of our CLAIMS to forestall or take account of real or anticipated CON-

---

4. The talk was given by Stephen T. Mayhew, then a sophomore in business administration at The Pennsylvania State University.   It was one of a series of speeches given in a basic speech course in November 1976; the title the students chose for the series was: "The Case of Marijuana: To Decriminalize or Not?"   Used by permission of Mr. Mayhew.

5. Stephen E. Toulmin, *The Uses of Argument* (Cambridge, Eng.: Cambridge University Press, 1958).   See especially chapter 3, "The Layout of Arguments."

DITIONS OF REBUTTAL that, if not guarded against, might make our CLAIMS seem too sweeping or otherwise unacceptable. Identifying and exemplifying these logical moves as we go, we want to show you the nature of Mayhew's reasoning in the excerpt we have given.

Mayhew opens by making a major CLAIM to his audience: There is often a problem with the validity of laboratory tests that have been made on marijuana. Why is this true? Because *subjective* interpretations creep into findings due to *emotional* issues raised in connection with marijuana itself. Using Toulmin's framework for analyzing such an argument, we can show what Mayhew has done so far (see figure 5-1).

We can see in this figure what Steve Mayhew gave his listeners to back up his claim about the validity of the tests. We also see something he did *not* give them: a justification or WARRANT for taking subjective interpretations as evidence of faulty validity. He *asserted* something was so about the laboratory tests, and he drew a conclusion about them without explaining how he could fairly get there from the DATA he gave. A logic professor might rightly tell him his argument was incomplete. But shall *we* complain or say Steve's proof would work poorly with his audience in their situation? No. Mayhew was talking to an audience of college students. He could expect that they would know enough about experimentation to see that to give subjective interpretations to objective, experimental data is to proceed invalidly, at least in some degree. Any listener who knew this much could privately *supply* a WARRANT to justify Mayhew's move from the situation he asserted as DATA to his CLAIM. The listeners might think something such as this: "Subjectivity makes for invalidity in experiments" or "You shouldn't let your emotions creep into experiments." Either kind of idea would make Mayhew's argument entirely satisfactory.[6]

There is something else we can see from this diagram of Steve's small argument. The word *often* occurs in the claim. What does that do? Toulmin calls terms like this QUALIFIERS of CLAIMS. They say how sweepingly the CLAIM is being made. Other common QUALIFIERS are "probably," "most of the time," "at least half the time," "sometimes," and so on. In Toulmin's conception a QUALIFIER is likely to be needed when some CONDITION OF REBUTTAL might be lodged against the CLAIM if it were not qualified. The QUALIFIER also indicates the strength the WARRANT exerts on the CLAIM. To show this we might rediagram an argument like Steve Mayhew's as shown in figure 5-2. Mayhew has protected his conclusion against a doubt by inserting the QUALIFIER "often." By doing so he may also

---

6. Those who are familiar with the term will recognize that we are here describing *enthymematic* reasoning.

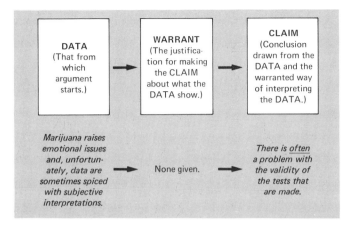

FIGURE 5-1.

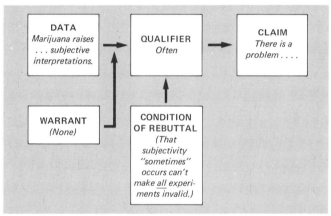

FIGURE 5-2.

be earning some credit *for himself* with the audience, for he is showing he does not claim more than he is justified in doing if the facts are as he asserts they are. We will return to this matter of earning credit and using one's self as proof in the next section of this chapter.

A final thing to notice about this simple argument is that a listener could believe Steve Mayhew *either* because he believed Steve's DATA, supplied the missing WARRANT, and was therefore led *logically* to the qualified CLAIM, or because he just *wanted* to believe Steve Mayhew. In short, although Steve offered an argument, no listener *had to* follow the argument to believe the CLAIM. One can even imagine someone who so distrusts a speaker that no amount of argument could convince him. "If *he* says it, it's probably *not* so" is a position you have heard expressed. We must recognize, then, that listeners may or may not choose to follow the rational proofs we give them; it is *their* choice that determines what is logical to them, not entirely the speaker's intent.

If Steve Mayhew had stopped with the argument we have so

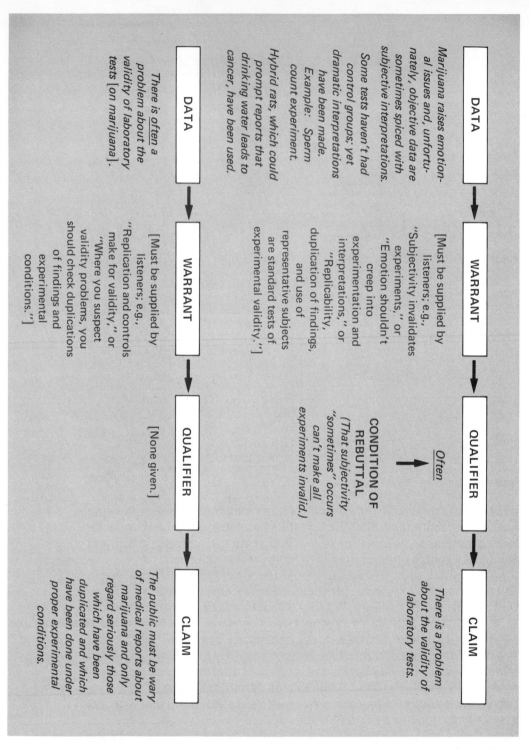

DATA

Marijuana raises emotion-al issues and, unfortu-nately, objective data are sometimes spiced with subjective interpretations.

Some tests haven't had control groups; yet dramatic interpretations have been made. Example: Sperm count experiment.

Hybrid rats, which could prompt reports that drinking water leads to cancer, have been used.

WARRANT

[Must be supplied by listeners; e.g., "Subjectivity invalidates experiments," or "Emotion shouldn't creep into experimentation and interpretations," or "Replicability, duplication of findings, and use of representative subjects are standard tests of experimental validity."]

QUALIFIER

Often

CONDITION OF REBUTTAL

(That subjectivity "sometimes" occurs can't make *all* experiments *invalid*.)

CLAIM

There is a problem about the validity of laboratory tests.

DATA

There is *often* a problem about the validity of laboratory tests [on marijuana].

WARRANT

[Must be supplied by listeners; e.g., "Replication and controls make for validity," or "Where you suspect validity problems, you should check duplications of findings and experimental conditions."]

QUALIFIER

[None given.]

CLAIM

The public must be wary of medical reports about marijuana and only regard seriously those which have been duplicated and which have been done under proper experimental conditions.

FIGURE 5-3.

134

far analyzed, he would have been rhetorically unwise because (1) whether his DATA were true and were really important had not been well settled for his listeners, and (2) what we have printed as the first paragraph of our excerpt would be too bold, too abrupt, for a conclusion to his talk. He wisely went on, heaping up DATA in support of his CLAIM. By the end of the excerpt the listeners had been given an extended argument such as that shown in Figure 5-3.

Looking at the entire argument Mayhew made shows several things about building rational proofs. First, if his examples are believed *and if they are seen as evidence of unsound experimentation,* they will add to the clarity and strength of his original assertion about what the facts (DATA) really are. At first look his first major argument has been made far stronger logically than it originally was; but look again! The instances he gives are not examples of "objective data [being] spiced with subjective interpretations." They tell us nothing about emotional or subjective *interpretations.* They tell us that some experiments were badly designed—lacked adequate controls. By standards of formal logic Mayhew has erred, but has he erred rhetorically? We think not, because the examples do lend support to his CLAIM that there are *problems* of validity in *some* laboratory tests. If his listeners had in their heads WARRANTS such as, "Control groups and representative subjects are necessary for experimental validity," Mayhew's argument would seem entirely valid. *Everything* that he has cited as DATA contributes in one way or another to his final CLAIM: There are reasons to be cautious in accepting scientific data about marijuana. So we may not have reasoning here that meets the tests of traditional, formal logic, but Mayhew has built a series of reasons (DATA and assumed WARRANTS) that hold together persuasively to support his conclusion.[7]

Mayhew's total argument also illustrates that we often need to give listeners *chains* of arguments. Believing his listeners would accept his first CLAIM, he uses it as DATA for another CLAIM. He has again left his listeners to think of the necessary WARRANTING ideas: (1) replication of results and (2) controlled conditions. These are criteria for determining whether experimental results are acceptable. He need not have done this. He could have said, in so many words, "You can't have a reliable experiment unless you have some 'natural' group to compare to your 'experimental group' (WARRANT), as Donald Campbell pointed out in his essay, 'Factors Relevant to the Validity of Experiments in Social Settings.'" (The citation of this authority would provide what Toulmin calls BACKING FOR WARRANT.) Add-

---

7. The inevitability of ambiguity and informality in general argumentation is given technical discussion in Leo Apostel, "Assertion Logic and Theory of Argumentation," *Philosophy and Rhetoric* IV (Spring 1971):92–110.

ing such words would have completed the argument, in Toulmin's terms, and would have made it more certain that no listener could misunderstand the full argument Mayhew was offering. But the practical question is: did Mayhew *need* to go to this length in this rhetorical situation?

Mayhew's listeners were college students who probably knew something about experimentation. Probably, then, he adapted wisely to them because they could supply the parts of the argument he left out. But if Mayhew had been speaking to a class of fifth graders, would his rational proof have been rational still?   Not if the fifth graders could not supply the omitted WARRANT and BACK it if need be. So we see, in another way, that what is rational always depends on what listeners can provide—especially on whether they can furnish out of their own experiences the ideas that *justify* allegations that certain DATA allow or require this or that CLAIM.

Our example should suggest to you several guidelines for practical speaking:

1. Building rational proof is really just showing that some DATA can be *justifiably* taken as supporting your CLAIM or conclusion. Your listener will compare your DATA and your WARRANT with his or her experience. If no conflict appears in either case the listener will find you reasonable. If you omit DATA or WARRANTS or do not state your CLAIMS directly, you will make a mistake unless you are confident your listeners can and will find these elements of rational proof in their own experience. Should your listener deny that your DATA are what you say they are, or deny that there is a justifying WARRANT for your reasoning, or consider that you have not taken into account the proper limits on your CLAIMS, that listener is apt to classify *you* as illogical. Not only will your attempt at building rational proof fail, but *you* will lose standing as a proof of what you say.

2. You should also have learned from our example that on such general, much discussed topics as decriminalization of possession of marijuana and a thousand other topics men and women discuss in public speech, it is useless to imagine that you can prove anything *finally*, as you might in geometry. If you understand this, you will undertake in speaking to invent patterns of rational thought that will be accepted as "more reasonable than anything else I know of." Your job is to train yourself to handle *probabilities* in ways *other people* will find credible according to their own knowledge and experience. This notion connects with a third thing we hope you have begun to infer from our example.

3. Rational justifications, like all other justifications in rhetorical speech, succeed or fail depending on how well you adapt them to particular sets of listeners. Your listeners' knowledge, their standards of evidence, and their conceptions of what is reasonable *in the*

present situation are the standards against which you have to work—no matter what *you* think is sufficient and reasonable in the particular case.

A mistake speakers make is to give only their own validations for ideas. Those who do this sometimes discover their listeners are unimpressed. The real audience may apply more exacting standards of justification than the speaker did. On the other hand, sometimes speakers bore listeners by trying to meet higher standards of rational justification than the listeners care for. To avoid such mistakes we suggest you make *two* kinds of judgments whenever what you say depends on its being accepted as rational. Ask yourself: (a) Is my proof sound enough so *I* believe in it, for myself? (b) How much *more* or *less* will the point require as support to satisfy my listeners in the situation where I will meet them? If what you say to an audience can be *made* sound enough to satisfy you when you make yourself the judge of it, you will meet your responsibilities as a conscientious speaker. If you adjust what you say to your listeners' demands, you will meet your responsibilities and aspirations as a practical communicator.

4. It is almost if not absolutely impossible in effective speech for rational justifications to occur apart from proofs and appeals that depend on the self-interests of listeners and the integrity (or lack of it) with which a speaker stands as a personal proof of his ideas. What did Mayhew accomplish by saying data are sometimes spiced with subjective interpretations? To some he surely implied that distortions of experimental results were deliberate. We have already pointed out that by carefully qualifying his first CLAIM with the word *often* he may have added some stature to himself as a responsible source of proof. Consider how the self-interests of his audience of college-aged students might have been aroused by his allusion to "those poor people [who] were locked up for four weeks" without being able even to see a female. In these and other ways Mayhew intermingled proofs resting on self-interest and on confidence in the speaker with his essentially reasoned proofs. It is always so in ordinary speaking. One kind of proving never exists entirely apart from the others.

5. Since almost nothing we ordinarily talk about can be proved *finally*, virtually any proof we offer is open to criticism on logical grounds. Put yourself in the frame of mind of an *opponent* of Mayhew's bit of reasoning. How many points can you find where you could attack him for not being tightly logical? We have pointed out two or three, but there are more. Do the same thing with Dr. Upcraft's speech in appendix B or any of the students' comments about his speech. But what does it prove if you can find holes in a rhetorical argument? It proves nothing until you have specified for what audience in what rhetorical situation the presence of the holes will make a difference.

The presence of logical holes in the expression of a piece of reasoning may make it bad science or bad philosophy, but that does not yet say anything about the probable rhetorical power of the reasoning in a particular situation. This is why we are not treating the formal principles of scientific or statistical validity or the principles of formal logic in this section. It seems to us that such rules are far too abstract and specialized to be fruitfully applied in speaker-listener relationships. There, private and cultural rather than universal standards of validity and adequacy normally operate. But there are, in Western culture, at least some principles that are very widely applied. We are going to express some of them baldly, crudely, because that is how they are applied in everyday listening. When you are trying to be reasonable, you lose if your listeners catch you:

1. Seeming to *contradict* yourself
2. Seeming to depend on DATA that are *irrelevant* to your CLAIMS
3. Seeming to choose your examples *unfairly*
4. Using WARRANTS your listeners *do not understand* or *deny*
5. Seeming to CLAIM *more* than your DATA can justify
6. Using incompetent or unqualified sources for DATA or for BACK-ING your WARRANTS

Centuries of experience and numerous experiments show that in the logic of popular communication, "One man's meat is another's poison." The tentativeness and situationality of the tests we have just enumerated show why that is true. Know your listeners' standards!

The Speaker as a Justification of Ideas

"Why should I listen to *you* on this matter?" is something asked about every speaker, and often. Aristotle pointedly stated the reasons for the question:

> The character of the speaker is a cause of persuasion when the speech is so uttered as to make him worthy of belief; for as a rule we trust men of probity more, and more quickly, about things in general, while on points outside the realm of exact knowledge, where opinion is divided, we trust them absolutely. This trust, however, should be created by the speech itself, and not left to depend upon an antecedent impression that the speaker is this or that kind of man. It is not true, as some writers on the art maintain, that the probity of the speaker contributes nothing to his persuasiveness; on the contrary, we might almost affirm that his character is the most potent of all the means of persuasion.[8]

---

8. From *The Rhetoric of Aristotle*, translated and edited by Lane Cooper, pp. 8–9, bk. I, chap. 2. © 1932, renewed 1960 by Lane Cooper. Reprinted by permission of Prentice-Hall, Inc., Englewood Cliffs, New Jersey.

It may seem strange to call upon so ancient an authority to explain the influence of speakers-as-their-own justifications. The fact is that although no topic has been more diligently studied by experimenters interested in rhetoric, there is still no more succinct and defensible statement on the practical role of a speaker's *ethos* than Aristotle's. He wrote:

> As for the speakers themselves, the sources of our trust in them are three, for apart from the arguments [in a speech] there are three things that gain our belief, namely, intelligence, character, and good will. Speakers are untrustworthy in what they say or advise from one or more of the following causes. Either through want of intelligence they form wrong opinions; or, while they form correct opinions, their rascality leads them to say what they do not think; or, while intelligent and honest enough, they are not well-disposed [to the hearer, audience], and so perchance will fail to advise the best course, though they see it. That is a complete list of the possibilities. It necessarily follows that the speaker who is thought to have all these qualities [intelligence, character, and good will] has the confidence of his hearers.[9]

Modern scientists have devoted a good deal of effort to exploring the dimensions of *ethos* or what we are calling "the speaker as justification for ideas." On the whole their findings argue that what listeners look for and weigh in speakers are a pair of attributes Aristotle called "intelligence" and "character" and that investigators of the past thirty years have variously called "competence-trustworthiness," "expertness-trustworthiness," "authoritativeness-character." Something similar to what Aristotle thought of as "goodwill" turns up in studies that indicate audiences are more readily influenced by speakers with whom they can readily identify and in other studies suggesting that we look for and respond to something called "dynamism" in speakers.[10] It is a limitation of virtually all studies of how speakers justify through themselves that the effects of *reputations* have been mainly explored. Yet what is most important to you as a speaker is how what you do when speaking affects listeners' judgments of your intelligence, trustworthiness, and your intentions.

We all know that our judgments of speakers' credibility change as we listen to them. That radical changes do occur has been demonstrated in a series of experiments in which college students listened to bits of tape-recorded speeches by the late civil rights leaders Malcolm X and Dr. Martin Luther King, by former president of the International

---

9. Ibid., pp. 91–92, bk. II, chap. 1.
10. A good summary of contemporary research on the *ethos* of speakers and the credibility of sources in general appears in Gary Cronkhite, *Persuasion: Speech and Behavioral Change* (Indianapolis–New York: The Bobbs-Merrill Co., 1969), pp. 172–78.

Teamsters' Union James Hoffa, by former governor of Alabama George Wallace, by Reverend Billy Graham, and by Richard M. Nixon speaking as president of the United States. In all tests listeners who were favorable to a speaker before he began to talk became *less* favorable to him after hearing a few moments of his talk, and listeners who felt unfavorably toward the speaker before hearing him felt *more* favorable to him after hearing him for a few moments! Very tentatively, Professor Brooks, who conducted most of these studies, proposes this generalization: "Audiences whose initial evaluations of speakers are clearly favorable or clearly unfavorable tend to shift in the opposite direction after a brief exposure to the source's recorded speech."[11] We should not conclude that if you are liked before you speak, you will lose ground as soon as you talk or that if you are initially disliked, anything you say will gain a bit of credibility for you. So far, experiments have used tape-recorded, introductory passages from speeches by controversial public figures about whom most listeners probably had stereotyped expectations. Nonetheless, the experiments do suggest that first minutes of talk are exceptionally important to any speaker's credibility. Perhaps the old adage, "First impressions are lasting," has more significance for speakers than had been supposed.

Modern experiments have given significance to Aristotle's proposition that listeners' trust needs to "be created by . . . speech itself, and not left to depend upon an antecedent impression that the speaker is this or that kind of man." All that is revealed by speech—knowledge, analytical power, organizational ability, verbal skill, delivery—can play a part in maintaining, strengthening, or weakening listeners' confidence in what you say. It is clear that as speakers we do, indeed, shape our credibility, even as we go through the early stages of composing speech.

To see that claims to intelligence, trustworthiness, and good intentions toward listeners can be built into speech, it is useful to look at examples of how speakers have done this. Consider first a man widely known as a scientist and, at the time he spoke, president of Harvard University: James B. Conant. He had just completed a section of an address in which he seemed to have opposed a view of the world based on a literal reading of the Book of Job and the scientific view offered by Marxism. Anyone who sets up an opposition of this sort invites a number of questions from listeners: So, where do *you* stand? Are you telling me *I* must choose between these extremes? What *are* you trying to do to *me*? As though recognizing that his reputation as a scientist made it necessary for him to answer such questions, Conant looked back to evaluate what he had just said:

---

11. Robert D. Brooks, "The Generality of Early Reversals of Attitudes toward Communication Sources," *Speech Monographs* XXXVII (June 1970): 154. This report (pp. 152–55) is based upon an earlier one. Robert D. Brooks and Thomas M. Schiedel, "Speech as Process: A Case Study," ibid., XXXV (March 1968): 1–7.

I have purposely placed before you a false dichotomy—the Book of Job taken literally or dialectical materialism. I have already suggested, I hope, my own predilection; I would not repudiate the nineteenth-century optimism about the continued improvement, with the aid of science, of all the practical arts (including the art of human relations). I would not, however, subscribe to any "in principle" argument about what science can accomplish. I would be certain that for the next century, under the best conditions, the areas of uncertainty and empiricism would remain enormous. As to the Book of Job, I would subscribe to the answer that the universe is essentially inexplicable and I would interpret Job's vision symbolically, using this as one entrance to the whole area of inquiry that can be designated as the universe of spiritual values.[12]

By candidly warning his listeners that he has overdrawn the conflict between spirituality and the scientific spirit, Dr. Conant encourages a favorable impression of his own integrity and, therefore, his trustworthiness as a rational interpreter and judge. His caution also enhances his trustworthiness. That Conant, a scientist, will "subscribe to the answer that the universe is essentially inexplicable" is surprising, perhaps. If so, the statement may render his viewpoint all the more acceptable because a listener might say to himself, "A scientist would hardly say a thing like that unless he had very good reason. His training should make him give the opposite answer." Perhaps the most important thing Conant accomplished in these moments was to assure his listeners that he had no intention of misguiding them through mere strategies. Although he "placed before you a false dichotomy" to emphasize a point, he promised by words and acts that he could be depended upon to give candid, unexaggerated appraisals of any points before leaving them. He appeared to be consciously trying to make himself more trustworthy than he would have seemed had he not explicitly displayed that he was alert to misinterpretations listeners might make of the ways he expressed things.

Establishing that one is *not* extreme or irresponsible is another way speakers can lay claim to listeners' trust. Perhaps no public figure in modern American history has been more obviously concerned to maintain that his positions were not extreme than Theodore Roosevelt. An astute critic writes that Roosevelt deliberately adopted "the rhetoric of concede-and-lead: concede the priority of the audience's self-interest and then on the basis of the good faith established by the concession lead them to commitments beyond self-interest." What this kind of strategy achieves, the same critic says, is this: "The demagogue reduces rhetoric to the first step alone; the idealist, to the second.

---

12. James B. Conant, "Science and Spiritual Values," a lecture delivered at Columbia University in 1952. In his *Modern Science and Modern Man* (New York: Columbia University Press, 1952), p. 92.

Roosevelt's formula was designed to correct the reductionism of each."[13]

On April 5, 1906, Roosevelt pleaded for moderation and regard for balance in the journalism of the muckrakers, some of whom had been carried far from fact by their zeal to expose corruption. His concede-and-lead habit in persuasion is evident in this excerpt from his famous speech, "The Man with the Muck-Rake":

> It is because I feel that there should be no rest in the endless war against the forces of evil that I ask the war be conducted with sanity as well as with resolution.
>
> The men with the muck-rakes are often indispensable to the well-being of society; but only if they know when to stop raking the muck, and to look upward to the celestial crown above them, to the crown of worthy endeavor. There are beautiful things above and round about them; and if they gradually grow to feel that the whole world is nothing but muck, their power of usefulness is gone.[14]

Like Dr. Conant, Theodore Roosevelt conveys an impression of trustworthiness through the care he takes in defining his position between sensationalism and complacency, while keeping himself on the side of reform. He not only implies this is a sane and sensible position, he declares its opposite is not very sane. He further asserts that he has adopted his position because he is against evil. His tactics in claiming credit for intelligence and trustworthiness are more direct than Conant's, but he is subtle also. His metaphorical imagery, borrowed from John Bunyan's *The Pilgrim's Progress*, could evoke religious or spiritual attitudes of approval in some listeners. Finally, we should note that by casting doubt upon the intelligence and trustworthiness of those he is criticizing, Roosevelt goes a step beyond Conant. He seeks deliberately to detract from the trustworthiness of his opponents.

These are representative ways by which speakers seek to enhance their own images. It is worth noting, too, that in the short excerpt from Dr. Boorstin's address to newspaper editors (pp. 126–27) he presumably drew some personal credit for goodwill and good character by associating himself so strongly with the virtues of *debate* (which editors would probably concede) and disassociating himself from *dissension* and *discord* (which editors were likely to disapprove).

There are other more obvious but often overlooked ways speakers justify their messages through justifying themselves as sources. In one of our classes a group of students decided to investigate apartment-leasing processes in their university community. They then

---

13. Harold Zyskind, "A Case Study in Philosophic Rhetoric: Theodore Roosevelt," *Philosophy and Rhetoric* 1 (Fall 1968):245.

14. In *American Public Addresses, 1740–1952,* ed by A. Craig Baird (New York: McGraw-Hill, 1956), p. 214.

made a presentation advising their classmates on renting apartments. The group presented a series of speeches to the class and, at the end, they asked whether there were any questions. Here is a transcript of just a few minutes of what was said in that question-answer period.

Questioner #1 in Audience: Did anything especially surprise you in your study?

Panelist #1: One thing that amazed me was that when we made a survey of students who rent apartments, we found an astonishing number of people who didn't even read their leases. That was one of our questions: "Did you read your lease? If you did, did you understand it?" There were an amazing number of people who hadn't read them at all.

Audience Questioner #2: But isn't it the situation that if you don't sign the lease, whether you read it or not, you don't get the apartment?

Panelist #1: These people signed the leases without even trying to read them.

Questioner #2: But even if you read it, you could hate it.

Panelist #2: That's just the point. There are important degrees of what's said in leases. And we found great differences in both leases and how renting companies treated them. We found one company that went over the leases with the renters, but another one had contract terms that were really bad, in fact amazing. Yet people didn't read, so they couldn't pay any attention to the differences.

Panelist #3 (To Questioner #2): I don't think you have the picture right. Leases can be full of tricky clauses. Now, when you look for an apartment, you have to file a lease application. At that time you'll *see* the lease. You file the lease application and you put down half of the required security deposit—it's either that or you deposit one month's rent. Now they'll send you the lease, and if you read it for the first time at this point and don't like it, and refuse to rent, you forfeit your deposit. That's all perfectly legal because you signed the lease application. But you're stuck simply because you didn't read the lease when you had the first chance. It *costs* not to read!

Questioner #3: I take it then that you found marked differences among leases.

Panelist #2: Besides the differences in requirements that we've talked about, another major difference was that some were long and full of details and others were short, direct, easy to read, and easy to understand.

In these exchanges the panelists impressed everyone listening because they so obviously knew their subject *thoroughly*. They also clearly understood what points they wanted to make in response to wholly unexpected questions. Panelist #1 was entirely clear on why failure to read leases was an oversight and not something forced on renters. Panelist #2 and panelist #3 were still more determined not to let Questioner #2 misunderstand either the group's finding or the significance of renters' neglect. Each had new information not before brought before the audience that focused sharply on the message the panel wanted to leave with the audience and that Questioner #2 seemed not quite ready to understand or accept in its full significance. When Questioner #3 raised a question that had already been answered (Panelist #2 had already said differences were marked), the panelist had the good sense to remind the audience that most differences had been discussed, but she had one more difference to add—which still related to the panel's immediate concern: *reading* leases before signing them.

Here was public speech (although very short speeches) in which the speakers made *themselves* proofs by (1) showing that they were thoroughly informed, (2) that they *knew* they were making an important point for the audience and were well organized enough to stick to that point although three panelists responded to three questioners. The speakers were *informed* and they were *organized*—even in handling unpredictable questions. Those are marks of intelligence and trustworthiness; in this case the panelists' concern to be rightly understood was also evidence of their good intentions toward the audience.

You have not the initial *ethos* of a Conant or a Theodore Roosevelt, but their methods are as open to you as to them. Your speaking ought always to acknowledge, as Conant did, the nature of your rhetorical strategies, the reliability of the ways you analyze and present your subject matter; these things gain for you and your methods strength and respect. It is as open to you as to Theodore Roosevelt to concede what deserves to be conceded, to make clear your avoidance of extremes that your listeners reject, to contrast the good sense of your chosen positions with the lesser wisdom of other views—all the while making clear that you are, for all your care, "going somewhere" in thought. Allusions that associate you and your ideas with that which is intelligent, candid, and in your listeners' interests are also as available to you as to Roosevelt. "I have seen it" or "I have been there" or "I have participated in an investigation that was thorough" or "It is important to you that you understand this rightly" are claims to respectful hearing you can use as readily as the panelists we have quoted. All those opportunities are as open to students as to anyone else.

Here is another excerpt from a classroom talk. The speech was given in 1971 by Robert Dike to a class in persuasion at the University of Delaware:

> As a resident of this state I'm not against normal industrial and population growth, but I am against this dam as a means to supply water for this anticipated growth. There are two basic reasons behind my opposition. The first is conservation; the second, for want of a better title, I've called "governmental injustice."
>
> Believe it or not, the White Lake Creek is the last clean stream

in this small state of Delaware.   If you ever go up into the area of the Creek, what you'll find is a quiet, scenic, very beautiful forest.   I was there recently and, believe me, it is, indeed, beautiful.   There are over 30 varieties of wildlife present—ranging from deer and foxes to the rare flying squirrel.   And some 143 species of birds and 20 different types of reptiles and amphibians.   Plant life is just as richly abundant —more than 250 species—43 kinds of trees and well over 200 varieties of wildflowers.

No one can doubt that this region is one of Nature's unique havens, but what will happen to this untouched beauty if the dam is built?[15]

Mr. Dike had earlier given his listeners the plans for a new dam. Having now announced his opposition and previewed his reasons, he was moving into a "conservation argument": water impounded by the dam would destroy the White Lake Creek area.   We believe he established himself as specially qualified on this point by revealing his personal acquaintance with the area and by the precision of his statistics, which made clear the care of his research and the thoroughness of his knowledge.   As with the students whose answers to questions we have quoted, persuasive impressions of *intelligence* and *competency* must have welled up in the minds of Dike's listeners.

Other methods of justifying ideas by revealing one's own qualities as a speaker relating to listeners can be illustrated briefly.   Franklin Roosevelt's famous salutation, "My Friends—" or his "you and I know" or any speaker's use of the pronouns *"we," "us," "our"* instead of *"I," "me," "my"* exemplify small expressions of goodwill and friendly identification with an audience.   They are open to anyone's use.   Simply to cite the best rather than a second-best authority hints that you have intelligence and knowledge.   A dispassionate recital of arguments for or against the position you are taking can suggest: "He's keeping his feelings under control and so is more to be relied on."   Demeanor, too, lends to source justification.   Listeners prize conversational directness, general pleasantness, and unself-conscious action, voice, and diction because they interpret these behaviors as signs that no ulterior intentions are diverting the speaker's attention from his business with us, his hearers.

A major thing we have been trying to show you with our examples is that, as Aristotle said, it is possible and important always to show listeners *through* your speaking that *you* are worthy of attention and belief.   To support a point, it is vitally important that you *build in* evidence that you know enough to deserve belief (intelligence),

---

15. This excerpt is from a recording of Mr. Dike's speech provided by Dr. Patricia Schmidt, formerly instructor in speech, University of Delaware, Newark, Delaware.

that you are both generally informed and careful about what you say (trustworthiness), and that you are keeping your listeners' interests and well-being in mind (goodwill). Your rhetorical resources do not end with your initial reputation as a person and speaker; all the choices you make as you begin to pull materials together for speaking will finally reveal *you* to your listeners as a personal proof of what you say. You are inevitably some kind of proof of what you say. The question is whether what you make yourself seem supports or undermines what you say.

In closing this section on the kinds of justifications speakers must use to support their ideas, we repeat what we said at the beginning of the section. We have had to discuss separately: justifications accomplished by using the personal interests of listeners, justifications accomplished by providing reasons and evidence, and justifications accomplished by establishing one's self as a proof. But in actual speaking these kinds of proofs occur together. Each kind of support reinforces or weakens the others. To extend a metaphor we have used before, to compose and deliver an ideal speech is to weave a fabric of thoughts—some having the color of reason, some of the color of personal interest, and some the color of yourself as proof.

A brief excerpt from a defense speech by a man who is still probably unmatched as a legal pleader in English will illustrate what we mean. Almost 200 years ago Thomas Erskine was pleading for his client, a defendant in what under modern laws would be called a divorce case on grounds of adultery. Erskine was already famed as both a prosecuting and defense attorney, and his opponent in this case had cautioned the jury that Erskine would try to sweep them out of their senses with rhetorical eloquence. Erskine's problem was to convince the jury that he would *not* become a spellbinder and that the proofs that his client had not seduced another man's wife required no eloquence from him but only the listeners' interests in getting at the truth of the matter and their understanding of the facts and the logic of the case. At one point in his plea he said to the jury:

> Now, to show you how little disposed I am to work upon you by any thing but by proof . . . I will begin with a few plain *dates*, and as you have pens in your hands, I will thank you to write them down. I shall begin with stating to you what my cause is, and shall then prove it—not by myself, but by witnesses.
> The parties were married on the 24th of April 1789. The child that has been spoken of, and in terms that gave me great satisfaction, as the admitted son of the plaintiff . . . , that child was born on the 12th of August 1791. Take that date, and my learned friend's [the plaintiff's attorney] *admission* that this child must have been the child of Mr. Howard [the plaintiff], an admission that could not have been rationally or consistently made but upon the implied admission that no

illicit connection had existed *previously.* . . .   On this subject, therefore, the plaintiff must be silent.   He cannot say . . . [his] parental
mind has been wrung. . . .[16]

All three kinds of justification operated in this bit of speaking
that would have taken less than two minutes to deliver.   The listeners'
interests in not being led astray and in getting at the true facts of the
case were used; Erskine's claim *and his demonstration* of his reasonableness were offered to enhance his own standing with the jury, and
his obvious invitation to the jurors to figure out the logic of (1) the
child's conception and (2) the opposing attorney's concession argued
formally that Erskine's client could not have had an affair with Mrs.
Howard before the child's birth.   If the listeners believed Erskine's
demonstration of reasonableness, they must believe the plaintiff
had *no claim* on their sympathies, at least up to August 21, 1791.
Each kind of justification reinforced the other to give credit to Erskine
and his argumentation and to *deny* sympathetic feelings toward Mr.
Howard, the plaintiff.

This is such a fabric of interrelated proofs as you must weave
in speaking.   Your goal needs the support of *all* the means of proof,
creating just the shadings of credibility required in your particular
rhetorical situation with your subject and your particular kind of
audience.

CLARIFYING AND REINFORCING IDEAS

Most ideas have to be justified in some degree before listeners
will accept them.   This requires that reasons and evidence (DATA and
BACKING FOR WARRANTS) be blended with emotional justifications
and evidence that the sources of ideas are credible.   Any cluster of
statements put into a speech for these justifying purposes will clarify
as well as justify.   But an attitude-awakening statement or a bit of
rational justification may not, by itself, convey enough knowledge or
allow time for a listener to apprehend fully what he is supposed to
accept.   Additional content, inserted primarily to clarify, to detail or
reinforce other ideas, is what writers on the art of public speaking have
long termed *amplification*.   We must therefore consider not just proving but the tactics speakers use to clarify, magnify, or otherwise

16. Thomas Erskine, "On Behalf of Mr. Bingham," a trial for adultery,
the court of King's Bench, February 24, 1794.   Text adapted from Chauncey A.
Goodrich, *Select British Eloquence* (New York: Harper and Brothers Publishers,
1880), p. 709.

intensify the likelihood that listeners will catch messages as the speakers mean them to. We call these *amplifying procedures* or tactics, but we will try to show how they can yield justifications, become forms of support, as they clarify and vivify.

Speakers clarify and amplify their ideas by at least nine common methods briefly discussed below. Notice that we are considering *methods* more than materials here; a single piece of material can serve more than a single amplifying or clarifying function.

Introducing Anecdotes

An *anecdote* is usually a brief narrative illustrating another idea with which it is connected. To clarify or emphasize the force of a tornado you might narrate how a storm picked a house off its foundations and dropped it in a field a half-mile away. Fables, parables, imagined episodes, or real incidents all allow you to amplify and clarify by narrating briefly. Narrating also allows you to dramatize the idea or event you have in mind. The chief things to consider when introducing anecdotes are that they need to be kept short and listeners must understand precisely what point or points they clarify or amplify.

An anecdote, like any other example, offers some rational justification of what it illustrates and clarifies. Moreover, an anecdote sets events before hearers in a dynamic, vivid way; this makes it easier to enlist listeners' personal interests and attitudes for or against what is being clarified. Anecdotes contribute more proof by eliciting strong attitudes than by furnishing grounds for rational justification.

Saying "thank you" is often awkward when an occasion is formal. Consider how William Howard Armstrong used an anecdote to show that he genuinely appreciated the Newbery Medal awarded him at the American Library Association's convention at Detroit, on June 30, 1970, for his story *Sounder*. "The boy" in *Sounder* has no other name. Armstrong used both his phrase "the boy" and an anecdote from his own life to amplify how and why receiving the equivalent of the Pulitzer Prize (but for children's literature) was a true source of gratitude. Said Mr. Armstrong:

> And now I find myself in the precarious position of having won a prize for a book called *Sounder*, written for anyone who might like to read it.
>
> Until I received a telephone call from Mary Elizabeth Ledlie some time in February, the word Newbery had *not* meant to me a man in England who stocked his bookshop with stories for children. [The award is named for such a man.] But Newberry had been a word to stir the deathless joy and remembrance of a small boy's Christmas. Because if that boy were especially good from somewhere around October 27th or November 12th until Christmas, his father would take him to Newberry's five-and-dime store in town. And after he had looked at all

the bows and arrows and red wagons, he could ask the jolly, red-coated Santa Claus—enthroned amid the incense of chocolate and peppermint—to leave them under the Christmas tree for him.

But Newberry's Santa Claus never brought the bow and arrows or the red wagon. So out in the back pasture the boy would cut a maple sapling with his two-bladed barlow pocketknife that he had won for selling Cloverine Salve—guaranteed to cure shoulder-gall for horse and chapped lips for man. Then with sapling and binder twine from the hayloft, the boy would make his own bow.

But tonight it is real. The boy will not have to go home and hammer the Newbery Award out of the top of a Campbell soup can or out of a washer off the axle of his father's hay wagon.[17]

Many people have said "thank you," but few have said it with more grace coupled with intense speaker-audience involvement than Mr. Armstrong—through the powers of anecdote.

To the extent that Armstrong's anecdote proves, it expresses his character as a sensitive and unpretentious man, even though he is a famous author. For a different, far simpler use of anecdote, look back at Panelist #3 responding to a questioner in the audience (p. 143). By putting his explanation in brief narrative form, imagining his questioner going through the steps of leasing an apartment, he quickly involves the questioner in a set of experiences taking place through time. By this simple means he injects *action* into his explanation and proves by invoking the questioner's own self-interests, involving *her* in the action of failing to read the lease when she could have.

Comparing and Contrasting

Comparisons and contrasts clarify, vivify, and often *argue*. One may offer metaphors, similes, or antitheses, or compare and contrast anecdotes, examples, whole arguments, or descriptions. Since we acquire many of our new concepts by comparing or contrasting the new with the old, these methods are especially valuable because they use familiar learning processes. Since conflict and similarity are fundamentally interesting to man, all contrasting and comparing vivifies.

An important distinction is that a comparison or contrast, used primarily to prove, needs to be developed with much more attention to the *literal* likenesses and dissimilarities than do comparisons and contrasts used merely to intensify or clarify. Consider this sentence from President Jimmy Carter's Inaugural Address in 1977:

17. William H. Armstrong, "Newbery Acceptance Speech." Delivered June 30, 1970, and published in *The Horn Book Magazine* XLVI (August 1970): 352–55. Printed by permission of the publisher.

> We will be ever vigilant and never vulnerable, and we will fight our wars against poverty, ignorance, and injustice, for those are the enemies against which our forces can be honorably marshalled.[18]

Carter did not, of course, mean "wars" in any literal sense; the goals he set for government were simply couched in war language for emphasis and to give listeners a sense of action and determination as they heard the president commit his administration against poverty, ignorance, and injustice. Everyone would recognize that Carter's uses of verbal comparisons and contrasts in this sentence were entirely figurative. He was under no obligation to show his administration's policies were literally like *war* policies.

However, the requirements were very different when Lady Barbara Ward Jackson, a British scholar in economics, addressed an audience at Herbert H. Lehman College in 1973 and undertook to show her audience that underdeveloped countries of the world had made great strides forward *under exceptionally difficult circumstances*. To prove this she built up a comparison between economic development in Europe and America in the nineteenth century and the more difficult economic circumstances in which underdeveloped countries must grow in the twentieth century. Here is the basic part of her comparison-contrast:

> Nineteenth-century industrialization created jobs, and the jobs, quite frankly, called for hands, mill hands. (Why mill hands? Because they only wanted their hands. They certainly did not want their brains.) In short, in the nineteenth century massive labor-intensive industry was the dominant technology. But in our century we have splendid, sophisticated, automated machines run by computers (which only break down about three times a year!). We have dispensed with the need for large reserves of manpower. And what is the result? The population curve goes up and the employment curve goes down. And on the edges of every major city [in developing nations] are the shanty towns where the environment for humans combines the worst of two centuries: nineteenth-century urban blight—bad sewage, cholera, and water-borne disease, and, added to all this, generally, the fancier sophistications of twentieth-century pollution—thermal, chemical, even nuclear.[19]

At this point in the speaker's address she had to present rational proof that the developing countries had in fact made their progress

---

18. Inaugural Address, January 20, 1977. Text as reported by United Press International news service.

19. From "Proposals for a Planetary Community," Herbert H. Lehman Memorial Lecture, Herbert H. Lehman College of the City University of New York, April 10, 1973, by Lady Barbara Ward Jackson, then Schweitzer Professor of International Economics at Columbia University. Text as published by Lehman College Publications, Number Nine.

against unusual difficulties.   Her proof was the comparison-contrast of industrialization in two centuries.   Each similarity and each difference she identified became DATA for the CLAIM that development in the twentieth century is exceptionally difficult.   Whether her CLAIM was believed depended on how *literally* listeners accepted the similarities and differences Lady Jackson identified.   Obviously Lady Jackson could not have met her situational needs by such quick, allusory, comparisons and contrasts as served President Carter's needs.

When you introduce comparisons or contrasts you will need to consider whether you want them to bear the weight of rational proofs or simply lend vividness and interest to what you say.   If your purpose is to prove by comparison or contrast, you must be careful to supply enough detail so listeners will see and believe the *literal* similarities and differences.

Defining

Defining may be accomplished in several ways.   Ideas are commonly defined (1) by classifying them; (2) by differentiating them from other ideas that belong to the same class; (3) by exemplifying them; (4) by inferring their natures from the contexts in which they normally occur; (5) by referring to the etymological derivations of their names; (6) by explaining what they are not; (7) by describing or explaining them from some special vantage point (such as specifying what a musical note is if we view it as a complex of sound waves); (8) by specifying functions, as when a child defines an automobile as a thing to ride in.

The most formal kinds of definition are overused in speaking. This is particularly true of dictionary definitions that classify terms and define them etymologically.   Definitions that compare, contrast, or exemplify are far more interesting and easier to understand.   Classifications and derivations usually demand that the listener think abstractly; therefore it is a good rule to offer these definitions only *after* other modes of amplification have been provided.   The formal definitions can then function to sum up other, easier-to-understand definitions, as in the first example below.

> To understand what a barge is, think of a railway coal car. [Example.] Take the wheels off the coal car and imagine the ends of the car are well sloped back toward the bottom.   [Further detail by example.] Now imagine the wheel-less car floating in the water—a river, a canal, or possibly the sea.   You have what is basically a barge: a floating cargo hauler, unpowered, low, and bulky.   [Functional definition with characteristics that classify the barge.]   A barge, then, is typically an unpowered cargo vessel used for hauling heavy freight.   [Most abstract, classifying definition.]

The following amplification through definition is less easy to take in at a single hearing, so less suited to speech:

> A barge is a large, flat-bottomed boat used for transporting goods. While there are powered barges, most are towed. Modern barges are usually bulky vessels used for hauling heavy freight.

The two explanations are the same in content, but the first proceeds from specific examples and comparisons to the abstract. The second proceeds in the opposite order, first confronting the listener with the most difficult form of amplification and only afterward providing specific, concrete information.

Only occasionally do etymological definitions interest and genuinely clarify. It does not help very much to know that the English word *define* comes from the Latin *definire,* meaning "to limit." It is better to say that *define* means to "explain or set forth the limits of something." On the other hand, if you are trying to explain what *habeas corpus* means in law, the shortest, quickest, and most vivid way to do it is probably to tell your listener that the literal Latin meaning of *habeas corpus* is "you may have the body." In short, etymological definitions are always available to you, but they ought to be used or rejected according to the *practical* help they will give your particular audience. Discussion of derivations is not inevitably clarifying or interesting.

Describing

When Aristotle noted that people like communications that set pictures before their eyes, he pinpointed the chief standard by which to judge the value of a description. Describing is a process of amplification.

Telling anecdotes, comparing and contrasting, and defining emphasize the special details of whatever is being talked about, but describing usually sets the *whole* of something before a listener. Unless intended to be humorous or ironic, description ought to focus attention on significant rather than trivial aspects of what is being described. It should also clarify interrelationships or patterns that give the subject its special character, and it should be as pictorial as the content will allow.

Description can contribute rational justification to discourse as well as clarity and liveliness. Since any describer fits together the elements that go into his description, he always implies that this is the best way of understanding what he is talking about. If we accept his description we accept his version of what is true of the thing described.

Notice the argumentative use of an imaginary set of circumstances described by a science fiction writer testifying before a House of Representatives committee on the subject of copyright laws:

> I am a science fiction writer, so I spend quite a lot of time thinking about the future, including the future of the publishing business. I'm not so sure that's a cheerful thing to think about. I have a great respect for books and for the printed word, but the traffic may be going all in the other direction.
>
> It's easy to imagine a time, perhaps not very far in the future, when every work of art—every story, every poem, every book, every painting—is stored in some great galactic computer, and when you want to read *War and Peace* or *Lust for Life* or *Slaughterhouse-Five* you can just punch a few buttons and it will appear for you on a cathode tube—in your bedroom, if you like, so you can watch it between your toes like the Johnny Carson show. Well, that might not be so bad. But from there it's only a step to having the computers write or compose or draw the things in the first place, and then we're all out of business. . . . The prospect of electronic information storage and retrieval will produce serious difficulties for writers.[20]

Obviously Pohl was pictorializing an amusing prospect for readers of the future, but it is likely he created the description as a *support* for the CLAIM made in the last sentence of our excerpt. The difficulties he implied and asserted in connection with his description were, in fact, supports of the final claim he made in his full statement:

> I think we're probably the only country of importance in the world that doesn't already have, or isn't about to get, a copyright law that protects the writer for his life plus 50 years. I think it's about time we did have one.[21]

Exemplifying

Exemplification is probably the most readily available and most useful of all modes of amplification and clarification. Whether factual or hypothetical, examples can focus listeners' attention on just those features of a subject that the speaker most wants understood. All of us have said perplexedly, "Can you give me an example?" We seem to understand specific cases more easily than generalizations, and most of

---

20. Frederik Pohl, science fiction writer and editor, testifying on June 18, 1975, The Gold Room, Rayburn House Office Building, Washington, D.C. Text as in *An Author's Symposium for Congress,* published by the Coalition for Fair Copyright Protection, no date or place indicated. Mr. Pohl's statement, from which this is an excerpt, appears on pp. 6–7 of the text of the symposium.

21. *Ibid.,* p. 7.

us gain more satisfaction from specific data than from abstractions. Exemplifying, whether as a part of defining or in the form of anecdote or as an element in description, is the speaker's ultimate weapon where clarification and vivification are his principal concerns.

When examples are used primarily to justify rather than simply to illustrate, they need to be checked carefully, for you must be sure they really support what they are intended to support. Furthermore, examples can become so interesting in themselves that even the points they are supposed to support or illustrate are lost. One of our students not long ago tried to illustrate what "spot reporting" is in radio journalism. His example was a tape recording of a network news reporter's on-the-scene, almost hysterical account of the unexpected murder of Lee Harvey Oswald (assassin of President John F. Kennedy) as Oswald was being transferred from his jail cell in Dallas, Texas. As the student might have foreseen, no listener remembered that this was supposed to be an instance of "on the spot reporting." Predictably all questions at the end of the student's talk had to do with details of President Kennedy's assassination and of Oswald's murder. Examples have great fascination for listeners; they need to be chosen to do exactly what you require of them—no more and no less.

Quoting

Quoting other sources can lend justification to what is said. This is especially true and important if your listeners do not consider you a person of authority on the matter you are discussing. Here's a clear example. We are not complete authorities on how this kind of evidence works in speech, but Professor James C. McCroskey has conducted a number of studies on the matter. So we will cite his statement:[22]

> ... we found that a communicator with moderate-to-low ethos could increase his ethos by including factual material and opinions attributed to qualified sources. This effect, however, was not found in connection with all topics. Whether the audience is familiar with the evidence the communicator uses, or with similar evidence, appears to determine whether the communicator may build his ethos by including evidence in his message. If the evidence is unfamiliar to the audience, it has a favorable impact. Otherwise it has no effect. It is important to observe, however, that the inclusion of evidence has never been

---

22. James C. McCroskey, *An Introduction to Rhetorical Communication*, 2nd ed. (Englewood Cliffs, N.J.: Prentice-Hall, 1972), pp. 72–73. Most of the findings referred to here come from McCroskey's "Experimental Studies of the Effects of Ethos and Evidence in Persuasive Communication," D. Ed. dissertation (The Pennsylvania State University, 1966). See also McCroskey, "A Summary of Experimental Research on the Effects of Evidence in Persuasive Communication," *Quarterly Journal of Speech* LV (April 1969): 169–76.

found by experimental researchers to lower a communicator's ethos, even if the evidence has been internally inconsistent.

If on reading our quotation and noticing our footnote you tend to think we probably are giving you solid information on the uses of quotation, our point is made. By citing an expert we have proved what we had to say about using quoted materials for rational justification of ideas.

But sometimes you will want to quote someone because he or she said things better than you could. For example, if you were talking about ambition you might conclude that the importance power has for ambitious men was especially well expressed by Oliver Wendell Holmes, Jr. when he said, "The reward of the general is not a bigger tent, but command." If you think so, that line might be a good one to quote in amplifying your own views. But as a *proof* the quotation would not function as strongly as our quotation above from McCroskey. If Holmes had said, "A general in the army is more interested in the size of his command than the size of his office or his tent," there would be no point in quoting Holmes. You could say the idea in your own words as well as he. On the whole, it is never worth quoting other people's words unless the quotation carries more *authority* than you can give or expresses ideas more clearly and wittily than you could.

Repeating and Restating

Repeating and restating are important amplifying tactics. To give their hearers second and third chances to perceive and understand, speakers need to use these resources often. Research on the usefulness of repetition suggests that with each of your first three repetitions of a thought or fact you further increase the likelihood that your listeners will actually grasp what you say. It appears that after the third repetition, the gains achieved by each succeeding repetition diminish. There is also evidence that repetitions work best when you distribute them through other material rather than repeating the same item two, three, or more times in rapid succession. Apparently this is not true with restatements—phrasing a given idea in several different ways. These *re*phrasings have strong impact if given in rapid succession. Notice the restating function of these two sentences from a talk by the president of Deere & Company to an audience of industrial analysts. Both sentences say the same thing, but the second says it differently from the first:

> Our second goal is to achieve a more stable rate of growth than we have managed in the past. We want to lessen the downside swings which periodically have affected our earnings. . . .[23]

23. Remarks of E. F. Curtis to members and guests of The Machinery Analysts of New York, May 26, 1976. From the text of "prepared remarks," published by Deere & Company, Moline, Illinois.

Obviously the corporation's president wanted to emphasize that steadier profits were the company's goal, not just stability for stability's sake. Restating the meaning of "stable rate of growth" as "lessen the downside swing" not only let him emphasize the policy but allowed him to touch the *financial* experts' special interests at the same time.

Any repetition—whether in the same or in different terms—increases the probability that the repeated idea will be perceived by a listener. Even unvaried repetitions tend to make listeners accept what they hear as true; so in this sense repeating and restating tend to justify the idea advanced even though the content may not change. You see and hear this principle used much in advertising, as slogans are repeated, sometimes in the same way and sometimes in different ways. The same practices are usually part of every propagandist's arsenal; Adolph Hitler wrote specifically that this was the way to sell "the big lie." True or false, it seems that what we hear often, we attend to and tend to believe. No speaker with command of his art will forget this.

Quantifying

Statistics clarify and often support or prove because they express quantity in the language of numbers. Therein lie the strengths and weaknesses of statistics as amplifying materials.

The danger of highway travel can be variously expressed. One can dramatize it through anecdote or example; one can compare it to the danger of air travel; one can describe congestion and consequent dangers. One can also express this danger statistically; but now one shifts from word symbols to numerical symbols. By this shift we gain much in precision, but we lose much in imagery. We may say there were 500 traffic fatalities in Powhatan County, which has a population of 1,500,000 people. This is a precise expression of traffic deaths in that country. But to get this precision, the conditions under which 500 people died, all the consequences of their deaths, and much other information have to be dropped out of the story. We have chosen to represent people and things by numbers. Moreover, the language of numerical expression has specialized rules—a kind of special grammar. What is it the numbers represent? Considering what they represent, and how the counting was done, what may not be inferred? What kinds of statistical manipulation are allowable, given these numerical representations of reality? Such are the normal questions any use of numbers raises. Unless you tell your listeners—in so many words—how your statistics may and may not be interpreted, there is a strong possibility your statistical amplifications will confuse or even mislead.

This means statistics *alone* are not very useful to listeners; they require numbers *plus* analysis of their meanings. It does not mean much to say that in 1960 Kennedy defeated Nixon for president by 118,550 popular votes. It means more to say that this was the voting margin and that there are more people than that in Topeka, Kansas, or Paterson, New Jersey, and that it's only a few thousand more than the population of Pasadena, California. Such localized comparisons would emphasize the *narrowness* of the margin—which would be the real point of citing the figure.

Even with their limitations, statistics are invaluable amplifying materials wherever quantitative attributes and relationships have to be clarified. Because they are so valuable for these purposes, it is all the more important for you to remember (1) that you must often compensate for the dryness of statistics, and (2) that it is usually not enough merely to supply statistics—you also need to explain their interpretations.

To compensate for the abstractness of statistics and to focus attention, it is well to round off figures (let 1,611 become "slightly over sixteen hundred"). It is also useful to present any series of statistics visually as well as orally. Concentrated clusters of statistics become confusing. Distribute them within your speech if you would hold attention. Finally, because statistics can only express quantitative attributes and relationships, amplify them by using imagistic materials.

Using Audiovisual Aids

Rightly used, audiovisual aids can give clarity, vividness, and personal interest and rational justification to what you say. The trouble is that audiovisual aids are so often unwisely introduced or clumsily used. The sensible reasons for using aids in public speech are to save or reinforce words, to bring ideas closer to listeners' live experience, to enhance attention by introducing change (but not for its own sake), and to relax listeners by letting them get information from a "new" source.

The audiovisual resources open to modern speakers are becoming more and more numerous. Every one of the following has been used to advantage in our speech classes: photographs, maps, charts and graphs, models, mock-ups, blackboard drawings, assistants who help with demonstrations, sound movies, slides, video tapes, musical instruments, disc and tape recordings, even the entire room in which the speaking was taking place! But with all these resources, it is still a fact that the most versatile and convenient audiovisual aid any speaker has available is his or her own body. You ought never forget this as a speaker. What else bends, smiles, points, sounds off, never gets out of focus, and keeps on communicating even when the electricity goes off? *You* are too easy-to-manage a resource to justify yourself with *unnecessary* gadgets.

There is a basic principle you should always apply when you think about amplifying or supporting an idea with audiovisual aids. It is this: Unless the aid is less complicated than the idea it will be used to clarify or amplify, *don't use it!*

Specific considerations are important, too. Any aid you use ought to be relevant to whatever point you want to clarify or amplify. Consider the facts about your speaking situation. Whatever audio aids you use must be hearable or they will be worse than nothing; visual aids must be seeable or there will be no point to introducing them. In sum, take thought in advance of speaking of the sight lines and the acoustics of the place where you will meet your audience. A good classroom exercise would be to discuss with your classmates what audiovisual aids would be appropriate in each of the settings we have sketched in chapter 10, pages 312–15. What problems would be encountered with each kind of audiovisual aid you can think of, in each situation?

Another specific problem that needs consideration in deciding whether to introduce audiovisual aids is the time they will consume. To take a pair of extreme cases: There is nothing wrong with an hour-long documentary film or a twenty-minute segment of an opera, but what public *speech* could *contain* these audiovisual units? To be more practical, think of the judgment the students whose critique is presented in appendix B had to make. They decided Dr. Upcraft's speech was not too long to present to their audience in full. They had thirty minutes for their presentation. Dr. Upcraft's speech was approximately twelve minutes long. That left the six panelists about eighteen minutes for their analysis of it. We leave you to judge whether they were wise to use the entire speech as an audio aid. What would you have done in their position had the speech been twenty minutes long?

There seems almost no end to the ways in which audiovisual aids can be misused in speaking situations; almost all misuses grow out of disregard for the fact that audiovisual aids potentially endanger the speaker's own mastery of purpose, audience, and occasion. "Who is in charge?" is always a pertinent question when audiovisual aids are brought in. The following true story presents a set of extreme circumstances, but it illustrates how and why unsophisticated use of audiovisual amplification can turn a speech into something very different.

The student's chosen subject was "The Treatment of Snakebite." Having introduced his subject, he startled his audience by releasing a white rat from a cardboard canister. The speaker announced that the rat's name was Maudie and whipped out a hypodermic needle. Plunging the needle into Maudie, he explained that he was giving the animal an injection of snake venom.   Maudie would expire within a few seconds.   Meanwhile, he would explain what steps a human being should take if bitten by a poisonous snake.   To clarify these steps the speaker now drew grease-pencilled lines and circles on his forearm to indicate where incisions should be made in cases of snakebite.   But Maudie was dragging herself about, gasping her last breath in full view of everyone.   Naturally, her troubles drew even the speaker's attention away from his explanations.   He interrupted himself to comment: "Oh, yes.   Bleeding at the mouth—quite natural at this stage."   The speech, of course, was a failure, as any thoughtful person could have foretold from the moment this speaker decided to introduce poor Maudie as an aid.

We charge this speaker with cruelty and bad taste, but what is more to the point for our present purposes, he exercised no rhetorical, situational sense at all.   The poisoning of a rat was foreseeably irrelevant to his purpose.   It was certain to set in motion situational forces he could not control.   It was predestined to draw attention away from what he alleged was his main message.   Movement, attitudes of revulsion, surprise, the life-death contest, suspense—all these would predictably work to grip listeners' attention.   No comparable forces could be arrayed to work for the speaker's message—however good his grease-pencil drawings or his exposition of them.   Had one of us not actually experienced this event, we would have thought such rhetorical stupidity about audiovisual resources could not be found on a college campus.   But we know lesser degrees of maladroitness are found everywhere.   You have certainly seen speakers introduce charts so detailed you could not understand them.   You have seen speakers pass items through an audience while trying to talk to the audience at the same time.   You have seen models and mock-ups whose many, detailed features so drew away your attention that you did not hear the two or three simple points their introducer wanted to make about them. You have been, then, in the presence of the fundamental mistake of Maudie's executioner: dullness as to the rhetorical potency of an aid.

What we want you to see is that audiovisual materials used for their own sakes can overwhelm speaker and speech.   "A picture is worth a thousand words," it is said.   But if pictures or other nonspeech content can convey one's entire message, the speaker ought to send the pictures and omit the speech.

We have no desire to minimize the values of audiovisual devices as clarifying, vivifying, amplifying resources for speakers.   Very often they are invaluable, even essential.   How many people know where Izmir is without having it pointed out on a map?   What is the best way to enable an audience to understand the differences between an emu and an ostrich?   To show pictures, of course.   To differentiate a diatonic from a chromatic musical scale?   Let them hear the two.   Audiovisual means of clarifying and amplifying are invaluable, rightly chosen and used. To remind you again of their variety here is a partial list:

- The object itself
- Models: complete, cut-away, mock-ups
- Motion picture film clips
- Photographic slides
- Photographic enlargements
- Maps
- Blackboard or other sketches, diagrams, outlines
- Graphs: bar graphs, pie graphs, pictorial graphs
- Schematic representations: organizational charts, genealogical charts, etc.
- Sound tapes and disc recordings
- Video tapes
- Other people: as demonstration assistants, examples, etc.
- Staged scenes

The list could be extended. Any device whatever that will present an idea to the five senses—sight, hearing, touch, taste, and smell—may help you clarify, vivify, and prove what you want to tell through speech. But to summarize our cautions as well as the potentialities of such aids, here are a few do's and don'ts it will be useful for you to remember:

1. Introduce visual and other external resources where you think your best verbal-personal presentation is likely to fall short of complete clarity.
2. Always *verbalize* what it is your listeners are *supposed* to see, hear, and understand from any audiovisual resources you introduce.
3. Where more than a few seconds are to be devoted to an aid, let your hearers know what they are to learn from it *before* introducing it; then restate what should have been learned *after* using the aid.
4. Design or edit all aids to eliminate or hide objects and material that are irrelevant to your immediate purpose. Eliminate whatever might send listeners' thoughts in directions you do not wish them to go.
5. Use your aid where you need it; then get it out of sight and hearing so your audience cannot dwell on it when you want them to attend to something else.
6. If possible, pretest sight lines and sound levels from all positions in which listeners will be during your speech. Pretest the workings of your aid if it has to operate in any way.
7. Give *your* attention to the audience when using audiovisual aids, not to the devices. You are still the *chief* messenger, and your listeners need your attention even though they are receiving part of your message through another source.

8. Always prefer the *simplest* form of audiovisual stimuli capable of doing what you need done. For the same reasons, keep machinery to the minimum for getting your task done.

The most important advice for all speakers who take advantage of audiovisual resources is: *keep yourself in charge and maintain the closest possible personal relation with your hearers.* You are still the chief messenger!

In the last half of this chapter we have set before you nine ways of clarifying, amplifying, and reinforcing ideas. They are resources that are not exclusively means of proving your spoken thoughts believable; yet each of these nine methods of communicating offers the possibility of giving vitality and clarity to what you say while it also *supports* your ideas rationally or psychologically or both. We cannot give you formulas for using these clarifying-amplifying-reinforcing tactics. We can only say: when you begin to compose any public speech, try to remember that all of these means of communicating are *available* should you need any or several at any point in what you plan to say. Ask yourself whether your speech material can be made to give your listeners the kinds of *variety* in development they like and that can specially clarify and reinforce the basic substance of what you will say. If you have any doubts in trying to answer that kind of question, look again at the nine ways of clarifying-amplifying-reinforcing we have discussed and illustrated on pages 147–60. There you will find artistic possibilities more subtle than the standard means of rhetorical proof.

In this chapter we have set out the importance of making clear, at least to yourself, the purpose of your communication. We have considered the possibilities and importance of combining personal-interest, rational, and source justifications so your listeners will find good reasons for listening to you and for believing you. We pointed out nine other ways available to you for clarifying, vivifying, and indirectly supporting what you believe. Exactly how you will blend these types of material will depend partly on your subject and partly on your relation to your subject and to the needs of your listeners and the social groups and systems to which they belong. What blend of content is right, only your judgment can determine. We hope to have offered sound suggestions for *ways* of thinking about such matters. If you *always* keep your listeners' needs, values, attitudes, and goals in mind when choosing speech materials, you will be taking the most important step toward sound inventional decisions.

What you want to accomplish with your audience puts some special constraint on rhetorical invention, of course. We therefore conclude our study of invention by considering in the next chapter what special tactics are yours, depending on whether you plan to inform, inquire, reinforce views, persuade, or entertain.

EXERCISES

Written

1. Before beginning other preparation for your next speech write out a "Choice of Subject" paper containing the following information: (a) an exact statement of your proposed speech subject; (b) an exact statement of your specific purpose; (c) a brief essay explaining why your subject and purpose are timely, significant for you and your audience, amenable to oral presentation, and manageable in the time available. Present this to your instructor for evaluation or have two or three classmates read it over and tell you whether they understand exactly what it is you plan and whether it seems a wise plan for the audience you will meet.

2. Evaluate each of the following statements. Indicate how well each meets the criteria for good expression of a specific purpose. Properly rephrase any statement you find unsatisfactory in wording.
   a. Don't adopt the sales tax.
   b. This is a speech to clarify the processes by which committee chairmen are chosen in the United States Senate.
   c. I want to explain that women ought to receive the same pay as men when they perform the same jobs and that in general their equality with men should be universally recognized.
   d. Economic and social effects of the growth in the United States' tourist industries since 1960.
   e. It takes study to appreciate the art of motion pictures.

3. As you prepare your next talk, label in the margins of your outline what *kind* of supporting or amplifying material you are planning to use at each point. Then write a short paragraph contending that you have achieved the best degree of *variety* in supporting material that is open to you. Discuss your defense with your instructor or one or two of your classmates.

4. Identify and evaluate (a) the kinds of justification and (b) the forms of amplification used in the following excerpt from Leonard Bernstein's lecture, "The World of Jazz":

   > But I find I have to defend jazz to those who say it is low-class. As a matter of fact, all music has low-class origins, since it comes from folk music, which is necessarily earthy. After all, Haydn minuets are only a refinement of simple, rustic German dances, and so are Beethoven scherzos. An aria from a Verdi opera can often be traced back to the simplest Neapolitan fisherman. Besides, there has always been a certain shadow of indignity around music, particularly around the players of music.
   >
   > I suppose it is due to the fact that historically *players* of music seem to lack the dignity of *composers* of music. But this is especially true of jazz, which is almost completely a player's art, depending as it does on improvisation rather than on composition. But this also means that the player of jazz is himself the real composer, which gives him a creative, and therefore *more* dignified status.[24]

---

24. From Leonard Bernstein's televised lecture "The World of Jazz," in *The Joy of Music,* p. 97. © 1959. Used by permission of Simon and Schuster, New York.

Oral

1. With a group of four or five classmates choose a subject to talk about. Almost any subject will do. Assign to each member of the group *one* of the nine ways of clarifying and reinforcing ideas discussed on pages 147–60. Have each member of the group prepare a one-minute statement about the agreed-upon subject, using primarily the single method of clarifying and reinforcing ideas that was assigned to him or her. After each group member speaks, discuss the advantages and disadvantages *any* speaker will face when he or she chooses to amplify ideas by that method.

2. Working in groups as suggested in Exercise 1 above, assign each group member the task of using *one* of the three ways of building proof discussed on pages 124–47 in a one-minute talk about some aspect of the topic the group has chosen. Following each presentation discuss how the one-minute talk could have been made stronger (a) by using additional kinds of justification for what was said and (b) by better use of the particular kind of justification assigned to the speaker.

3. Using a group like that suggested in Exercises 1 and 2 above, choose a subject for an imaginary speech to be given in a situation you have imaginatively worked out. In group discussion phrase the ideal central idea for the imaginary speech, agree on what main points ought to be made about it, and make a list of what tactics of invention would be especially important in developing each point.

4. Prepare and deliver a one-point informative speech in which you use at least four forms of amplification.

5. Prepare and present a short speech on some aspect of a subject you know your classmates disagree about. Try to build enough rational justification into your speech to satisfy a skeptical listener. After the speech, invite a listener who agrees with you and one who still disagrees with you to evaluate how well you proved your point. Conduct a class discussion of their evaluations of your proof.

6. Present an oral report on an advertisement or advertising campaign. Discuss the ways in which personal-interest, rational, and source justifications are used in this advertising.

7. With a group of three or four others in your class, or alone, choose one of the figures in chapter 10 (figures 10-3, 10-4, 10-5, or 10-6) and (a) analyze whether the setting makes visual aids desirable and if so why, (b) what sight lines a user of visual aids needs to be especially concerned about in this setting, (c) what would be the best *kinds* of visual materials to use in this setting if any at all proved desirable. When you have made your analysis, report your conclusions, with reasons, to your class.

6

INVENTION IN RELATION TO PURPOSES

This chapter concludes our consideration of the discovery and selection of what to say in a speech. In chapters 3, 4, and 5 we tried to think about all speeches and all speakers. But, as we stressed in those chapters, as a speaker's sense of purpose becomes firm his or her options narrow. The normal objectives in speaking publicly are to inform, to induce inquiry, to reinforce, to persuade, and to entertain. If you focus clearly on what you want to accomplish in a rhetorical situation, one of these goals will dominate your efforts. That is as it should be; but as soon as you settle on one of these dominant goals some inventional *moves* become more important than others. It is on those special requirements that we focus now, looking at the constraints of each conventional goal in speaking.

SPEAKING TO INFORM

There are times when speakers are fully satisfied if their hearers understand what is said. Then we tend to think of their talk as *informative*. We could as easily call it explanatory or expository. A teacher's lecture and a physician's explanation of how a disease must be treated are examples of this kind of speech. To a considerable extent the committee of students whose presentation appears in appendix B had this kind of goal, as Dr. Upcraft certainly did not when he addressed the mass meeting of students on his university's drinking policy.

Whether understanding is a speaker's overall objective or the objective of only a part of his or her talk, the aim to inform requires the speaker to find particular kinds of material and use them in special ways that meet the distinctive standards listeners impose when asked to accept knowledge understandingly.

What kinds of content are especially appropriate when you set out to inform? Any material clarifying such attributes and relationships of a subject as are listed on pp. 94–95, excepting the attribute of desirability, are appropriate. Also, whatever clarifies any of the five relationships listed on page 95 will be potentially informative. Material that concerns the *desirability* of anything is never purely informative. It implicitly or explicitly raises questions about debatable matters: "goods," "bads," "betters," "poorers." Material that affirms or denies desirability forces speaker and listener into the realm of persuasion.

The standards peculiar to informative speaking are: (1) *accuracy*, being true to fact in both detail and proportion; (2) *completeness*, being comprehensive enough to cover the subject promised by the specific purpose; and (3) *unity*, providing knowledge that will be intelligible as a whole. Like many other propositions about oral communication, these standards of informative speaking are simply the expectations of audiences. When a speaker indicates he or she wants us to understand, we begin watching whether what he or she says seems true, whether there is enough detail to allow us a full understanding, and whether what we are being told adds up to anything that seems to fit together.

Mistakes in Explaining

A speaker who undertakes to explain the nature of the modern bicycle will err if he or she seems to say that all bicycles have several speeds and gears (racing and other bicycles do not); the speaker will err in a different way by neglecting to point out that modern bicycles are specially built for different uses; and there will be a third error if the speech fails to include recognition that the main object of bicycle design is to interrelate human strength to speed of movement on some preconceived range of surfaces. If a speaker makes all three errors, he or she will have violated all the basic demands people put on those who profess to inform them. The speaker will be excused from talking about *all* kinds of bicycles if explanation of only certain kinds is promised. One's promise defines what one must be accurate and complete about. Any speaker may excuse himself or herself for exclusions, provided neither essential completeness nor unity will be spoiled.

Failure to meet the requirement for unity or wholeness is frequent among information givers. A way to protect yourself against this is to write out your specific purpose and then examine it carefully to see that your statement expresses all, but no more than, you want your listeners to understand. A very good practice is the following. Write the words: "When I finish I want my listeners to understand *that. . . .*" Insert after "that" a single clause completing the sentence and expressing what you want to accomplish. "When I finish I want them to understand *that* the Battle of Gettysburg was a battle of maneuver rather than firepower" is a precise subject sentence. "When I finish I want my listeners to understand the Battle of Gettysburg" is useless as a subject sentence because it gives you no focus and promises the listener no limits on what it is he or she is supposed to learn.

Even if audiences did not need so much help in discovering what you do and do not intend to cover, your own self-interest argues for taking great care in phrasing subject sentences whenever you plan to talk informatively. Without expressing your purpose to yourself in exact terms you are likely to try to cover too much, gather material you cannot use, and have trouble organizing your ideas.

Maintaining Interest

Maintaining interest is also often difficult in talking to inform. Some material does not have inherent qualities that draw attention. Then you will need to choose special materials that associate these qualities with what you explain. Through special attention to style and delivery you may also be able to intensify the attention value of what you say. Specific examples, comparisons and contrasts, brief narratives, and real and figurative analogies are especially useful. So are all facts that are close to the experience of your listeners—even facts that appear threatening.

The physical features of a one dollar bill scarcely seem a subject on which to build an engrossing speech, but a student speaker did just that by finding unusual, concrete, and newsworthy amplifying materials. First, he prepared a blowup of a dollar bill, showing all details of both sides. Then, he related some unusual historical details and some long forgotten interpretations of the specific words and images on the bill: it was copied from the Spanish dollar; beneath the scales of justice are thirteen stars—representing, of course, the original states; the Latin phrases mean "One nation out of many states," "God has favored our undertakings," "the new order of ages," and the last two are borrowed from the Roman poet Virgil; the pyramid was chosen as a symbol of the Union; and so on. For each feature of the bill the speaker had some informative and interesting datum to establishing for his listeners that "the design of our dollar bill has significance dating back to the time of George Washington."[1] When so commonplace an item

---

1. This talk was given by Anthony Damiani of Herbert H. Lehman College as a classroom speech in a basic speech course.

as the one dollar bill can be given significance by careful choice of materials, it is hard to see why any speaker in full command of the art of public speech should fail to interest listeners in subjects that have initial importance in a rhetorical situation.　One *can* find information and methods of speech that will compensate for remoteness, technicality, or ordinariness in matters that need to be lucidly explained.

Speakers often neglect another opportunity when explaining difficult subjects.　It is the opportunity to treat the subject matter *as if* it were other than it literally is.

No one has ever seen a sound wave.　Sound waves do not behave precisely like the water waves we call ripples.　Nonetheless, it is customary to explain part of the behavior of sound waves *as if* the waves acted as ripples spreading outward when a stone is dropped into water.　There are many aspects of sound that cannot be explained properly by this *as-if* treatment; nevertheless, the treatment will serve as long as we confine our attention to specific aspects of how sound waves spread out from their source.　The whole point of hunting for *as-if* treatments is that people build new knowledge upon the knowledge they already have—through comparison and contrast.　Some aspects of a steel rolling mill can be made both clear and interesting if we think of the steel *as if* it were dough and the mill *as if* it were equipped with kitchen rolling pins.　One must be careful that listeners understand that an *as-if* treatment is not a discussion of actuality; yet, informative speakers should search for such potentially useful ways of explaining.

Other Valuable Materials

Several other kinds of materials are especially valuable in informative speaking.　Types of material that clarify were discussed in chapter 5 (pages 147–60).　Of special use are comparisons and contrasts, definitions that exemplify and specify functions, descriptions, examples, restatements, and visual aids.

We have been discussing informative speaking *as if* information giving really existed completely apart from inquiry, reinforcement, persuasion, or entertainment.　It seldom does, but we can talk clearly of only one thing at a time.　Clear explanations persuade us to believe; they encourage us to seek more knowledge; they reinforce our feelings; and they are often entertaining in the sense that new learning is pleasing.　Good informative speaking frequently persuades.　When President Carter announced his energy policy in 1977, he *explained* the policy and also sought to persuade people to accept it.　Or consider a different situation: If a speaker tries to explain methods of contraception, he or she will almost surely be interpreted as endorsing their use.　On controversial matters pure explanation is almost impossible just because speakers are naturally thought to stand with whatever they present, however dispassionately they present it. It is also often the case that the strongest persuasion is the clearest exposition of how and why things *are* as you say.

To summarize, your main goal may be to inform people. When it is, the important thing is to specify to yourself (and usually to your auditors) exactly what you want understood. Information about any characteristic of what you explain *may* be useful, except that statements about its desirability will always involve you in persuading listeners to accept your *endorsement* of the subject as well as your explanation of it. When your main business is to clarify and amplify, comparisons, contrasts, references to what is familiar, examples, narratives, and analogies are likely to be especially useful to you because these materials tend to provide built-in elements that draw and hold attention. You ought not forget that those who inform accurately, fully, and pointedly often turn out to be the most persuasive of communicators!

SPEAKING TO INDUCE INQUIRY

Do speakers ever address others without having the answers? Unquestionably, although the audience is then apt to be specialized. A chairman meeting his staff or a planning committee raising a problem with its community must present problems *for* discussion before solutions can be arrived at. A city manager may have to describe a water-supply problem to a mass meeting of citizens or a committee of doctors may present a hospital problem to the entire medical staff for solution.

Creating a Spirit for Inquiry

If group problem solving is a part of the work of your class, you will notice that creating a spirit of inquiry is the primary goal expert chairmen seek to attain in their opening remarks. A formal speech to induce inquiry is simply a longer presentation of the ideas that under different circumstances would have formed the agenda of an inquiring discussion group.

If you look about you, you will see more speech aimed at inducing inquiry than you may have expected. One apartment mate may notice a sink drain is slow. What shall we do? Consult the landlord or superintendent? Let it go? Try to fix it ourselves? Call and pay a plumber ourselves? The person noticing the problem may bring it up with his or her partners, describing and estimating the problem, expressing what ought to be, and reviewing the possible actions.   A research committee finds we have a choice.   Which product shall we buy?   One committee member or all may speak for a few moments. They may not inform in the usual sense but not really persuade in the usual sense either.   The extent of persuasion may merely be to make others see that the subject deserves serious reflection *now*.   In such situations speakers usually want to set out the conditions within which a solution needs to be found and to stimulate listeners to look for, evaluate, and choose a desirable solution.   They may even be trying to encourage discussion in open forums that they expect to follow their remarks.[2]

Questions and Answers

The subject sentence of any remarks to induce inquiry ought to express a precise question to be answered.   Such a sentence might be put thus: When I (we) finish I (we) want the audience to be prepared and motivated to answer the question, "............?"   The words "be prepared and motivated" represent key aspects of the inquiring speaker's assignment.   Whether or not you put these words in a formal statement of purpose, the function is always to pave the way for a serious search for real answers.   A person or group must explain the problem and, insofar as possible, suggest directions in which a viable solution might be looked for.   These parts of the task are primarily informative, but unless you can also answer the hearers' ever-present question, "Why should *I* care?" little will result from the speech.   Whoever undertakes to induce inquiry must accept the dual responsibilities of preparing and motivating his or her audience to try to solve a problem.

The fact that people who speak to induce inquiry do not know the answers frequently keeps them from even identifying the proper *questions!*   People can be sensitive to difficulties and have standards or goals by which to measure solutions and yet possess no clear idea of what question needs solving.   An English writer, Arthur Young, noticed this state of mind among the revolutionists in France in 1792:

> I have been in much company all day, and cannot but remark, that there seem to be no settled ideas of the best means of forming a new constitution. . . .   In these most interesting discussions, I find a general

---

2. Exposition of this kind of speaking may also be found in J. H. McBurney and Ernest J. Wrage, *The Art of Good Speech* (New York: Prentice-Hall, 1953), chap. 13, "The Methods of Inquiry."   Recognition that formal speaking of this kind does occur can be found in the writings of Cicero and Quintilian and even in the works of lesser but earlier authors.   Our discussion of this topic draws upon many of these sources and, at several points, goes somewhat beyond what has heretofore been said.

ignorance of the principles of government; a strange and unaccountable appeal, on one side, to ideal and visionary rights of nature; and, on the other, no settled plan that shall give security to the people for being in future in a much better situation than hitherto; . . .[3]

Young identified a great source of difficulty in France at the time of the Revolution. Most leaders simply lacked the wisdom or experience to distinguish among: questions inviting inquiry, questions that must be debated to choose or not choose a solution already known, and philosophical questions ("rights of nature") to which no *final* answer could ever be found. They framed and debated philosophical questions, not questions of practical action. Some of the excesses of the period occurred because they debated their philosophical questions as though they were issues of absolute and practical right and wrong.

A campus speaker who says he wants to raise the question, "What is student government good for?" or "What are the inalienable rights of women?" or "Is racism eradicable in America?" is in the same difficulty as the French leaders. The speaker senses that problems exist but frames questions having no clear, final answers. The questions invite interminable debate about definitions and values; they postpone the possibility of practical, improving action. The poser of such questions does not recognize, as most philosophers do, that for every philosophical proposition about a definition or value there is, somewhere, an alternative proposition; this is the reason definitions and values are matters of debate from generation to generation. Meanwhile people have to *choose* from among *available* definitions and *choose* among conflicting values to get their daily business done. The student speaker we are imagining really wants to alter events, but he poses questions as though matters concerning "good," "inalienable rights," and the *future* of "racism" could be *settled* by discussion and debate. If change must wait for agreement on such questions, there will be little change at all.

Differences in Questions

Anyone wanting to induce inquiry for other than purely learning purposes needs to recognize that questions of fact (especially *future* fact) and philosophical definition can only be *judged;* they do not in themselves generate thinking about practical alternatives. Questions of policy and of action serve best to generate inquiry because people

---

3. Arthur Young, *Travels in France*. Quoted in *The Debate on the French Revolution, 1789–1800*, ed. Alfred Cobban (London: Nicholas Kaye, 1950), pp. 51–52.

can agree—temporarily at least—on *practical* definitions and move from these to the *apparent* wisdom of alternatives.   Our campus speaker must decide whether to try to invoke inquiry about practical alternatives or seek philosophical reflection, without limits, on the uses of government in general.   This speaker needs to decide whether listeners are to think about student government *as a concept* or search for answers to specific problems existing *in* student government on a specific campus.   It is equally necessary to decide whether listeners are to study how to produce some kind of "Bill of Rights for Women" or try to locate *actions* that could enhance the day-to-day rights of women.   On racism the issue is whether to invite a search for some prophetic pronouncement about the future or a search for courses of action that might minimize or eliminate racially discriminatory behavior.

Our point is that if you want to open practical inquiry instead of lengthy philosophical discussion or extended debate, you need to be very careful about what your questions *seem* to ask your listeners to do.   If you phrase questions so you seem to ask for decrees, definitions, and decisions about ultimate values, you may not be replaced by Napoleon as the French revolutionaries were, but you will tend to invoke exchanges that produce only opinions but not actions.   It is therefore especially important that your subject sentences in speaking to inquire be precisely phrased to invite exactly the *kind* of inquiry you want.

Phrasing your subject sentence is important also because the sentence must not only define the kind of inquiry wanted but pose a problem that can be dealt with in the time at your listeners' disposal, and it must be solvable through the listeners' available knowledge and other resources.   Problems need not be *completely* answerable to be worthy of inquiring consideration, but at least your listeners ought to be able to make satisfying progress toward a final answer.   If they have too little time or too few resources to allow any decisions at all, your invitation to inquire can only frustrate them.

Distinctive Aspects

With a single exception, the kinds of ideas that can be pertinent to inquiry are like those appropriate to informing.   The exception is that *desirability* is a topic that *must* be treated if the problem to be explored involves *policies*.   For example, whether campus conduct should be regulated by student government finally becomes a question of whether such regulation would be desirable.   It is the same with virtually all questions about courses of action or about how values ought to be applied.   The desirability of actions or applications must at some point be explored, either by you or by those who pick up the inquiry after you have stimulated it.

The distinctive pattern of organization into which main ideas fall in a speech of inquiry is discussed in chapter 7 (pages 214–16). The divisions of an inquiry are useful guides to the materials needed in developing speech of this kind.

Inquiring speech normally begins with discussion of a problem and proceeds toward solutions deserving consideration by reasonable people. This kind of thought movement is not inherently interesting. The speaker, and therefore the listener, moves from point to point with judgment suspended. Even at the close, the inquiries may or may not have revealed a preferred solution. There are, thus, few natural climaxes. There is no inherent sense of energetic progress or satisfying release from tensions. In return for asking listeners to defer judgment and to sustain the tensions of inquiry, speakers ought to repay them by using the most interesting clarifying and vivifying materials available. They ought to use those amplifying tactics that do the most to aid auditors to grasp the message (see chapter 5, pages 147–60).

An inquiring speaker assumes a special leadership role. He or she presides over a collaborative search for a "best choice." In this role he must be careful to demonstrate his own knowledge of the subject, his impartiality concerning the decisions he is asking his listeners to make, and his candor in dealing with both content and listeners. Few tactics are more resented than attempts to maneuver audiences toward a preselected conclusion under the pretense of inviting them to inquire freely. This applies to group presentations also.

Questions, not propositions, stimulate inquiry; so the subject sentences of speeches to induce inquiry ought to express answerable questions. However, when several people collaborate to present a message to induce inquiry, it may well be that some individual speeches will be chiefly aimed at informing—especially those that present aspects of the problem. Finally, however, an individual or group presentation intended to evoke inquiry must pose clearly and sharply the question to which the audience is to address its thought. If this is not clear, in the end listeners will be left asking, "What do you want from us?" That is not a question that yields decisions or actions or clear-headed thinking about issues.

SPEAKING TO REINFORCE BELIEFS AND FEELINGS

From time to time rhetorical situations require that we speak to reinforce beliefs and feelings listeners already have. We speak of the values of education on commencement day; we assure a friend that she is right in claiming that women's salaries do not equal men's for equal work. Then we aim to make the listeners feel or believe something more strongly than ever, or perhaps we speak to inspire confidence or faith in what is already believed.

Speaking of this kind is *persuasion*. We are considering it apart from what we shall shortly call *persuasion* for two reasons. The materials you need for reinforcement are unique, and when you develop points and themes in this kind of speaking you will amplify more than you will justify.

Limitations on Ideas

When you set out to reinforce beliefs or feelings, your search for discussable ideas becomes limited to ideas your listeners already have some knowledge about. Whether you talk about education, physical fitness, or scientific method you will locate your most useful ideas for reinforcement *in the knowledge and attitudes your listeners already possess*. When you have found these, your task is to develop those themes in ways that connect them *with important values the listeners have*. The essential process of reinforcing beliefs and feelings is connecting familiar ideas and attitudes with *high* (or low) values. To this extent, speaking to reinforce allows you the least intellectual freedom of any customary type of speaking. You work within the framework of your listeners' *existing* beliefs, feelings, and value systems. This is why speaking to reinforce can be heard in all societies, no matter how totalitarian or censorious. Even where freedom of speech is closely restricted, there will always be some approved ideas and *proper* values that can be extolled. There also will be certain *improper* ideas that can be connected with *improper* values for purposes of denunciation. Hence, speaking to reinforce (positively and negatively) occurs in all known cultures and social systems.

Uses of This Type of Speaking

Despite its limitations, speaking to reinforce beliefs and feelings has important uses. Through it religious congregations are sustained and social and political virtues such as pride and mutual respect are maintained as active forces. Indeed, the values that bind us into social groups form the subjects of most of the important reinforcing communication that occurs. Without reinforcement through speech and other media, social bonds would begin to atrophy and any society would begin to drift toward anarchism.

The audience determines on what subjects a speech of reinforcement may be made. Whatever the audience already believes or disbelieves and whatever values they hold in high esteem or plainly reject can become subject matter. (One can reinforce disbelief or rejection as readily as belief or acceptance.) But not every existing belief or disbelief is appropriate for discussion at any time. People who attend meetings of ethnic groups indicate by attending that their beliefs about nationality or race are, just then, of high importance. Whoever addresses such a meeting must recognize that beliefs about nationality or race are to be reinforced, not, say, beliefs about commerce or education. But many persons who attend such meetings will also be members of business, educational, and political groups; nonetheless, during an ethnic gathering these people will be only secondarily conscious of their other associations. They will be unready to hear commercial, educational, or partisan talk unless ethnic values are stressed. The same people may on another day gather as businessmen or as political partisans. Then there will be occasion for reinforcing beliefs about business and politics. The same general situation applies in religious convocations, educational commencements, lodge meetings, voters' groups, and so on. Wherever there is an identification among all or most listeners, there is occasion and often need for reinforcement of beliefs and feelings.

What we have just said implies that rhetorical situations inviting speech that reinforces are often ceremonial but not invariably so. Anniversaries, religious and other observances, rituals of various sorts, kick-off meetings, locker-room half-time sessions, and rallies of all sorts, are among the situations that invite speech that reinforces beliefs and feelings. So also are dating and love making!

Procedure

Assuming a moderately formal circumstance for reinforcing speech, how does one proceed after having taken inventory of the listeners' known ideas, attitudes, and values? You ask what the exigences are—the special needs—of the situation and select a theme or a special subject that fits those needs. Now it will be time to formulate a subject sentence that can guide you in searching for further materials and in composing an appropriate message. You will help yourself and your listeners if you adopt the following formula for framing subject sentences in this type of speaking. Write the words, "When I finish I want my listeners to (believe, feel) (more, less) strongly *that* . . . ." Compose a clause to follow the word "that." Decide whether it is predominantly *belief* or *feeling* you wish to intensify or diminish, and eliminate either *more* or *less* according to your intention. A finished subject sentence might read: "When I finish I want my listeners to *believe more* strongly *that* personal acts of pollution control are worth doing."

The unique feature of a subject sentence for reinforcing is that it ought to express the *degree* of intensification or diminution for which you will strive. It is useful to express, too, whether it will be ideas or emotions on which you will concentrate. Our formula will remind you of both needs.

Except for the limitations we have discussed, the reinforcing speaker's search for ideas differs little from the searching we discussed in chapter 4. Any of the attributes we commonly assign to things and people and any of the relationships we commonly assert or argue (see pp. 94–95) can suggest potentially discussable themes that justify greater or less belief or feeling. There are, however, two special bits of advice that can help you when you aim to reinforce.

We borrow our first piece of advice from Aristotle, who observed that in his day speeches of reinforcement consistently made beliefs or feelings impressive (or unimpressive) by connecting them with recognized goods or their opposites. He saw speakers linking ideas with justice, courage, temperance, grandeur, liberality, gentleness, prudence, wisdom, and so on. He contended that ideas seem more or less impressive depending on how much they contribute to or are consistent with these qualities and others that listeners admire. If you will listen to reinforcing speech in our own day, you will find it working in just this way. So in amplifying your themes or *points* you will be well advised to show that the *beliefs* or feelings you are magnifying or diminishing enhance or diminish the major *goods* your listeners prize generally and prize specially because of the rhetorical situation they are part of.

The other item of special advice is: it is better to develop a train of thought that is simple and clear than to try to render an idea impressive in several different ways. Enlargement of an idea is preferable to multiplying its features. An ancient Greek speech is still an ideal model in this respect. In his famous funeral oration commemorating the bravery of Athenians who had died in the first year of the Peloponnesian Wars, Pericles expressed the pith of his whole discourse thus:

> Taking everything together then, I declare that our city is an education to Greece, and I declare that in my opinion each single one of our citizens, in all the manifold aspects of life, is able to show himself the rightful lord and owner of his own person, and do this, moreover, with exceptional grace and exceptional versatility.[4]

His whole address, as Thucydides reports it, merely amplifies these tightly related thoughts concerning the city for which the dead had

---

4. Thucydides, *The Peloponnesian War,* trans. Rex Warner (Baltimore: Penguin Books, 1954), p. 119.

fought.   A lesser speaker might have insisted on discussing the way the heroes died, the justice of the war, the qualities of victories and defeats, and the gratitude of living Athenians—all in a misguided effort to multiply listeners' feelings of gratitude to the dead.   Pericles wisely chose a single theme and amplified it: Athens' worth ennobles its fallen soldiers.   His speech had focus.

Distinctive Aspects

What makes speech to reinforce successful?   You need to amplify hitherto unnoticed connections between *goods* your listeners already value and the *idea* or attitude you want to reinforce.   Some examples illustrate ways of doing this.

Before the Seattle Shriners in 1976, the bicentennial year of the United States, Charles Boyle, a writer and consultant, turned his listeners' negative memories and historical knowledge into supporting material for the proposition that "this age" will deserve to be looked upon as "the good old days."   In the major portion of his speech Boyle contrasted the "good old days" of pre-World War II (which many of his middle-aged and older listeners were fully aware of) with 1976.   On topic after topic Boyle argued or suggested that the world was better off now than then.   Finally he arrived at his conclusion that the United States has never been without serious problems but *thrives* on adversity, so the "drummers of despair" should be distrusted because if "people . . . do their jobs one step at a time" their "great grandchildren will be looking back at this age and saying, 'Those were the good old days.' "   We may suppose that this was what Boyle's middle-aged and senior listeners wanted to believe; his reminders of their former "hard times" were calculated to encourage their inclinations to endorse the status quo.[5]

Winston Churchill used the same general methods of associating values, making vital and important the rather platitudinous notion that the British and the Americans should "never cease to proclaim . . . the great principles of freedom and the rights of man which are the joint inheritance of the English-speaking world."   To reinforce this idea he said:

> . . . this means that the people of any country have the right . . . to choose or change the character or form of government under which they dwell; that freedom of speech and thought should reign; that courts of justice, independent of the executive, . . . should administer laws which have received the broad assent of large majorities or are consecrated by time and custom.   Here are the title deeds of freedom which should lie in

---

5. Charles Boyle, "The Bright Side of Adversity," *Vital Speeches of the Day* XLII (May 1, 1976): 436–38.

every cottage home.   Here is the message of the British and American peoples to mankind.[6]

Undoubtedly Churchill's careful choice of value-laden words helped to make the virtues of self-government, freedom of speech and thought, and independent courts of popular law dignify the importance of "proclaiming."

Abraham Lincoln used the same general methods at Gettysburg; however, he found the virtues he would speak of by studying the *setting* for his speech.   He found them in the familiar dedicatory scene. Simply to "dedicate this cemetery" would not sufficiently dignify the occasion, he seems to have thought.   To the ordinary act he attached the value-laden concept "dedicate ourselves."   This idea was in turn associated with still higher *national* goals.   Thus, he reinforced the notion that the military cemetery was important as both a personal and a national symbol.

Although magnifying and diminishing ideas and values are frequently ceremonial functions, purposiveness and clarity are essential. This is worth emphasizing because speakers attempting to reinforce frequently tend to ramble among headings not closely related to one another.   This is probably because the ideas of the headings are general and familiar, but focus is no less important to listeners to this kind of speech than to any other.   Once focused on purpose, your tasks in reinforcement become (1) to amplify familiar ideas and values that serve your purpose by means of (2) pointing up hitherto unthought-of attributes and relationships.

We now turn from this special form of persuasion to the more typical problems of persuasive speaking.

SPEAKING TO PERSUADE

When you try to create greater changes than just to reinforce beliefs, you confront troublesome questions of what counts as success. To be realistic you have to set your goal on achieving as much change as your rhetorical situation allows.   You cannot always ask for great changes of beliefs and attitudes.   To do so when listeners oppose your views or hold firmly to views somewhat different from yours is almost sure to turn them off, as we pointed out in chapter 3.   You must accept that speakers often wish for changes they cannot completely achieve.

---

6. "The Sinews of Peace," delivered at Westminster College, Fulton, Missouri, March 5, 1946.   The text of this speech (also called "The Iron Curtain Speech") is available in many sources.   Quoted here from *The Sinews of Peace: Post-War Speeches by Winston S. Churchill,* ed. Randolph S. Churchill (Boston: Houghton Mifflin Company, 1949). p. 97.

That involves no necessary failure in persuasion. It is not *absolute effect* that testifies to the excellence of persuasion; the measure of *effectiveness* lies in the *comparison* between the influence you actually achieve and what was reasonably possible considering all the circumstances. Dr. Upcraft was successful in the speech quoted in appendix B; he was able to turn the audience around. But a persuader like the conservative speaker-writer-broadcaster William Buckley must be counted as successful if he achieves small changes in public opinion. He speaks—and speaks very well—for a set of political and religious views the majority of Americans simply refuse to accept in full. So he effectively reinforces the views of those who already agree with him and tries to alter general public opinion on a point here and a point there. It was much the same with the perennial spokesman and presidential candidate Norman Thomas. He never won an election or had a law named after him in more than three decades of trying to persuade Americans to socialist doctrines, but he did popularize a number of ideas about reform that were later adopted as their own by Democrats and Republicans. It would be absurd to say his public persuasion was unsuccessful because he won no office. In persuasion you need to set your sights on what is practically possible in your situation; to persuade is not necessarily to convert.

Special Demands

Understanding, then, that you will aim at varying *degrees* of persuasion in the different situations you will enter, what special demands will be imposed on you because you are trying to shift beliefs and attitudes to some extent?

Justifying is always essential. All speaking ought to motivate, but in persuasion motivation is crucial. Hearers' own interests must be enlisted as justification for change. This point was forcefully put by the Scottish rhetorician George Campbell. His language and psychological theory seem quaint, but his point concerning motivation in persuasion is unmistakably sound:

> . . . when persuasion is the end, passion also must be engaged. If it is fancy which bestows brilliancy on our ideas, if it is memory which gives them stability, passion doth more, it animates them. Hence they derive spirit and energy. To say that it is possible to persuade without speaking to the passions, is but at best a kind of specious nonsense. The coolest reasoner always in persuading addresseth himself to the passions some way or other. This he cannot avoid doing, if he speak to the purpose. To make me believe it is enough to show me that things are so; to make me act, it is necessary to show that the action will answer some end. That can never be an end to me which gratifies

no passion or affection in my nature. You assure me, "It is for my honour." Now you solicit my pride, without which I had never been able to understand the word. You say, "It is for my interest." Now you bespeak my self-love. "It is for the public good." Now you rouse my patriotism. "It will relieve the miserable." Now you touch my pity. So far . . . [is it] from being an unfair method of persuasion to move the passions, that there is no persuasion without moving them.[7]

A twentieth-century psychologist might reject Campbell's technical distinctions among fancy, memory, and passion, but he would agree that there is no changing attitudes or feelings without engaging the desires that Campbell called "passions." The modern psychologist would agree with Campbell that "the coolest reasoner" must certainly fail to change views unless aided by feelings. This necessity of enlisting active desires is one of the special demands the persuader's aim imposes on you.

In order that active drives may operate within hearers, it is sometimes necessary to refrain from expressing all that you believe. You may avoid asking for all the opinion change you would really like to attain. The reason is that what men cannot yet understand, what they are not intellectually or emotionally ready to receive, is more likely to trouble them than persuade them. St. Paul's sermon on Mars Hill (pages 108–9) illustrates how audiences' limitations affect what persuasive speakers dare say. Paul deliberately claimed less than he might have if his audience of Athenian philosophers had been intellectually and emotionally ready to examine his teachings without bewilderment. Most persuaders find themselves in comparable situations and dare not claim all they would like to claim for fear of destroying their opportunity to change *some* beliefs. The situation is not unlike that of a teacher who must teach what the students are now ready and able to learn; if the teacher goes farther, he or she will perplex and perhaps frustrate, not teach. The persuader's situation is often still more critical; if the persuader goes too far the audience may reject the entire position.

Consulting All Sides

The general controversiality of the things we persuade about can create special problems in persuaders' preparation. There are sources of information so strongly committed to the various sides of controversies that they cannot give a whole view of the issues and

---

7. George Campbell, *Philosophy of Rhetoric*, ed. Lloyd Bitzer (Carbondale, Ill.: Southern Illinois University Press, 1963), bk. I, chap. 7, p. 77. Originally published in 1776.

evidence.   One does not expect to receive the whole story about a labor dispute at either the labor union headquarters or from officials of the disputing corporation.   Nor is one likely to get all the facts from hearing the witnesses for only one side in a court case.   Less obvious but equally biased sources of information abound on almost all controversial issues.

You need to consult all sides in your research: read *The Nation* and *The National Review, The New York Times* and *United States News and World Report* if your subject involves a liberal-conservative controversy in politics.   See that you get the positions of union and management if your subject concerns a labor dispute.   Getting both sides will not necessarily give you the whole story.   You are likely to come away from this kind of investigation with a good deal of extraneous information.   But you will know where opponents differ and where they agree.   Where they agree you may probably accept; where they disagree you must search for more facts by firsthand investigation and by consulting the most impartial sources available.   Using both modes of research you will ultimately acquire a reliable body of material for the construction of arguments.

What we have just said may sound idealistic, but it is practical, too.   Of all speakers, the inquirer and the persuader must be most jealous of their reputations for integrity.   Persuaders, like inquirers, presume to lead and advise.   Thereby they place their own reliability at issue.   You do not readily accept the advice of people who know less about the matter than you do.   So it is with all persuadees.   What they especially want from their advisers is consistent evidence that the adviser fully understands and reasons well about the matter at issue, and that he or she counsels in their own best interests.

An important way a persuader can show that he or she is both informed and fair is to recognize the existence of other views as he or she talks.   Experimentation has almost uniformly shown that recognizing opposing views in persuasion has more durable influence than giving one-sided presentations.   Only when an audience already agrees or when it will never be exposed to other sides does it seem safe to be one-sided.   But two-sidedness raises the further question: shall we present our own views before or after conflicting views?   A great deal of research has been carried out on this and related questions, especially on whether what is discussed first (primacy) or what is discussed later (recency) has greater impact on persuadees.   The findings are not definitive, but the following seems a fair statement of what experimental research suggests at this point to practical persuaders.

It is plausible to think that when a listener hears the other side of an argument and hears it refuted or otherwise taken care of, he is conditioned or *inoculated* against that side.   It will thereafter require more persuasion to get him to accept that other side than it would had he never heard that side discussed.[8]   On this principle, then, you ought to make your own position as attractive as possible *before* you handle counter views.   You will thus take advantage of the fact that ideas seem to gain adherence over competing ideas when they are attractively presented *first* in a series.   Once your own position has been established you ought to recognize conflicting views and show that they are less credible than your own.   In this way you may inoculate your listeners against competing conclusions and, at the very least, give your own stand the best positioning advantages you can.   To all of this we add two thoughts: (1) a persuader who recognizes and reasonably disposes of other views is showing that he both knows his subject and can reason about it; and (2) if listeners think the opposition was *justly* handled, his *ethos* is apt to rise.

Constructive and Refutational Discourse

What we have just said about the importance of recognizing opposing views implies that effective persuasion normally involves both constructive and refutational discourse.   *Constructive* argument builds up the persuader's side of his subject; *refutational argument* challenges or otherwise exposes weaknesses in contrary views.   The technicalities of developing these two sorts of arguments are best studied in courses devoted specifically to persuasion and argumentation.   As a beginning student of speaking, you can carry out your work if you follow these guidelines in developing constructive and refutational arguments:

1. No matter what motivational justifications you offer for your position, you must satisfy your listeners that you have not taken your position irresponsibly.   You must give some kind of evidence that you have taken it for sensible and essentially rational reasons.   (Concerning the development of rational supports see chapter 5, pages 129–38.)
2. You need to show your listeners why the position you have adopted

---

8. The classic studies of one-sided *vs.* two-sided persuasion were done during World War II and were reported by Carl I. Hovland, Arthur A. Lumsdaine, and Fred D. Sheffield in *Studies in Social Psychology in World War II*, vol. 3: *Experiments on Mass Communication* (Princeton: Princeton University Press, 1949), see especially pp. 201–27.   A significant essay concerning one-sidedness and two-sidedness in informal communication is James C. McCroskey, Thomes J. Young, and Michael D. Scott, "Effects of Message Sidedness and Evidence on Inoculation against Counterpersuasion in Small Group Communication," *Speech Monographs* XXXIX (August 1972): 205–12.   On the role of personal involvement and responses to persuasion that counters listeners' attitudes, Edward M. Bodaken and Kenneth K. Sereno, "Counterattitudinal Advocacy, Ego-Involvement, and Persuasive Effect," *Western Speech Communication* XL (Fall 1976): 236–48, is especially informative.

is more sensible and responsible than other positions they may have heard of (or may hear of in the future). This usually means you must give your audience both rational and self-interest justifications for rejecting alternatives to the position you endorse.

3. The ultimate justification for any position will be, for your audience at least, your constructive proof that your position is better for them. Hence, the bulk of persuasion is constructive.[9]

What chiefly distinguishes the persuasive speaker from the informant, inquirer, or entertainer is that his *primary* test in choosing available materials for proof or amplification is always, "Has this material enough promise or threat for my listeners so I may expect their outlooks to shift a bit because I have used it?" He or she must be unusually sensitive to George Campbell's previously quoted reminder: "That can never be an end for me which gratifies no passion or affection in my nature." A persuader dares not stop the search until he or she finds materials that will make a psychological contribution toward altering human experience.

SPEAKING TO ENTERTAIN

When a speaker decides to *entertain*, he commits himself to hold attention agreeably by diverting listeners' thoughts from matters of high seriousness. Often, although not invariably, the task is to provide amusement. Another way of defining entertaining speech is to say it so completely interests listeners that they have almost no sense of working to acquire the full significance of what is said.

Notice that entertainment *may* be amusing but is not invariably so. A first-rate travelogue can be entertaining but not basically amusing. Many narratives and descriptions entertain us with varying degrees of humor. So a speaker planning to entertain listeners should recognize that being humorous is not the only option open.

Treatment of Subject Distinguishes This Type

Any subject—any theme that will hold attention agreeably in a diverting rather than highly serious way—is a potential subject for entertaining talk. The *treatment* of the subject is the distinguishing

---

9. For an excellent, detailed treatment of these responsibilities in argumentation, see Douglas Ehninger and Wayne Brockriede, *Decision by Debate* (New York: Dodd, Mead, 1963), especially pp. 81–95 and 252–66.

mark. Treat any subject lightly, divertingly, and you can make it entertaining.

Typical occasions for entertaining talk allow extraordinary latitude for choosing subjects. These occasions tend to be convivial gatherings or situations where no stronger motivation than curiosity has brought people together. Wherever listeners are willing to be diverted from the usual and the serious there is a rhetorical situation for entertaining speech.

Where casual curiosity has created the speech situation there is occasion for entertaining speech that is not predominantly humorous. Light, straightforward treatment of whatever subject is the speaker's specialty is usually expected. Consider two of many possible settings. A Rotary Club invites the public to a postluncheon period during which Mr. So-and-So will talk about his recent visit to India. A sorority invites Miss Blank who won a gold medal in Olympic competition to a coffee hour. Obviously Mr. So-and-So's trip and Miss Blank's Olympic achievement prescribe each speaker's subject. Few listeners in either place will be deeply informed or consumingly interested in either India or Olympic competition. Most will be there chiefly to see the traveler or the champion. The traveler has to say things in a fairly formal way because of the structure of his situation. Miss Blank will doubtless be asked to "tell us" at some point or points during the coffee hour. But in both places the speaker's task will be to give special information in popular terms that will satisfy the listeners' casual curiosity. This dictates that each should be prepared to give prominence to whatever is most colorful, most human, most tantalizing about the prescribed subject. Whatever discourse has these characteristics is almost certain to be entertaining. It need not be as objective or as comprehensive as a speech on India or Olympic competition prepared with a purpose of informing.

Distinctive Aspects

From what we have said, one may draw several important inferences. (1) *Speech that entertains differs from other speech primarily in the way subject matter is treated.* The more agreeable and diverting the amplification and delivery of ideas, the more entertaining speech will be. The difference between informing, inquiring, and persuading on the one hand and entertaining on the other is chiefly a difference of manner, not of matter. (2) A second inference is that *to be entertaining a speaker must regard the pleasure of his audience more highly than the logic of his subject.* This does not mean that to be entertaining one must be inaccurate; on the contrary, accuracy at least in some details is essential. What arrests us is usually some disproportion of attention to specific details: detailed attention to the colorful garb of Indian women without much attention to, say, the social significance of their dress, or ludicrously detailed attention to the rigors of training for Olympic competition without much attention to the results of it.   The entertaining speaker must remember that the interesting *parts* of his subject are often more important than the *whole*.   It is in this sense that he sacrifices the logic of his subject to the pleasure of his audience.   (3) A third inference to be drawn about speaking to entertain is that *although good humor is always entertaining, entertainment does not necessarily hinge upon the presence of humor*.   This inference has been amplified by our earlier examples.

Since it is the *treatment* of material that makes speech entertaining, you will want to give special attention to stylistic resources in developing speech to entertain.   (See chapter 9, pages 246–79.) However, to create entertaining language you first find ideas that lend themselves to entertaining treatment.   Once again, a review of the attributes things and people possess and the relationships that may exist among these attributes (pp. 94–95) can suggest potentially entertaining thoughts.   Any attribute of anything has potentially humorous possibilities if examined in enough detail or distorted in some fashion. Charlie Brown and Lucy and Linus in the comic strip "Peanuts" constantly create humor by treating the *existence, nonexistence, forms,* and *possibilities* of things absurdly.   George Bernard Shaw played trenchantly but amusingly with the attribute of *degree* and with *causality* when addressing students at the University of Hong Kong:

> That war [World War I] was made by people with university education. There are really two dangerous classes in the world.   There are the half-educated, who have destroyed one-half of civilization, and there are the wholly educated, who have nearly completely destroyed the world.[10]

The Reverend Richard Whately, Anglican Bishop of Dublin and also an able rhetorician, developed an entertaining refutation to arguments denying that Jesus lived by applying the tests of *possibility, causality,* and *existence* too strictly to the life of Napoleon.   He thereby proved that Napoleon could not have lived.[11]   "The Conspiracy Against Lefty" was the title of one of several delightful, informal talks we have heard left-handed students make by exaggerating (while preserving some realism) what it is like to be left-handed in a right-handed world.   The young woman who alleged "conspiracy" deftly jumbled *causes* and *possibilities* together when she established that the entire horse-breeding, training, and equipping industry is managed by "right-wing

---

10. "Universities and Education," delivered February 12, 1933.   Reported in *The New York Times,* March 26, 1933.   Note Shaw's exaggeration—one of the most common techniques for creating humor.

11. *Historic Doubts Relative to Napoleon Bonaparte* (1819).

plotters" who "brainwash" every newborn foal to resent all left-handed persons who try to approach in "a natural and convenient manner." Any subject—idea, person, object, experience—has or can be given amusing relationships to other ideas, persons, objects, or experiences. It is for amusingly *conceivable* attributes and relations that entertaining speakers hunt when their special goal is to amuse.

Interrelated Points Concerning Entertaining

Three other, interrelated points need to be made concerning the content of speech that entertains. They can be stated briefly, but their importance is considerable.

1. *Only in entertainment is it sometimes advantageous to make no sense.* Sometimes the nonsensical bears just enough similarity to the sensible to amuse us. Here lies much of the fun of Lewis Carroll's *Alice in Wonderland* and David Brenner's outrageous "analyses" of noses, air travel, and South Philadelphia customs.
2. *What entertains in speaking is that which is quickly and easily understood.* Private jokes or asides and private experiences are not entertaining. In entertaining speech all meaning is public— familiar and easily grasped. Even nonsense must contain a semblance to sense, or the response is not amusement, only bafflement. It is true that working puzzles can be entertaining, but puzzling speech is not. The reason is that speech moves swiftly through time, leaving listeners no opportunity to work puzzles as they appear.
3. *An entertaining speaker may properly disregard or even do violence to the natural logic of his subject, but he will please his hearers best if his speech has some kind of thematic logic.* This will give the audience the satisfaction of having been pleased by *something*, not just some *things*. Even the nightclub gag man recognizes this audience demand for structure in entertainment. If artful, he will separate his mother-in-law jokes from his insurance-company jokes, giving each group the status of a thought unit within his patter. As though further adapting to the preferences of modern audiences, more and more comedians now develop entire monologues around single themes treated humorously. In so doing they emulate the practice of the best among entertaining speech makers.

Entertainment can be used without being the dominant objective of a speech. Comprehensive speech of serious intent certainly can contain subordinate units of entertainment, provided they do not becloud the serious content.

In closing our three-chapter survey of how content for speeches is discovered and selected we have examined the special opportunities and difficulties that arise when you set out to inform, induce inquiry, reinforce beliefs or feelings, persuade, or entertain. We have seen that some of these special purposes limit the range of ideas from which you may draw content, and that each kind of purpose imposes its special manner of treating ideas after they are found. If any generalization is to be drawn from our survey in this chapter, it must be that you cannot be wholly successful until you have determined your specific purpose in speaking. Without understanding your specific task you cannot know what materials are useful to you nor can you know precisely how to treat them.

It would be an error to infer from what we have said that mixed purposes never occur in good speech. Informing, persuading, and entertaining, for example, can all be found in almost all first-rate speech. But if speech is first-rate, one purpose will dominate, nor will there be any confusion about which purpose dominates any *part* of the speech. If your primary intention is to persuade, your informing sections will have the features of informative speaking but will plainly serve your dominant persuasive intention by providing a base for it. Entertaining subsections will provide momentary diversion without distorting your information-giving processes or demeaning the importance of your persuasive content.

EXERCISES

Written

1. Write a brief essay on differences between speech materials that prove propositions and those that amplify ideas.
2. Choose a general topic such as "The Cost of Living" or "Clothing" and outline three kinds of speeches that could be given on some aspect of the topic. For example, outline a persuasive, an informative, and an entertaining speech on "The Cost of Food Is Rising."
3. Read a speech of your own choosing and write a critique in which you:
   a. Identify what seems to have been the speaker's dominant purpose in speaking.
   b. Identify any subsections of the speech in which the purpose of communication seems to have shifted temporarily (e.g., from a dominant purpose of informing to a subordinate purpose of entertaining or persuading).
   c. Evaluate the speaker's success in making shifts from primary to secondary aims and back to his primary aim. (Did he indicate to his listeners that he was shifting purpose? Did he indicate why he was doing this? How successful was he in keeping his dominant purpose clear despite temporary shifts? Was the total impact of his speech strengthened or weakened by temporary changes in purpose? If weakened, how might this effect have been avoided?)

Oral

1. With two other members of your class choose a simple topic such as earth, tools, or books. Let each member of the group prepare and give to the class a two-minute talk that makes three points about the chosen topic, one talk giving information, another persuading, and the third entertaining. Afterward compare and contrast the different kinds of materials each speaker used and the different ways he or she had to use them.

2. Prepare and give to your class a short speech of inquiry on a question such as "What is the best way we could conduct our class to get helpful feedback from the audience in our next formal speeches?" When you have opened the problem and suggested directions in which a solution might be sought, preside over a class discussion seeking to devise a plan for handling feedback and criticism during a forthcoming set of classroom speeches.

3. Among the more difficult topics on which to inform are those in which abstract or aesthetic concepts have to be made clear. For practice with this kind of speaking prepare and give a two-minute talk on how people should go about understanding or appreciating some specific artistic object (a statue, piece of jewelry, architectural form, bit of poetry, or other).

4. Prepare and present an oral report on the kinds of content used in some speech to entertain. Indicate also what special treatment was given this content. (Speeches by Mark Twain or Will Rogers or recordings by such entertainers as Mort Sahl or Bob Newhart could be chosen for this exercise.)

5. Prepare and present a brief talk on one of the following subjects or some variation on one of them:
   a. It is unwise for speakers trying to inform to color their content with extensive use of personal opinions.
   b. A speaker seeking to persuade needs to reveal his or her own attitudes toward subject matter.
   c. Some differences between appropriately expressing attitudes toward information in speeches seeking to induce inquiry and speeches seeking to persuade.
   d. Kinds of proof especially useful in reinforcing beliefs in the value of the family (or any other subject you choose).

6. With four or five colleagues assess why some allegedly good speaker failed in a major attempt at persuasion. (Certain campaign speeches by, say, Adlai Stevenson, Jimmy Carter, or Gerald Ford might be examined. Or you might consider a television editorial you have recorded, or any other short unit of oral persuasion.) When your group has completed its assessment, organize a group presentation like that illustrated in appendix B. Your purpose, as a group, could be either to persuade your class that your group's judgment is "right" or just to inform them of what happened. As you plan your group presentation, pay attention to the specific purposes of your different speakers and to the different materials each needs to accomplish his or her specific purpose.

Disposition: Organizing Materials

. . . form is the creation of an appetite in the mind of the auditor, and the adequate satisfying of that appetite.

Kenneth Burke, "Psychology and Form"[1]

In his book *The Image*, Kenneth E. Boulding points out that a modern view of physical processes assumes an ever-present tendency "for things to run down." He continues, "The end of the universe, according to this picture, will be a thin, uniform soup without form. It is toward this comfortless end that all physical processes are moving." By contrast, Boulding insists, the record of history exhibits another tendency, "the tendency for the rise of organization":

> It is the capacity for organizing information into large and complex images which is the chief glory of our species. . . . Our image of time . . . goes far beyond that of the most intelligent of lower animals, mainly because of our capacity for language and for record. . . . Closely associated with the time structure of his [man's] image is the image of the structure of relationships. Because we are aware of time, we are also aware of cause and effect, of contiguity and succession, of cycles and repetition.[2]

The organization of an oral message is the application of this distinctive human capacity and appetite for organizing our environment into ideas we want to give to other people. This is more easily said than done.

---

1. From Kenneth Burke, *Counter-Statement,* originally published in *The Dial* LXXIX (July 1925): 34–36, quoted from Morton D. Zabel, ed., *Literary Opinion in America* (New York: Harper & Row, Publishers, 1962), II, p. 668.
2. Kenneth E. Boulding, *The Image* (Ann Arbor: University of Michigan Press, 1956), p. 25. See chapter 2, "The Image in the Theory of Organization."

The thought of a swimming pool, in your mind, may be encrusted with what are *for you* memories of friendships made while relaxing beside the pool; pleasing sensations of cool water on hot days; cookouts; and so on. But you can never implant this entire cluster of remembrances in anyone else's mind. The elements of the cluster must be detached from one another. They must be verbalized in some sequence that allows the other person to create another cluster of images and sensations comparable to yours. This he or she must do out of (1) your message and (2) his or her own experiences. The more special and private the images and relationships you present, the more difficult it will be for your listener to associate them with his or her experiences. Yet, to communicate with one another at all we must combat these difficulties. For important communication, that takes planning and careful organization.

DEMANDS FOR ORGANIZATION

Happily, in most matters that we speak about publicly we can cast our ideas in structured forms that reveal their internal natures. That we share conceptions of the relationships we call time, cause, effect, contiguity, cyclical succession, and repetition makes it possible to communicate at least our basic experiences and thoughts. Even listeners with poor perceptions can see relationships if we organize our thoughts with careful regard for the patterns all men are accustomed to. A speaker must invariably remember, however, that (1) listeners do not take in as much detail as readers, so the speaker must show relationships very plainly; (2) the object of all effort to organize ideas for public speech is to shape the speaker's thought into patterns that a particular audience will recognize; (3) it is foolish to try to organize the ideas before most of them have been located and the specific purpose has been identified.

Audiences insist that they be helped to understand what a speaker says. Listeners naturally wish to see the interrelationships among ideas. They like to know which ideas are primary and which are subsidiary and to be able to detect the rationale behind the overall pattern. When you depart from an order of thought anticipated by your listener or from an apparently logical order of thoughts, you had better explain why; otherwise your hearer will find the flow of thought chaotic. He or she may suspect you of deliberately trying to mislead.

Listeners lose interest when discourse does not seem to be advancing toward a psychologically meaningful goal. Because they are human beings with a need to organize, listeners demand progression and a sense of constructive variety. They want cumulative, psychologically satisfying effects. A speech, then, must build, point by point. Somewhere a climax must be reached. This high point is usually near the end of the discourse, but it may and sometimes does occur earlier. In either case it will be psychologically satisfying if points along the way are given time, detailed development, and intensity proportionate to their relative weights within the total structure. Listeners anticipate that somewhere in your speech all the necessary information will be in, all arguments developed to the point of acceptability. They expect, in short, that all roads will lead to Rome. In this they are simply displaying the chief glory of their species.

Not all decisions about organization of oral communication derive from the natures of audiences. Some ought to depend on your own responses to the structure of your ideas. If you find your plan too complicated to use easily, you have probably created a poor organizational structure. Uncertainty about organization is often a main cause for lack of confidence in yourself and your materials. It is only when you are satisfied that *you* understand how each piece of supporting material is related to each other piece that you will be able to proceed with assurance.

Content can impose patterns of organization, too. Once material is discovered and gathered, you will begin to sort it. Sorting may show that materials such as anecdotes, questions, examples, and statistics tend to group under a particular set of topics or arguments. Thus, materials about topography or scenery will lend themselves to spatial organization, producing description. Historical materials may virtually demand to be handled in narrative, chronological form.

How materials ought to be weighted in relation to one another may also be determined by your research. As you move through the inventional processes we discussed in chapters 4, 5, and 6, you may evolve an image of your speech that will have to be changed when you undertake to structure all you know. You may be startled by how little there is to say about a pet idea, for example. Then you have the choice of discarding a seemingly weak contention or of backtracking to search for new information.

More often, you will find that you have too much material for the available speaking time. Upon sifting and sorting data you may discover that you have support for twelve or thirteen significant ideas. You may then discard those ideas that are least fruitful, those least likely to gain audience acceptance, those least necessary for your purpose. On the other hand, you may decide to regroup and reorganize your material. Very often when material seems to yield too many main points the problem is that secondary ideas are being mistaken for broader ones and ought to be used as support or amplification for the larger concepts.

The processes of elimination or reorganization may seem painful. You may have to cut your speech repeatedly. Should you discover that your speaking time has been encroached upon by unforeseeable circumstances, you must sacrifice still more material and do it without destroying form. It happens even to the famous. Franklin Roosevelt found it necessary to cut his 1932 speech accepting the presidential nomination. The plane in which he flew from Albany to Chicago was hours late, which meant that he would appear before an audience wearied by waiting to hear him. He wisely decided that his speech would have to be shorter than he had planned. Samuel Rosenman, who assisted him with the speech, writes:

> With each radio report, we were falling further and further behind schedule; and more and more paragraphs came out of the acceptance speech. This lopping off of material on which we had worked so long and so hopefully was a painful process. I know that there were some jewels dropped on the airplane floor that day. It is likely, though, that the cutting process hurt us more than it did the speech.[3]

Such may be your feeling; yet rejection and red-pencilling will often result in conciseness and sharper focus. The tightening that comes from excision usually enhances the organic unity of a speech.

Often regrouping is less difficult than it at first seems. Many good speakers insist that the fewer points in a speech, the better. If you are giving a short speech, you ordinarily ought to assume you have time to develop three or four main points at most.

By slicing your material in a new way those twelve or thirteen points will fit under three or four main heads. One or two of the thirteen may now appear expendable; others will probably prove to have been subpoints all along. If you keep the audience in mind, you will realize that two or three points acceptably substantiated are more valuable for most purposes than a half-dozen points lightly touched and dropped.

Arrangement of main points according to strength deserves serious consideration. When you have decided upon the points to be amplified or supported, questions arise about their placement. Knowing that audiences are likely to pay closer attention and to be least tired during the early part of a speech argues for putting your strongest point first. But knowing that listeners are also likely to remember the ideas they have heard most recently argues for placing your strongest point last. As we indicated in chapter 3, despite numerous experiments, there are no rules by which you should choose between these alternatives.[4] All you can be sure of is that the first and last positions in any series are more impressive than the other positions. Therefore, it is sensible to place ideas of less importance in the intermediate positions.

---

3. Samuel I. Rosenman, *Working with Roosevelt* (New York: Harper & Brothers, 1952), p. 75.

4. Ernest Thompson, "Some Effects of Message Structure on Listeners' Comprehension," *Speech Monographs* XXXIV (March 1967): 51–57.

Experienced speakers employing three points favor placing them in 1-3-2 or 2-3-1 orders of strength. In dealing with four points they favor 1-3-4-2, 1-4-3-2, 2-3-4-1, or 2-4-3-1 orders of strength. Your final decision has to be one of *judgment*. It ought to rest on whether special features of content or situation lead you to "bet" that primacy or recency will here be the position of greatest emphasis for your particular audience.

Although we usually think of organization or disposition of entire speeches, the principles of clear organization also operate for the various points within discourse. If you use narrative, chronological order is almost inescapable. Interrupting narrative for expressions of personal opinion almost always diverts attention from the main movement of thought. Yet, there may be circumstances where spontaneous insertion of definitions or other clarifying details is necessary if you are to adapt to your audience. The questions to be asked about any break in an established order of ideas are: "Is this departure relevant? Will this deviation from the thought pattern *help* to achieve my purpose?"

Occasions and settings influence organization of ideas less often than do audience, speaker, and material. The occasion may require initial acknowledgments or personal greetings, but these are minor adaptations. A setting may also more severely narrow your choice. For example, a Washington's birthday celebration may call for a eulogy of George Washington. Speakers have found that eulogies are successful when the praise of the man is structured by recounting incidents in his life or describing his traits of character. When speakers depart from a pattern because the occasion itself is unexpectedly changed by some distraction such as the rattle of jackhammers outside the window, a sudden power failure, or the unexpected appearance of an important personage, modification of the message is as much a matter of audience adaptation as of adaptation to the occasion.

Plainly the disposition of ideas, their orderly arrangement, is not random. Nor can it be done by rule. Organizational choices are wisely made only after careful consideration of the audience's expectations; the speaker's capabilities; the nature of the data used to achieve the speaker's purpose; and, incidentally, the circumstances prevailing at the time of delivery.

MAIN COMPONENTS OF A SPEECH

The number of *parts of a speech* has been an issue of debate for centuries. Today's convention is that a speech should have an introduction, body, and conclusion *unless* there are strong reasons for building it otherwise. The proportions of these parts depend upon the subject matter, the situation, and the speaker himself, but most often they depend upon the audience's expectations and motivations. There will also need to be clear connections that link the three main portions. These linking parts are transitions. A speech has a beginning, a middle, an end, and internal transitional elements. We will consider these separately.

Introductions

The introduction to any speech or series of interrelated speeches ought to establish the relationship of what is to be said to the rhetorical situation. Since the introduction is a beginning it must (1) attract the initial, favorable attention of the audience; (2) provide necessary background for the audience so they may comprehend what follows; (3) be suitable to the occasion; and (4) contribute to your own ease during a crucial period of adjustment. In addition, the introduction ought to be coordinated with and must relate to the body of the speech. It is not a preamble nor a prelude without relation to what follows.

At the outset you must gain attention in such a way that your listeners will want to go on listening. Any of the methods for achieving attention may be employed, but the most useful ways are to refer to something familiar or something novel. You may start with a reference to the occasion, to its purpose, or to other things about which the audience already knows. You may begin with greetings, an anecdote, or analogy. Tradition may dictate what you will say at the beginning. Or you may need to awaken the audience by sharpening the focus of their attention. Where this is so, unusual facts or stories, shocking or startling assertions, unfamiliar statistics, telegraphic headline fragments, or other striking materials may enable you to create curiosity or suspense. Reference to your own interests and needs, especially if they are similar to those of your audience, may create common ground and cause your audience to want to listen. A modest statement of your qualifications for speaking on the subject you have chosen can make your listeners want to hear more.

Most audiences want to be given reasons for listening. They are always ready to ask, "Why should *I* listen? What's in this for *me?*" Often, they want directions about what to listen for. The ways in which you can touch off an audience's powers of concentration are limitless; yet none is truly useful unless it will at once seize attention and favorably dispose your audience to what follows.

It is often essential for you to provide background knowledge your hearers must have from the outset. It may be necessary to provide preliminary information about new materials, details you will use in amplification, or the relationships between main points and your central proposition.   Such basic information may be provided by way of a preview that will furnish a context for what you are going to say.

If you will look at Joe's introduction to his group's presentation in appendix B (page 391), at Dr. Upcraft's introduction to his speech (paragraphs 1–4, pp. 391–92), and at Kathy's analysis of Upcraft's introduction, you will see most of the functions we have just enumerated being carried out, then pointed to by Kathy. The function given least attention by Joe and by Dr. Upcraft was attracting attention to the subject.   Given their situations, this is understandable.   The classroom group was *scheduled;* the audience knew beforehand that the group was to present a critique, although the listeners did not know what speech was to be examined nor did they know Dr. Upcraft, himself, would be present.   It was background and indications of how the group's subject related to the audience that Joe needed chiefly to focus on.   Before his audience Dr. Upcraft scarcely needed to establish attention because the meeting he addressed was about his subject.   More for his own purposes than for the audience's feelings or interest, he needed to give the historical background of the policy he had to defend. He needed also to acknowledge the audience's invitation to him, which he did in a single sentence.   However, in neither Joe's nor Dr. Upcraft's situation was there need to do what you may have to do in a classroom speech: draw an audience's attention *away* from other things *to* a subject for which only you can prepare it.

The subject matter with which a speaker deals may require that special kinds of material be included in an introduction.   It may be necessary to define unfamiliar terms to be used later, or to define familiar terms so the audience will understand special meanings you plan to assign to them.   A short, historical review such as Dr. Upcraft offered may help.   For him history set the context within which the policy he must defend emerged.   In other circumstances where argument from precedent is involved or where your subject is one that listeners have not thought a great deal about, it is useful to employ a history of the question.

Definitions and histories are sometimes supplemented or replaced by statements of those matters you will or will not deal with in the body of your speech.   Items so singled out because you intend to pass them over or because they seem irrelevant are often called *waived materials*.   You simply state that you will not consider them and give your listeners your reasons.   Giving main points to be developed later by amplification or support is what the Romans called *division;* today it is sometimes called *initial partition*.   The tactic is useful when your audience needs to know the path you intend to take.   Of course, you would not offer such statements if you wished to preserve suspense or feared that revealing your entire plan so early might make some listeners defensive.   Initial partitioning is not a useful introductory tactic in speeches developed inductively or in those designed for unfriendly audiences.   There, even the subject sentence is often withheld until the end.

In speeches constructed on a deductive pattern you ought to include the subject sentence of your speech as a final item of your introduction or as an initial item in the body of the speech.   As we have already said, the subject sentence is delayed in most indirect sequences.   Wherever it appears it ought to be carefully expressed in a single, economical, unambiguous sentence, as was pointed out in chapters 2 and 5.

Not all the items we have mentioned will be included in any one introduction.   What your listeners *need* to know before you proceed should dictate how much and what kinds of orientation material you offer.   In addition to the illustrative introductions in appendix B, an introduction for a speech appears in the exercise section of this chapter on page 219.   In each example you will find the speaker taking some of the steps we have just discussed, omitting others because of the nature of the situation, the subject matter, or the speaker's role in the situation.

The introduction is a part of the speech that, given the right circumstances, may be omitted altogether.   It is not necessary if an audience is already attentive and interested in your subject, if they expect you to speak, if they already possess the background information, if they are highly motivated, or if the occasion exerts no special pressures.   College professors can often dispense with introductions after the first few lectures.   If their audiences are oriented and motivated, introductory remarks become superfluous.   You, however, should be cautious about omitting introductions.   Rarely can an introduction be omitted when you speak to an audience for the first time; never, when your audience is not entirely ready to pay attention from the outset.

Body of the Speech

The body of a speech comprises (1) the main points, (2) the material that supports or amplifies these points, and (3) transitional phrases or sentences.   The same requirements hold for a group presentation of a subject.   Consider the extent to which Kathy, Ron, Patti, Greg, and Stephanie fulfilled these obligations in presenting the body of their group's report (see pages 395–98).

Earlier we discussed sorting and sifting materials to arrive at main points and determine their psychological weighting and placement.[5]   When these stages of preliminary analysis have been completed and you know your main points, you next word the main ideas.

---

5. See pp. 194–95.

Where possible, main points ought to be worded in parallel phrasings to provide balance, thus making them easier to remember. They should also be worded to elicit the responses you seek from your audience. Main points for informative speeches should be simple, clear assertions. In speeches of inquiry the main points are often worded as questions that are then explored or answered with information. Main points for persuasive speeches should be assertions, slanted in wording to express your point of view and to support the main proposition embodied in your subject sentence. These main points should be *contentions* or reasons closely linked to the subject sentence so they become the foundation stones upon which the core idea rests. Main points for speeches of reinforcement are framed in essentially the same ways as those for speeches of persuasion. For speeches designed to entertain, main points again take the form of assertions.

In all cases the final form of your main points should respond to the interrelated demands of the material, the audience, and your habitual mode of expression. The ways of arranging these main points into patterns are discussed later in this chapter. Under the discussions of the various patterns you will also find some examples of wordings for the different purposes.

Transitions[6]

Listeners cannot easily review what you have said after it has been spoken, as they might turn back and reread the pages in a book. Therefore, you will need to provide careful transitions if your speech is to be clear at all points. *Transitions* are words, phrases, sentences, or groups of sentences that join ideas together. If clear and smooth, they contribute to the organic unity and the clarity of your speech.

Transitions are like signposts. They tell your audience where you have been, where you are, or where you intend to go. They are most frequently needed at the completion of a main idea, before you move on to the next one; but you may also need them as connections between subsidiary points or phrases leading to the ideas in single sentences.

· Since we have already considered that . . . , we should adopt . . . .
· In addition to . . . there is another outstanding reason (element, factor, consideration, fact) . . . .
· We have seen . . . , yet it remains for us to observe . . . .
· But . . . is only one important viewpoint. Equally important is . . . .

----

6. This section is based in part upon an explanation of transitions originally written by Harry P. Kerr, University of Maine, Farmington, Maine. Used by permission.

· Since . . . is so, what can be said of . . . ?   (Questions can often be useful as transitions.)

Where the thought connection to be emphasized is between subpoints, or where the thought relationships are easy to comprehend, a phrase or even a single word such as *so* or *yet* may be adequate to tie ideas together.   Some examples of such phrasings are:

· More important than all this is the fact that . . . .
· In contrast to . . . .
· Looked at from a different angle the problem seems to be . . . .
· This last point raises a question: . . . ?
· What was the result?   Just this . . . .
· On the other hand . . . .
· When this has been done . . . .
· And so you can see that . . . .

When more than one person participates in presenting a report or argument, transitions become very important as the flow of talk shifts from one speaker to another.   If the speakers' total message is to hold together for the listeners and have strong impact on them, it is necessary that someone emphasize how the several parts of the pre- sentation relate to one another.   Sometimes this is done by having a chairperson make transitional connections between subtopics developed by different speakers; sometimes, as in the presentation in appendix B, it is left to the speakers who precede and follow one another.   Either way, good transitions here or within individual speeches should (1) show that communication is moving from one idea to another, (2) demarcate completed ideas, (3) indicate the relationships between the ideas involved, and (4) remind speaker and listener of the overall sequence of thought.

Seek variety in transitions.   Avoid using only stock phrases or repeating the same few phrases over and over.   Although you should not be afraid to be obvious in your transitions, you should avoid being too brief.   A mark of an unpolished speaker is his tendency to use only *and, also,* or *like* as transitions.   He gives the impression of having tacked his ideas together, of having joined them to one another care- lessly.   Yet he is in a better position than the speaker who melts from point to point or vaguely gropes his way from topic to topic.

Conclusions

The final segment of your speech, its conclusion, performs functions demanded by the audience, the material, the occasion, and yourself.   In this segment the audience normally expects at least (1) a restatement of your core idea or (2) a summing up of main points that clarify or prove your thesis. Both restatement and summary may be needed. Almost any body of material needs a final rounding out that fuses subject matter with intent. To emphasize a detail or simply to fade into silence obscures meaning. The audience should not feel at the end of a speech that they have been left hanging, that the speech ended too abruptly, or that the subject is still up in the air. *The final moments of a speech ought to be used to drive home the core idea.* The audience should know that you have finished, and you should feel satisfied that you have accomplished your purpose and produced an intended final impact. This does not mean that your final sentence ought always to be a restatement or summary. True, recapitulation is the main function of most conclusions, but one's last sentences are often strongest if devised to challenge the audience to further thought or action or to operate as a coda to one's central theme. Final sentences may echo the beginning sentences or constitute a return to a text or refrain, thus providing a frame for all you have said. A "thank you" at the end of a speech may detract from the central idea and an otherwise strong final impression. Indeed, any remarks of appreciation used as last sentences ought to be carefully considered since they may destroy the focus of an otherwise effective conclusion.

Joe's conclusion (appendix B, p. 398) illustrates some general and special points about concluding a presentation. This conclusion would have been more effective if Joe had reviewed *which* rhetorical processes his group had shown contributed most to Dr. Upcraft's rhetorical achievement. He neglected this and so missed the opportunity to reinforce the group's findings. Not unlike many other speakers, Joe had the additional concluding task of controlling *what was to happen next.* He could have been far more incisive in directing the next happenings. Did he want Dr. Upcraft to respond to the criticism or did he want questions from the audience? He left this unclear. Fortunately Dr. Upcraft chose to make some impromptu responses. This particular example should remind you that in concluding any communication you need to make sure—by what you say—that you leave the rhetorical situation exactly as your purpose requires.

As we have said elsewhere, it is conceivable that you will speak in a few situations where you need not utter concluding words. These circumstances will be rare. The most common ones are those in which someone else will conclude what you have said very briefly, as when one person explains that the treasury is empty, knowing that a colleague will immediately make an appeal for money. Dr. Upcraft had the special circumstance that a hearing would continue. He had only to be available, having spoken.

Introduction, subject sentence, body, transitions, and conclusion will, with rare exceptions, be parts of every speech you will deliver, although they may be cast in different designs from speech to speech. It remains for us to consider the most common structures or designs employed in arranging materials.

EFFECTIVE PATTERNS OF ORGANIZATION[7]

Four conditions will usually determine the most appropriate pattern for a given speaking situation: (1) the particular type and degree of response you seek from the audience; (2) whether the audience is favorably, unfavorably, or apathetically disposed toward your subject, your central idea, and you as a speaker; (3) how much knowledge your listeners possess about your subject; (4) how you can best relate your specific purpose to the pertinent interests and desires of your audience.

The standard *patterns* commonly used in structuring ideas in practical speaking include: (1) chronological, (2) spatial, (3) topical, (4) ascending and descending orders, (5) causal, (6) problem-solution or disease-remedy, (7) withheld proposal or indirect sequence, (8) open proposal or direct sequence, (9) reflective sequence or pattern of inquiry, (10) Monroe's motivated sequence, and (11) elimination order. Each is explained in some detail below.

Patterns may be thought of as primarily logical or primarily psychological. The chronological, spatial, topical, causal, and problem-solution are structures that are primarily logical. Ascending and descending orders, withheld- and open-proposal sequences, and elimination order are methods that may be considered primarily psychological. The reflective sequence and Monroe's sequence are at once logical and psychological in that they adapt material to audiences psychologically by offering it in a problem-solution structure.

We make these distinctions to show you that psychological patterns of audience adaptation may be superimposed upon logical patterns. For example, ascending or descending orders may come into play as you arrange ideas topically or spatially. In like manner elimination order may be employed in treating causes, effects, or possible solutions. In some instances two psychological orders can be used in handling a particular logical arrangement. For example, ascending and

---

7. The descriptions of the cause-effect, problem-solution, withheld proposal, and open-proposal patterns in this section are based upon explanations originally written by James A. Wood of the University of Texas, El Paso. Donald E. Williams, University of Florida, prepared the original explanation of the reflective sequence. Used by permission.

withheld-proposal orders may be used as you develop a topical pattern.

Patterning ideas is not an either-or affair; it is a matter of clar-ifying psychological and logical relationships by adding the meanings of various structural systems to the basic meanings of speech content.

You should bear in mind that a pattern need not be followed rigidly or in its entirety to be useful as a general scheme for organizing materials. It may be used for the organization of a whole speech, for only a particular segment, or for a relatively brief statement you might make in a discussion. For example, in a speech you might have a chronologically arranged section within the introduction and a problem-solution arrangement in the body; or you might have a cause-effect pat-tern for the problem section of a problem-solution speech. Generally speaking, introductions ought to be organized independently of the bodies of speeches, and the conclusions usually reflect the patterns of organization used in the bodies of speech materials they conclude.

Chronological Pattern

The *chronological pattern* is a time order, enumerating occur-rences in the sequence in which they happened or giving directions in the order to be followed in carrying them out. Material will often dictate this kind of ordering. Chronology, an order most useful in recounting events, is almost mandatory in narration. Chronological patterns may be used in all kinds of speech units. They are used com-monly in connection with informative purposes. A time sequence usually allows climactic development, arousing curiosity and creating suspense. Segments of speeches chronologically developed can be found in the narrations of circumstances leading to crime in Clarence Darrow's famous summation at the trial of Loeb and Leopold, or in Daniel Webster's classic speech for the prosecution in the Knapp-White murder case. William Armstrong (pp. 148–49) used a short narra-tive (chronology) as a means of amplifying how different receiving a literary prize was from the unfulfilled dreams of his childhood. Within the total structure of the group presentation in appendix B, Patti and Greg (pp. 396–97) develop their particular points by following the line-by-line or time sequence of Upcraft's speech. In many eulogies, speeches of nomination, historical lectures, demonstrations, and in-structional discourses, the entire body of the speech is chronologically organized.

One weakness of chronological patterning is that important con-siderations such as cause, effect, desirability, and form cannot easily be emphasized without interrupting the movement in time that gives chronology its chief interest value.

The *spatial pattern,* as the name implies, is a structure based on the relationships of parts of a whole as they exist in space. In building such a pattern you proceed systematically, describing how something looks or functions. Normally you will describe from left to right, top to bottom, bottom to top, or front to back. Sometimes you will describe by moving from that portion at the center to those on the periphery. For instance, you might describe the control panel in an airplane by pointing first to those centered instruments most often used before moving out toward the surrounding instruments less frequently used. You would then be using a pattern of descending importance, which happens here to become identical with the pattern of spatial description. In all spatial arrangements you will need to mention each part or aspect *according to plan;* haphazard coverage makes spatial relationships hard to understand.

Spatial structure is especially useful in giving information. A space rocket on its launching pad might be described from top to bottom, a painting from right to left, the floor plan of a house from front to back or story to story. The order in which to proceed when describing spatially will ordinarily be up to you. Your decision on which space portion to take up first ought to hinge on your estimation of how you can be clearest for your audience while highlighting the important relationships among parts. If these standards leave you more than one good way of describing spatially, choose the one that is easiest for *you* to present.

The *topical pattern* is really one in which there is no easily labeled speech structure. The label *topical* is assigned to organizational schemes we cannot otherwise account for. Some call them *classification orders* to denote that some kind of orderly categorization accounts for the patterning. Some would say topical patterns are those that arise from the subject matter, that these are patterns evolving out of the natural parts of the subject, its aspects, types, or qualities. The word *topical* gives us a clue. A communicator trying to order his ideas asks himself where the places are to which we go for argument or clarification and comes up with an answer such as: "We often look at social, political, or economic aspects of arguments." Thus he *invents* a *special* classification of materials. It may be only one of several schemes of organizing data. Another might have been: public interests versus private interests. Dr. Upcraft (pp. 392–93) developed a series of aspects of his policy problem from paragraphs 5 through 10. In the students' discussion of Upcraft's speech Ron presented two points that were: (1) use of examples and (2) Upcraft's argument that the university had no choice. The points are related only by the fact that they both "redirect the hostility," and in that sense they constitute topics of proof.

In this way we think of the topics we might use, select from them; and they, as we choose to arrange them, become the bases for organizing ideas. A topical pattern is an arbitrary grouping of themes pertinent to a particular subject and speech purpose. It is adaptable to any purpose but inquiry. The only demand upon such a pattern is that the audience accept the divisions as reasonable and suitably comprehensive.

Ascending and Descending Orders

Should you choose to use *ascending* and *descending orders* you place patterns, aspects, types, or qualities in sequence according to their increasing or decreasing importance or familiarity. That is, you move from the most to the least important or from the most to the least familiar points or vice versa. You start with the strongest argument and move to the weakest or start with the weakest and move to the strongest. You may start on common ground and move into unfamiliar territory, or you may begin with an unusual aspect or argument and lead the audience to what they already know or to what is already uppermost in their minds. In the case of descending order, for example, you would explain how pulp is processed for the manufacture of paper by taking up the most commonly used process, the ground-wood process, and move through your speech to the soda, sulfite, and alkaline processes, which are used less frequently and are less familiar to most people. Similarly, in a speech on population control, the familiar argument that natural resources of the earth will soon be used up would precede less striking arguments about political and cultural consequences of an exploding population. If you simply reverse the sequence so less known or weaker arguments come first, you achieve ascending order.

Ascending-descending orders are suitable in speaking to inform, to persuade, or to reinforce. The pattern might also be adapted for use in a speech to entertain. The choice and construction of ascending and descending orders hinge on your judgments of the relative importance of your materials; on your estimate of what will help your listeners remember and give them a sense of climax; and, sometimes, on whether you have time to develop enough points to make ascent or descent psychologically meaningful.

Causal Sequences

Causal patterns are used in situations where one set of conditions is given as the cause for another set. In such cases you may begin with a given set of conditions as the cause and allege that these will produce certain results or effects; or you may take a given set of conditions as the effect and allege that these resulted from certain causes.

In most uses of this pattern the specific purpose is to urge elimination of those conditions that function as causes. To achieve this specific purpose, however, you may need to persuade your audience of one or more of these things: (1) that the effects are really undesirable to them; (2) that the alleged causes are truly responsible for these effects; and (3) that elimination of these causes will not result in other, undesirable consequences. The first two concerns must either be evident to the audience or must be proved. The third may sometimes be safely disregarded.

The most common use of this pattern is one in which a speaker points out that certain undesirable conditions (*effects*) now exist and then explains that these are caused by certain other conditions (*causes*). The speaker *may* carry his reasoning through a chain of two or more effect-cause relationships to get from the present undesirable effects to the cause he asks his audience to eliminate. This kind of development might run thus:

I. The nations of the world now spend billions of dollars on armaments. (Present undesirable effect.)
II. This money is spent because the people of the world live in perpetual fear of war and aggression. (Establishing first effect-to-cause relationship.)
III. People live in such fear because there is no international authority strong enough to prevent war. (Second effect-to-cause relationship establishes the real cause of the present undesirable conditions.)
IV. Billions of dollars and much warfare will be saved by establishing stronger authority in the United Nations. (Audience urged to adopt proposal eliminating prime cause and thereby eliminating effect.)

Frequently, a speaker will point out that certain existing conditions will cause undesirable effects in the future and so should be eliminated. The normal sequence is to begin with the present causes and then describe the anticipated future effects. Sometimes a more artistic sequence can be achieved by visualizing the future effects for the audience first, then linking these effects to the present undesirable causes. One might structure a unit of speech thus:

I. The world is drifting toward exhaustion of its fossil fuel supplies.
   (Future undesirable effects portrayed.)
II. This drift is caused by unmanaged consumption of these fuels.
   (Present conditions cause the future effects.)
III. Therefore, all nations should be required to submit fuel conserva-
   tion programs to a United Nations planning commission. (Appeal
   to audience to support a policy to eliminate present causes to avoid
   the future effects.)

Sometimes a speaker draws an analogy between a cause-effect
relationship and another similar cause-effect relationship already accepted by his or her audience:

I. At the present time essential human rights are being disregarded
   despite commitments to human rights in the United Nations
   Charter. (Establishing present conditions as a potential cause.)
II. Because the League of Nations failed to force Hitler and Mussolini
   to observe human rights they achieved an unchallenged power
   that allowed them to threaten the entire world. (Referring to a
   past cause-effect relationship.)
III. In a similar way country X's repressive policies could generate a
   world threat. (Drawing parallel undesirable effects from parallel
   causes.)
IV. Therefore, the United Nations should force X's obedience to the
   U.N. Charter's stipulations concerning human rights. (Appeal to
   audience to eliminate present causes to avoid future effects.)

Although causal patterns are generally used to advocate the re-
moval of some condition, they can be used to advocate that certain
conditions be encouraged. In this use you would show how something
desirable to your audience (effect) results from other things (causes);
therefore, they should set these causes in operation to secure the effect.
Such a pattern might run:

I. We want lower inflation rates in the United States. (Establishing
   condition, effect, as desirable to the audience.)
II. Diminished inflation is possible only if federal deficits are reduced.
   (Establishing a cause as capable of producing the desired effect.)
III. Therefore, let us insist upon smaller federal deficits. (Appeal for
   audience support for conditions designed to cause the desirable
   effects.)

Causal patterns are also often used in informing to describe the
relationships of parts of what is being explained, such as the causes of
inflation or the effects of X-rays on human tissue. On occasion,
speeches to reinforce and entertain are cast in this pattern.

Often the biggest difficulty in using causal patterns in either persuasive or informational speaking is making clear that a valid cause-effect relationship actually exists between the two sets of conditions. The demand to be met is primarily the listeners' need to see a clear and logical demonstration that genuine and significant (for them) causal relationships do exist. In turn, to use causal patterns requires that a speaker be capable of cogent thinking and that the materials used in the speech lend themselves to rational, casual development.

Problem-Solution Sequence

The *problem-solution pattern* presents an audience with a problem and proposes a way to solve it. This pattern is also called the *disease-remedy* or the *need-remedy pattern*. Here, you point first to the existence of a problem or evil and then offer a corrective program that will be (1) practicable and (2) desirable. The corrective program must be capable of being put into effect, and it must be capable of eliminating the problem or the evil in question. It must also be one that will not introduce new and worse evils of its own. This is an issue long debated regarding the control of nuclear weapons. Does the proposed control erode national sovereignty in ways more dangerous than nuclear arms?

The specific purpose of speaking in a problem-solution pattern is to urge listeners to adopt the conditions embodied in the solution. This type of organization usually serves well in the following situations.

1. When the audience is aware that a problem exists and is interested in finding a solution to it, you may advocate one solution as the best of several possible answers. Although you will generally describe the problem briefly, you will be primarily concerned with showing how your particular solution will solve the problem in the best possible way and how any alleged disadvantages of your solution may be avoided. This latter concern, avoiding new difficulties, will frequently involve you in anticipatory refutation, which means you will have to dispel arguments against your proposal even though they have not yet been advanced by anyone.

2. Where the audience is only dimly aware of a problem or need, the problem-solution pattern still serves well. Listeners can be made aware of the problem's exact nature; then, perhaps, the solution will become evident. This is what Dr. Upcraft does in paragraphs 4 through 9 of his speech in appendix B, pages 392–93. Here the goal is to focus listeners on crucial aspects of the problem. They must see that their interests are involved in both problem and solution. The concern is to show that a specific, serious problem does exist. When your

audience is not initially aware of their difficulty, it is unlikely that in a single speech you can do more than establish a precise sense of need; but not even in these circumstances can you disregard the solution section of your sequence completely. If you do, you will leave the hearers up in the air. You must at least indicate that there *are* ways of solving the problem.

     3. There are situations where the major concerns of both the preceding settings are combined. Sometimes you can carry your audience from awareness of a problem through to a readiness to act on a particular solution.

     Now your task is (1) to sharpen awareness of the problem and (2) to show why your solution is the most suitable. Such speech might be structured thus:

I. A serious problem of unemployment now exists in the United States. (Referring to felt need.)
  A. This problem poses a threat to our national economy. (Establishing importance of problem to audience.)
  B. This problem costs us millions of dollars in unemployment insurance. (Again, establishing importance of problem to audience.)
  C. The problem is particularly acute for those under twenty-five years of age. (Focusing felt need on particular audience.)
II. The problem of unemployment can be solved by providing jobs through government and private industry for those who need them. (Statement of solution to the problem.)
  A. With a government program that provides jobs that will do things such as rehabilitate slum areas, improve our national parks, and ease the work loads in government agencies, we can help solve the problem. (Showing *how* proposal will solve problem.)
  B. Private industries can also help by expanding plants so more jobs are available. (Also showing *how* proposal will solve problem.)
  C. Since both sectors of the economy will participate, the solution would not result in a socialistic system as some may fear. (Meeting objections to proposal.)

     Variations on the problem-solution pattern are sometimes used. One variation is that of alternating or staggering portions of a problem with portions of the solution. For example, the cost of a project may be seen as one aspect of a problem, the workability of the project as another. Finding time for the project may be a third. Taking each up in turn and providing the solutions for cost, workability, and time as you present these aspects of the problem may psychologically satisfy your audience better than if you had discussed all of the problem and then its total solution. A second variation occurs in informing, as when you *show how* people were faced by a problem and how they solved it. One might report how halfway houses came to be established to meet the problems faced by people seeking to overcome drug addiction. Or, like Dr. Upcraft in paragraphs 8 and 9, one may offer a solution already arrived at as the only one possible. The pattern may be used to inform even if the solution is not yet in effect, provided the answer has been decided and is no longer a question for debate. Problem-solution arrangements may also be adapted to reinforce belief and feeling or, more rarely, to entertain.

From what we have said it can be seen that problem-solution patterns are direct responses to audiences' needs. An audience must feel or be made to feel that a problem exists or that an evil is present before it will accede to a solution. Often the felt need will originate in you so you have the initial need for this pattern. When this is true you must make the audience feel that the needed action is justified in terms of their interests. Speech materials also affect your choice of this organizational pattern. They must be capable of being divided into clear-cut problems and solutions. The occasion will determine to some extent those items you select to depict a problem and to explain a solution. Thus, all forces in the communicative setting are at work in the final determination of how and whether a problem-solution pattern ought to be evolved.

Withheld Proposal or Indirect Sequence

The *withheld proposal* or *indirect sequence* presents individual cases or instances as the bases for a conclusion about additional members of the same class.

The most important characteristic of the indirect sequence is that when using this pattern you give your audience examples, or some basic assumptions and facts, before you present any generalized inferences or conclusions of your own.

This inductive pattern is especially useful when you speak to a hostile audience. Logically the pattern is usually inductive; psychologically it leads listeners gradually toward a conclusion. This is why it may be the only pattern that will enable you to persuade. It permits you to begin an argument with material your audience knows to be true or with assumptions they accept. A common ground of agreement is established with the audience; when inferences are drawn logically from these accepted materials, the audience must either attack the logic involved or admit that you may be right. This pattern is also effective because it reflects man's normal thinking processes—reasoning from examples and assumptions to reach decisions.

Indirectly structured speeches generally operate in one of two basic patterns. In the first a number of examples is given, and a generalization is inferred. The plan might be:

I. Our city was charged with polluting the lake by improper sewerage control during last year.

II. Regulation 73 on smoke abatement was enforced against only three companies in the city during the first six months of this year, although fourteen complaints were filed.

III. Days on which air pollution alerts were officially announced to city residents increased during the last six months by 35 percent over last year.

IV. Three of five retirees from the pollution-abatement office of the city were not replaced last year.

V. This city administration is not living up to its pledge to improve the quality of our physical environment.

In using this pattern it is essential that your induction meet your own and your listeners' logical tests for acceptable generalizations.

In a second type of indirect pattern you first give basic assumptions or premises acceptable to your audience; then you give the facts of the specific case about which you are speaking; finally you apply your basic premises to the specific case.

I. The property tax is our primary source of public support for education.

II. Property taxes have more than doubled since the 1960s.

III. The property tax particularly oppresses the elderly.

IV. The property tax oppresses low-income workers who own their own homes.

V. We have no choice but to redesign our tax structure.

Several specialized, indirect patterns usefully support central ideas. One of these is the *applied-criteria pattern* in which propositions of fact or value are argued by first setting up criteria or standards and then showing that the alleged fact or value matches them. Another specialized use of indirect presentation develops when what at first appears to be a pattern of inquiry (described below) concludes by showing or strongly implying that only one solution solves the problem. The so-called implicative pattern resembles an incomplete, indirect pattern in that description, narration, and exposition are used for persuasive purposes. Word pictures, stories, and explanations hint at conclusions. Arguments presented may or may not be stated in formal fashion. In any case, the method is implicative because the audience is left to draw its own final conclusion or application.

As we have noted, indirect sequences are useful in dealing with hostile audiences and where materials can be divided into acceptable and known, unacceptable and unknown. Concerns of speakers also invite use of this pattern. If you are more adept at presenting materials indirectly, in the soft-sell manner, than at approaching audiences directly, you may favor this pattern. Furthermore, indirect presentation is feasible regardless of the speaker's purpose.

Open Proposal or Direct Sequence

The *open-proposal* or *direct-sequence pattern* of organization is in one sense a deductive order and stands in contrast to the indirect sequence. In using this pattern you urge the audience to accept a proposition on the grounds that its validity, morality, or practicality necessarily follows from accepted axioms or principles.

The direct sequence is simple to use. Essentially, it consists of telling your audience what you intend to prove or explain and then giving the arguments or clarifications that support your thesis. On many occasions you will use several different arguments or divisions of clarification supporting your subject sentence, and these can be grouped into categories. A person advocating certain legislation might develop arguments showing it is morally right, legal under the constitution, of economic benefit, and practicable. A speaker explaining road building might cover route planning, grading, and surfacing. These divisions could form the main heads of the body of a speech. They could be arranged in a sequence that gave additional climactic or logical force to the development (the proposal is *desirable; it is also practical;* moreover it will have *no significant disadvantages*). Your major concern in applying the open-proposal sequence should be that the subpropositions be arranged in the clearest, most natural, and most logical order.

The direct or open-proposal sequence includes, among its variations, the topical arrangements so common in giving information. It also includes the *list-of-advantages pattern* for persuasion. In this scheme the case for a proposition of policy is structured to present a list of benefits arising out of the proposed policy. This variation is closely related to problem-solution organization in that each alleged advantage implies or demonstrates a problem and solution.

In general, an open-proposal sequence is most suitable when listeners are fairly familiar with your subject and when they have favorable or open-minded attitudes toward your position. There are at least two significant advantages in this system of organization. First, you can give a number of arguments or kinds of clarification efficiently while keeping your audience always aware of what you are trying to prove or clarify. Second, the very openness of this way of organizing can enhance your credibility because there seems little possibility that you are hiding anything.

As in the case of the indirect sequence, whether you adopt or avoid the direct-sequence presentation depends on the outlook of your audience, the way subject matter may be reasonably divided, your skill with direct versus indirect presentation, and the tone or spirit of the occasion.

Reflective Sequence or Pattern of Inquiry

The *reflective sequence* or *pattern of inquiry* is a pattern of organization based upon five steps in reflective thinking outlined by the philosopher John Dewey—(1) locating and defining a problem, (2) describing and limiting the problem, (3) suggesting possible solutions, (4) evaluating and testing the solutions, and (5) selecting the preferred solution.

To use this pattern you and your listeners must be willing to suspend judgment about a problem. This willingness comes from experience and reflection; life teaches us that snap judgments are often wrong, and that sound opinions are usually based on careful consideration of numerous factors. An inquiry and its reflective pattern of organization are appropriate when you are willing to assemble information and ponder various solutions with your audience before reaching a decision.

In a state of mind touched by doubt you invite your audience to join you in a quest for the best solution or the best answer to a question. You develop your speech so your listeners feel the problem is their problem, not yours alone. You do all you can do to give the audience and yourself a better basis for coming to a sound decision. This is the function of a speech of inquiry.

Such speaking is obviously both informative and persuasive. It persuasively asks hearers to ponder, to weigh and consider, to explore; but it does not ask audiences to adopt all of your opinions.

An inquirer both resembles and differs from an informative speaker. The person who gives us information is conversant with his or her subject and aims to impart that understanding. An inquirer, on the other hand, does not enjoy the same degree of certainty. An inquirer is experiencing a degree of discomfort about his or her subject. He or she either is unable to settle on a really satisfactory choice among competing solutions or for some reason is determined that the listeners must think their own ways through solutions. Such a speaker is certain of some things, having studied and thought about the problem that vexes. Usually the inquirer is ready (or can get ready) to do these things in communication: (1) formulate and clarify the question that poses the problem; (2) explain the background, causes, symptoms of the problem, and the forces at work to intensify or diminish it; (3) explain what criteria a satisfactory solution to the problem ought to meet; (4) identify and explain some or most of the solutions that seem to be available.   This kind of speaker either has doubts about the relative worth of the solutions or, like a teacher or counsellor, has decided not to give *the* answer but to encourage his or her audience to choose for themselves.   The speaker's aims are thus to impart information and to enlist the listeners in the task of choosing final answers.

To orient listeners to his or her subject, an inquirer first provides them with an understanding of the problem they share.   He or she informs them of its troublesome symptoms, its causes, and the forces at work to aggravate or ease it.   In this process it will be especially important that he or she help the listeners see the differences between the symptoms and the cause(s); else they will be inclined to cure symptoms rather than actual causes.   This process of informing the audience may also require a review of historical developments and how controversies, if any, have grown up around the issues.

The speaker does not stop there, however.   He or she next considers the criteria an acceptable answer must meet.   This is an important and often-missed step.   The speaker must be satisfied that he or she has formulated the right criteria, since the acceptability of any solution will depend on what standards are chosen.   Although he or she must consider criteria in every case, inquirers do not always find it necessary to present and justify them in the speech.   Some are obvious and readily taken for granted: safety on the highways, democracy, speed in settling legal cases.   Such standards hardly need formal presentation and if they do, they require no justification.   Sometimes criteria need to be presented but are too complex for explanation apart from discussion of solutions.   This might be the case with the aims of a foreign policy or with the nature of the good life.   In such cases criteria will be presented piecemeal as various solutions are discussed.   But consideration of criteria is integral to inquiry, so formal presentation of criteria is usually advisable.

Having clarified a problem and said what is necessary concerning standards, an inquirer using the reflective sequence turns to the alternative solutions or answers.   This is generally the most important element in the speech, hence you should allow sufficient time for it, restricting preliminary sections to what is absolutely essential.   For each solution you explain and assess, explain the solutions or answers and assess or evaluate each thoroughly and fairly in light of the pertinent criteria.

In concluding his or her speech an inquiring speaker should try to make the audience continue to inquire.   Their reflection on the subject should not stop when the speaker stops.   In fact, inquiry on a large scale—group inquiry—often begins after a speech of inquiry has been delivered. The speaker may well conclude by presenting the salient questions his or her listeners should consider as they continue their search for the best solution. Or the speaker may point out the *direction* in which he or she thinks the best answer will be found.

A speaker who would really inquire may suggest, but will not urge, acceptance of a special solution. He or she may omit Dewey's fifth step altogether. All five steps need not be included in every inquiry. Indeed, some inquiries go no farther than steps two or three. Others omit step one. The pattern, in short, is subject to considerable variation according to the requirements of speaker, audience, and occasion.

The speaker's own state of mind comes first in justifying this pattern of organization. The readiness of the audience to accept a pattern that does not provide for the conclusive settlement of a problem may also be a consideration. Speech materials have less influence on the selection or rejection of this pattern since the same materials at once lend themselves to informing, persuading, or questioning. The occasion is a determinant in that the situation must be one in which people can deliberate. An atmosphere of puzzlement, of careful consideration, will most often suggest to you that a pattern of inquiry is your best scheme of organization.

Monroe's Motivated Sequence

Professor Alan H. Monroe of Purdue University developed the motivated sequence pattern of organization, which bears his name. Based on the normal process of human thinking, the *motivated sequence* is thought to be especially effective in motivating listeners' responses to speakers' purposes. The sequence consists of five steps: attention, need, satisfaction, visualization, and action.

In persuasive speeches, which Monroe also sees as speeches to actuate and to reinforce, all five steps are used. The speaker (1) gains attention; (2) establishes a need for change of some sort; (3) shows how the change needed can be brought about or satisfied; (4) visualizes what will happen if the need is or is not met—that is, pictures the good or bad results of following the course he or she suggests; and (5) appeals directly for action, either mental or physical.

In the speech to inform, Monroe's fourth type, only the first three steps are used, and the "need" step becomes the "need to know" rather than the "need to believe" or the "need to act." In the speech to entertain, his fifth and last kind, only the "attention" step is used, or others are used as the entertainment becomes a parody of informative or persuasive speaking.

This sequence, more than any other, is psychologically planned to lead your audience's thinking naturally and easily from a vague interest in your subject to a definite acceptance of the attitude or action you are advocating. Each step in the sequence is built on the preceding steps. The motivated sequence can be used in a variety of speeches, but it is chiefly useful when you face an audience that has little interest in your subject or when you want to arouse a strong and specific response in your listeners. Here is how the pattern might be developed:

I. A recent survey shows that the average shopper can squeeze as much as 14 percent more out of his shopping dollar by becoming a smart shopper. (*Attention*)
II. You really need to save money in these days of severe inflation. (*Need*)
III. By reading ads skillfully, by knowing what questions to ask before you buy, and by buying at the right time you can save those precious dollars. (*Satisfaction*)
IV. If you do as I suggest you may be able to take that trip to Europe you've been dreaming about, buy that motorcycle you've had your eye on, or replenish your wardrobe and become the best dressed man on campus. (*Visualization*)
V. Although you cannot stop inflation you can outflank it by starting *today* to follow the tips I've given you so you won't continue to throw your dollars away. (*Action*)

You will notice that you have been exposed to and perhaps have used this pattern of ideas before! But do not miss the fact that the structure is psychologically sound for promoting international cooperation, rousing lethargic voters, showing people how to study better, or even giving a speech to entertain.

Because it is both logically and psychologically based, Monroe's motivated sequence is in whole or in part usable with most kinds of material, in a wide variety of situations, and by any speaker willing to work his or her ideas into the most psychologically inviting form to which they are amenable.

Elimination Order

Elimination order is a pattern of organization wherein several or all possible interpretations of a subject or solution to a problem are considered, and all but one are eliminated as undesirable, impractical, or incorrect. This strategy is sometimes called the *method of residues* because whatever remains at the end is the matter to be accepted by the audience.

The method of elimination is often used as the fourth step of what is otherwise a reflective sequence. This adaptation is especially advantageous when you wish to present an investigation for the purpose of persuading rather than inquiring. At the point of considering solutions you may eliminate all known solutions except the one you advocate. The same pattern may be applied during the second half of a problem-solution speech when more than one solution or remedy must be considered. Thus, this pattern may be thought of as a variation that can be incorporated within either reflective or problem-solution systems or it may be treated as a scheme of organization applicable to a whole speech.

Your choice of this organizational system will depend on the situation and your own concerns. Both you and your audience must be willing to investigate more than one kind of "answer." The system must allow discussion of more than one course of action or possibility. Time must be available for full explanation and for testing the possibilities, and the atmosphere must favor a several-sided consideration of the subject.

We began this chapter by considering man's special need to find relationships and speakers' consequent needs to clarify and show the movement of thought. Disposition of the content of a speech is further adaptation. It is adaptation to the human propensity to search for structure and unity in all things. Our examination of the normal parts of speeches (introduction, body, and conclusion) and of patterns of organization has been a survey of various ways by which speakers have learned to answer the universal demand for organization.

Most of the time a reasonable adaptation to the rhetorical situation will make it necessary that speech begin by orienting the listener to speaker and subject (introduction). Properly adapted speech will continue with a message that makes listening easier and surer by offering a structural pattern familiar to both listener and speaker. It will conclude with some reinforcement of the total experience of hearing the speech.

We have discussed the standard patterns of organization, first, because public speech is an art form through which relationships are exhibited in familiar, public terms. The standard patterns of organization are simply the most familiar—the most public—systems our society uses in verbal communication. Second, although not all speech can be effectively structured according to one of the patterns we have discussed, all speech will have at least a segment that can be best conveyed according to one of them. These patterns, then, are optional systems among which you will constantly choose. We hope that by understanding what they can accomplish and what they cannot, you will be able to choose wisely.

EXERCISES

Written

1. a. Choose a subject area, such as air pollution, current methods in secondary education, or the Democratic party in America today.
   b. Carefully write out three subject sentences for the subject chosen. One sentence should be devised for a speech of *information,* another for a speech of *persuasion,* and the third for a speech of *inquiry.*
   c. Write out the main heads for each of the three subject sentences you have composed.
2. Write an essay in which you evaluate the following introduction according to the requirements for a good introduction found on pages 197–99.

DRUNKEN DRIVERS

From the wreckage of the crash, two persons extricate themselves. The first seems to be an elderly, well-dressed businessman, who, after surveying the wreckage, pulls out a young man and helps him to his feet. The young man obviously needs help; his gait is unsteady, his eyes are bloodshot and bleary, and his speech is almost unintelligible. The onlookers are convinced by these signs that he is drunk, which is confirmed by the strong smell of alcohol which is obvious a few feet away.

As the police cars pull up, the crowd is assured that the young man will get what is coming to him. He can get out that his name is William Schultz, and he is a taxi driver, but he is unable to give the police his address, does not know where he is by a few miles, yet insists that he had nothing to drink. The officers dutifully administer a test commonly known as the "Balloon Test" to him. After the balloon is blown up, the contents are passed through a tube containing a purple liquid on what looks to be a wad of cotton. The purple color disappears if the air passing through it is filled with alcohol, the policeman explains, and the faster the color disappears, the drunker you are. At the end of the test, however, the purple color is still there, causing some bewilderment among the spectators and the policemen. Some more tests will be taken down at the station.

It is now the older man's turn for examination. As expected, he gives a good account of himself. He is Milton P. Jones, an executive, on his way home from a business conference. He admits to having had a few drinks two hours earlier with his lunch, but the policemen are unable to smell alcohol on his breath. He is also asked to take the balloon test, and, within a fraction of a minute, all color disappears in the glass tube. Befuddled, the policemen take them both down to the station for further examination.

From the evidence before you, every person in this room must have some thoughts as to who the guilty party is. Young Mr. Schultz appears to have all the physical attributes of a drunk, while Mr. Jones is surely the victim of this terrible crime. We'll come back to these men and their particular case in few minutes.[8]

---

8. This introduction was composed by Renee Ehrlich for an introductory course in public speaking. Used by permission.

3. Assume the following sets of main heads have been taken from the bodies of outlines for speeches. Evaluate each set for (a) the wording of the main points, and (b) the overall pattern of organization. Give detailed reasons for your judgments.

    a.   I. Every speech should have an introduction, body, and conclusion.

           II. Should the introduction get attention and make the speaker's purpose clear?

          III. A conclusion should summarize and put the entire speech into focus.

    b.   I. The social, political, and economic instability of underdeveloped countries is a potential breeding ground for communism.

          II. We must increase our financial aid and technical assistance to these countries to head off the threat.

    c.   I. Economical and efficient means of smoke prevention have been devised.

          II. Heavy smoke darkens the sunlight.

         III. Smoke is harmful to public health.

         IV. Smoking is a bad habit.

         V. The annoyance, filth, and unhealthful effects of smoke have caused an agitation for smoke prevention in large cities.

         VI. Gas and electricity may replace coal for many domestic uses.

        VII. Imports of residual oil cause much unemployment in coal fields.

      VIII. Since smoke is injurious and preventable, immediate steps should be taken toward its elimination.

         IX. Efficient smokeless furnaces have proved a success.

         X. Smoke hinders good ventilation.

        XI. Smoke prevention in large cities should be compulsory.

       XII. Electric locomotives may be used in place of diesels.

      XIII. Many fires are caused by faulty furnaces.

      XIV. Coal smoke damages the lungs.

      XV. One important step is to sign the Anti-Smoke League petition.

4. Locate the text of a speech in an anthology of speeches, an issue of *Vital Speeches,* or a volume of the Reference Shelf series (H. W. Wilson Co.) devoted to speeches. Read the speech carefully. Identify the structure or structures. Defend your labeling of the patterns in a paragraph or two in which you cite specifically what led you to choose the labels you did.

Oral

1. a. In class discussion choose several subject sentences for impromptu speeches. Sentences such as: "The automobile is primarily a vehicle for human transportation"; "Donation of blood to the Red Cross is worthwhile"; "Everyone should have a hobby" will serve.

    b. Assign each of the subject sentences chosen to three members of the class, and also assign to each of them *one* of the usable patterns of organization discussed in chapter 7, e.g., chronological, spatial, problem-solution, causal.

    c. Allow time for each of the three students to prepare two- to three-minute impromptu speeches using the patterns assigned.

   d. After hearing the speeches, discuss the suitability of each pattern to the subject sentence assigned. Also evaluate the speaker's ability to produce a recognizable pattern of organization on short notice.

2. Make a two-minute speech about a classroom you are familiar with. Treat *at least* these main headings:
   - Blackboard areas
   - Lighting
   - Seating arrangements
   - Virtues and flaws as a classroom

   Determine and be ready to defend the sequence in which you order your points and your choice of a central idea. Be sure to append appropriate introductory and concluding remarks.

3. Here is a problem in isolating a usable central idea and in arranging main points and amplifying material. The miscellaneous facts below have (or can be given) relationship to one another. Using them as your basic material, give a two-minute talk in which you have at least two major points amplifying whatever central idea you choose. Be sure to show by clear transitions how the main points relate to the central idea (and to each other if that is important). Here is your basic material:

   In dealing a hand of 13 cards from 52 in bridge, the probability of drawing a perfect hand (13 spades) is 1 in 635,013,559,600. In a four-handed poker game, the chances of getting the highest possible hand (royal flush) are 1 in 649,739. If you are a white, female American, aged 19, insurance companies estimate that you have 57 more years to live. If you are a white, male American, aged 19, the estimate is that you will live 51 more years. If you are a girl and 19, there is 1 chance in 8 that you will marry within a year, but if you are a male and 19 there is but 1 chance in 25 you'll marry within a year.

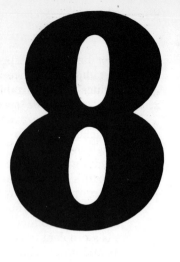

Disposition: Outlining

Constructing an outline insures that your ideas will be arranged and sufficiently supported or amplified to meet the needs of your rhetorical situation. Outlining further insures that you will consider the logical relationships among ideas and the weights and emphases you need to give them. Finally, the act of outlining and the use of an outline are exceptionally helpful in setting your ideas firmly in your mind so you can command them confidently as you speak.

The detail in which you outline for public speech depends primarily on the uses you are going to make of the outline. You may need only a skeletal map of a talk, or you may need such a complete plan that your outline becomes almost a manuscript of the speech.

FUNCTIONS OF OUTLINES

Your own needs and preferences and the requirements of assignments will probably determine what kind of outlines you prepare. In some classroom situations you may be asked to construct *content* or *technical outlines* to show a teacher your planned content and strategies. You may be asked for *full-sentence, phrase,* or *key-word outlines*. In any case, you will surely need to outline your speech plans in some degree of detail. To do so is a far better preparatory procedure than writing a talk in full before you have inspected its basic structure.

If you are a beginner you will find sentence outlines most helpful. Full sentences express complete thoughts and using them enables you to frame each thought fully and to think out its proper relationship to all other complete thoughts in your speech plan. Thoughts may, of course, be symbolized on paper by single words or phrases or, indeed, by symbols even simpler than words, such as crosses, circles, and the like. But most beginners and most of the expert speakers we know find themselves handicapped in speech planning if they use shorthand outlines of very abbreviated sorts. Experienced speakers do, of course, come to speak from very abbreviated sets of notes, but somewhere in the planning stages there was usually a more comprehensive, outlined plan.

Fundamentally you outline to serve *yourself.* Audiences seldom see outlines, so usefulness to *you* is the mark of a good outline. Outlining is a part of dealing with the inescapable problem the ancients talked about under the heading "memoria." You will find this general subject discussed at some length in appendix A, "Rhetorical Theory: A Heritage." (See pp. 381–85.) Whoever speaks has the problem of foreseeing where he or she is going, keeping ideas organized for the listeners' sake, and generally executing some plan while under the tensions of speaking. In our civilization all kinds of complicated procedures have been proposed to help speakers remember their plans; the procedure of outlining is simply the most modern and most practical of your alternatives. In learning situations, however, outlining may serve additional purposes.

You are likely to be asked to submit an outline to your teacher. The reason will be to allow you to receive constructive criticism. Your outline, then, is no longer a private paper. It is, instead, a record of preparation to be shared with another interested person who is to make suggestions. This shared paper must be understood by your teacher as well as by you. Since this is so, you must take special care to make ideas and their relationships clear both visually and verbally. You and your critic must agree upon a system of outlining. You may be asked to employ full sentences, at least to begin with, because your reader can understand them better than phrases or words. A single word offered in support of another single word may not be comprehensible to your teacher, and it will not indicate whether you have thought through your ideas. For instance, you may know what you will say when you have written the word "economic" and listed "cost" and "profit" as supporting ideas, but your teacher may not see clear-cut connections between these sketchy symbols. He may be led to conclude that at this particular stage of speech preparation your ideas have not been fully enough refined, that they are still in vague or fuzzy condition. In fact, you may really have slipped in your own thinking.

For your reader's sake and for your own you must take special care in preparing your papers so your ideas and their relationships are beyond misunderstanding.

As a teaching method your instructor may ask you to construct a content outline showing the ideas in your speech and then to add technical labels. He or she may ask you to indicate your kinds of proof and amplification, sources of attention, or the pattern of structure exemplified. When these labels are added to an outline, you have in reality two outlines. One maps ideas to be uttered; the other maps strategy and tactics. It is common for the inexperienced to mix these two types of mapping. In making outlines you will not give symbols to the introduction, body, and conclusion, because these are not parts of the idea structure of the speech. It is useless in constructing a content outline simply to write "story" or "statistics" beside a subpoint number without indicating what you intend to say. To identify your tactics or methods enables you to straighten out in your own mind just what it is you are doing as you order ideas and just what kinds of ideas you are ordering. Sometimes your teacher may ask you to use the technical labels to test you. But such labels alone will not enable you to tell others what you will say. An outline reading as follows would be of little help were you to try to determine what the speaker who made it intended to say.

INTRODUCTION
  I. Story—using novelty, stereotypes, familiarity; chronological order
 II. Subject sentence
III. Definitions
     a. By function
     b. By classification

BODY
 I. Argument—open-proposal pattern
    a. Quotation—familiar
    b. Statistics—visual aids
II. Argument—developed inductively
    a. Report of experiment
    b. Report of second experiment

CONCLUSION
 I. A summary

This record would be of little value either to a teacher aiming to evaluate supports or proofs, subject sentences, or attention values, or to a speaker trying to recapture from personal files what he or she said six months ago.

COMMON PRACTICES

No hard and fast rules can be made about outlining, but certain practices promote clarity, organic unity in speeches, and the adaptation so necessary in successful speaking. They yield a practical, visual image of a speech plan—one you or anyone else can follow easily. Here are practices it is wise to follow:

A CLEAR INDICATION OF THE BASIC DIVISIONS OF THE SPEECH: INTRODUCTION, BODY (SOMETIMES LABELED DISCUSSION OR PROOF), AND CONCLUSION. Since these labels are not parts of the idea structure of the speech but are technical notations, they will not normally be given symbols. Numerical and alphabetical symbols ought to be reserved as indicators of relationships. Usually the names of the basic divisions of your speech are centered on the page and go unsymbolized. This placement insures that you have an introduction and a conclusion and that you are aware of what constitutes these portions of your speech. In those infrequent instances when no introduction is used, its absence is readily apparent if one forms the practice of identifying each division actually included.

A CONSISTENT SYSTEM OF (A) SYMBOLIZATION AND (B) INDENTATION. This aids in clarifying relationships and in helping you to remember those relationships. The system of symbols you use is up to you; consistency in their use is essential. It matters little whether Roman numerals, capital letters, or Arabic numerals are used to indicate main heads and subheads. What matters is that each time a type of symbol occurs it signifies that the ideas thus identified are of approximately the same importance or weight. Uniformity in symbolization will indicate clearly the values you assign to your material, and the different symbols assigned will show which ideas are subsidiary to which. Since you will be working out a structure idea by idea, you should place only one symbol before any one idea. This serves as a caution against composing compound sentences containing more than one thought. If you follow the rule: one symbol for *each* idea, you will be reminded to break compound statements in two. You will need to check very carefully in making a phrase outline to see that each symbol stands beside an idea rather than beside a fragment of one or a phrase that represents—for you—several ideas.

Indentation, the physical arrangement of ideas, further reveals values assigned and stirs the memory. If each new idea has a clear indentation, that fact announces to you when it is time to embark on a new phase of your thought structure. Ideas subsidiary to other ideas should be indented under the subsuming thought. In this way it will be easy to see supports and amplifications as subordinate points. Your visual image of your speech will then be of a network of ideas with the least important ones indented farthest from the left-hand margin of the page. Although none of the ideas you set down on the page is, ideally, expendable, it will be less of a calamity should an idea given minor weight (one farthest indented) be forgotten.

In outlining inductive patterns, a common practice is to symbolize and indent points and subpoints in the same way you do for deductive patterns, then to place supporting or amplifying subpoints in parentheses. Such practice indicates that the examples, statistics, and definitions subsumed by a point are to be presented *before* the point being amplified or supported.

ABSENCE OF SINGLE SUBPOINTS. Whenever one idea is subordinated to another, this indicates a splitting of the subsuming idea for purposes of amplification or support. Usually more than one piece of information is needed to develop a point adequately. Yet, one definition, one example, or one opinion sometimes may suffice to clarify or prove to an acceptable degree. Point I. B. of the outline for a speech on "A Slice of the Bronx" on p. 236 is an illustration of this. Neither the speaker nor the audience needs to know, for this speech, any more about Mr. Philipse's loyalism than that his bridge was taken from him. But usually a single subordinate item needs the reinforcement of other, parallel items; otherwise, it ought often to be combined with the idea to which it appears to be subordinate. In any case, any outline containing many single subpoints should be viewed suspiciously. It is likely that the ideas contained in it have not been developed to the point of audience acceptance and that necessary information and proof have been overlooked. Only when you are absolutely sure that one and only one piece of proof is necessary should a subpoint be allowed to stand alone.

DISCRETENESS OF IDEAS. In outlines ideas should not be lumped together nor should they overlap. An outline is a structure intended to display relationships clearly. This fact dictates that each idea stand separately within the structure. The need to reveal the relationship of each idea to other ideas is an additional argument for full-sentence outlining. Sentences, if correctly constructed, are expressions of complete thoughts. Be wary of the compound sentence in outlining; it contains more than one idea, making it impossible to follow the principle of one symbol, one idea. Therefore, "and" and "or" should rarely appear in the sentences of an outline; they bear special checking when they do appear.

APPROPRIATE SYMBOLIZATION AND PLACEMENT OF SUBJECT SENTENCES. Since the core idea (subject sentence, main proposition, central idea, or specific purpose) is the most important idea in the speech, it deserves the highest rank in symbolization. This main proposition or assertion should be unmistakable in your outline. Some teachers and students prefer to label this proposition or assertion "central idea," "main proposition," "subject sentence," or "specific purpose," rather than affix number or letter symbols, because it is of highest rank in the hierarchy of ideas symbolized in the outline.

In the sample outlines at the end of this chapter and in the diagram on page 230 we have both symbolized and labeled the central idea, indicating that either method is acceptable and that both are common in outlining. No matter which of these practices is followed, the central idea should never appear as a subpoint nor should it be indented beneath any other point. In deductive patterns this central sentence will usually appear near the end of the introduction or near the beginning of the body of the speech. Wherever it appears, the central idea should be designated by a symbol or label indicating that it is of most weight or value. Graphically, it should at least be accorded the same rank by indentation as the other most important items in the section. The same is true in symbolizing or labeling and in indenting the central idea when outlining inductive patterns, such as the withheld-proposal sequence. The main idea should be given the symbol and/or label and indentation that reveals it is a statement not outranked in importance by any other ideas in that section of the speech. Whether the central idea appears in the introduction, body, or conclusion, it is the most important idea in that division of your outline.

CLEAR TRANSITIONS. Transitions should be uniformly indicated and set off from the rest of the structure. Points of linkage and internal summaries should be clearly indicated. This is more than a mere technical matter. It is at the points of shift from one line of thought to another that your memory is most likely to fail you while speaking and it is at these points that listeners are most likely to lose the connections among ideas unless you give them special help. If transitions are symbolized and indented in the same manner as other parts of the outline, they should be given technical labels such as "transition" or "internal summary." A common practice is to treat these portions of the speech differently from main points or subpoints, omitting symbols but marking them off by enclosing them in brackets or parentheses. This practice shows that you have given careful attention to how you will move from one point or subpoint to another, and it will remind you of the necessity for repetition and review in speaking.

If you observe the above practices, a diagram of your outlines will look like that printed below. For a short speech you may not need to outline in as full detail as this diagram indicates, but we have included the fullest detail we think you are ever likely to need.

TITLE

INTRODUCTION

I. ....

    A. ....

    B. ....

II. (Central Idea) ....

       (Transition: ....)

BODY

I. ....

    A. ....

    B. ....

      1. ....

        a. ....

        b. ....

      2. ....

        a. ....

        b. ....

    C. ....

      1. ....

      2. ....

        a. ....

        b. ....

          (1) ....

          (2) ....

        (Transition: ....)

II. ....

    A. ....

      1. ....

        a. ....

        b. ....

        c. ....

      2. ....

        (Transition: ....)

    B. ....

      1. ....

        a. ....

        b. ....

          (1) ....

          (2) ....

          (3) ....

            (a) ....

            (b) ....

        c. ....

        d. ....

          (1) ....

          (2) ....

2. ....
    a.   ....
    b.   ....
    (Internal Summary: ....
    ....)

III. ....
  A. ....
    1. ....
      a.   ....
      b.   ....
    2. ....
  B. ....
    (Transition and/or Internal Summary ....
    ....)

CONCLUSION

I. ....
  A. ....
  B. ....
  C. ....
II. ....

BIBLIOGRAPHY
(OR STATEMENT OF SOURCES)

....
....
....
....
....
....

Two items appearing in this diagram remain to be considered: title and bibliography or statement of sources.

TITLES

The final act in composing a speech ordinarily is to select a title. Informal situations make titles less necessary than situations in which you will be introduced, but a title provides a label anyone reporting your speech, recording it, or referring to it can use handily. Of course, if your talk is part of a group's public presentation, it will be the group's subject that will need to be titled.

Whether it is an individual or group presentation that you are seeking a label for, you ought to make the title brief, clear, and provocative.   You will want it to arouse interest and reveal in some degree what the talk or report is actually to be about.

A title needs to be brief for practical reasons.   An audience will stop listening before the end of a title such as: "The History and Significance of the Indian Tribes in the Western New York Area from the Years 1770 to 1790 with Special Emphasis on the Youth between the Ages of Twelve and Eighteen and Their Roles in War Making."   At first glance that looks completely ridiculous, but actually it might represent the substance of a talk or a symposium at a historical society.   However, a title that would serve practical purposes and not suggest the speaker(s) lacked rhetorical sense would be: "The Warring Indian Braves of Western New York in the Late Eighteenth Century."   This would be practical for publicity purposes, short enough to fit on a program or poster and into a one- or two-column newspaper head for a report on the presentation.

When a presentation has no title or a long and unarresting one, chairpersons are apt to invent one.   One of our students told his classroom chairman, "Oh, I'm going to talk about fishing, you know."   The chairman brought him on with, "Now you all know the trout season opened this week, so John's going to tell us what all those people are doing out there along the trout streams."   Actually, John had an excellent speech on how tie-flies, artificial lures, are made.   He, of course, had to correct the chairman's announcement before he could begin his talk—a problem he would not have had if he had formed a clear title of his own and had given it to the chairman.   Famous speakers get into similar difficulties.   President Franklin D. Roosevelt once gave an untitled speech to the Teamster's Union in 1944.   It was a broadly ranging political defense of his policies in conducting the Americans' part in World War II.   Reporters, needing a *short* title to fit their headlines and reports, seized on one small segment of the speech and created a title from it.   In this part of the speech Roosevelt referred to his black Scottie dog, Fala.   The title "The Fala Speech" has stuck to this address ever since, although that title quite misrepresents Roosevelt's subject matter and the rhetorical situation in which he gave the speech.

Titles for presentation, whether by individuals or groups, ought to fairly characterize the presentation and arouse some curiosity about it.   Two kinds of mistakes get in the way of these goals: using vague, "umbrella" titles and using titles that are all but riddles.   "A Hope for the Future," "You Ought to Try," "A Happy Solution," are not only vague, but they might announce any number of speeches on utterly diverse subjects.   They cover everything and nothing.   Some other titles we have heard offered in classrooms have drawn attention—but to what? Consider these: "Little Fences and Barriers," "Pins and Needles," "The Big Fraud" (see pp. 238–40), "How to Be Fit."   Each is unnecessarily a riddle.   "Little Fences and Barriers" could have been "Fences and Barriers of Prejudice."   "Pins and Needles" might have been "Healing

Pins and Needles," since it was the title of a speech about acupuncture. "The Big Fraud" might have been "Social Security or Insecurity?" or "The Social Security Fraud." The group reporting on an investigation of physical-fitness programs would have conveyed its general message more clearly through the title, "Which Way to Physical Fitness?" In this case the group's report was an *evaluation* of the relative effectiveness of different programs and systems of exercises.

A title for any presentation ought to do specific work: convey a promise that can be understood and do it with quick provocativeness.

BIBLIOGRAPHIES

The educated person knows the sources of his or her knowledge and opinions. Such a person is able to acknowledge how and where ideas and facts were acquired and does so voluntarily. In preparing outlines and manuscripts a speaker or any composer ought to annotate ideas and quotations not his or her own for at least two reasons. To do so is a natural recognition of other people's contributions and it creates a record that can be referred to at a later time.

For both of these reasons you are apt to be asked to include a bibliography or "statement of sources" with final outlines. Occasionally acknowledgments of sources may appear in the outline proper. They should certainly appear there when the sources are mentioned in the speech itself. More often, such acknowledgments will be appended at the end of the outline as a communication to the instructor or other reader. Your teacher, as a critic, wants to know what you actually found useful, and you, yourself, may at some future date wish to relocate the sources.

There are many forms for bibliographical entries. The important objectives are to be complete and consistent. The following forms may be used when you are asked to cite your sources. Comments on the scope and value of printed sources follow each source in brackets. The notes on other materials are given in informal description.

OBSERVATION:

During the week of August 12–19, 1977, I took part in NROTC naval maneuvers and saw the things I describe under point I of the introduction.

INTERVIEW:

On May 12, 1976, I talked with President J. B. Smith of X Company for about an hour and got the ideas on management's problems, which appear in section III of this outline.

      I have drawn at many points on the courses I have taken in business, economics, and oral and written communication.

BOOK:

Johnson, Bonnie McDaniel, *Communication: The Process of Organizing* (Boston: Allyn and Bacon, 1977).
[*The first chapter, "Images of Organizing," gave me the idea for my first main point, that this university is organized on "classical" or "design" or "machine" notions. I also used Johnson's criticisms of this organizational theory and others throughout the speech.*]

ARTICLES:

A. From Periodicals:

    Wiley, Richard E., "Family Viewing: A Balancing of Interests," *Journal of Communication* XXVII, no. 2 (Spring 1977): 188–92.
    [*The first part of this article was my main source for how "family viewing" came to be a programming concept in network TV programming. The author participated in some of the negotiations.*]

B. From Books:

    Kauffmann, Stanley, "The Film Generation," in eds. Allen Kirschner and Linda Kirschner, *Film: Readings in the Mass Media* (New York: Odyssey Press, 1971), pp. 151–63.
    [*Some of the material I used concerning the role of sex in current films (see point II) is taken from this essay.*]

C. From General Reference Books:

    "John Donne," *Encyclopaedia Britannica,* 9th ed. (New York, 1878).[1]
    [*Most of the biographical material in my speech came from here.*]

NEWSPAPERS:

A. From Signed Articles, Editorials, and News Accounts:

    Fairlie, Henry, "Our Misguided Defenders of the English Language," *The Washington Post* (May 29, 1977), sec. B, p. 8.
    [*My argument that grammatical mistakes are not in themselves the sources of failures in communication is based on Fairlie's argument that what you have to say is the most important thing in communication.*]

B. From Unsigned Articles, Editorials, and News Accounts:

    "City Schools Need You on Board of Education," *The Philadelphia Inquirer,* June 3, 1977, p. 7–B.

---

    1. In citing any *Britannica* since 1932 it is advisable to use the date of printing: "John Donne," *Encyclopaedia Britannica* (1971).

[This editorial gave me my example of how complex nominating procedures make it likely that school board members in large districts will be picked on the basis of who-knows-whom.]

PAMPHLETS (WHERE THE AUTHOR OR EDITOR IS NOT CREDITED):

The Crime of Genocide. United Nations Office of Public Information (New York, 1959).
[The text of the convention (international agreement) passed by the General Assembly in December of 1946, which I quoted, is contained in this source.]

SAMPLE OUTLINES AND SPEAKER'S NOTES

The two outlines that follow illustrate good outlining procedures and preparatory methods.   The first is an outline for a speech of information five minutes in length.   It not only is a good example of organization and the mechanics of outlining but it illustrates exceptionally careful adaptation of material to a specific audience in a specific rhetorical situation.   (See footnote 2 for details.)   You will profit by reflecting on the large amount of material the speaker must have excluded from her talk because it would not fit closely enough the audience and even the room in which she would speak.

Both outlines furnished here are probably as detailed as any you will ever make.   Your own needs and your instructor's expectations may allow you to prepare less comprehensive outlines than these, but the principles of outlining and of documenting source material are fully illustrated here because at some time you may need to prepare in this much detail.

A SLICE OF THE BRONX[2]

INTRODUCTION

I. Kingsbridge Road is familiar to all of us in this classroom because it lies just outside the room we are in.
   A. But do we really know about it?

---

2. Adapted from an outline prepared for an informative speech in a beginning public-speaking course at Herbert H. Lehman College, City University of New York.   The author of the outline was Alma Lajara Franco.   Used by permission.   The classroom in which this speech was delivered overlooked Kingsbridge Road and was approximately one-half block from the park where Edgar Allan Poe's cottage is now located.   It was two blocks from the Kingsbridge Armory and approximately six blocks from Fordham University.

B. For instance, it was not until January of 1874 that even the township of Kingsbridge became a part of New York City.

(Central idea)

II. I want you to understand some of the interesting historical facts about Kingsbridge Road and vicinity.

BODY

I. Let's first examine how Kingsbridge Road received its name.
   A. In 1693 Fredryck Philipse was granted a ninety-nine-year franchise to build the twenty-nine-foot King's Bridge over Spuyten Duyvil Creek.
      1. Philipse was allowed to collect tolls from everyone crossing the bridge except for the king's troops.
      2. Only this bridge connected Manhattan Island with what is now the Bronx, so Philipse tended to overcharge.
      3. Nonetheless, the bridge remained the Philipses' property until near the end of the Revolutionary War.
   B. Unfortunately Mary Philipse was a Loyalist in the Revolution.
      1. All her property, including the bridge, was confiscated by the patriots.
II. The bridge, the road, and the area played further roles in the Revolutionary War.
   A. British General Howe had a plan to trap General Washington and his troops on Manhattan Island.
      1. He was to sail up the East River, march to Westchester County, and then block the King's Bridge.
      2. This would cut off Washington's only means of escape.
      3. Washington outsmarted Howe by cutting him off in Westchester.
   B. Howe did eventually capture Manhattan by other means and held it for seven years.
III. In the 1800s the Kingsbridge Road area was affected by the construction of the New York and Harlem Railroad.
   A. This brought in new people who were trying to escape a congested Manhattan.
      1. The railroad had a stop near where Fordham University is today.
      2. One of the people who moved into the area was Edgar Allan Poe who lived in this area from 1846–49.
         a. Poe's cottage was across the street on the east side of Kingsbridge Road near 192nd Street.
         b. The cottage was moved to the new Poe Park in 1902 and in 1966 was declared an official city landmark.
   B. The fast-growing community around Kingsbridge Road needed medical care, of course.
      1. Thus, the first hospital established in the Bronx was Fordham Hospital.
         a. It was then located on Valentine Avenue near Kingsbridge Road.
         b. It had a maximum of twenty-five beds and was open chiefly for accident and emergency cases.

2. The United States Veterans' Hospital building on Kingsbridge Road was purchased by the government in 1921 for use by veterans suffering mental and nervous disorders.

C. Another project with which you are familiar was begun in 1895— the Reservoir.

   1. The Reservoir, as you know, is located right behind Lehman College.

     a. It has two basins capable of holding 2 billion gallons of water.

     b. As it was being dug, many Revolutionary War relics were unearthed: cannon balls, bayonets, swords, and even what turned out to be the skeleton of a British soldier.

D. If you ride the train to school, you have passed the Armory on Jerome Avenue and Kingsbridge Road.

   1. It houses the 258th Field Artillery regiment of the New York State National Guard, and that group has an interesting history.

     a. Its original organization was as an artillery company founded in 1784.

     b. Part of the original company formed the honor guard for George Washington when he was inaugurated president of the United States.

E. In other days you could not only get to this area of Kingsbridge Road by train, you could come by trolley.

   1. The trolley climbed up Kingsbridge Road west of Sedgwick Avenue.

   2. The trolley was one of the 1701 series—among the last models of trolleys to be built.

     a. The car was so long that it was often derailed.

     b. This trolley was finally retired in 1942.

CONCLUSION

  I. Kingsbridge Road, the street we are on, had interesting roles both before and during the Revolutionary War because it was a means of access to Manhattan Island.

 II. The Kingsbridge area became a historic suburb of New York City.

III. As the area flourished, it became the site for a variety of historic and curious projects which have contributed to making the Bronx now a city-within-a-city.

BIBLIOGRAPHY

BOOKS:

Van Pelt, Daniel, *Leslie's History of the Greater New York* (New York: Arkell Publishing Co., 1898), vol. 1.

Wells, James L., *The Bronx and Its People* (New York: Lewis Historical Publishing Co., 1927).

PAMPHLETS:

Peterson, Everett A., and Smart, Mary F., *Historical Handbook of the City of New York* (New York: City History Club of New York, 1934).

Ulton, Lloyd, *The Bronx in the American Revolution* (New York: Bronx Historical Society, 1975).

OBSERVATION:

On Saturday, October 16, I visited the Bronx County Historical Society at 3266 Bainbridge Avenue in the Bronx. There I studied several displays depicting the involvement of the Kingsbridge area in the Revolutionary War and secured other overall information about the area.

THE BIG FRAUD[3]

INTRODUCTION

(Central Idea)
I. Beware of social security: a poor investment.
  A. Students preparing to enter the work force will be more affected and have the least to gain from social security insurance.
    1. They will contribute for forty-six years at the highest rates in history.
    2. Their contributions will far exceed what they could ever hope to achieve in benefits.
  B. They must be alerted to the inequities of this system.
  (Transition: Before telling you more about this fraud, I'd like to mention a few of the facts.)
II. Social security insurance was born at the height of the depression when 22 million were unemployed.
  A. It was a crash program to free citizens from economic fear, care, and want.
    1. It provided money with dignity to those in need.
    2. The requests for welfare were reduced.
  B. The present system is not fulfilling the promise made back in 1935 with regard to financial security.
  C. It is predicted that the present system will exhaust its contingency fund of $45 billion by the early 1980s.

BODY

III. In the beginning social security insurance was a good deal.
  A. Until 1939 whatever money the worker contributed was returned to either the retired worker or his estate.

---

3. This outline was submitted by Mary M. Collins. Used by permission.

  1. This "money-back guarantee" was cancelled in 1939.
 B. Ida Fuller was the first person to receive benefits and is still receiving them—$12,000 later.
  1. She paid in less than $70 to the plan.
  2. She participated in the plan for only two years.
 (Transition: For *Ida* it was a good deal; for *you* it's *not!*)
IV. Under present law social security insurance is not a good deal.
 A. A person now eighteen will contribute at least $19,270 by the time he reaches sixty-five and will not receive interest on his money.
  1. If deposited in a bank, the contributions could earn presently 5½ percent interest.
  2. Money doubles every fourteen years in a bank.
 B. The maximum benefits one could receive assuming one lived till seventy-nine years of age would be $80,888.
  1. Internal Revenue actuarial tables show life expectancy at 71.9 years.
 C. There are many inequities in this system.
  1. Participation is compulsory.
  2. This "insurance" does not have the restrictions and regulations imposed on private insurance plans.
  3. The plan used is "pay as you go"—no reserves.
  4. Funds can be used for any purpose the government decides upon.
  5. This "gift" can be revoked, increased, or decreased by Congress.
  6. There are gimmicks attached that prohibit receiving checks under certain circumstances.
 V. The solution is to get the government out of the insurance business.
 A. Encourage growth of private investment plans rather than hamper them.
 B. Manage your own money in your own way rather than entrusting it to Uncle Sam.

CONCLUSION

VI. After three decades the promise of financial security is still unfulfilled.
 A. Constant clamoring for more indicates that social security is not enough.
 B. Let's do all we can to abolish social security insurance.
 C. The fraud is being perpetrated on *you*.   Beware!

STATEMENT OF SOURCES

Anonymous, *Social Security—Medicare Simplified* (Washington, D.C.: *U.S. News and World Report*, 1969).
  [This book was easy to understand and provided basic material. Pages 219–23 were especially useful.]
Ellis, Abraham, *The Social Security Fraud* (New Rochelle, N.Y.: Arlington House, 1971).
  [Ellis suggested leading arguments and some of the wording of main points. My title was also suggested by this source.]

Koeppel, B., "Big Social Security Rip-Off," *Progressive* XXXIX (August 1975): 13–18.
[This general article made some points very similar to some of those I will make in the speech.]

McKinley, Charles, and Robert W. Frase, *Launching Social Security: A Capture-and-Record Account, 1935–1937* (Madison, Wisc.: University of Wisconsin Press, 1970).
[I found most of this book much too technical, but historical aspects were helpful.]

Shore, Warren, *Social Security: the Fraud in Your Future* (New York: Macmillan, 1975).
[Chapter 8, "The Generation of Victims," was very specific in providing amplifying material for IV. A. and B.]

Social Security Benefits for Students, 18–22, United States Department of Health, Education and Welfare, Social Security Administration Pamphlet No. SS1-48 (Washington, D.C.: U.S. Government Printing Office, October 1969).

Social Security Benefits—How You Earn—How to Estimate, United States Department of Health, Education and Welfare, Social Security Administration Pamphlet No. SS1-47 (Washington, D.C.: U.S. Government Printing Office, January 1970).

Treat, Charles, "Another Day of Hunger for the Aged," *New York Times,* November 28, 1976, sec. 21, p. 30.
[Discusses the failure of social security to supply aged and handicapped survivors and couples enough to meet living costs in Nassau county.]

Van Gorkom, J. W., *Social Security—The Long-Term Deficit* (Washington, D.C.: American Enterprise Institute for Public Policy Research, 1976).
[This pamphlet contained statistics supporting point II. C. in my outline.]

Speaker's Notes

The speaker's notes for the speech outlined above might have looked like this:

THE BIG FRAUD

INTRO: Beware of social security = poor investment
Students entering work force—you—most affected
· Contribute 46 yrs. at highest rates
· Contributions exceed benefits
Program born at height of Depression, crash program

BODY: In beginning, good deal!
· Money-back guarantee—cancelled
· Ida Fuller, example—how worked well
At present, *not* good
· 18 yr. old, by 65 = $19,270: vs. money in bank

(doubles every 14 yrs.)—no interest on yours
· S.S. maximum at 79 = $80,888
Six inequities of system:
    1. Compulsory
    2. No regs. (as there are for private ins. co's)
    3. Pay as you go—*no reserves*
    4. Funds can be used for any purpose
    5. Congress can revoke—increase or decrease
    6. Gimmicks
Solution: *Get Gov't out of business!*

CONCL: Promise—still unfulfilled
              Don't let it happen *to you*. Beware!

Note that the brevity of these notes would make it possible for the speaker to fit them on two or three 3″ × 5″ cards, which might be used unobtrusively on the platform.

      An outline is the basic tool by which an extemporaneous speaker fixes the design of a speech as a composition, tests the reasonableness of that design, represents to self and others the relationships among his or her thoughts, and fixes the speech plan firmly in mind. A completed outline is a visual representation of how speech materials are going to be disposed or handled in the speech to come. Both making an outline and reviewing it are invaluable aids to what ancient writers on rhetoric had in mind when they used the Latin term *memoria*—the speaker's ultimate command of material, plan, and his or her own thinking processes in the moments of delivery. These being the justifications for outlining, the mechanics of the process are good or bad in proportion to how well they serve you for these purposes. To sum up, we have said that six common practices are invariably helpful:

1. Clear identification of the basic divisions of the speech: introduction, body, and conclusion
2. Use of consistent systems of symbolization and indentation to signal the relative importance of the relationships among ideas
3. Recognition that the appearance of single subpoints in an outline is likely to indicate that a relationship has not been clearly thought out
4. Firm adherence to the rule of discreteness in outlining; one thought per symbol; one symbol per thought
5. Clear and unmistakable identification of the central idea or subject sentence
6. Clear and unmistakable identification, in uniform fashion, of important transitions and internal summaries

The sample outlines we have provided for your study and analysis conform to these practices in most details.   They illustrate the general principles of disposition we have discussed in chapter 8.

EXERCISES

Written

1. Arrange the eleven statements below as an outline for a main point in a speech.   There is no title, introduction, or conclusion.   Select the sentence containing the main point and give it proper place and status in your outline.
   · Political bribery may be increased considerably due to heart transplants.
   · Some feel the poor man deserves it.
   · The families of the poor cannot afford prolonged private care without surgery.
   · *Saturday Review* of February 3rd reports an incident in which a prominent New York politician used his influence to have a half-hour conference with Dr. Christiaan Barnard when he was in Washington, D.C., to discuss the possibilities of his securing a heart transplant.
   · Heart transplants are ethically questionable.
   · Some feel the rich man who can afford surgery should receive it.
   · The poor are the only means of support for their families.
   · The January 6th *Science News* states, "A million dollars could buy a patient almost anything . . . including a new heart."
   · There are inequalities shown in deciding whose lives are to be saved through the miracle of heart transplants.
   · How many other unreported incidents of this sort will be revealed in the near future?
   · Some feel it should be the man or woman with special talent.
2. Make a list of suggestions for improvement of the outline entitled "The Big Fraud" (see pages 238–40).
3. In a sentence or two evaluate each of the following speech titles:
   a. "What You Must Do"
   b. "Acres of Diamonds"
   c. "Billy the Kid—Juvenile Delinquent?"
   d. "A Case for Euthanasia in the United States Today with Special Emphasis upon the Role of the General Practitioner in the Rural Areas"
   e. "Goya"
   f. "From Trees to Paper"
   g. "Drug Addicts: The Living Dead"
   h. "Some Evidences of the Pedagogical Philosophy and Techniques of Quintilian as They Are Found in Modern Speech Education"
   i. "The Sleeping Dragon"
   j. "The Eternal Verities"

Oral

1. Outline a speech by one of your classmates as you listen to him or her deliver it. Arrange for a conference during which you compare the outline you composed with the outline he or she used. Look for similarities and differences between the outlines and discuss why these occurred as they did.
2. Compose an outline for a six-minute speech of information or persuasion. Observe the suggestions made in this chapter and in chapter 7.
3. Here, in proper order, are the items of a blank outline. Choose a suitable subject, organize the items of the outline with proper symbols and indentations, and fill the blanks with ideas appropriate to the subject you have chosen. Be prepared to give this short speech extemporaneously at your next class meeting.

   · I wonder whether you have thought enough about _____(subject)_____ .
   · I would define _____(subject)_____ like this: _____ .
   · You can see what I mean by thinking of these examples:
   · My first example is: _____ .
   · Another example is: _____ .
   · What causes (or results from) _____ is this:

   _____ .
   · An example of how this happens is _____ .
   · Another example is _____ .
   · We usually think of _____ as something remote from our everyday lives, but there are cases where it makes a lot of difference to people like you and me.
   · One everyday influence it has (had) is (was) _____ .
   · Another influence is (was) _____ .
   · My conclusion is that the next time we hear people talk about _____ or think of it ourselves, we ought to remember it is no vague thing but something that can touch our lives as closely as in (refer to examples used) .

Style

Among all other lessons this should first be learned, that wee never affect any straunge inkehorne termes, but to speake as is commonly received: neither seeking to be over fine, nor yet living over-carelesse, using our speeche as most men doe, and ordering our wittes as the fewest have done.

Thomas Wilson, "Arte of Rhetorique"[1]

Man's expression of inner self probably emerges more clearly in his style than in any other aspect of his communication. The verbal ways in which a speaker symbolizes thought reveal his capacities to discriminate among meanings, to conceive ideas clearly, to represent them precisely. Styles reflect men's adjustments to their times. The relatively unguarded expression found in speaking mirrors habits of thinking with special sharpness. Thus examination of style provides information for conclusions both about accommodations to society and about society itself.

Speech consists of ideas converted into words. *Acoustic* words are the basic symbols of oral communication. When we speak, these acoustic symbols stimulate the listeners, and they stand for our ideas. We encode our thoughts and express our emotions in sound, hoping the listeners have the necessary aural repertoire of meanings to decode the message accurately or nearly so. The fundamental problem of oral style, then, is to find and use language true to our actual meanings and within the capacities of particular listeners to interpret with a high degree of accuracy. Hence, Thomas Wilson's advice to Englishmen learning to use English for formal purposes is still applicable: not the strange but the "commonly received," not the "fine" and not the "careless" but the precise and telling—for listeners—are the goals in developing a style for speaking. The work of speaking is not finished until ideas and feelings are *couched in the language of speech,* voiced, and given further meaning through bodily action.

---

1. Thomas Wilson, *Arte of Rhetorique* (London, 1585), p. 162.

The words we choose as symbols of our ideas, their capacities to stir meanings in listeners' minds, matter. There is a great difference between saying: "A girl in a red dress hesitated at the head of the flight of steps to look over the railing at the other young people who were waiting for her to come down," and saying, "A debutante in a scarlet gown paused at the top of the staircase to peer over the balustrade at the other adolescents who were anticipating her descent." Some people would see most of the words in these two sentences as synonyms—as words having substantially the same meanings. But it is very easy to see that although the sentences are similar in idea, they do not communicate the same images. The alternative words and their combinations create nuances that change the message you receive.

Through such stylistic choices speakers ultimately control what their audiences perceive. Since the primary concern in oral communication is to arouse precise meaning, success depends very much upon the speaker's ability to choose and combine symbols for aural reception. If we are to be practical, then, we must each be concerned with the art of creating an efficient, telling style. It is not a matter of being concerned with niceties of language or of playing with words. We have to be concerned because we use words symbolizing ideas whenever we speak. This being so, it is simply common sense to study seriously this aspect of our communication.

THE NATURE OF STYLE

Oral style is that part of rhetorical art that emerges from choices and combinations in language. The force of style derives from the meanings of words, their grammatical construction, and their collective psychological impact. We define *oral style* as the personal manner of utterance or expression giving ideas impact and movement. Style in this sense is the result of the most complex and personal of all the adjustments involved in human communication. You will be creating and controlling the processes of style as soon as you have selected an idea or have begun to arrange ideas in logical and psychological sequences. Some language decisions are made during stages of invention and disposition; but whole speeches almost never exist, even in the mind, until after the problems of language have been faced directly.

You will not always speak extemporaneously even though that mode of speaking finds most favor with most people. On the other hand, people do not ordinarily speak off the tops of their heads or even from just a few notes at inaugurals, commencements, dedications, or funerals, or in making technical reports. These occasions hold great significance; they are often once-in-a-lifetime events for those involved.

Whether everyday situations or special ones, all call for care in choosing symbols and often they dictate writing down one's verbal choices ahead of time. The more formal or technical the situation is, the more vital care becomes.

Our purpose in this chapter is to discuss resources you have when you need to make careful choices in solving the problems of style. We also consider the general role style plays in oral communication of all serious sorts. We use the term *style* in a limited sense. Style may be thought of as a quality pervading all of a communication, including the way it is uttered. Gestures and facial expressions operate as symbols to stir up thought, so style in delivery is worthy of consideration. However, in this chapter we consider style only as it relates to verbal composition, the conversion of ideas into words. The selection of words and their combination into thought units are our special topics in the pages that follow.

We want to emphasize at the outset that we conceive of style neither as decoration nor as the exhibition of mere facility with language. Many think that style is, as Lord Chesterfield said, "the dress of thoughts." They think of verbal style as clothing or covering, as something you *put on* ideas or *do to* them. Ideas are looked upon as windows to be trimmed or as Christmas trees; composition then becomes work from which you step back to see if the baubles and tinsel you have applied give interesting effects. This view we reject.

This concept of style as exornation, as superimposed beautification, is often associated with an equally erroneous conception that the object of working on problems of style is to produce something to be exhibited. When speakers try to dazzle their audiences with clever wordings or to impress them with long or archaic words or with quaint expressions, we think they misconceive the function of oral language. They miss its necessary relationship to idea, audience, and situation.

We believe that when language is truly effective it arises *from* and is at one *with* thought. Rather than worrying about how to exhibit a thought, we believe one should try to think clearly in the first place. We agree with Abba Eban, an exceptionally eloquent speaker:

> It's not a technique. I think it's really a function of intellect, like having a musical sense. It's a result of the shape of your mind and the gathering of resources by reading fine prose.

This was Eban's answer to a questioner who asked whether he spoke the same way in each of the five languages he knows fluently.[2] He insisted that "if you have any originality" the pursuit of good oral style is the same in all languages.

In the remainder of this chapter we try to help you to see ways

---

2. Unsigned interview with then Israeli Foreign Minister Abba Eban, "in late June of 1967" and published under the title, "Speaker," *New Yorker* XLVI (November 14, 1970): 45–48. The passage quoted is on p. 46.

to develop your personal style in speaking. Topics we treat are: how oral style differs from written; how to improve the style you have; constituents of effective style; and the resources of language as they relate to style.

ORAL AND WRITTEN STYLE

Speaking is not writing. Both deal with words, sentences, and language in general. Written style often has oral elements. Still, to compose for the ear is not to compose for the eye.

James A. Winans once said, "A speech is not an essay on its hind legs." He meant that an essay is not oral even though it may be rhetorical. The chances are that your essays, themes, and term papers, if read aloud, would lack some of the traits your spreaking ought to have. Proof of the differences lies mainly in everyday experience.

What little experimental evidence there is argues that the differences between oral and written style are differences not of kind but of degree.[3]

Available research and our personal observations provide the following hypotheses, which we invite you to test in your speech making. In contrast to written prose style, good oral style uses:

1. More personal pronouns
2. More variety in kinds of sentences
3. More variety in sentence lengths
4. More simple sentences
5. More sentence fragments
6. Many more rhetorical questions
7. More repetition of words, phrases, and sentences
8. More monosyllabic than polysyllabic words
9. More contractions
10. More interjections
11. More indigenous language
12. More connotative than denotative words

---

3. See, for example, Gladys L. Borchers, "An Approach to the Problem of Oral Style," *The Quarterly Journal of Speech* XXII (February 1936): 114–17; Gordon Thomas, "Effect of Oral Style on Intelligibility of Speech," *Speech Monographs* XXIII (March 1956): 46–54; Joseph A. De Vito, "Comprehension Factors in Oral and Written Discourse of Skilled Communicators," *Speech Monographs* XXXII (June 1965): 124–28; James W. Gibson, Charles R. Gruner, Robert J. Kibler, and Francis J. Kelly, "A Quantitative Examination of Differences and Similarities in Written and Spoken Messages," *Speech Monographs* XXXIII (November 1966): 444–51. The last study includes a valuable survey of contemporary studies of oral and written style.

13. More euphony
14. More figurative language
15. More direct quotation
16. More familiar words

Aristotle recognized much the same differences when he said:

> . . . each kind of rhetoric has its own appropriate style. The style of written prose is not that of controversial speaking. . . . A knowledge of both the written and spoken style is required. . . . The written . . . style is more finished; the controversial is far better adapted to dramatic delivery. . . . On comparison, speeches of the literary men sound thin in the actual contests; while those of the orators sound well but look crude when you hold them in your hands—and the reason is that their place is in a contest.[4]

When students are working on speech manuscripts, we urge them not to worry about how the speech looks on paper. Some sentences will look strange, and many constructions will depart from the writing patterns learned in a class in English composition. Criteria of writing for the eye such as the principles of paragraphing have limited relevance in composing for the ear. Neither Cicero nor Patrick Henry ever heard of a paragraph, but they did know about shorter thought units! Outstanding speakers use widely varying practices for major and minor ideas on the page. Editing, then, is for the convenience of the speaker, not for general readers.

The same is true of sentences. Speaking appropriately requires many more sentence fragments than formal writing. Every novelist who is expert in writing dialogue and every good playwright knows this. So to apply formal standards of sentence construction and sentence completeness in evaluating the manuscript form of a speech would be to force the communication to follow rules that do not normally apply. Consider a fragment from Franklin D. Roosevelt's address, "The Philosophy of Social Justice Through Social Action."[5] Using the best available records, L. LeRoy Cowperthwaite's judgment of what Mr. Roosevelt actually said in Detroit is quoted below. Notice how little the language resembles what we ordinarily call polished writing *for the eye*. Notice the broken sentence structures. Doubtless they were rendered smoothly meaningful by pause and vocal inflection.

---

4. From *The Rhetoric of Aristotle,* translated and edited by Lane Cooper, p. 217, bk. III, chap. 12. © 1932, renewed 1960 by Lane Cooper. Reprinted by permission of Prentice-Hall, Inc., Englewood Cliffs, New Jersey.

5. The text of President Roosevelt's speech excerpted here is based on an official stenographic report, his own manuscript, and a recording. This text appears in full in C. C. Arnold, D. Ehninger, and J. C. Gerber, eds., *Speaker's Resource Book* (Chicago: Scott, Foresman and Co., 1966), 2nd ed., pp. 135–39.

Notice the reinforcement gained by repetition of the words "crippled children"—reinforcement that writing for the eye might achieve in less obvious ways.   This is a very carefully established sample of the *oral* style of one of the most successful political speakers in the history of the United States.   This is the way he *talked:*

> Take another form of poverty in the old days.   Not so long ago, you and I know, there were families in attics—in every part of the Nation —in country districts and in city districts—hundreds and thousands of crippled children who could get no adequate care, crippled children who were lost to the community and who were a burden on the community.   And so we have, in these past twenty or thirty years, gradually provided means for restoring crippled children to useful citizenship; and it has all been a factor in going after and solving one of the causes of poverty and disease.

Other differences in oral and written style will reflect the sixteen special qualities listed above.   Usually the text of a speech ought to exhibit fewer "howevers," "thuses," and "therefores" than an essay might; it ought to contain words and phrases such as "but," "and so," or "the result of high cost is."   These last examples are simply the connectives of normal conversation.

Speeches ought to contain few indefinite pronouns.   "This" and "that" are ambiguous words for a listener.   They always require him or her to remember some noun used earlier.   It is often hard to recall that the "this" now heard actually means the "cathedral" heard five or ten seconds ago.

Whether you are writing or speaking, you will convey meaning more forcefully and usually more clearly if you use verbs in the active voice.   There is more efficient meaning and more action in "The dog bit the man" than in "The man was bitten by the dog."   "It is believed by most observers that a decision will be made by the president on Thursday" is awkward writing and poor speaking.   Listening is neither easy nor a highly efficient way of absorbing information.   Good oral style compensates for these limitations by its directness; one of the easiest, most obvious compensations is to use active verbs as much as possible, in the present tense where that is appropriate.   There are times when the detachment produced by the use of passive voice is desirable, but ordinarily active voice serves best.

Scientific evidence does not justify an unqualified declaration that using the sixteen characteristics we enumerated above and keeping your talk in the active voice as much as possible will result in successful oral style.   The point we want to stress is that oral style needs to develop in the context of the special situation where speaking takes place.   It is crucially important that speaking is heard, not read.   This is what dictates that oral style be conversational, personal, and responsive to the thought processes of listeners. If you try to make choices conducive to developing the qualities of spoken language, you will begin to increase your conversational quality and rid your speaking of a written sound that disturbs and hampers efficient listening.

THE DEVELOPMENT OF YOUR STYLE

We have been implying that you can improve your speaking style. You already have your own particular manner of utterance—good or bad. Consider the other members of your speech class. You will notice that some of them have distinctive styles. One may help you see more visual images, let you see and feel the things talked about. Another may have a rough-hewn style—terser, plainer, or more home-spun in wordings. Still others may be abstract, may habitually use colloquialisms, cliches, or slang, or may be exceedingly precise in explanations. Why these styles impress you as different from one another may be difficult for you to determine, but every speaker has habits that favor particular kinds of language and certain stylistic devices. Each one consciously or unconsciously endows his or her speech with particular characteristics. Each style, including yours, has its hallmarks.

These styles differ partly because each of you works differently. When you revise and reword, you modify and change ideas to say what you mean. Or you just don't think ahead about language. Do you really make full use of your linguistic opportunities? Even when you speak extemporaneously, you need to express yourself as accurately as possible. Even then you can try out wordings as you work from your outlines or your speaker's notes. You need not freeze wordings. You can build a reservoir of alternative, effective phrasings. At every point in composition you can make choices that will make your style uniquely yours. It is important to remember that although readers may flip back through a book to reread thought, listeners seldom relisten to your speech. It must, therefore, be clear to them upon first hearing, and your style can help to make it so.

A style of some sort, then, is yours at the outset. You have a vocabulary at some stage of development and special habits of expression. Your background, prior education, and methods of writing have exerted their influences. Some of your habits of expression are good ones that need emphasis. Others are faults to be eradicated. Improvement comes from developing your strengths and removing your weaknesses. You start by surveying your present speech style and work from there. It takes a long time to change a style. Developing an effective style is a slow process. You cannot expect fixed changes to emerge overnight, but you will be surprised at how you can gradually modify your style through conscious attention and experimentation.

Your aim ought to be to nurture variety. An inflexible style will not meet the demands of enough different speech situations. As Herbert Spencer said, "To have a specific style is to be poor in speech."[6] The many adjustments necessary to meet the demands of specific speaking situations preclude the use of any one style in all cases. The style of a chemistry or mathematics lecture would hardly be suitable for a popular lecture on the advancement of science. An inspirational sermon would be poorly couched in the jargon of a salesman. In a sense, then, improvement involves developing *styles* within a general way of talking that is both effective and your own.

Situation, not purpose, governs the characteristics of a style that is practically effective. Some people think that informative speaking is distinguished by language of fact and explanation, the diction of definition, example, comparison, and literal vocabulary. Such broad generalizations are unsatisfactory. It seems to us that the *situation* for information rather than the *purpose* determines what is appropriate. Thus there is no section in this book in which style is matched to speaking purposes. No one characteristic of style is exclusively associated with any one purpose. What you need is a personal, distinctive manner of utterance within which many variations may be made as you adapt to the requirements of ideas, audiences, occasions, and your own needs. What is it that you are to adapt? The resources imbedded in language itself.

What sort of program for long-range improvement should you follow? To manage your speech well, try to:

1. *Become language conscious.* Become sensitive to good and bad uses of words. Discover your faults in grammar and those points of style where you seem to be most limited. Ferret out weaknesses such as want of vividness, poor syntax, malapropism, use of clichés. Listen carefully. Read widely. At times read aloud to test the *orality* of your language.

2. *Increase your speaking vocabulary.* It is alleged that the average college student's day-to-day, working oral vocabulary is about 250 words. Is it any wonder that many students' speaking style lacks precision, color, and rhythmic variety? To improve your style try consciously to extend the number of words and phrasings at your command. You do not have to go out of your way to master unusual words and unique phrases; learn the meanings of the language you normally encounter but do not understand. You are after the most accurate and appropriate words. Keep a dictionary handy and refer to it when you see or hear unfamiliar words. *Roget's Thesaurus* will also help, but

6. Herbert Spencer, *The Philosophy of Style* (New York: D. Appleton, 1920), p. 47.

look up its synonyms in the dictionary to fix precise meanings in your mind.

3. *Write.* By expressing yourself on paper you will learn to make conscious word choices. Writing will improve your vocabulary and the accuracy with which you use words. Aim for the best written expression when writing for the eye and the best oral expression when writing for the ear.

4. *Rewrite.* Experiment with parts of an extemporaneous speech by writing and rewriting them—not for the purpose of producing *a* way of saying an idea but for the purpose of discovering several good ways of saying it. The best speakers put their speeches through several drafts, even when not planning to speak from manuscript. Benjamin Disraeli, a great parliamentary debater, experimented with phrasings of key portions of his speeches, then rehearsed alone and before friendly critics, and rewrote again—to speak extemporaneously! Franklin Roosevelt, a master of the craft of manuscript speaking, put some of his speeches through as many as twelve drafts before he was satisfied. The point is that if you write and rewrite portions of speeches you can smooth out wordings, correct unclear constructions, tinker with phrasings, rearrange ideas and their linkages. All the while you will be expanding your verbal resources and, even when you speak extemporaneously or impromptu, these added "ways of saying" will be available in your mind.

5. *Study published and live speeches.* Note what makes for success and failure in style. Take cues from the good models. Avoid the faults of bad ones. Imitate the style of others, but for practice and exercise only. Do not study the style of great speakers to copy them; study them to incorporate their best attributes in a distinctive style suited particularly to you.

6. *Speak in public.* Take advantage of opportunities to refine your expression of ideas in both conversation and public address. Speak as often as possible. The more you speak, especially in the extemporaneous and impromptu modes, the better you will become at finding ways to finish phrases and statements effectively no matter how you started them. The more experience you have with thinking on your feet and symbolizing your ideas as they develop in your mind, the more fluent and attractive your style will become.

CONSTITUENTS OF EFFECTIVE STYLE

A useful way of looking at style is to consider the general qualities or traits of language that contribute to effectiveness. These are qualities that combine to constitute a speaker's personal, distinctive way of speaking and the variations within it. They are attributes or constituents of style *as listeners view style*.   Whether they understand the uses of language well or not, your listeners are always asking themselves whether what you say is *accurate* in relation to what you probably mean.   They also ask whether what you are saying is *clear, appropriate,* and *economical* in relation to the task you have undertaken.   Listeners respond specially to *forceful, striking,* and *lively* language that keeps interest up and gives ideas the right emphases.   From listeners' points of view your speech, however individualistic, must seem good in at least these six ways.

Accuracy

Whatever is said has some degree of accuracy; any thought expressed has some amount of precision or fuzziness.   Your accuracy depends on your ability to choose words that will represent as exactly as possible what you want your listeners to understand.   The precision and range of your vocabulary will partially determine your accuracy. If you use "infer" for "imply" or vice versa, no listener can get your meaning precisely.   Would it be better to say, "I *telephoned* my father" or to say, "I *contacted* my father?"   The first is more specific, more accurate, and, therefore, clearer.   You will solve problems of accuracy best by concerning yourself with the concreteness and exact meanings of words.   What saps the strength of our language is the failure, usually through laziness, to search out the accurate and sometimes unexpected word.   Too few of us take the trouble to find out the differences in meaning between words such as *institution* and *corporation* or *ghost* and *banshee*.

Grammatical accuracy—observing the convention your listeners respect most—ought to guide you in putting words together in meaningful combinations.   It has been said since classical times, and modern experiments and surveys have repeatedly confirmed it, that whatever listeners take as slips in grammar will negatively affect your image as a speaker.   Conventional usage is expected by audiences unless the immediate situation contains unique features.   With educated audiences your standards ought to be the same as Cicero's:

> . . nobody ever admired an orator for correct grammar, they only laugh at him if his grammar is bad, and not only think him no orator but not even a human being; no one ever sang the praises of a speaker whose style succeeded in making his meaning intelligible to his audience, but only despised one deficient in capacity to do so.[7]

---

7. *De Oratore*, trans. H. Rackham (Cambridge, Mass.: Harvard University Press, 1948), vol. II, pp. 41–42, bk. III, chap. 14, sec. 52.

The literature of experimental research done with college students as subjects confirms each of Cicero's points, although it appears that college-educated listeners do not so much laugh at as regret grammatical inaccuracies in speaking.

A third concern in achieving accuracy ought to be for what is correct for one's situation. Matters of accuracy, correctness, and appropriateness come into blended consideration here. If you need to produce a particular tone or feeling, you may need to choose between several levels of language, any of which might be accurate to your basic meaning. For example, the formality of an occasion may force a special choice. In a parliamentary situation, "I agree with George's idea" may accurately reflect your attitude, but it is both inaccurate and inappropriate to the ways of doing parliamentary business. "I support the motion presented by George Green" would have both accuracy and propriety for this situation. Your level of abstraction and the technicality of your language can be *both* accurate and appropriate only if your immediate audience understands what you say and the occasion justifies the way it is said. The most convivial gathering of astronauts would allow levels of technicality and precision that would be bafflingly imprecise and inappropriate for a high school class in general science. The same could be said of the "in" language of motorcycle buffs.

What is accurate enough to be efficient in speech is always modified by who speaks, to whom, on what idea, and under what circumstances. The right language must meet all these tests at once.

Clarity

What listeners demand as clarity involves more than the precision discussed above. At the beginning of his discussion of style in *The Rhetoric,* Aristotle said: "We may therefore . . . regard it as settled that a good style is, first of all, clear. The proof is that language which does not convey a clear meaning fails to perform the very function of language."[8] So you must ask yourself, "How clearly have I expressed the idea?"

Aristotle went on to say: "Clearness is secured through the use of name-words [nouns and adjectives] and, verbs, that are current terms. . . ."[9] His judgment is still sound. Listeners prefer concrete to abstract words. Good transitions and simple, familiar sentence structures help them, no matter what their levels of sophistication. So the

---

8. *The Rhetoric of Aristotle,* translated and edited by Lane Cooper, p. 185, bk. III, chap. 2. © 1932, renewed 1960 by Lane Cooper. Reprinted by permission of Prentice-Hall, Inc., Englewood Cliffs, New Jersey.
    9. Ibid.

more directly you say what you have to say, the more likely you are to be clear.[10]

What your listeners are *ready* to understand ought also to help you decide *how much* you can say and still be clear. How far you can go in amplifying or giving details must be determined by how much your listeners already know—or how little. It is easy to say so much you are unclear. Some years ago a commencement speaker, early in his speech, said,

> We place less and less emphasis on the joy of achievement—and more and more on the achievement of joy. . . . And when you grasp the full implications of our altering philosophy of work, you can no longer regard it with equanimity.

We are confident that his listeners had no notion of what he was talking about because he had not yet prepared them by clarifying what "achievements" and what "philosophy of work" he had in mind. His nice antithesis and his strong assertion of a danger were wasted because his audience was not yet ready to understand exactly what either referred to.

To put this point another way, you may be entirely accurate about an idea and still be unclear. This is important to remember about both general and technical material. Except among specialists and people who already agree with you and each other, clarity requires that you interpret ideas precisely by filling in definitions of terms, analogies, contrasts, and the like. But there another danger must be watched for and avoided. *Mis*information can be communicated clearly. To explain the transmission of sound it is clarifying and accurate, up to a certain point, to ask listeners to think of sound waves as spreading out as ripples do when a stone is dropped into water. The comparison and the associated language having to do with water can help an uninformed listener greatly. But if he is allowed to think of sound waves as *looking like* ripples, he will be misinformed. The "water language" must be quickly abandoned once the image of the spreading movement has been established, for sound waves travel through walls and holes as water waves do not.

As the examples above suggest, clarity is a goal you work for relative to a particular audience, but your idea, itself, is inevitably a controlling factor, too. The occasion on which you speak may influence you if it is of a special nature. But your own preferences should influence you least in making choices of language. There is the rub! Your clarity, for yourself, will tempt you to disregard your listeners'

---

10. You will find Rudolph Flesch's *The Art of Plain Talk* (New York: Harper & Brothers, 1946) exceedingly helpful and informative on this point and others. The work deals chiefly with writing, but the principles and methods discussed are valuable to speakers.

clarity, the opportunities your subject offers you, and special aspects of your occasion. Clarity thus becomes a matter of *self-discipline*.

Propriety

Propriety, or appropriateness, is also characteristic of any good oral style. Speaking, unlike the writing in an essay or a novel, is meant for a particular audience gathered in a particular place at a particular time. Particularity and close adjustment are the goals of oral style, not universality or adaptation to respondents in all places at all times.

One's style must, of course, be appropriate to the subject matter treated. "The style again," as Aristotle declared, "should not be mean nor above the dignity of the subject, but appropriate. . . ."[11] To describe a commonplace operation, such as changing a tire, in flowery language would be ridiculous. Such menial subjects are not good ones for stylistic experimentation. To depict a sunset in plain vernacular is to rob the subject of meaning and of its inherent emotional quality. To say "the sky was kind of red, sort of like a tomato or a radish," would be as inappropriate as to say of a tire, "the shiny black vulcanized rubber besmirched by dust and grime, ought to be carefully loosened from the band which girdles the wheel."

As we have said, audiences as well as subjects impose standards of appropriateness. You could hardly use the same vocabularies or phrasings when talking to a group of college alumni, to a group of boy scouts, and to persons lacking in formal education. The words used for these groups would vary as would the amount of elaboration. Yet in adapting to each particular audience you must still be careful always to be yourself. You must not sell yourself *or* your listeners short. A college graduate who tries to sound at different times like a farmer at a Grange meeting, a juvenile delinquent at a boys' reformatory, and a college professor in the classroom is play acting. Somewhere he will slip and become ridiculous. So in tailoring your style to an audience, do not forget that you can and must tailor it to yourself—and to your listeners, the occasion, and the subject. *Your style*, as Buffon noted, *is you*, yourself. It is a very personal thing. It forms your manner of expression. Straining too hard or trying too strenuously to adapt to an audience or striving for a special level of style, as some beginning students do, usually results in style that smells of the lamp or sounds like a caricature. You, as you are, define what *can* be appropriate for you, even after all other controls have been considered.

Style must be appropriate to subject matter, audience, and speaker, and to the particular occasion. To use the same style in a

---

11. *The Rhetoric of Aristotle*, p. 185, bk. III, chap. 2.

corporate meeting or at a professional meeting as you would use for informal remarks at a fraternity gathering would be to court disaster. On certain occasions it is traditional to be formal. On other occasions it is more appropriate to be relaxed, informal, and to indulge, with taste, in slang and colloquialisms. Common sense will usually let you solve these problems of adjustment—if you think about them.

Economy

Most of us use too many words when we speak. We clutter thoughts so even when we are not obscure, we irritate. Listeners want efficiency. That is why they want clarity and interestingness.

By economy in language we mean the right choice of words, in right amount, and in best order for instantaneous intelligibility.

In his *The Philosophy of Style* Herbert Spencer emphasized the importance of economizing the "mental energies" and "mental sensibilities" of auditors or readers. "To so present ideas that they may be apprehended with the least possible mental effort, is the desideratum towards which most of the rules . . . point," he said.[12] Spencer claimed that the secret of effect lies in right choice and collocation of words, the best arrangement of clauses to clarify the ranks of principal and subordinate propositions, judicious use of figures of speech, and creation of a rhythmic sequence of syllables. He summarized his "principle of economy" thus:

> A reader or listener has at each moment but a limited amount of mental power available. To recognize and interpret the symbols presented to him requires part of his power; to arrange and combine the images suggested requires a further part; and only that part which remains can be used for realizing the thought conveyed. Hence, the more time and attention it takes to receive and understand each sentence, the less time and attention can be given to the contained idea; and the less vividly will that idea be conceived.[13]

Extreme brevity is characteristic of passionate language, but the fewest number of words for effective expression is not always the smallest number possible. Economy of attention is economy only if the idea is fully clear and understandable. At times, economy in style means not brevity or frugality but the necessary amplification. A further fact to consider is that speech needs to be more ample than writing. One reason is that listeners cannot review unless speakers provide the necessary words.[14]

---

12. Spencer, *The Philosophy of Style*, p. 11.
13. Ibid.
14. This point is discussed on pp. 249–52 in the section on "Oral and Written Style."

No one can tell you exactly how to judge in advance when you have thought out just enough to say about a point. But as you speak you have one major way of gauging what is needed. You can watch listeners closely, looking for facial and other evidences that they have or have not understood, have or have not accepted what you are saying. If you have prepared sufficient material and several different ways of stating things, you will find it possible to enlarge your discussions of ideas when you see signs of uncertainty and to cut out unneeded bits when you receive signs of acceptance. It is, in fact, a great advantage that in planning and rehearsing for extemporaneous speaking you can and probably will evolve several ways of saying most things. In final presentation, then, you can work from the briefest to the amplest expression of any point if feedback from listeners shows that *more* than a minimum of right words in best order is needed for intelligibility.

Force

Listeners like language that has drive, urgency, action. It compels them to pay attention as it propels ideas forward. Economy, precision, and simple grammatical constructions produce force. Spencer supplies the link when he says, ". . . other things equal, the force of all verbal forms and arrangements is great in proportion as the time and mental effort they demand from the recipient is small."[15] Modern research in linguistics and stylistics bears him out. The simplest, easiest, and so most forthright construction in English is the simple, subject-verb-object or modifier. This form you first experienced when you first read "I see the ball." Interfere with the sense between "I" and "see," and you will complicate understanding and also lose force: "I, to the best of my judgment, see the ball." The complexity of an idea or the character of your situation may make the more complicated kind of construction all but inevitable (e.g., "The measurement, taken at 70 degrees Fahrenheit, is 60 millimeters"), but you should know that force and simplicity are sacrificed if you interfere with your listener's simplest thought movement from the subject to the predicate.

Some words are more forceful than others. It appears that it is not length or the origin of a word that makes it complex and unforceful. It is the number of "interior" meanings the word contains. Rudolph Flesch explains:

> Language gadgets . . . are of two kinds: words by themselves, like *against,* and parts of words (affixes), like *dis-*. The more harmful of the two for plain talk are the affixes, since the reader or hearer cannot

---

15. Spencer, *The Philosophy of Style,* p. 33.

understand what the gadget does to the sentence before he has dis-
entangled it from the word it is attached to.   Each affix burdens his
mind with two jobs: first, he has to split up the word into its parts and,
second, he has to rebuild the sentence from these parts.   To do this
does not even take a split second, of course; but it adds up.[16]

You need not avoid all complicating and force-diminishing affixed
words, but whenever there is a choice you ought to prefer the simplest
word that will be accurate.   The student who said, "Your response is a
variant of the teleological argument for the existence of God," was unnecessarily complex.   He was, therefore, less forceful than he could
have been.   He could have said, "Your answer is like the argument that
the world seems orderly, so a God must have organized it."   He would
have used more words, but they would have been simpler.   His grammar would have been a bit more usual, and the gadgety word
teleological would not steal force and clarity.

There is no clear empirical proof of it, but experience argues
that listeners like active terms more than passive ones and pictorial
words and phrases more than abstract ones.[17]   You can choose words
that denote or suggest actions.   You can also keep as much of your
talk as possible in the active voice.   Then both vocabulary and grammar will work toward successful communication.   Any college student
can approximate the precision, clarity, appropriateness, economy, and
force that Leonard Bernstein attained in a televised broadcast.   He was
doing the difficult job of speaking about a musical composition:

> Whether you call this kind of weird piece "cool" or "crazy" or "futur-
> istic" or "modernistic" or whatever, the fact is that it is bordering on
> serious concert music.   The arrangement begins to be a *composition*.
> Take away the beat, and you might not even know it's jazz at all.   It
> would be just a concert piece.   And why is it jazz?   Because it is
> played by jazz men, on jazz instruments, and because it has its roots
> in the soil of jazz and not of Bach.[18]

All the constituents of style we have so far discussed are present in this short passage from the speech of a brilliant expositor.
Notice especially, however, that *no* subject is separated from its verb
by intervening thought; of eighty-six words only about fifteen (depending on cne's method of analyzing) are gadget terms; action words and

---

16. Flesch, *The Art of Plain Talk*, p. 42.

17. See pp. 269–78, "Figures of Speech" for fuller discussion of the second
of these points.

18. From Leonard Bernstein's televised lecture "The World of Jazz," in
The Joy of Music.   © 1959.   Used by permission of Simon and Schuster, New
York.   The text of this lecture is also available in Arnold, Ehninger, and Gerber,
eds. *The Speaker's Resource Book*, pp. 67–76.

descriptive words are scattered throughout; and the passive voice is never used. The English language offers you the same resources for creating straightforward, forceful style. What is required of you is forethought about simplicity and force and, of course, clear ideas to begin with.

Striking Quality

The characteristic of style we choose to call *striking quality* gives speech heightened effect. Writers have called this characteristic "interestingness," "impressiveness," "vividness," or "beauty."

We reject "beauty" because speaking is a utilitarian art. Its primary function is never to be beautiful. A speech admired for the sole reason that it aroused the imagination as a poem would be suspect as rhetoric. A speech whose main virtue is that it is euphonious is also suspect. Beauty alone will not do in practical art. Moreover, the ugly can sometimes be useful; the revolting as well as the attractive can draw attention and have useful effect. "Striking quality" seems to us the better concept because it recognizes the many aspects of language that can seize and guide thought. The unknown writer called Longinus said in his *On the Sublime:*

> . . . the choice of proper and striking words wonderfully attracts and enthralls the hearer, and . . . such a choice is the leading ambition of all orators and writers, since it is the direct agency which ensures the presence in writings, as upon the fairest statues, of the perfection of grandeur, beauty, mellowness, dignity, force, power, and any other high qualities there may be, and breathes into dead things a kind of living voice.[19]

Longinus also pointed out, ". . . stately language is not to be used everywhere, since to invest petty affairs with great and high-sounding names would seem just like putting a full-sized tragic mask upon an infant boy."[20] Georges Louis Leclerc, Count de Buffon, echoed him: "Nothing is more inimical to this warmth [of style] than the desire to be everywhere striking."[21]

---

19. Longinus, "On the Sublime," trans. W. Rhys Roberts, in J. H. Smith and E. W. Parks, *The Great Critics,* 3rd ed. (New York: W. W. Norton, 1951), p. 95.

20. Ibid., pp. 95–96.

21. Georges Louis Leclerc, Count de Buffon, "Discours sur le Style," in *The Art of the Writer: Essays, Excerpts, and Translations,* ed. Lane Cooper (Ithaca, N.Y.: Cornell University Press, 1952), p. 151.

The quotations from Longinus and from Buffon suggest the delicacy of deciding how to express ideas verbally. From one side aspirations for accuracy, clarity, economy, and simplicity ought to tug at any speaker, but from another side the wish to make at least some ideas striking ought to draw him too. It is probably not too much to say that the history of John F. Kennedy's life will continue to be something a little special to Americans because he uttered the uniquely formal sentence, "Ask not what your country can do for you—ask what you can do for your country." The turn of phrase embedded a familiar idea within history and made it one specially associated with Mr. Kennedy. The college student who said "The Inner City does this—it crushes and shatters thousands; it is our shame" struck a strong blow for serious consideration of urban decay. In telling of his summer's work in Harlem he wanted very much to shake up his fellow students on the subject. His striking phrasing helped to accomplish that; and you may have similar needs from time and time.

Striking quality in language comes from giving poetic turns to words while keeping them prose, from painting word pictures that stir listeners' emotions, from combining words in unexpected and sometimes alliterative or euphonious ways. It is the *unique* expression that seizes listeners' attention specially. In most circumstances at least a bit of uniqueness can serve almost any speaker's purposes. Aristotle's advice was, ". . . it is well to give the ordinary idiom an air of remoteness; the hearers are struck by what is out of the way, and like what strikes them."[22] *Remoteness* presumably leaves the impression we have called *uniqueness* in expression. But as Longinus and Buffon warned, not everything is important enough to bear the honor of unique phrasing. So the subject matter you are handling at any moment of speaking severely controls whether you should apply striking phrases. Of course, what your listeners are familiar with will define what will prove striking to them. Your own taste can also govern, but not alone. You may be fond of imagery, pleasing sound combinations, and unusual turns of phrase. As long as this fondness does not produce exhibitionism it is all to the good, and striking quality is likely to become a mark of your oral style. But it does not follow that effective speaking cannot be accomplished without striking quality; the passage just quoted from Bernstein is an illustration of that fact. Or is Bernstein's very simplicity striking?

Particularly important in any decision to try for the striking is the occasion. Ritualized occasions for speech cry out for touches of originality. Awards are presented and accepted constantly, and welcomes and farewells must be said. The usual has been said many times, in usual ways. In such circumstances a speaker's major goal

---

22. *The Rhetoric of Aristotle*, p. 185, bk. III, chap. 2.

might be to speak the old in a fresh way, to seek striking variations on old, familiar themes.

Liveliness

Force, economy, and striking quality contribute to *liveliness* in oral communication. If the mission of rhetoric is to endow ideas with movement and if its goal is, as C. S. Baldwin said, "the energizing of knowledge and the humanizing of truth,"[23] there is no more important stylistic quality oral discourse can have than liveliness.

Aristotle recognized the basic devices that generate liveliness when he said that listeners ". . . like words that set an event before their eyes; for they must see the thing occurring now, not hear of it as in the future."[24] The speaker, he said, must "aim at these three points: Metaphor, Antithesis, Actuality."[25] He thereafter advised speakers to make their verbal pictures move—to make them motion pictures rather than still photographs as modern photographers might put it. The goal is not still-life images but "objects . . . invested with life," and thereby "an effect of activity."[26] The successful stylist is one who ". . . makes everything live and move; and movement is activity."[27]

In discussing "actuality" Aristotle says,

> We have said that liveliness is secured by the use of proportional metaphor, and by putting things directly before the eyes of the audience. But we still have to explain what is meant by setting things "before the eyes," and how this is to be effected. What I mean is, using expressions that show things in a state of activity.[28]

Liveliness comes from animation, conflict, suspense, actuality (or realism), specificity, and proximity in what you say. It comes from using the present tense and the active voice. It comes from economy in wording, from simple rather than complex structuring, from vivid imagery, and from any other resource of language that sets moving images before the minds of listeners.

Relate events in a "you are there" rather than an "I was there"

---

23. *Ancient Rhetoric and Poetic* (Gloucester, Mass.: Peter Smith, 1959), p. 247.

24. *The Rhetoric of Aristotle,* translated and edited by Lane Cooper. pp. 207–8, bk. III, chap. 10. © 1932, renewed 1960 by Lane Cooper. Reprinted by permission of Prentice-Hall, Inc., Englewood Cliffs, New Jersey.

25. Ibid., p. 208, bk. III, chap. 10.

26. Ibid., p. 211, bk. III, chap. 11.

27. Ibid., p. 212, bk. III, chap. 11.

28. Ibid., p. 211, bk. III, chap. 11.

fashion.   Take your audience with you as you relive the suspenseful moment when your boat capsized or your car crashed.   Let the audience feel the tape breaking across your chest at the finish line of a race, the touch of your friend's hand at the moment of good-bye, the pull of your muscles as they lift a rock or kick a football.   Make your images cumulate and build.   Let your appeals to sight, touch, taste, hearing, and smell, to thermal and kinesthetic sensitivity, so combine that images in the mind are experienced.   Combining images and constructing a *past* experience in the *present* tense might produce such a passage as: "I smell the pines.   The morning air is crisp, and I hear the crunch of snow beneath me as I plod up the path.   My tired muscles seem to cry out at every step."   In this sequence, four kinds of sensory images combine to bring a whole experience to reality.   These are ways to make use of those rhetorical features for which listeners are always ready, as we said in chapter 3 (pp. 73-76).   Experiment with animation, actuality, and imagery and you will find that your speeches can attain realism and movement.   What you say can run to its goal rather than limp to its conclusion.

Bouncing, vigorous, hard-muscled style fits some situations and not others.   An extremely lively style may be out of place at eight o'clock in the morning.   The solemnity of a commencement or a worship service may call for gentle pace rather than for vigorous movement.   But whatever the occasion, clear, concrete images are never out of place. Liveliness through metaphor, antithesis, realism, and progressive movement of ideas is possible with or without high excitement.   That is fortunate for some speech materials lend themselves better to lively discourse than others.   Narratives are especially susceptible to animated treatments and committee reports and speeches of inquiry often demand your diligent search for the means to liveliness.

To say that liveliness is the most important of all qualities of good oral style is no exaggeration; it is a forthright summary of all we have just said.   Accuracy, clarity, propriety, economy, force, and striking quality are constituents of good style, but they are constituents of the ultimate virtue of speech that influences—liveliness.

THE RESOURCES OF LANGUAGE

Words are symbols; they stand for and suggest ideas.   No word has exactly the same meaning for any two individuals.   Words uttered are combinations of sounds that travel through air.   We endow them with meaning.   The meaning assigned depends upon the human being who perceives the sounds.   Background makes him or her interpret word symbols in particular and sometimes peculiar ways.   Parental authority, environment, and learning combine to determine exactly what a word will mean to any one of us.

Connotation and Denotation

As sounds or print, words always have at least two kinds of meaning: denotative and connotative. Some words denote much and connote relatively little—for most people. *Denotative words* seem more logical, objective, impersonal, and extensional. They refer explicitly to objects and actions outside the mind that are verifiable through observation. Many denotative words require few further words of explanation. A fairly denotative statement would be, "President Jones called the meeting to order. Secretary Smith read the minutes of the last meeting."

Connotative words are those that, for most people, have important emotive, subjective, personal, and intensional meanings. Their meanings turn toward the self. Meanings are private, suggestive, and depend upon the individual's emotions. Words such as *mother, homecoming, democracy, black,* and *lover* are rich in connotation. They arouse emotional responses, create images in the mind, and evoke the established attitudes of the listener. These words can be explained—rendered precise or public—only through the use of other words.

Most words, of course, are both connotative and denotative because their objective meanings touch off personal reactions. The word *house* can in many cases be considered denotative, as in a sentence reading, "There are twenty houses in the 300 block of Elm Avenue." This same word in other contexts may call to mind a particular house or a particular experience with a house and thus becomes strongly connotative.

In distinguishing between the two kinds of meaning, Professor S. I. Hayakawa is helpful:

> . . . the extensional meaning is something that cannot be expressed in words, because it is what the words stand for. An easy way to remember this is to put your hand over your mouth and point when asked to give the extensional meaning.
>
> The intensional meaning of a word or expression, on the other hand, is that which is suggested (connoted) inside one's head. Roughly speaking, whenever we express the meaning of words by uttering more words, we are giving intensional meaning, or connotations. To remember this, put your hand over your eyes and let the words spin around in your head.[29]

---

29. S. I. Hayakawa, *Language in Action* (New York: Harcourt, Brace, 1946), p. 47.

The fact that words have connotations and denotations shows that our systems of language are imperfect as precise representations of reality. *Semantics*, the science of word meanings, deals with some of these imperfections. It is enough to say here that confusion in meanings poses many problems for speakers. It is almost too much for them to hope they will stir up the exact meanings they intend. Almost any symbol may mean one thing to a speaker and quite another to his listeners. So speakers must make choices and revisions to maintain practical control over intended meanings.

A word choice is a mistake, of course, if it implants an unintended message in the mind of a listener. Mental pictures are altered and modified by changes in wording. To say "I saw a *red* bicycle" prompts a different image from "I saw a *pink* bicycle" or "I saw a *fuchsia* bicycle" or "I saw a *vermilion* bicycle" or ". . . a *Chinese red* bicycle" or ". . . a *Coca-Cola red* bicycle." The manufacturers of nail polish could extend the list of reds *ad infinitum*. Similarly to say "The child skipped *gaily* down the street" is different from saying the child skipped *merrily* or *joyously* or *boisterously*, or even *happily*. But a change of adjective or adverb is secondary to a change of noun or verb. Substitute *lad* or *youth* or *teen-ager* or even *girl* or *boy* for *child*, and the meaning changes markedly. Or substitute *shuffled* or *skated* or *strolled* for *skipped* and the mental picture is again modified drastically. To stir up an intended meaning, just any word will not do even though it conforms to all grammatical conventions.

At times the wrong choice of word, a malapropism, can make meaning ludicrous or spoil the mood created by a speaker, undoing several minutes' work. We think of the student who said that a speaker's body was "stagnant" when he meant "static," and of the student who spoke of "illiciting" rather than "eliciting" audience responses. We also think of the student speaker who, in describing a thief's actions during a robbery, coined a new word when he declared that the thief "slurked" around the corner. Whether the intended meaning was "slunk around" or "lurked at" or "sneaked around" was found out only by questioning the speaker. When he was questioned something fundamental came out: the idea, the image, was not exactly clear in the speaker's own mind. His coined word was in fact a way of evading clear, denotative meaning. From these examples, we gain two basic guidelines for making meanings serve rather than hinder you: (1) Determine your own exact meaning. (2) Once you know your meaning select from the accepted terms the one or ones that conform most closely to the meaning in your mind. But select those terms that are unlikely to connote anything incompatible with your immediate rhetorical purpose within the situation you plan to enter or have entered.

To do this you will, of course, have to be sensitive to the changing character of language.

Word Changes

A resource (and possible source of trouble) is that language is a system of meanings in continual flux. Meanings of words change with locality and with time. Some words are indigenous and even peculiar to geographical areas. In one region of the country people buy sandwiches called *heros*. But in other areas they buy *submarines* or *grinders* or *hoagies* or *wedgies* or *poor boys*. In all cases they are purchasing the sort of sandwich that originated in the Blondie comic strip. The sandwich was first dubbed the *Dagwood*, a name taken from the character who first made such gastronomic creations.

Verbal expressions come and go as fads change; other sayings have special meanings to particular "in" groups at particular times. Depending on your speech situation, you may speak clearly and appropriately of *motorcycles* as *motorbikes, cycles,* or *bikes*. If you are talking about the 1950s, a young person wandering about the country had better be called a *beatnik,* but the same kind of person wandering about later could be better identified as a *hippie* or by saying he joined the *street people*. A *skin flick* was a *stag film* on campuses some years ago; today the term equates for many with *X-rated movie*. *Black* and *Negro* have become especially sensitive terms, and you need to know an audience well to determine which will carry precisely the denotation and connotation you want. Some words are added, some are replaced, as noted in our Dagwood illustration. Words and expressions also become tired and worn out. Certain expressions become clichés: "black as pitch," "blue as the sky." It is rare for the vocabulary of any society or person not to shift. It grows, it shrinks, and the word shadings change.

These shifts in our way of symbolizing meaning present opportunities and problems to speakers. In deference to an audience you may need to speak their particular language, of their particular time, and according to their judgments of what is appropriate to the immediate situation. If you can fit into that "language system" naturally, you will have considerable rhetorical advantage. Happily, if you cannot use their language system and still be yourself, almost any audience will accept with good grace the standard usages and meanings of General American speech and standard English grammar. So the fluctuating character of language systems gives you two options for communicating effectively: (1) Adjust to the language system of your audience when it is natural for you, and (2) in all cases of doubt adopt the current patterns of language that are understood and respected across regions, groups, and decades.

Language and meanings shift, but certain ways of saying things seem always to work in fairly predictable ways. The Greeks seem first to have noticed and catalogued those influential forms of linguistic expression we know as *figures of speech,* or *rhetorical figures.* Most of these forms achieve special impacts in all modern languages, so you ought to be aware that they exist and are in common use. It is particularly important that you recognize that most of these recurring forms of phrasing can *argue* as sharply as the arguments illustrated in logic and debate books. The importance of this last point has been given proper attention only in the last half of this century.

The Belgian philosophical writers Chaim Perelman and L. Olbrechts-Tyteca have written one of the best discussions of these resources of language. Here are some excerpts from their *The New Rhetoric.*

> From antiquity, and probably from the moment man first reflected on language, one has noticed certain modes of expression which are different from the ordinary, and they generally have been studied in treatises on rhetoric: hence their name, *rhetorical figures.* . . . Rhetorical figures increasingly came to be regarded as mere ornaments that made the style artificial and ornate. . . . If the argumentative role of figures is disregarded, their study will soon seem to be a useless pastime, a search for strange names for rather farfetched and affected turns of speech.
>
> In order that there may be a figure, the presence of two characteristics would seem essential: a discernible structure, independent of the content, in other words a form (which may, under the divisions recognized by modern logicians, be syntactic, semantic, or pragmatic), and a use that is different from the normal manner of expression and, consequently, attracts attention.[30]

Later these authors point out that figures such as they are considering can function *either* as arguments or as simply adding color to what is said:

> We consider a figure to be *argumentative,* if it brings about a change of perspective, and its use seems normal in relation to this new situation. If, on the other hand, the speech [utterance] does not bring about the adherence of the hearer to this argumentative form, the figure will be considered an embellishment, a figure of style. It can excite admiration, but this will be on the aesthetic plane or in recognition of the speaker's originality.[31]

30. Chaim Perelman and L. Olbrechts-Tyteca, *The New Rhetoric: A Treatise on Argumentation,* trans. John Wilkinson and Purcell Weaver (Notre Dame: University of Notre Dame Press, 1969), pp. 167, 168.

31. Ibid., p. 169.

When it is understood that these forms of expression can either enliven speech or argue, or both, the importance of recognizing these forms as resources and of understanding how they work on listeners becomes plain. Unfortunately many of the forms have acquired ancient names that are now obscure, but it is far less important that you know their names than that you see what these verbal schemes can do for you—and what they do *to* you when others use them. We will not draw your attention to all such figures, but here are the ones most often used in ordinary speech. We identify, describe, and illustrate each and try to explain what each can accomplish for a speaker.

Simile is a *direct comparison* between things that are essentially dissimilar except in the particular qualities alluded to in the simile. This kind of comparison contains the words *like* or *as*. For example, "There are voices hot, like scorching blasts from a furnace . . . and others cold as if they came from frozen hearts" (Peter Marshall, "Letters in the Sand").[32] Or

> The policy towards Ireland . . . was similar to that of the avaricious housewife who killed the goose who laid her golden eggs . . . and you will deserve the reputation for being the lineal descent of that goose if you be such ganders as not to declare . . . that no longer shall this system of plunder be permitted to continue. (Daniel O'Connell, "Speech at Tara.")[33]

Metaphor is an implied comparison between two essentially dissimilar things. Words such as *like* or *as* are omitted. As you can see, the dictionary's distinction between simile and metaphor is wholly technical and of no practical consequence. We might be wise to go back to Aristotle's unpedantic position that the term *metaphor* is a sufficient word with which to talk about *any* stylistic comparison between essentially different things. Does it matter, in the practical impact, that *like* or *as* is missing from Robert F. Kennedy's remark below? We think not. Said Kennedy: "Yet I suppose that the end of the academic year is one of those watersheds of life where a backward and then a forward look become almost mandatory" (Robert F. Kennedy, "Speech Delivered at California Institute of Technology, Pasadena, California").[34]

From a practical standpoint the important thing about Mar-

---

32. In Catherine Marshall, *A Man Called Peter* (New York: McGraw-Hill, 1951), p. 322.
33. From text collated by William E. White in "Daniel O'Connell's Oratory on Repeal," unpublished dissertation (University of Wisconsin, 1954).
34. In Thomas A. Hopkins, ed., *Rights for Americans: The Speeches of Robert F. Kennedy* (Indianapolis: The Bobbs-Merrill Company, 1964), p. 246.

shall's, O'Connell's, and Kennedy's verbal tactics is that each *made a claim and implied an argument* by means of them. Marshall implied that we should prefer hot voices to those from "frozen hearts"; O'Connell's goose analogy implied that tolerating English rule of Ireland was both wrong and, worse, stupid; and Kennedy implied that commencement was a point of change in life where you do something predictable. (But see *irony* below.) Whether or not these speakers were conscious of it, all three made quick arguments through metaphoric comparisons. If Marshall did not wish to denigrate "cold" voices, he used the wrong verbal form. If O'Connell did not intend to magnify the injustice he talked about, he used the wrong verbal form. If Kennedy did not mean to treat commencements lightly, he spoke with the wrong kind of metaphor.

Metaphors (and similes) have serious effects, then. They can enhance, denigrate, or embellish. They are stylistic procedures we all use, and you will be wise to consider their probable impacts and use them often but in ways that will serve your purposes precisely.[35] You will make metaphoric comparisons. We all do. They enliven speech and affect listeners' attitudes. They therefore need to be chosen purposefully and with a sharp eye to your listeners' tendencies and biases. Then, they will work for you rather than against you.

Rhetorical question is a question designed to produce an effect but not to evoke an overt answer unless, perhaps, an answer verbalized by the speaker. For example, "Now how is this news determined? A small group of men, numbering perhaps no more than a dozen anchormen, commentators, and executive producers, settle upon the 20 minutes or so of film and commentary that's to reach the public" (Spiro T. Agnew, "Television News Coverage").[36] Whether answered in the minds of listeners or answered explicitly by a speaker, the question form *reinforces* its own answer. If the listener answers within himself, he strengthens his own commitment to that answer by producing it in his own terms. If the speaker answers his own rhetorical question, as Mr. Agnew did above, he makes his answer seem more significant than if he had not used the question form. His answer now has the added importance of being a response to a live and specific query; the answer cannot seem to a listener a statement without an excuse for being. There is, of course, a limit to when and how rhetorical questions can

---

35. For valuable and thorough treatments of the rhetorical metaphor, see: Michael M. Osborn and Douglas Ehninger, "The Metaphor in Public Address," *Speech Monographs* XXIX (August 1962): 223–34; John Waite Bowers and Osborn, "Attitudinal Effects of Selected Types of Concluding Metaphors in Persuasive Speeches," *Speech Monographs* XXXIII (June 1966): 147–55; Osborn, "Archetypal Metaphor in Rhetoric: The Light-Dark Family," *The Quarterly Journal of Speech* LIII (April 1967): 115–26; Osborn, "The Evolution of the Theory of Metaphor in Rhetoric," *Western Speech* XXXI (Spring 1967): 121–31.
36. In *Vital Speeches* XXVI, no. 4 (December 1, 1969): 99.

argue by emphasizing. It is unsafe to raise rhetorical questions unless you are sure your listeners *will* produce answers agreeable to your purposes. Otherwise their internal answers or their uncertainties about how to answer a rhetorical question create more problems than they solve if listeners are not certain to accept your answer completely.

Antithesis (an-ˈtith-ə-səs) is a parallel construction of words, phrases, or sentences that contains opposed or sharply contrasting ideas. Expressing the antithetical ideas in similar (parallel) language injects an additional claim that the matched ideas really are opposed or contrasting. John F. Kennedy said, "Let us never negotiate out of fear. But let us never fear to negotiate" ("Inaugural Address," 1960).[37] The paralleled wordings of the two parts of Kennedy's antithesis tend to argue that fearful negotiations and negotiating out of fear are genuinely opposed things we should never do. (Notice that in this construction Kennedy created an opportunity to *repeat* his key injunction, "let us never.") By emphasizing in this verbal matter the oppositions you want to talk about, you, too, can add touches of strength to your general claims that they are indeed opposed. By using parallel wordings in expressing things that are *alike* you can similarly emphasize through verbal form that they are indeed alike in the ways you say. This structure is usually called *balanced phrasing.*

Onomatopoeia (ˌän-ə-ˌmat-ə-ˈpē(y)ə) occurs when you choose a word in which sound suggests the meaning of the word. Notice the suggestive, descriptive function of "clattering" in this example: "The free Irishmen marching everywhere today to the tune of 'O'Donnell Abu' and 'The Wearing of the Green' are a dramatic contrast to the clattering of hobnail boots on darkened streets, the sound that marks the enslaved nations" (Robert F. Kennedy, "Speech Delivered to the Friendly Sons of St. Patrick of Lackawanna County, Scranton, Pennsylvania").[38] The symbol of enslavement, the "hobnailed boots," is surely made a bit more threatening because Kennedy chose to make them "clatter" rather than just "sound." He might have achieved a similar but slightly different effect if he had said, "the *thud* of hobnail boots." *Thud*, like *clatter*, is an onomatopoeic word. So are *ripple, crunch, slither,* and many other standard English words. All are available to you as means of adding realism and sometimes threat or promise to points you want to make.

Pun is a word substituted for another having a suggestively different meaning or a suggestively similar sound. For example, "Churchill said aptly, that Jaw, Jaw is better than War, War" (Hubert

---

37. In Linkugel, Allen, and Johannesen, eds., *Contemporary American Speeches*, 2nd ed., p. 300.

38. In Hopkins, ed., *Rights for Americans: The Speeches of Robert F. Kennedy*, p. 195.

H. Humphrey, "The Open Door").[39]   The effects here are several.   The
parallelism of sound (Churchill, an Englishman, would have said
"waw, waw") reinforces the contrast Churchill and Humphrey want to
stress: talking is *much* better than warring.   In short the sounds stress
the antithetical qualities.   But there is also a touch of humor in equat-
ing *talking* or *negotiating* with *jawing,* thus suggesting that even the
crudest talk is better than "waw."   In all, Churchill's phrasing plus his
dialectal way of saying the word *war* constitute a subtle argument that
all negotiation is preferable to warring.

Less subtle uses of puns may inject humor without much
argument.   The problem is, one may seem to try too hard for the
humor.   Obvious puns like, "She seized the hen; fowl deed!" have
caused some to call puns "the lowest form of humor."   We suggest that
they need not be low forms and that truly imaginative puns can be
valuable linguistic resources to speakers.

Irony implies something different from, usually the opposite of,
what is stated.   Sarcasm is a form of irony.

> To guarantee in advance that the President's plea for national unity
> would be challenged, one network trotted out Averell Harriman for the
> occasion.   Throughout the President's address, he waited in the wings.
> When the President concluded, Mr. Harriman recited perfectly.   He
> attacked the Thieu Government as unrepresentative; he criticized the
> President's speech for various deficiencies; he twice issued a call to the
> Senate Foreign Relations Committee to debate Vietnam once again; he
> stated his belief that the Vietcong or North Vietnamese did not really
> want military take-over of South Vietnam; and he told a little anecdote
> about a "very, very responsible" fellow he had met in the North Viet-
> namese delegation.   (Spiro T. Agnew, "Television News Coverage")[40]

There have been a few attempts to discover empirically what
persuasive effects irony (and the related form, satire) has.   The findings are by no means definitive, but they suggest that these forms of
saying-other-than-what-you-mean do not *change* attitudes very much
but may be excellent ways of reinforcing existing attitudes.[41]   Agnew,
of course, was seriously argumentative in saying that Harriman "re-
cited perfectly," but ironic statements can also be playful.   The man
who said, "Sin is something to be looked at with gentle, sad hatred"

---

39. In Linkugel, Allen, and Johannesen, *Contemporary American
Speeches,* 2nd ed., p. 244.

40. In Carroll C. Arnold, *Criticism of Oral Rhetoric* (Columbus: Charles
E. Merrill Publishing Co., 1974), p. 368.

41. Two studies by Charles R. Gruner encourage these judgments.   See
"An Experimental Study of Satire as Persuasion," *Speech Monographs* XXXII
(June 1965): 149–53 and "A Further Experimental Study of Satire as Persuasion," ibid., XXXIII (June 1966): 184–85.   We are of course, inferring that the
effects of irony are probably comparable to the effects of its sustained form, satire.

was being more playful than intensely persuasive, but his irony also argued subtly concerning the nature of temptation.

Climax is the arrangement of words, phrases, or sentences in series according to increasing value or strength of impact. For example,

> There is no place in this Republican Party for those who would infiltrate its ranks, distort its aims, and convert it into a cloak of apparent responsibility for a dangerous extremism.
>
> And make no mistake about it—the hidden members of the John Birch Society and others like them are out to do just that!
>
> These people have nothing in common with Republicanism.
>
> These people have nothing in common with Americanism.
>
> The Republican Party must repudiate these people.
>
> I move the adoption of this resolution. (Nelson Rockefeller, "Extremism")[42]

There has been much discussion and experimentation seeking to determine exactly how climactic arrangement persuades. This problem, which exists in disposition, is duplicated in miniature when we consider climax as a stylistic device. The best conclusion seems to be that structuring language in this fashion *can* add persuasiveness, but that under some circumstances creating an anticlimactic structure in which the strongest thought comes first rather than last can yield at least an equal persuasive force. We cannot advise you beyond saying that to emulate Governor Rockefeller when you feel it would be wise to build up to a telling point cannot possibly take away from the force of your key idea and may significantly strengthen it.

Repetition is the reiteration of words or phrases or sentences to reinforce ideas. Evidence drawn from experience and experiments indicates that repeating is one of the surest of all means of giving ideas emphasis. That new immigrants are accepted as Americans much more readily than blacks is certainly made unavoidable as a proposition in this excerpt:

> If you and I were Americans, there'd be no problem. Those Hunkies that just got off the boat, they're already Americans; Polacks are already Americans; the Italian refugees are already Americans. Everything that came out of Europe, every blue-eyed thing, is already an American. And as long as you and I have been over here, we aren't Americans yet. (Malcolm X, "The Ballot or the Bullet")[43]

Here Malcolm X combined the power of repetition with the force of antithesis (white versus black experience) to contend that his point was inescapably true.

---

42. In H. Bruce Kendall and Charles J. Stewart, eds., *On Speech and Speakers* (New York: Holt, Rinehart and Winston, 1968), p. 322.

43. In Irving J. Rein, *The Relevant Rhetoric* (New York: The Free Press, 1969), p. 49.

Alliteration is repetition of sounds in words or in stressed syllables within words. Judiciously used, the repeated sounds can hold listeners' attention to an emerging idea and can sometimes render the idea easier to remember. The first of these functions is surely served in the question, "Shall we sit in complacency, lulled by creature comforts, until we are engulfed in chaos?" (Hubert H. Humphrey, "The Open Door").[44] Sometimes repetition combines repetition of idea plus sounds that further reinforce the idea, as in Lincoln's sentence, "As our case is new, so we must think anew and act anew." The sound, therefore the meaning, of "new" is thrice repeated and "newness" is made easier to remember.

Personification is the endowment of objects, animals, or ideas with human attributes. They can by this means be given qualities that seem attractive, unattractive, powerful, weak, and so on. Or motives may be assigned to things that ordinarily would not be seen as motivated. Consider Leonard Bernstein's "For Gilbert and Sullivan, along with those other geniuses, Johann Strauss and Offenbach, had led the American public straight into the arms of operetta" (American Musical Comedy").[45] Bernstein makes "the American public" fall in love with—not just accept—operetta as a musical form, and by doing so he probably reports more accurately than if he had said the public "accepted" or "became interested in" operettas.

Personification offers an exceedingly valuable way of making persuasive statements about abstract or inanimate things and ideas. Congress may be seen as a giant enmeshed in procedural details. The personifying metaphor clearly argues that congressional inactivity has a particular kind of cause and that the human capabilities of Congress are more or less painfully constrained. The possibilities of thus activating, humanizing, and arguing on behalf of your ideas should always be thought about as you make final choices in preparing to speak.

Synecdoche (sə-'nek-də(ˌ)kē) is the substitution of parts for wholes or of wholes for parts of things. For example, "We tie all countries close together, put each doorstep on a universal ocean, but how are we to direct these accomplishments to improve the basic qualities of life?" (Charles A. Lindbergh, "The Future Character of Man").[46] As Chaim Perelman and L. Olbrechts-Tyteca point out, what happens when a part is made to stand for the whole of something or vice versa is that attention is focused on a characteristic aspect of a whole (the characteristic dramatized by the part) or attention is drawn to the class to which a specific thing belongs (by naming the class rather than the

---

44. In Linkugel, Allen, and Johannesen, eds., *Contemporary American Speeches*, 2nd ed., p. 243.
45. In Kendall and Stewart, eds., *On Speech and Speakers*, p. 287.
46. In *Vital Speeches* XX (March 1, 1954): 294.

thing itself). Thus *sail* for *ship* or Lindbergh's *doorstep* for *geographical boundary* argues that the power-source of the sailboat or the entrance-exit features of a country are the major things one should think about just now. Conversely Lindbergh implies that every individual, international decision belongs to a grand class that is of crucial importance, decisions affecting "the basic qualities of life."[47] In each case the figure of speech focuses attention on specifics or on the general and makes a subtle argument that whatever listeners associate with *those* entities are the factors they should think of just now.

Hyperbole (hī-ˈpər-bə(ˌ)lē) is exaggeration or overstatement used for purposes of emphasizing without deceiving. This tactic works in the same general way as synecdoche; here the aspects that are exaggerated or overstated are emphasized as uniquely important at the moment. Malcolm X once emphasized the monetary wealth of a university audience in this way: "And if you realize that for anybody who could collect all of the wages from persons in this audience right here for the next month, why they would be so wealthy they couldn't walk" ("A Debate at Cornell University").[48] Perelman and Olbrechts-Tyteca show that the function of hyperboles is "to provide a reference which draws the mind in a certain direction only to force it later to retreat a little. . . ."[49] Exaggeration taken seriously in any literal sense that deceives cannot function as dramatization of a "right direction." It cannot overdraw or magnify so the listener will willingly retreat to what was really meant. Bernstein's phrase, "led the American public straight into the arms of operetta," is truly hyperbolic as well as a personification. The public did not literally have a love affair with operetta; any listener knows that and knows that is not what Bernstein means. Seeing the real truth of the matter, the listener willingly retreats to the *true* position that the public became exceptionally fond of operettas. The truth of Bernstein's point becomes more credible because the listener has actively participated in locating the degree of enthusiasm that rightly represents historical reality.

There are additional, less well-known figures of speech that we add here because they are more often used by speakers than by writers. In all likelihood you will hear these three figures in the speeches of others more often than you will use them yourself. You are almost sure to use the first more than the other two. In any case, knowing these three figures will help you to analyze and criticize speeches heard or read.

Epanorthosis (ˌepəˈnȯ(r)ˈthōsəs) is retracting or cancelling what one has already stated. To say, "The town was aflame—I mean

---

47. For a more general discussion, see Perelman and Olbrechts-Tyteca, *The New Rhetoric*, pp. 334–37.

48. In Haig A. Bosmajian and Hamida Bosmajian, ed., *The Rhetoric of the Civil Rights Movement* (New York: Random House, 1969), p. 80.

49. Perelman and Olbrechts-Tyteca, *The New Rhetoric*, p. 291.

of course the center of the town" specially emphasizes that the fire was at the *center* and not everywhere else. If the *correct* location were not especially important, the speaker would presumably not bother to correct himself. Leonard Bernstein once used this method of retraction to alter the direction of his listeners' thinking and to argue the special importance of a new perspective on what he had already said: "By this time I've probably given you the impression that jazz is nothing but Blues. Not at all. I've used the Blues to investigate jazz only because it embodies the various elements of jazz in so clear and pure a way."[50]

Aposiopesis (ˌap-ə-ˌsī-ə-'pē-səs) is the practice of breaking off utterance of one thought without finishing it, to express another, due presumably to the emotional state of the speaker. The cause of self-interruption might be anger, sorrow, fear, or some other strong feeling. In this sense perhaps the figure should be called a figure of delivery, but it *is* rhetorical and it explains many sentence fragments in speech. For example,

> Property rights, property rights is what the United States Constitution is based on. You should know that. . . . Property rights. People who didn't own property could not vote when this country was first founded. (Stokely Carmichael, "Speech at Morgan State College")[51]

Carmichael effects a special claim for the importance of "property rights" in two stylistic ways: (1) he interrupts himself to say, "You should know that," and so claims "property rights" is so important a concept that he is almost "carried away" by its importance, and (2) the very breaking up of his own grammatical structure gives him occasion to repeat the phrase three times for further emphasis.

Apophasis (ˌap-ə-'fā-səs) is the ostensible omission or concealment, through denial, of what the speaker has really declared. For example: "I am not pleading so much for these boys as I am for the infinite number of others to follow, those who perhaps cannot be as well defended as these have been, those who may go down in the storm, and the tempest, without aid. It is of them I am thinking, and for them I am begging of this court not to turn backward toward the barbarous and cruel past" (Clarence Darrow, "The Plea of Clarence Darrow").[52]

Darrow was in fact pleading for his clients, but by denying the primary importance of the Loeb-Leopold case he could make their case a part of a larger and perhaps more significant set of issues. A particularly unpleasant use of the tactic of apophasis occurs in statements

---

50. In Arnold, *Criticism of Oral Rhetoric*, pp. 320–34. Excerpt is on p. 330. Quotation from Bernstein, "The World of Jazz."
51. Bosmajian and Bosmajian, eds., *The Rhetoric of the Civil Rights Movement* p. 120.
52. In Maureen McKernan, *The Amazing Crime and Trial of Leopold and Loeb* (New York: The New American Library, 1957), p. 192.

like, "I could of course dwell on my opponent's record of mishandling funds, but I won't." Psychologically such a statement functions much like Darrow's. The idea denied is emphasized because the denial calls attention to it. But Darrow's use of the form is much less transparent than the second statement; moreover, it could have been true to Darrow's real intent.

The catalogue of figures of speech could be continued for there are other ways of bending language to the service of special or emphatic meanings. The figures we have identified are those that are probably already in your day-to-day speech. They are figures that are common in English usage but are too seldom focused on as *usages that can drive points home with the strength of complicated arguments*. They are not, however, the forms of speech we use all of the time. We seem to save them for special moments of meaningfulness; hence, each startles listeners mildly and so momentarily rivets attention and potentially makes a unique set of claims about ideas and things.

A skilled speaker needs to know these special ways in which he or she can achieve special emphasis and direct minds persuasively if subtly. A speaker who does not know and understand at least the usages we have discussed simply does not know the affective possibilities his language system offers him. He is inept, resembling a landscape contractor who knows everything about his business except the conditions under which plants thrive or die. To refine your access to the resources of language, reflect on why these figures of speech work as they do. Look for them in speeches you hear and read, examining what they achieve or fail to achieve for those speakers. Learn, too, the distinctions between figures of speech that prove functionally useful and those that stand out ostentatiously and distractingly. In preparing to speak, review at some stage how figures might help—or hinder—when emphasis, vividness, and subtle argument are needed. There is nothing unusual about using figures of speech to create effects in listeners; what differentiates expert speakers from casual ones is that the experts choose their figures and understand their workings and casual speakers only follow habits and fads without knowing why.

Style emerges from choices and combinations of language. Its psychological impact has been the subject of investigation in the preceding pages. It is not decoration but a facet of speech making derived from reasonable and imaginative management of words.

Wording and thinking are inseparable processes wherever communication deserves its name; hence, style in speaking must always be viewed as one more means to winning a particular set of responses under particular circumstances that comprise the rhetorical situation you enter as speaker.

What we call oral style cannot be separated from the whole act of speaking, except for purposes of analysis and discussion. Style, good or indifferent or bad, is present in all speech. Its qualities color listeners' perceptions of the entire rhetorical situation. Nonetheless, there is no universal set of stylistic qualities appropriate to all speakers although they speak in comparable situations. This is why we have contended that each speaker must understand, for himself or herself, the various resources of language. With such understandings each individual can develop the particular patterns of verbal style suited to his or her needs and talents. Happily audiences and rhetorical situations allow for and respond favorably to individuality in speakers, provided that individuality does not disregard the general principles upon which language operates as social force.

Language is so complicated no one as yet fully understands its workings. There are, however, basic features of linguistic influence that we can all understand in an elemental way. These are the features speakers need to appreciate. Words have denotative and connotative meanings. To a degree at least these are open to speakers' artistic use and control. Figures of speech offer special resources for achieving clarity, force, and even argument and persuasiveness. Attention to what dictionaries, thesauruses, and good models offer as guides to linguistic resources enlarges any speaker's capacity to meet the demands of different rhetorical situations. But only your sensitive judgments of the demands of your subject, your audience, the situation in which you will find them, and your own abilities can guide you toward effective language choices. We can point out your resources; we cannot offer you language for all occasions. There is none. We can stress that all listeners in all situations ask their speakers for accuracy, clarity, propriety, economy, force, striking quality, and—above all—liveliness in verbal expression. But your listeners, not we or you, will define these stylistic virtues. Even so, college students, statesmen, ministers, lawyers, teachers, and others have consistently demonstrated that with understanding of language, they can adapt, plan, and practice appropriate style as we have defined it: *the personal manner of utterance that gives movement and impact to ideas.*

EXERCISES

Written

1. Below are the first, second, and final versions of a statement from Lincoln's "Gettysburg Address." In a paragraph or two discuss what language problems Lincoln tried to eliminate as he worked on the speech and which of the successive changes he made yielded gains (or losses) in effective communication of the ideas. Be sure to say *why* each change was an improvement or a regression in stylistic effectiveness.

- *First draft:* We have come to dedicate a portion of it as a final resting place for those who died here, that the nation might live.
- *Second draft:* We have come to dedicate a portion of it as a final resting place for those who here gave their lives that that nation might live.
- *Third draft:* We have come to dedicate a portion of that field, as a final resting place for those who here gave their lives that that nation might live.

2. Choose a speech from *Vital Speeches* or from an anthology of public addresses. Study it carefully. Write an essay in which you (a) identify the major stylistic devices the speaker used to support his ideas; (b) point out particular word choices that give special clarity, propriety, and economy to the language; and (c) identify instances in which figures of speech function argumentatively or otherwise persuasively.

3. Rewrite the following sentences for oral delivery:
   a. Therefore, it is evident that before you can provide an elucidation of the operational functions of the system for the propagation and dissemination of information you would be required to make a thorough investigation of the public relations branch of the corporation.
   b. If one had one's preference, one would be likely to hold a preference for one's own photographic equipment with which to photograph one's own favorite subjects.
   c. Easily seen is the fact that the playing field is surrounded by a large metal fence over which the ball often passes when a home run is made.
   d. Even although I had been selected to represent my college, had planned my itinerary to the meeting, which incidentally was held sixty miles from the college itself, had packed my clothing for the journey, which I did the night before, had reserved my seat in the airplane, which was a jet and was flight 107, and had persuaded my close friend, whose name was Mark Smith, to convey me to the airport, I was still in fear that the weather would prevent my going to the convention at all.
   e. "Like I said," she said, "Jane's cheeks looked as red as roses, however, I discovered that the effect was all due to the application by her of cosmetic in large quantity."

4. Rewrite the following paragraph in such a way as to give it the motion-picture quality discussed in the section of this chapter devoted to liveliness.

My most embarrassing experience was when I was a boy. It was the result of my getting into a place I had no business being. I had crawled under our old back porch and had found some paint cans. I pried off the tops with a stick. Then I had put my hands into one can after another. First I put them into a can of green paint. Then I put them into a can of red paint, and then into a can of yellow. The color which resulted was an ugly brown. When I finally finished, my clean clothes had paint dribbled all over them. I was a mess. What was embarrassing though was that I couldn't get the paint off. After a licking by my mother, a bottle of turpentine was given to me, and I tried to get the paint off with that. I rubbed and rubbed with a cloth, but there was so much paint it just wouldn't come off. I was embarrassed for a whole week because it was summertime, and I looked as if I were wearing a pair of brown gloves. I guess I felt most foolish when my piano teacher came to give me my lesson, and I had to explain why my hands were as they were. I also felt very foolish on Sunday. I was sure that everybody was looking at my hands when I was up there singing in the choir.

5. a. Identify the kinds of imagery used in the following passage taken from a speech by a college student.

> The quiet rural atmosphere had been effectively shattered. Chickens and feathers flew fast and furiously from both sides of the road. Cattle, only a moment before peacefully pastured, ran in aimless directions. Farmers' horses became frightened and reared into the air. A low-slung sports car, flashing and brilliant yellow in the afternoon sunlight, thundered through the rural village, a beautiful blonde movie queen at the wheel. An aroused policeman hauled the straw-haired beauty over to the side of the road, arrested her, and brought her before a justice of the peace who fined her five dollars. The indignant beauty thrust a 10 dollar bill into his hand and stalked out of the courtroom. "Just a minute," shouted the judge, "your change." "Keep it," she hurled back as she hopped into the auto, "I'm going out of here a hell of a lot faster than I came in."[53]

b. Identify the figures of speech used in the above passage.
c. List the kinds of imagery *not* used.
d. Write a paragraph commenting upon strengths and weaknesses for speech in the rhetorical style of the passage.

Oral

1. Compose and deliver a two-minute persuasive talk in which you use (a) at least three figures of speech and (b) at least three kinds of imagery.
2. Using a speech you delivered during a prior session of your class and drawing upon what you now know about style, rework the speech or a portion of it and deliver it again. Discuss the effects of your deliberate stylistic changes with your listeners.
3. Some subjects are harder to talk about in words than others. For example, it is more difficult to find words to describe an abstract painting than it is to find words to describe an automobile. As an exercise in expanding your awareness of linguistic resources, prepare a short talk on one of the following subjects or a comparable subject:
   a. How abstract art tries to communicate.
   b. *Form* as communication.
   c. Red and yellow are warm colors.
   d. "Quick hands" are essential in a basketball player.
   e. Charisma is a quality public leaders need.
   f. Here's what to look for in (a statue, a piece of jewelry, tailoring in clothing, a top-quality first baseman, or other quality-oriented items of a similar sort).
   g. The reason this (car, book, movie, music group) was the best I've seen or heard is . . . .

---

53. From the manuscript of a speech entitled "Seven Years of Silent Excitement," by Nelson T. Joyner, Jr.

10

Delivery

After surveying empirical research on delivery as an influence in communicative speaking, an author wrote:

> In summary: (1) visible action does not harm communication and perhaps helps; (2) certain deficiencies in the audible code, though listeners consider them unpleasant, do not affect comprehension. The conclusion to draw from the second point is not that speakers should cease striving for excellence, for clearly good delivery does no harm. The meaning rather is that in the whole complex of content, style, arrangement, and delivery no one presentational element, such as fluency or voice quality, is likely to affect the outcome significantly.[1]

There is still no clear evidence that any particular presentational behavior will surely affect your listeners' responses if that behavior is within those listeners' range of previous experiences. Nonetheless, problems of oral delivery have preoccupied speakers and theorists since the beginnings of Western thought about speech communication (see pages 374–81).

One is tempted to believe that this pervasive concern with aspects of delivery reflects the inner needs and insecurities of speakers more than the pragmatic demands of speech situations. Indeed, the psychology of speaking and the enthusiastic searches for rules of delivery in modern times tend to confirm this suspicion.

Because we believe the *way* you *think* about speaking is very

---

1. Wayne N. Thompson, *Quantitative Research in Public Address and Communication* (New York: Random House, 1967), p. 92.

important to whether you speak well or ill, we want to preface discussion of *your* delivery with some comment on the chief ways delivery has been thought about in the last hundred years. We think important cautions for all of us are embedded in that record.

Energetic attempts to create rule-bound systems exemplify man's desire to guard against uncertainties in speech. We do take risks when we speak. Physical and vocal activities furnish cues by which other people judge our worth and self-control. The crucial question for those who practice the art of public speaking is: can the risks of speaking be minimized by adopting rules of delivery? This is a question men and women of Western culture have been disputing since the days of Gorgias and probably before.

Four approaches have been made in attempts to arrive at a mode of superior delivery: the *imitative* (which recommends copying the delivery skills of others); the *mechanical* (which attempts to arrive at rules based upon empirical analysis); the *impulsive* (which throws all cautions to the winds); and *think-the-thought* (which may or may not ignore the action of body and voice as it emphasizes concentrating upon ideas).[2]

During the past decade there has been renewed interest in delivery, especially in bodily action as communication. Scholars and popular writers have turned their attention to action communication, action language, body language, and nonverbal communication. Their interest is akin to that of the elocutionists (see pages 377–79) in that they are attempting in scientific ways to chart, annotate, and explain the aspects of human behavior that do not involve words. Exactly what that does and does not mean is difficult to state. Abne Eisenberg and Ralph Smith say:

> All communication except that which is coded in words is generally referred to as *nonverbal communication*. This rubric is in one way unsatisfactory. The term "nonverbal" aggregates different kinds of behavior which have in common only the quality of not being structured by a linguistic system. Like the term "nonhuman," which covers an infinity of life forms from protozoa to gorillas, nonverbal denotes that which is *not* included in the concept "verbal," but it tells us little about what *is* included.[3]

---

2. These approaches may be investigated by consulting: S. S. Curry, *The Province of Expression* (Boston: The Expression Co., 1927), pp. 301–25; Richard Whately, *Elements of Rhetoric*, Douglas Ehninger, ed. (Carbondale, Ill.: Southern Illinois University Press, 1963), especially pp. 346–53; Frederick W. Haberman, "John Thelwall: His Life, His School, and His Theory of Elocution," *The Quarterly Journal of Speech* XXXIII (October 1947): 294; Joshua Steele, *Prosodia Rationalis: Or An Essay Towards Establishing the Melody and Measure of Speech, to Be Expressed and Perpetuated by Peculiar Symbols* (London, 1779), and Gilbert Austin, *Chironomia or a Treatise on Rhetorical Delivery* (London, 1806).

3. Abne M. Eisenberg and Ralph R. Smith, Jr., *Nonverbal Communication* (Indianapolis: Bobbs-Merrill Company, Inc., 1971), p. 20.

Some distinctions, helpful to understanding these specific concerns, are made by other investigators. (1) Nonverbal communicative functions are continuous whereas sounds and letters have definite beginnings and ends. Because of starts and stops anyone can choose *not* to talk verbally but no one can choose not to communicate nonverbally. (2) Nonverbal communication is taken in through several senses simultaneously. You can feel, smell, see, and hear a message and its source at one and the same moment. In contrast, verbal cues are taken in by fewer of the sense organs.[4] (3) Nonverbal cues yield less cognitive content than verbal ones, because language can easily indicate objects and relationships. (4) Nonverbal cues are in many instances better suited for projection of emotional states.[5]

The kinds of nonverbal communication investigated by those working in this field, as classified by Jurgen Ruesch and Weldon Kees, are: (1) *sign language,* the use of gestures in place of words, numbers, and punctuation signs; (2) *action language,* such as walking, eating, drinking, and making love; and (3) *object language,* comprising the intentional or unintentional use of objects such as furniture, clothing, and architectural elements in communicating feelings and ideas.[6]

Others have classified what is included in the study of nonverbal communication differently. Some speak of paralanguage, proxemics, and kinesics. The study of *paralanguage* is concerned with voice set and nonverbal vocalizations. The influence of vocal properties such as resonance, rhythm, rate, and pitch and the effects of sounds such as *ums* and *ers* and silences between words fall within the purview of this class of nonverbal communication. *Proxemics,* a second broad category of nonverbal communication, deals with the spatial relationships that exist between a speaker's body and other people or objects in communicative settings. *Kinesics* or body movement has been viewed as a separate kind of communication by means of facial expression, head action, posture, walking, and gestures made by the arms and hands. Kinesics as defined by its originator, Ray Birdwhistell, is a system for classifying body language much as linguistic systems classify elements of language. Kinesics, however, has come to be used as a term signifying all study of all body movement. Birdwhistell says:

> Kinesics is concerned with the abstraction of those portions of motion activity which contribute to the process of human interaction....

---

4. Jurgen Ruesch, "Nonverbal Language," in Robert Cathcart and Larry Samovar, eds., *Small Group Communication* (Dubuque: William C. Brown & Co., 1970), pp. 260–63.

5. Eisenberg and Smith, *Nonverbal Communication,* p. 22.

6. Jurgen Ruesch and Weldon Kees, *Nonverbal Communication: Notes on the Visual Perception of Human Relations* (Berkeley: University of California Press, 1956), p. 189.

Kinesics is not concerned, as such, with the movement potential of the human species, but rather with those portions of the movement spectrum which are selected by the particular culture for patterned performance and perception.[7]

This scholar goes on to say that research in kinesics has so far been largely devoted to refining procedures for describing and classifying patterned physical behavior as a foundation for developing kinesics as a science.   Studies in *prekinesics*, a subarea of kinesics, define the movements of which the human body is capable.   Birdwhistell estimates that the human face is capable of 250,000 different expressions.[8] Albert Mehrabian says that 55 percent of the impact of a face-to-face spoken message derives from facial expression and 38 percent from vocal features; however, these estimates seem to apply only where a listener sees the verbal and the nonverbal messages as inconsistent with one another.   A generalization coming from experimentation with eye movement asserts that the closer people are to one another the less they make direct eye contact in communicating.[9]

Such findings underscore the *presence* and the *possible* symbolic significance of body and voice as channels of communication, but just how speakers and listeners ought to *use* this knowledge remains unclear.   A psychiatrist and a psychologist have put the situation thus:

> We do not know (unambiguously) how we interpret body messages and we disagree (to some extent) about the end results of our interpretations.   Was so-and-so being defensive, rejecting, or shy?   Do vivid gestures indicate lively emotionality and spontaneity, or merely a hysterical and basically shallow search for theatrical effects.   Do presentationally still waters run deep?   Is it true that a person whose pelvis and lower extremities move awkwardly is emotionally out of touch with his lower body? . . .   Until the present, psychology and the social sciences have . . . expanded the disagreements by elaborating various incompatible procedures for eliminating ambiguity.   Something parallel to criticism . . . in the arts is needed in the social sciences.[10]

The research accruing from the renewed interest in nonverbal behavior has for the most part failed to take *public* communication into consideration.   What is chiefly implied for public speech is that recog-

---

7. Ray L. Birdwhistell, *Kinesics and Context* (Philadelphia: University of Pennsylvania Press, 1970), p. 190.
8. Birdwhistell, *Kinesics and Context*, p. 8.
9. Albert Mehrabian, *Nonverbal Communication* (Chicago: Aldine-Atherton, 1972), p. 182.
10. John Spiegel and Pavel Machotka, *Messages of the Body* (New York: The Free Press, 1974), p. 345.

nition and adaptation to nonverbal feedback from audiences may be
even more important and subtle than has been supposed. One pair of
authors has said:

> The effective group member or public speaker constantly surveys his
> auditors to judge their reaction to him and his ideas. Even a group
> or audience that appears to be relatively passive sends many messages
> about their degree of involvement and acceptance of what is being
> said. Failure to look at the speaker, small nervous gestures, an overly
> relaxed posture, can all signal boredom.[11]

We will be referring to the importance of such interchanges of nonverbal signals repeatedly as we explore the general potentialities of
delivery in the remainder of this chapter.

DELIVERY AS ADAPTATION

The approach to delivery we advocate is a modification of
Richard Whately's theory reinforced by the teachings of James A.
Winans. We hold that to think your thought is not enough, although
it is primary. You ought to achieve both a keen sense of communication and a vivid realization of your idea at the moment of utterance,
and you should work to control all the channels of action—mental,
physical, and vocal—to support and reinforce ideas. There are no
hard and fast rules for this. Delivery must be adapted to all the
demanding elements in the speech situation: the material, the audience, the occasion, and the speaker himself. None of these elements
is ever frozen or absolutely set; all make fluctuating demands. Even
so, there are certain principles that may be followed to achieve effective, adaptive delivery.

General Principles

The most important thing to remember about delivery is that
*good delivery helps the listener to concentrate on what is being said; it
does not attract attention to itself.* If you adopt this as your governing
principle in actual speaking, the following principles will be relatively
easy to observe.

1. *You will not speak to perform or to exhibit yourself.* You
will concentrate on meanings. Delivering what you have to say will be

---

11. Eisenberg and Smith, *Nonverbal Communication*, p. 64.

viewed as a means to an end, not as an end in itself. Your mission should never be to show off your body, your grace, or your clothing.

2. *Your mind will be on the meaning of what you say, as you speak.* To create or recreate ideas vividly at the moment they are being uttered means that you reactivate a subject and ideas to support it, that you regenerate the enthusiasm that led you to speak in the first place. This enthusiasm must last from the first moments of preparation through the last syllable of your speech. You must be in control of assimilated ideas so they are at your bidding. You must have become so intimately acquainted with them as you structured, worded, and orally rehearsed them that no matter what happens during the actual presentation of your speech, you will be master of your feelings and of your audience's responses. Professor Winans, who formulated this precept, put your needs well when he said:

> . . . there should be full and sharp realization of content. And this in-cludes more than bare meaning; the implications and emotional con-tent must also be realized. The reference here is not merely to those striking emotions commonly recognized as such, but also to those attitudes and significances constantly present in lively discourse: the greater or less importance of this or that statement, the fact that this is an assertion and this a concession (with an implied "granted" or "to be sure"), this is a matter of course while this has an element of sur-prise, and so on through all possible changes.[12]

The ideas you work with must be in your grasp so you can support them through your own behavior. The ideas you have pains-takingly worked over must come alive. They must flow. You must be able to lose yourself in your speech and still maintain control of your experience.

No matter how well you know your materials, you ought to give the impression of meeting the ideas for the first time. You ought not be serving up limp remnants from creative experience. What was alive as you prepared and as you rehearsed must come to life again in the actual speech situation. The process of speaking, you should remember, is one of creation, then re-creation for the sake of listeners.

3. *Cultivate a keen sense of communication.* This third prin-ciple we also borrow from Professor Winans. Thinking of public speaking as dialogue rather than as soliloquy will help achieve this keen sense. Talk *with* the audience, not *at* them. Dwell on ideas until you are sure of the response for which you work. Try to feel on the platform what you experience during verbal exchanges with your

---

12. From *Speechmaking,* by James A. Winans. Copyright, 1938, D. Ap-pleton-Century Company, Inc., p. 25.

friends over the dinner table, on the athletic field, or in bull sessions. We experience this sense of sharing minds daily; trying to recapture the same sense in public speaking makes for lively delivery. By assuming an artificial mood we rob public speaking of the urgency and eagerness it ought to have. As Professor Winans said:

> We should make sure in our efforts to bring this communicative tone into our delivery that it springs from mental attitude; for it, . . . should [not] be assumed as a trick of delivery. The attempt to assume it is likely to result in an over familiar, confidential, or wheedling note which is most objectionable.[13]

4. *Be direct.* People are seldom evasive when they are in earnest. Look the audience in the eye. If you look at your audience, they will look back at you. Looking at a spot on the back wall will not produce directness. You will give the impression that you are in a trance. A dead-fish stare while you call up ideas and wordings will not do. Neither will darting your eyes from person to person or addressing one side of the audience to the exclusion of the other. In the first instance eye contact will be so fleeting that it will be no contact at all. In the second, a whole segment of the audience will think that you have ignored them.

Your eyes are decidedly expressive parts of your face. Haven't they been called "the windows of the soul"? Eyes and mouth more than other parts of your body, reveal your emotions. So you should face front and direct your eyes to your listeners. Try looking at a segment of the audience or at one or two people in a particular area of the room as you develop an idea. When you have finished with that idea, and as you start the next one, direct your gaze to another part of the audience. As you move to subsequent ideas, refocus each time. Then you will talk with your audience, not at them or past them.

Directness is fundamentally a matter of direct eye contact. Attain this much and the probabilities are that you will also be tolerably direct mentally, vocally, and physically.

5. *Punctuate and support your ideas with your body and your voice.* Channel your physical resources to reinforce your message. Let your bodily actions and your vocal intonations operate as warm, emphatic communication. In speech making, facial expressions, gestures, pitch changes, variations in vocal rate and volume, pauses, shifts in posture, and walking take the place of the commas, italics, exclamation points, and question marks in written communication. Therefore, intelligibility and clarification often depend greatly upon support and emphasis from your physique. Learn to use *yourself* often and with control. Some special considerations in this connection are discussed below under the heading "Bodily Action" (pages 292–95).

---

13. Ibid., p. 28.

6. *All aspects of your delivery should promote conversational quality.* If the ways you say things have the qualities we have referred to in discussing the five principles above, your speech will tend to be much like your best conversation: meaningful, reflective of content, clearly intended for listeners, direct, and supported by natural physical and vocal behavior. But the larger your audience and the more formal your situation, the more your presentation will need to differ mechanically but *not in manner or intention* from everyday conversation. We noted differences between conversation and public speech in chapter 1 (pages 8–9). There we observed that public speech contrasts with conversation in that we speak more loudly, are relatively uninterrupted, focus attention more sharply, are more systematically prepared, and have less opportunity to perceive auditors' responses in detail. But effective formal speaking still retains important characteristics of good conversation: directness, spontaneity, animation, and emphasis. It is, therefore, conversational in *quality* though not in *style*. Reproduced conversation does not satisfy. Public speech needs to sound like conversation enlarged—more dignified, more systematic, and more forceful than conversation under informal circumstances. Yet as far as is possible, a speech maker has to suggest to his listeners that his *attitudes* toward them remain essentially those of one person conversing with others.

7. *Focus the attention of the audience on meaning.* Influence of some sort is any public speaker's goal. Manner must direct attention to the meaning of the moment. The task is not to direct attention toward only stimuli bearing basic meaning; one must also act in ways that exclude irrelevant stimuli that might produce interfering noise. Manner of delivery can often displace distractions that come from other sources—a flapping window shade, a smell from a laboratory down the hall, your listeners' fatigue. If strong stimuli stem from your own behavior such interference can be overcome. Bodily movement and vocal variations are always available to you as means of specially focusing or refocusing listeners' attentions.

8. *Monitor delivery to generate and respond to emotional and physical experiences of listeners.* A recent survey of theoretical and experimental literature relating to audience response or feedback in communication emphasizes that an adequate account of how human communication works must recognize that *both* speakers and listeners have *personal goals* that *each* party must (a) recognize and (b) adapt to if ongoing communication is to succeed.[14] Accordingly, your delivery must clearly communicate your goals to your listeners. It must also signal that you are receiving and adapting to signals from your

---

14. Donald A. Clement and Kenneth D. Frandsen, "On Conceptual and Empirical Treatments of Feedback in Human Communication," *Speech Monographs* XLIII (March 1976): 11–28.

listeners implying their goals—their rising or declining interest, their physical and psychological needs. To a large degree your own signals that you are aware of and are responding to your listeners' goals are the cues listeners read to discover whether you mean what you say and whether you are being direct toward them.

What listeners see and hear also causes them to have physical and emotional reactions resembling what they see signs of. If you seem fidgety your audience is likely to become so. If they detect you are tense and rigid your listeners may experience similar physical states. If you are confident or indecisive, smiling or depressed, tough or soft in manner, listeners will feel so, too. Your manner thus determines experiences listeners have and whether they are pleasant or unpleasant. So a fundamental task once invention, disposition, and language choice have been completed is to conceive of the sort of delivery that will *show* your full meanings to your audience.

Just thinking about and discussing how speakers maintain lively contact with listeners and generate desirable emotional and physical experience can make your behavior more natural and conversational. A recent experiment showed that inexperienced speakers who had considered and discussed using feedback from listeners subsequently used dramatically fewer "ahs," "ers," and other vocal signs of unease than similar speakers who had given no special thought to capturing and responding to feedback cues from audiences.[15] In short, just knowing there *are* messages for you out there and determining to respond to them are likely to help you monitor your delivery and generate among listeners the kinds of emotional and physical experiences that will reinforce your message.

Bodily Action

We implied earlier that the chief instruments of delivery are physical actions involving the face, limbs, and torso and expressive use of the voice. The broad principles we have just outlined apply to any aspect of delivery, but bodily communication deserves some special consideration.

Any speaker must understand that his or her actions are of two kinds: overt and covert. *Overt action* is open to inspection, easily perceived by an audience. *Covert action* is covered or concealed. An audience may sense even concealed action. For example, you may have sensed that a speaker's throat was tight or that he or she was

---

15. Steven C. Rhodes and Kenneth D. Frandsen, "Some Effects of Instruction in Feedback Utilization on the Fluency of College Students' Speech," *Speech Monographs* XLII (March 1975): 83–89.

gripping the table even though you could see no physical muscular activity.

Strong feeling often turns covert into overt action, and this fact can be an advantage to you or it can be a disadvantage. You have seen a spectator at a football game wish so strongly for his team to score that he crouched or leaned, reproducing the thrust he wanted the ball carrier to prepare for or enact. He will not perform the action completely; he will empathically (see pp. 303–4) perform it only partially. The involvement in the *meaning* of the moment causes the spectator's subtle enactment of the event, and the same thing can happen and ought to happen in speaking. The question is whether you will enact bodily your positive or your negative feelings toward your content and your relationships with your listeners. To feel an idea so strongly that you automatically rap your knuckles on the lectern is to reinforce your meaning bodily. To lean away from your audience, expressing a covert wish to escape, is to minimize your meanings by bodily action. In short, if you *like* your listeners and build inner enthusiasm or intense meaning, both covert and overt action will support your communication. In this sense it is true to say that most problems and achievements in bodily action arise from your attitudes toward your meanings and your listeners.

Gestures

We have just asserted that gestures—generally thought of as movement of hands and arms—ought to grow out of your own feelings and meanings. This is true, but you should also recognize that you can use gestures *descriptively* as well as suggestively. If you refer to a straight line, why not *draw* one in the air? If you refer to the blackboard, point to it—but do not stare at it; maintain contact with your audience. It may be more efficient to make an angle with two hands than to stop to draw the angle on the blackboard. Gestures are expressions of feeling and meaning, yes; but gestures can also be descriptive visual aids. To support your ideas fully, you should use gestures in this way as well as to suggest attitudes and feelings.[16]

To communicate effectively, gestures of any sort need to be energetic, well coordinated, well timed, integrated with other bodily movement, normal for you, and appropriate to your meaning and feeling. The inadequacy we see most often in student speakers is failure to gesture *fully*. Inner meaning causes a hand to be raised or a finger

16. For a useful discussion of the roles of gesturing in interpersonal communication, some of which also occur in public speech, see Paul Ekman and Wallace Friesen, "The Repertoire of Nonverbal Behavior: Categories, Origins, Usage, and Coding," *Semiotica* I (1969): 49–98.

to be pointed at something or someone, but the movement is only partial so it does not really communicate its meaning. The hand only flutters or the finger only flinches. When inner meaning tells you to communicate with your body, *do it;* but do it *fully*, not indecisively.

It is also worth remembering consciously that the larger your audience, the broader your gestures will have to be to be easily seen and understood. Intimate situations allow subtle movements to communicate, but large rooms and halls do not.

Qualities of Effective Bodily Action.

From our general discussion of bodily action and our remarks about gestures, certain specific qualities of effective bodily communication can be drawn. They are these:

1. Action should be in key with audience temperament and should prompt the reactions sought.
2. Action should suit the occasion.
3. Action should reinforce, enhance, and emphasize meanings.
4. Action should never belie what the speaker is saying.
5. Action should refine the focus of attention.
6. Action should contribute to the speaker's comfort by being easy and unlabored.
7. Action should reveal the speaker's total concentration upon communication of his or her message.

The questions students ask about delivery tend to be: how shall I walk? How shall I stand? How shall I move about? What shall I do with my hands? How can I show the right feelings in my face? Such questions are natural, but they are posed in the wrong way. They imply that some mechanical planning and execution of movement will achieve genuine communication of meanings. Possibly this is true for some actors some of the time, but it is almost never true for ordinary speakers. We cannot answer the questions with prescriptions. We can only point to the qualities we have just listed and urge you (1) to aim at achieving them and (2) to strip away from your behavior all habits that inhibit you from attaining these qualities.

Demands for Action

Special audience requirements for action derive from the ages of listeners. A group of small children listening to a talk on Africa may wish the speaker to be the elephant he describes. The five-year-old demands much action, for his attention span is short and his comprehension level, comparatively speaking, is low. His imaginative level is high, so he responds with delight when a speaker is literal and offers representational action in amplifying ideas. At the other extreme, if you were to address a gathering at a home for the aged, you would disturb your audience if you used a great deal of action or action that was especially fast. Unless you aimed at humorous effects, you would not assume your hearers had never seen an elephant. The postures and gestures that gave joy to the child by seeming to represent the trunk of the animal are absurd in the sight of the mature adult. In general, the younger the audience, the more plentiful and suggestive action may be. The older the audience, the more likely it will be that reserved and subtle action is meaningful and fitting.

Each message, too, exerts special demands for bodily action. Since the listener's eye reads only the speaker's body and its surroundings, it receives whatever signals the speaker gives to clarify his message. As we have noted, action is part of the punctuation of a speech. A sensitive listener knows that an index finger shaken in the right way or brought down forcibly upon a table is in reality an exclamation point, just as a spread palm in horizontal position may serve to underline. Some material requires special bodily action for proper emphasis. Often, too, material calls for clarification through extensive bodily movement. A step or two in a new direction during a transition breaks and refocuses listeners' attention as a speaker moves from point to point. Other material calls for literal, physical description. For example, the easiest way to suggest spherical or square shapes is by gestures. During demonstrations of techniques in military, gymnastic, or dance instruction, action is not just inherent in the material, action *is* the material, a part of the message to be conveyed.

Situations may also govern action, as in religious ritual. Quick, jerky movement in a softly lit, sedate, ceremonial setting would normally be as inappropriate as would lazy, languid movement at a political rally. Even the time of day influences what is appropriate. When it is late and an audience is tired, speakers do well to increase the flow and variety of their movements.

Action can be helpful to you. Speakers who experience tensions and lack confidence can disperse these strains by moving meaningfully. This is why visual-aid speeches are often assigned early in speech courses. When you can—even by forcing yourself—move *with meaning,* you will adjust yourself to speaking and your speaking to your listeners.

Voice

It is impossible to conceive of ordinary speech consisting of gestures alone. All public speech requires vocal ability.

Management of your voice, then, ought to be of concern to you. You must be able to use your voice flexibly. Yet, a sound course in public speaking cannot be a course in voice training. Voice improvement is best achieved by individual work on poor habits or by a separate course of study. Poor vocal habits ought to be remedied by private exercise and practice. Public, group exercises consume valuable time that ought to be devoted to speech making,

Minimal vocal competence means you will (1) be heard, (2) be understood clearly, and (3) be free from annoying vocal habits and distortions. Most of us can fulfill these minimal requirements. Some fail to meet them simply because they have acquired poor habits in forming particular sounds—a *p* sounds like a *b*, a *th* like a *d*, or an *l* like a *w*. Others' voices rasp or squeak, so the quality distracts from what is being said. But most of us are endowed with adequate physical equipment for acceptable voice production. We make sounds that are usually heard and understood. We may be sloppy and inaccurate, yet every day we convert ideas into sounds that convey meaning. But it is still universally true that everyone can do better. Even the Laurence Oliviers and Paul Newmans, after years of experience, continue to exercise their vocal mechanisms to improve intelligibility and quality.

Voice, like action, must be under the speaker's control. You must think what you are saying. You should not be affected or "speak with your mind on your larynx," but you ought to pay attention to understandability and vocal flexibility. To attain clearness and variety a speaker needs to be generally acquainted with the process of producing meaningful sounds and with the variables of vocal expression: articulation, volume, rate, pitch, and quality. He or she cannot otherwise exercise control.

VOICE PRODUCTION. Speech is an *overlaid function* of the speech organs because each of them has some other primary purpose such as breathing or swallowing. Inspiration takes place as air is taken into the lungs through the nose and/or mouth, passed through the pharynx (throat), the larynx (voice box, vocal folds, or Adam's apple), the trachea (windpipe), the bronchi, and bronchial tubes. (See figure 10–1.) As air fills the lungs, they expand; the chest walls within which they are contained move outward and upward to create the partial vacuum that causes this lung expansion. The muscles that control the actions of the ribs come into play in this raising of the ribs and consequent expansion of the rib cage. During this action, the front wall of the abdomen also expands as the diaphragm—the muscular floor of the chest and the roof of the abdomen—moves downward compressing the visceral organs. When the rib muscles and the diaphragm relax, the latter moving upward in a recoiling action, the size of the chest cavity is again reduced and the air forced out of the lungs and through the trachea. As this exhalation takes place, the air passes through the larynx, between the vocal folds that vibrate to produce

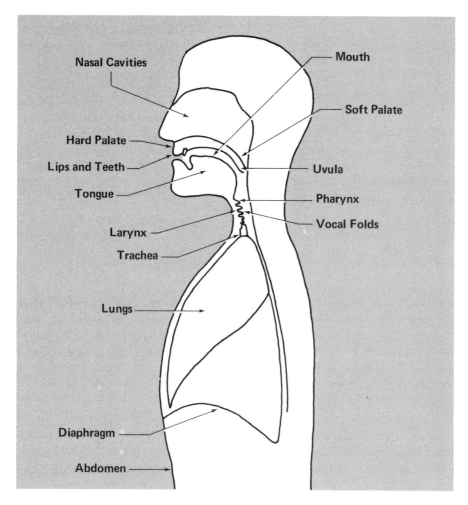

FIGURE 10-1. *Diagram of the Vocal Tract.*

sound as the air passes through the glottis (the opening between the vocal folds). The length and thickness of the vocal folds and their state of tension are responsible for the pitch of the voice produced.

The voiced and unvoiced sounds produced during exhalation are given character and quality as they are resonated from the surfaces of the pharynx, mouth, and nasal cavities. The sounds are reflected from these surfaces and reinforced by them. Finally, certain sounds are turned into consonants by the articulators: the tongue, the teeth, the lips, and the soft palate, which controls the passage of air between the mouth and nose. These sounds combine to form words, and the cycle is complete. (See figure 10–2.)

From this simplified description we see that the production of

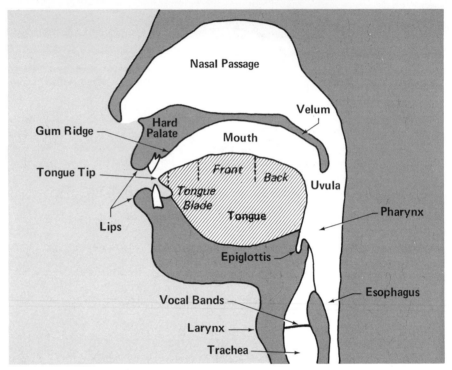

FIGURE 10-2. Diagram of Speech Mechanism.

voice is a motor process involving breathing; a phonation process involving the vibration of the vocal folds; a resonation process involving the reinforcing surfaces of the mouth, throat, and nose; and an articulation process involving the formation and codification of specific sound symbols.

The cycle we have described repeats itself over and over as we speak, and what happens at the various stages in the cycle is responsible for the distinctive attributes of the voice. The physical adjustments and modifications that take place during speech and the general physical condition of the speaker are responsible for the individuality of each human voice. It has been argued that our voices are as distinctive as our fingerprints. Certainly we know we can readily identify one another by voice alone, that by the sound of the voice we know who is at the bottom of the stairs or around the corner.

ARTICULATION. What can you do with this knowledge? You can apply it in eliminating habits that interfere with your meanings. You do not have to slur words, drop off word endings, run sounds together. In private you can pay some attention to how you are using your articulators: your tongue, teeth, lips, and soft palate. Just attending to what is going on (but not in public!) will make you more precise.

You do not have to say "ath-a-lete" for "athlete," "ex-scaped" for "escaped," or "a-crost" for "across." Here you have added sounds. Nor need you omit sounds by saying "reg-lar" for "regular," or "nuff" for "enough." You need not substitute one sound for another by saying "hyp-motism" for "hypnotism," "car-toon" for "carton," "ya" for "you," or "fella" for "fellow." These are all matters of choice. There are situations in which your choice matters little, of course, but there are other situations, including most situations for public speech, where the only safe, fully communicative choice is *pronunciation in accordance with the conventions of dictionaries, community leaders, and experts* in the field in which a given word is commonly used. Here is perhaps the most important point: no speaker loses influence by conforming to the best standards—provided he or she is businesslike, relaxed, unlabored, and unaffected.

VOLUME. Appropriate volume is the degree of loudness that meets the needs of the audience and the physical setting. Without straining, an audience ought to hear every word a speaker says, no matter what the size of the place in which he or she speaks. When loud, strong utterance is required, a speaker ought to be able to produce it, but when the situation calls for soft or soothing utterance, a speaker must be equal to that necessity.

Beginning speakers are often unskilled in assessing the demands of audience for vocal force. Some beginners speak in tiny, whispery, subdued voices that cannot be heard beyond the fifth row because they are unable to judge how forcefully sounds must be produced to reach the rear of the room. Just as often, a beginning speaker speaks with too much volume. He unnerves his audience with too much force because he erroneously thinks that all speeches ought to be delivered loudly. He is like those people who think they must shout into the telephone to be heard at the other end of the wire. Often this speaker thinks that to be intense he must increase volume. Much intensity is, of course, of a very quiet sort and achieves its influence by its very want of volume.

To make proper adjustments to situational demands for volume requires experience and practice. When a student speaker repeatedly misjudges, a hearing test is in order. It may be that he does not hear himself accurately and as a result is using more or less force than needed.

RATE. Optimum effectiveness in speaking requires a rate of speaking suited to the abilities of the audience to comprehend and to the emotional coloring or mood to be conveyed. Beginners tend to race through formal speeches, stumbling over words, slurring them and blurring articulation. The audience cannot then keep up. Ultimately, listeners may come to feel they are running a losing race and so give up. The remedy is disciplined self-control on your part. If you pace utterance to *meaning,* your listeners will have little cause to complain.

When ideas are not under control, rate may become inappropriately slow, lagging behind the listeners' abilities to comprehend. The too-slow speaker breaks ideas within thought groups so meaning is distorted or lost; his pauses are too often stops during which he collects his thoughts. Or the silences of the stops are filled with "uhs" and "ers." When such utterance occurs, disfluency becomes so severe that it destroys meaning and is often taken as a sign of lack of substantive knowledge or capacity to organize. The remedy is clear: careful preparation and a strong sense of the sequences of ideas.

Too-rapid speech often comes from want of the sense of communication we have already discussed. Concentration on meaning and the audience are the only serviceable remedies. The too-rapid speaker does not take time to group words into meaningful thought units; nor does he or she stop often enough for the audience to catch up. Both behaviors signal disregard for the listeners' needs.

A skilled speaker controls rate as he observes cues that signal listeners are or are not absorbing his message. If he sees frowns or puzzled looks, he may slow down, at the same time modifying content by repeating what he has already said or by adding new ideas to make his point clearer and more acceptable. If he sees his listeners staring vacantly or assuming indifferent bodily postures, he may speed up or slow down to produce variety and thus recapture attention. If he sees knowing smiles or heads nodding in agreement and understanding, he may speed up since he has been given a "go" signal that says what he is saying is understood and he need not belabor it. In all these ways speakers can respond adaptively to feedback.

The content of speech often demands variations in rate and certain quantities (meaning elongation of particular sounds, usually vowels). A blow-by-blow description of a boxing match would sound ludicrous if delivered at largo pace and with elongated vowel sounds. Similarly, to describe a quiet, calm canoe ride in rapid rate, sounds of short duration, and abrupt, staccato rhythms would neither reinforce meaning nor create appropriate mood. Just as rate ought to match comprehension, it ought to suit the material's emotional tone.

If rate is correlated with meaning, mood, and feedback, it will be varied. To speak at the same rate throughout is monotonous and invites listeners to turn their attention elsewhere if it does not lull them to sleep.

PITCH. Flexibility in pitch is a major quality by which listeners judge speakers as indifferent to or interested in what they are saying. Monotony in pitch, volume, and rate can destroy the meaning of even the best ideas and the attentiveness of the most willing listeners.

Each of us has a pitch level that is natural and normal. Theodore Hanley and Wayne Thurman say, "Research findings for superior young adult male and female speakers are that their average (habitual) pitch levels are C_3 and $G\#_3$ respectively ... or one octave and two musical notes, respectively, below middle C."[17]   These authors and other authorities recommend that no one institute a program for relocating his or her habitual pitch without prior medical consultation. They further add:

> Pitch (frequency) is a function of balances among length, tension and mass in the vibration of a taut string, which your vocal cords resemble to a considerable degree. In your vocal mechanism these balances or adjustments have been arrived at over a span of many years. Your average level changed from infancy to childhood to young adulthood, where you now stand. In the absence of better information, we believe, it should be assumed that your physiological maturation has been as normal in the larynx as it has been in your upper arm, or ankle, or any other anatomical locus. If this is true, if you have normal cords that vibrate under normal tension, then the frequency at which they vibrate most often is the best, most effective, most efficient frequency, the optimum pitch level, the one at which you can produce sounds longest, with least effort. Temporary movements away from that frequency are good, for obvious reasons. But an ill-considered shift of any magnitude away from that habitual level can result in vocal strain and other more serious effects. . . .[18]

Some speakers unintentionally adopt pitches too high or too low. This is especially true at the beginnings of speeches and at points where tenseness and nervousness impair ability to vary pitch levels. From any such artificial pitch it is difficult to inflect upward or downward for emphasis or meaning. Thus a speaker who does not take steps to reduce tensions such as those that were discussed in chapter 2 will find himself adopting pitch levels that do not allow reasonable expression of meaning.

Changes in pitch are effected by raising or lowering the key of the voice either gradually or abruptly between or within words. Gradual changes in pitch are referred to as *slides*, since we actually slide from one key to another. Abrupt changes are called *steps*. The ways in which we modify pitch often determine what we mean and the degree of emphasis we place upon an idea. Through inflection it is possible to convey meaning opposed to the meanings of one's words. "Oh, no" inflected upward by means of a step may convey disbelief. "Oh, no" inflected downward by means of a slide may indicate indecision. "Oh no" inflected upward by means of a slide may indicate dismay or may mean "yes."

---

17. Theodore D. Hanley and Wayne L. Thurman, *Developing Vocal Skills*, 2nd ed. (New York: Holt, Rinehart and Winston, 1970), p. 184.
18. Ibid., p. 185.

Demands for pitch changes come most often from the material of speech. If public speech is to have conversational quality, inflection and stress must resemble the inflections and stresses of lively conversation. In ordinary conversation we do not think much about pitch inflections, stresses, or changes of key; we automatically make changes consonant with meanings. So you need to respond to material as you would under normal circumstances; then your pitch patterns are unlikely to belie your words. But if your habitual pitch and stress patterns do not serve you well in impromptu and extemporaneous speaking, we suggest that you seek the help of a speech specialist who can competently analyze your speech patterns and devise a program of retraining. The public setting is not a suitable place to think about pitch and stress; there, the task is to *use* the conventional patterns you have elsewhere learned to command.

In addition to variety in pitch, an audience demands the comfortable empathic responses that result from appropriateness in inflection. If an audience perceives from inflection that you are not thinking about what you are saying or that you lack enthusiasm or are falsely enthusiastic, if they see that you are uncomfortable and therefore unable to move freely within your pitch range, you cannot expect them to respond appreciatively or comfortably to your message.

Your own need for flexibility in pitch arises from your need to avoid feelings of strain. Also, you listen to your own voice as you speak and are stimulated or bored by what you hear.

Situations, too, must be considered in establishing pitch controls. Pitch helps to establish mood. High pitch can create impressions of tension and excitement; low tones can help to convey solemnity or calmness. Pitch and the power to project adequate sound are related. To fill a large hall or to speak above competing noises you must adopt your most comfortable and efficient pitch range so all resources of a relatively relaxed vocal mechanism are at your disposal in overcoming the difficulties imposed by the setting.

QUALITY. Quality is produced by changes in the shapes and sizes of the resonators: pharynx, mouth, nasal passages. It is common to say that an ineffective speaker's voice is breathy, nasal, denasal, guttural, or strident. These terms are really attempts to say something about what is happening along the path of the breath stream that produces sound. To say a voice is *nasal* means that an unusual amount of the breath stream emanates from the nose strongly reinforced by resonance in the nasal passages. To speak of a voice as *denasal* means that there is little nasal resonance on the *m, n,* and *ng* sounds due to some closure of the nasal passages. You can hear this quality in almost anyone with a severe head cold.

Guttural voices are those that seem especially reinforced low in the back of the throat. Sometimes harshness is associated with this kind of speech production. In any case, guttural quality or harshness is one of the qualities of voice that listeners repeatedly identify as "unpleasant."

Breathy and *aspirate* describe voices produced by inadequate control over the breath stream. When more breath is released than is needed to vibrate the vocal folds efficiently, the result is a whispery sound, usually of inadequate volume. Often the reason for this phenomenon is that the vocal folds are not firmly approximated; the air passing between them causes *some* vibration but also some sheer escape noise comparable to the sound of whispering.

The ways you tense the muscles of your vocal system and your general physical condition determine your vocal quality to a large extent. Tensed muscles are likely to produce harsh, guttural, strident qualities, which listeners in turn "read" as signs of tension. Too much relaxation is likely to produce unconventionally breathy and nasal sounds. Listeners are apt to interpret breathiness as a sign of weakness or (especially in women) coyness or want of intelligence. Nasality or denasality tends to be interpreted as simply disagreeable. What these facts add up to for practical speakers is that speakers must strive for full, efficient, relatively relaxed use of their sound-producing and resonating apparatus. For those with full command of all muscles this usually means: focus on meaning and the importance of the people out there. One should not try to perform vocal or articulatory experiments during public communication; that is a time to reveal the precision of muscular and qualitative control that private experimentation and reflection have established as natural to you. You ought to experiment with your vocal and bodily resources to enlarge your communicative powers, but do so in private with a view to establishing the habits and versatility essential to evoking favorable, empathic responses from listeners.

Empathy

We have mentioned the term *empathy* several times. Something more needs to be said about it, for a major part of what is achieved through delivery comes about from "the ability to project ourselves into other people's personalities," as David Berlo says.[19] What does this mean?

The German word for empathy, *einfühlung*, provides a clue to distinctions we ought to make between sympathy and empathy. *Sympathy* is ordinarily thought of as a feeling toward another person

---

19. David K. Berlo, *The Process of Communication* (New York: Holt, Rinehart and Winston, 1960), p. 119.

or being, a feeling for him or it. Empathy—*einfühlung*—is a "feeling in with." Our natural ability to take the role of another vicariously is the source of our empathic behaviors. Laurance Shaffer, B. Gillmer, and Max Schoen have said these ". . . empathic actions, postures or expressions are not deliberate mimicry and the persons displaying them are usually unaware of what they are doing. As nonvoluntary acts, therefore, they are explained in the same manner as suggestion."[20]

It is plain that people who listen to others *do* involuntarily "feel in with" those who talk with them, if the talk is effective. When you speak, therefore, you need to act and sound in such ways that the audience receives sensations (or suggestions) that draw them to feel "in" with your meanings. They must perceive your behavior as invitations to *participate in* your message. There is no such thing as *not* emanating communicative cues; the task is to emanate cues that invite identifications with your meaning. This is what adaptive delivery is— being sensitive to listeners' reactions, identifying them, reacting to them, and guiding them. The most effective speakers plan very little of their delivery. They reach out and invite naturally; they watch for cues that listeners are joining in; and they try by voice and action to illustrate full participation in the meanings of what they are saying.

You will be able to generate empathic support for your ideas if you develop conventional vocal and bodily behavior and add to that full realization of your meanings at the moment of utterance. Coordination of matter, manner, and listeners' perceptions is less the product of inspired moments than of moments of communication prepared for by careful inventional and stylistic choices fixed within your natural control by rehearsal.[21] Empathic response is harder to achieve when speeches or parts of them are read from manuscripts or notes, but reading is sometimes necessary. We turn next, therefore, to the topic of reading speech materials in public situations.

READING IN PUBLIC SITUATIONS

When the Speaker Reads

Almost anyone who functions in a community or other public role sooner or later has to read while trying to place ideas before listeners. The material may be your minutes of a meeting, your report for a committee, a special passage supporting the ideas of your otherwise

---

20. Laurance F. Shaffer, B. Von Haller Gillmer, and Max Schoen, *Psychology* (New York: Harper & Brothers, 1940), p. 195.
21. For extended discussion of extemporaneous speaking and rehearsal for this kind of speaking, look back to chapter 2, pp. 37–39; 42–44.

extemporaneous speech, or an entire speech prepared in manuscript form because of some special demands of the occasion. At such times you become a public reader as well as a public speaker. Assuming such a role means that you take on the responsibilities of an interpreter —one who stands between an author and an audience. When he presents his work from memory, a speaker similarly stands between the author he was and the speaker he is. Since the position of a reader is intermediate, the primary demands upon him come from the material. The situation and its conventions force only minor modifications in behavior. His personal skill affects his communication, but the material to be read chiefly determines what he ought to do as a reader.

If we put aside private reasons such as personal convenience or uncertainty, there remain but two good reasons for reading to an audience: (1) to bring something new and unusual to the fore or (2) to give listeners meanings they would not get from reading the material by themselves either silently or orally.

Reading a speech or a portion of it involves stirring up meanings in those who listen. By uttering the sounds signified by black marks on a white page, you translate the marks into meaning. You must endow the printed words with the meanings their composer, or you, if you happen to be the author, intended them to have. If you were the composer, you presumably know what the words mean; the problem is to revitalize your own ideas. If someone else composed what you choose to read, you must understand what that author meant before you can give the meaning to others. Whether you undertake to revitalize your own ideas, or to bring to life what another author meant, you have analytical work to do before you read.

Most people read badly because they are not aware of what is involved in getting and giving meaning. This is sufficient reason for discouraging beginners from reading their speeches. We cannot treat oral interpretation fully, but we can offer basic suggestions to public communicators who must sometimes read. Since a public speaker's reading is primarily for utilitarian rather than aesthetic purposes, the observations that follow focus on reading to convey practical meaning, leaving out of consideration the equally legitimate object of giving pleasure.

General Principles

The following suggestions are arranged in the approximate order in which you are likely to confront problems.

Discover Author's Purpose and Method. To determine an author's purpose and method, sift the material for clues. Is the communication essentially utilitarian?   Aesthetic?   Or does the author's intent fall somewhere between?   At the utilitarian end of this imaginary continuum might stand a technical report or the minutes of a business meeting.   At the aesthetic end you would expect to find love lyrics. Any author's purpose will lie somewhere along the line between these types.   Consider the different communicative purposes that distinguish a news report, an editorial, a personal essay, a fictional narrative, a scene from a play, a ballad, a sonnet.

When an author's purpose is practical, as the news reporter's and editorialist's purposes usually are, he may explain how a thing can be done, why it should be done, or how to get people to do it.   He may simply describe.   Or he may explain through abstract proof.   Most authors have the same purposes you have: to inform, persuade, reinforce, inquire, or entertain.   This tells you what tone or mood to adopt in your general delivery.   It also gives you a framework for further analysis of the material.

DISCOVER THE COMPLETE MEANING.   One of the chief causes of poor reading is failure to obtain complete meaning from the material.   To discover the purpose is not enough.   You should learn what the material says and what the author's attitude is.   In so doing you may have to turn to other materials and read about the author or read critical essays written about the material if you did not write it.

Getting the full meaning entails knowing the meanings of all the words.   You must know their dictionary meanings and their denotative and connotative meanings.   You will also have to study the context of these words before you can interpret them precisely as *this* author meant them.   Associations and the responses words touch off are important.   Make sure, then, that you are aware of the referents intended by your author.   Examining language carefully, a task you may find glorious or laborious, will be essential if you are to grasp the material, to reconstruct suggested meanings, and to respond empathically to the ideas.

To achieve complete meaning you will sometimes have to study the setting for the material.   The historical period depicted or to which the piece belongs may be as much a matter for concern as its objective meaning.   You may have to answer for yourself questions such as: who is saying this?   Why is he saying it?   Who is the intended listener? Whether the words were spoken on the steps of the nation's Capitol during an inauguration or in the give-and-take of a legal debate will affect the manner in which you read them.

Knowing the author's mood—his or her attitude—is a related requirement.   You, as the middleman, must reflect feelings in harmony with the author's and for that reason, unless you are an experienced and accomplished reader, sight reading can be dangerous.   The establishment of mood is especially important to effective presentation of materials with aesthetic purposes. You cannot quote poems and stories effectively unless you understand and are able to transmit mood. Even your reading of utilitarian material is enhanced if you can adopt the manner that reflects your author's feeling toward the subject about which he or she wrote.

Sometimes paraphrasing a passage or writing a précis will aid you in assimilating its full meaning. You must undertake whatever research, peripheral reading, or review is needed to discover complete meaning. Only if you understand the whole can you understand how to read a work or any of its parts.

DISCOVER THE STRUCTURE AND UNITY OF THE SELECTION. Every well-written composition—even a passage—has perceivable structure and unity. Some planned development of ideas dominates the work. If you can see what lines of thought or feeling contribute most to the structural pattern and the unity of the material, you have important hints about what to emphasize in reading. If you quote at length, you have need to examine the form the author has chosen as his or her medium of expression. News story, prose narrative, ballad, sonnet, and dramatic scene have distinctive structural patterns. For example, the most important facts or meanings are usually found near the start of a news story, but near the end of a dramatic scene. What is worth quoting, what is representative of the author's meaning, and what must be emphasized are all revealed by attention to the structure and unity of the work and its parts.

Discovering structure also means examining grammatical constructions so you can see minor relationships. Paying close attention to transitions can also help. Whether you are concerned with minor or major structural features, your purpose is basically to discover what relational patterns you must express by your manner of utterance.

CULTIVATE A SENSITIVITY TO RHYTHM. Some of the subtlest shadings of meaning achieved through language are conveyed by changes in rhythm, changes in the beat or measure of sounds. This is especially true of poetry but it is also important in some prose. If you choose to quote Daniel Webster, Winston Churchill, John F. Kennedy, or Martin Luther King, you will seldom convey the full meaning of a passage if you do not express the rhythmic patterns so characteristic of these speakers' prose. Only by preserving rhythm, or by breaking it, can the meaning of some authors be conveyed. It is seldom necessary to do so with poetry. If you quote poetry you should be careful not to let meter dominate your utterance to such a degree that you destroy meaning. The extreme example of this fault is the small child's sing-song recitation of poetry. Your capacity to "hear" rhythmic meanings and reproduce them will often determine what you should and should not try to quote.

CULTIVATE IMAGINATIVE CAPACITIES.   A further requisite for good reading is imagination, the power to see what others cannot in a combination of words.   Watch for authors' unique achievements, their use of special patterns of expression, new relationships between ideas, and new word pictures.   The more aesthetic the author's purpose, the more valuable imagination is in interpreting his or her material.

Imagination comes from experience and from temporarily divorcing yourself from reality.   It comes, in part, from a capacity to dream.   Let your mind range as you work over material to be read. Visualize the possibilities.   Create several versions of possible meaning in your mind; then choose the best one for your final interpretation. All of this is useful even if you are quoting yourself.

CULTIVATE ABILITY TO GROUP AND PAUSE.   Grouping or phrasing is the art of breaking a text up into ideas or speech units.   A word is a grammatical unit; the idea is the speech unit.   According to W. M. Parrish:

> When we are creating thought as we go along, as in conversation, we generally make the grouping clear to our hearers, that is, make our ideas distinct.   In reading from the printed page, our eyes must be trained to run quickly along the succession of words and organize them into proper groups before the voice attempts to utter them.   If the voice fails to communicate this grouping to one's hearers, it fails to communicate meaning, for meaning lies in the grouping.   And if we make a false grouping, we falsify or destroy meaning.[22]

In reading poetry the inexperienced tend to group mechanically at the end of each line, a practice to be avoided.   You must learn to group by thought.   Realistic grouping is no less necessary in quoting prose, although the problems are less complex.

You should be aware that there are two types of punctuation, oral and written.   Oral punctuation makes meanings clear to an auditor by noticeable changes in voice or action, as written punctuation makes similar meanings clear to a reader.   The two kinds of punctuation do not always coincide.   There are many times when you will want to ignore the written punctuation altogether.   Pausing at every comma, semicolon, or period does not always enhance meaning.   It may confuse.   One who reads aloud must determine in advance which

---

22. Wayland Maxfield Parrish, *Reading Aloud,* 4th ed. (New York: The Ronald Press Co., 1966), p. 21.   Copyright © 1966 The Ronald Press Company. Used by permission of the publisher.

written punctuation will assist him or her in grouping audible thought and which will not. Punctuation in oral reading, as in speaking, is achieved by changes in volume, rate, or pitch, and by gestures and other bodily movements that make groups of words stand out clearly and so convey units of meaning incisively.

A pause is a psychophysiological event. Proper pausing does more than any other one thing to make reading natural and realistic. "There is never any need to pause for breath alone, as the pauses for thought are so many that the lungs may always be full, a necessary condition for good voice support. . . . We must learn to fill the think tank and the lung tank, automatically and simultaneously."[23] A pause is not mere silence. It is not a dead stop. In a true pause silence is pregnant with meaning. When the voice stops for a true pause, thought continues. The reader sees ahead and gains command of the next idea; the listener digests what has been said and becomes curious about what is to come. Pauses help both reader and listener to apprehend the relationships among the words and phrases.

Professor Parrish explains why young readers do not pause. He says:

> First, they lack confidence. The excitement of reading before others causes a nervous acceleration of what is normally too rapid a rate of utterance. Under such circumstances, the cessation of vocal activity for a fraction of a second seems an ominous silence full of dreadful possibilities. The reader feels that his audience will begin to wonder whether he has not broken down. . . .
>
> A second reason why young readers seldom pause is just that they do not *deliberate*. They skim. Their minds do not *dwell* upon the ideas to be communicated. As surely as the mind begins to dwell upon the ideas being expressed, there will be focusing on separate word-groups (How else *can* one think?), and these word-groups will generally be separated from each other by pauses.[24]

We add, parenthetically, that Parrish's observations are true of speakers as well as of readers.

CULTIVATE ABILITY TO SUBORDINATE IDEAS. You must realize in reading, as in speaking, that ideas are not all of the same value. Some ideas are subordinate to others. They support and amplify. In your analysis of material to be quoted you must look for these relationships. Then you must try to *convey* these relationships of degree by voice,

---

23. S. H. Clark and M. M. Babcock, *Interpretation of the Printed Page* (Englewood Cliffs, N.J.: Prentice-Hall, 1940), p. 5. Don Ihde says in his *Listening and Voice: A Phenomenology of Sound* (Athens: Ohio University Press, 1976), p. 168: "Word does not stand alone but stands in a ratio to the unsaid. . . ."

24. Parrish, *Reading Aloud*, p. 36.

gesture, and movement. Emphasize the most important ideas and deemphasize the less important ones. If you read every word in the same way with the same rate, pitch, and volume, you will be boring. The variety of enlarged conversation clarifies the meaning in printed material. Thinking the thought, feeling the meaning, and releasing voice and body to reinforce these experiences are your best means of expressing discovered relationships.

CULTIVATE ABILITY TO MAINTAIN VISUAL DIRECTNESS. Preserving visual directness is a greater problem when reading to an audience than when speaking to it. Speakers who bury their noses in books or who gaze at papers on the lectern destroy the liveliness that ought to prevail during public speech or reading. As Ben Henneke says,

> The reader has a special eye problem. He must look at his manuscript and still maintain eye contact with his audience. His best answer is a compromise. His eyes should follow the manuscript until he is certain of what he is going to say. Then he may look at his audience until he has completed saying that phrase or group of phrases.[25]

In this way speakers may read without wholly destroying the intimate speaker-audience relationship that gives speech its special social meaning.

Preserving visual contact with an audience during reading is a skill attained only through practice. To take in a group of words, then to lift your eyes and focus upon the audience as these words are uttered, requires that you remember what the eye first took in long enough to deliver it meaningfully and without interruption. The process demands a high degree of physical coordination with memory. Some beginning students who find it difficult to achieve this resort to memorizing quotations. The better way is to familiarize yourself thoroughly with all quotations or excerpts before speaking. If you proceed wisely in this task you will find you are following precisely the steps of analysis and practice we are recommending on this and the immediately preceding pages.

In short, visual directness—or its absence—usually reveals whether the reader has thoroughly or haphazardly prepared to read.

CULTIVATE THE "ILLUSION OF THE FIRST TIME." Flexibility and variety are essential for all good speaking or reading. In extemporaneous speaking one responds afresh to ideas, sifted though never fixed by preparation, but in reading from the printed page it is fixed content

---

25. Ben Graf Henneke, *Reading Aloud Effectively* (New York: Rinehart, 1954), p. 143.

and form that must be recaptured. The oral reader's material is inevitably static. The material is precisely that thing to which he or she responded again and again during preparation. Thus, the illusion of fresh experience with content is much harder to convey when reading than when speaking.

It is not limitations of vocal and bodily equipment that constrain most speakers who read; it is inability to recapture whole meanings and to respond with full powers of intellect and imagination while under the stresses of public communication. There is no easy remedy. As is true with other arts, so it is here: given understanding of how to study material and of the resources of delivery, practice, evaluation, and more practice produce the controlled and lively responses that superior reading requires. The "illusion of the first time," to which audiences enthusiastically respond, is largely the result of experience and painstaking practice. For the speaker who reads only brief passages in the midst of extemporaneous speaking there is this encouraging fact: careful analysis, modest experiments with the resources of delivery, plus less than formidable amounts of practice can produce meaningful readings of utilitarian prose and uncomplicated kinds of poetry.

DELIVERY AND SETTINGS

Whether you speak extemporaneously, read, or both, the physical features of your situation are resources and restraints. Your relation to *things,* and your listeners' relations to them and to each other, are objects and forces to be commanded by your manner. Of course, in an open, spacious setting you will ordinarily have to move considerably more and use broader gestures than in a more confining space. But students of *proxemics,* the study of distances and their influences on communicators, draw attention to more subtle influences of space and distance on communicative effect.

In almost all manners of speaking, space and communicators' relations to space contribute significant parts of the total message. Your relation to space is *not* a matter of taste or haphazard choice. Yet you, yourself, may have passed opportunities to look, before speaking, at what spaces and furnishings were available for your use in a room where you were to speak. Very many speakers fail to test, before speaking, what kind of vocal modulations a room allows or demands. Salesmen, lecturers, and even office personnel often study systematically what positions, postures, and furnishings give them advantages and disadvantages in relation to their clients or audiences.

One cannot give rules for regulating and adjusting to physical

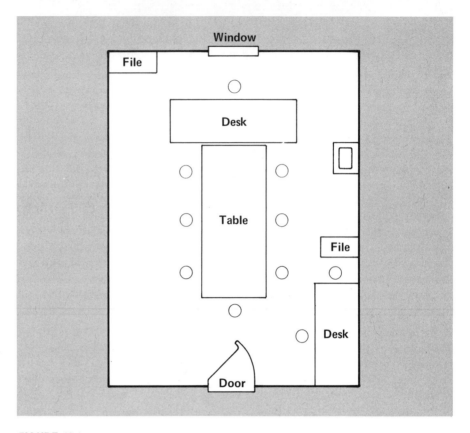

FIGURE 10-3

features of a setting. All we can do is urge you to look carefully in advance at what space and furnishings will *do to you* as a communicator and how *you* can manage them to your advantage. Common sense will usually tell you some adjustments to make. If, for example, there is no lectern or desk about which to center your speaking and thus provide a point of focus for the audience, what will you do? You can still succeed. How? A way of learning to think about how to use space and furnishings is to test out alternatives.

Figures 10–3, 10–4, 10–5, and 10–6 are diagrams of rooms in which we have both made speeches and taught, and we have watched students like yourself try to make speeches and conduct meetings in these spaces. We invite you to consider: (a) What does the arrangement of the office space pictured in figure 10–3 "announce" about the two faculty members occupying this space? (b) How would you want to rearrange this office if you and the other desk occupant wished to communicate to others that you were of *equal* importance? (c) Where would you stand or sit to make a report in this room?

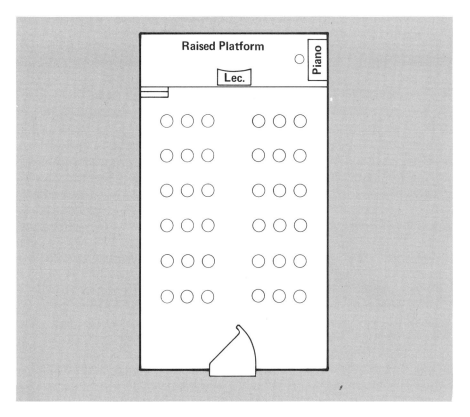

FIGURE 10-4

Ask further how a sensible speaker ought to direct his movements behind and around the lectern as it is placed in figure 10–4. What would a speaker have to do with his movements to maintain effective communication with the audience indicated in figure 10–5? Where would you position yourself in figure 10–6 if you were to preside over a meeting or make a report to ten people gathered in the room with the furniture arranged as indicated? Would you move any of the furniture? If you will make your judgments on these and like matters and discuss them with friends and colleagues, you will have begun to sensitize yourself to the uses (and abuses) speakers can make of the physical settings in which they talk.

Another benefit of considering carefully the physical settings in which you speak is that you will often discover they have persuasive effects. It is no accident that portraits of the leaders of the party are often displayed in the halls where national political conventions are held or that flags, bunting, emblems of brotherhoods or unions, of parties and patriotism adorn the walls and platforms of meeting rooms. These create atmospheres and moods that modify the persuasiveness of

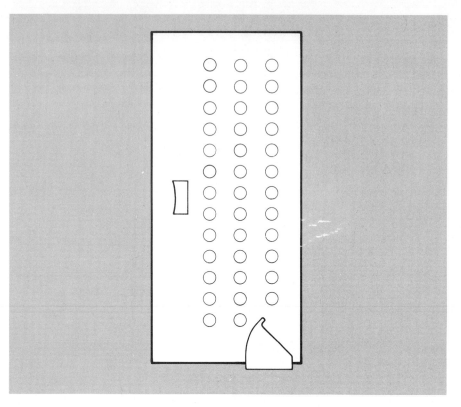

FIGURE 10-5

what is said in such places. These inanimate symbols have meanings and stir up memories. They are there because it has long been known that they are important in reinforcing certain kinds of speaking. It was not by chance that Hitler often spoke in gigantic stadiums at night with flags massed, torches flaming, and drums beating or that there were bugles blaring before his entrance into these carefully staged settings. Nor was it by chance that Mussolini always spoke from balconies, which he had built to order when none was available. Neither is it strange that speeches before mobs seem to get most effect if delivered from elevated places above the crowds or before symbolic façades. Words uttered in such settings have different meanings from the same words delivered in the sometimes sterile and cold setting of college lecture halls.

The place in which you deliver a speech, then, is first a space in which to move; second, it creates a part of the situation, especially if it contains visible symbols that will reinforce what you have to say or detract from it. Your task is to calculate ways to use or counteract

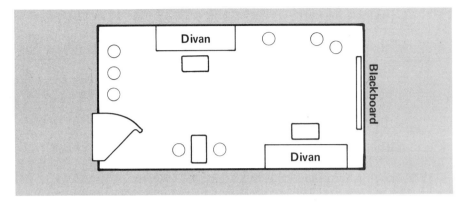

FIGURE 10-6

the space and the symbols in the midst of which you try to attain your purposes.

In this chapter we have examined delivery as a means to an end rather than as an end in itself. It seems sensible to approach personal presentation of speeches by first recognizing that constructively communicative behavior arises as controlled but free response to thought and feeling fully experienced. If physical and vocal behaviors are means rather than ends in speaking, a general standard for good delivery is easily found: *Good delivery helps the listener concentrate upon what is said; it does not attract attention to itself.*

There are, as we have tried to show, general principles of bodily and vocal action that encourage free and full use of the human body in reinforcing thought and feeling. There are also specific behaviors to be learned if listeners are to empathize favorably with speakers' messages. In essence, however, it is a speaker's attitude toward his ideas, himself, and his audience that govern the functional value of his delivery. We have offered suggestions concerning constructive use of body and voice and on reading for public speaking. But our belief is that it is from knowing and reflecting upon the possibilities of communicative action, and from private drill to achieve conventional and variable habits, that effective delivery ultimately emerges in informal or formal public speech.

EXERCISES

Written

1. Write a description of the bodily action used by one of the following:
   a. A professor during a lecture

b. A classmate delivering a speech

c. Your roommate as he goes about his or her daily activities

2. Write an analysis of your voice after listening to a recording of it. Comment especially upon volume, rate, pitch, and quality.

3. Listen to a live speech delivered in person or over television. Write a description of the speaker's delivery with these questions in mind: What did the speaker do to support his ideas visually and vocally? What did he do with his body and voice that detracted from what he was saying?

4. Observe one of your classmates as he or she delivers a speech and during an informal conversation. Write a comparative account of his or her use of body and voice in these two situations. Note the similarities and differences in vocal and visual elements.

Oral

1. Make a short speech during which you read aloud from at least three literary forms: news account, scientific report, fictional prose, sonnet, ballad, essay, or dramatic scene.

2. Prepare and deliver a speech three to six minutes long in which you explain some procedure requiring much action: how to do a dance, how to perform artificial respiration, how to handle a fencing foil, how to execute wrestling holds, how to direct calisthenics, or some similar subject. (Note: If you feel unduly nervous about speaking to a group, you will find this exercise or something of its kind particularly helpful in reducing your tensions.)

3. If bodily movement is not your style in communication, try this exercise. Below are a series of common events that need at least *some* nonverbal communication whatever you say about them. Put the items in some narrative or make an explanation that will allow you to use each idea; then give a brief talk in which you convey the meanings physically as well as by words.

a. A man was out-of-doors and, for some reason, *he studied the sky.*

b. A *small* cloud intrigued him. It seemed about the size (choose a size) and it was *shaped* like this (choose the shape and communicate it verbally and nonverbally).

c. For some reason his thoughts drifted to air travel (perhaps he hears a plane), and he looked toward the horizon *somewhat to his left.*

d. He had a thought of *great importance* (to you, to your audience, or both). Perhaps it was about pollution, how small the world is, or whatever you choose.

e. You would like *to offer us* your own interpretation of this thought.

The italicized ideas are spots at which some kind of movement, if only of eyes, will be essential if you are to observe the speaking conventions of our culture.

4. Explain the layout of a supermarket. Tell your listeners, in your own words, that as one enters past the shopping carts into the main display area, the fresh produce will be on one side, the frozen foods will be on the other, the meat department in a far corner, and so on. Without being dramatic, try at least to *suggest* by some kind of action and vocal variety

the spatial pattern of such a store. (Note: If you need practice in broader physical movement, try this exercise using a large space and *demonstrate* the spatial positions; or use a blackboard drawing if you need experience in using visual aids.)

5. If using your hands in communication seems unusual or awkward, try this exercise. Give a two-minute talk on "Some Geometric Figures We Couldn't Do Without." You might try describing rectangles of different sizes, an octagon, various shapes of triangles, or others. If you refuse to use a blackboard or other externally derived visual aid, you will discover (a) that you have to describe with hands, arms, and other movements, and (b) that these are quite natural and easy things to do.

6. Assign each of the following sentences to three or four members of your class. Ask each person to say or read his or her sentence with an emphasis different from that used by the preceding person, changing the meaning of the sentence each time it is read. Following the readings, discuss the differences in volume, pitch, and rate employed to achieve the differences.

   a. Whom do you suppose I saw in class today?
   b. Oh yes I'd love to go.
   c. You aren't really sure of that are you?
   d. I've never seen such food.
   e. There are always a lot of men at the movies on Saturday night.
   f. It was the most spectacular yet peculiar race you ever saw.
   g. There was the book just where I'd left it, rain soaked and falling apart.
   h. No I simply can't believe that that is so.
   i. Whoever heard of a person doing such a thing?
   j. Oh my dear what have you done?

Judging Public Speech

A liberally educated citizen ought to be able to explain what happens when speech occurs. Such a listener ought to be able to describe the speech he or she hears and to explain why and how it contributed to the results that follow. If people could do these things expertly in all cases, interpreting and judging speech would be a science, and speaking would be human engineering. But no one has achieved precision in observing and analyzing public speech, nor is anyone likely to, but we all can do better.

Even the most highly educated people find it difficult to recognize all the components of speech as they listen to it. It is even more difficult to judge the effects speech has on other people. As Robert S. Cathcart has said, "Usually we know whether we like a speech, but being able to judge that speech as effective or influential is quite another matter."[1] Those who have carefully studied the theory and practice of speaking judge qualities and effects more reliably than those who have not, but even experts are by no means infallible. This does not mean it is useless to try to understand how and why our own speech and the speech of others work. It means we have to discipline ourselves to understand the influences of speech at all. Like reliable criticism of fiction, poetry, or painting, reliable evaluation of speaking depends on practical and theoretical knowledge of what is possible and impossible. With that kind of disciplining knowledge the Ciceronian

---

1. Robert S. Cathcart, *Post Communication: Critical Analysis and Evaluation* (Indianapolis: Bobbs-Merrill Company, 1966), p. 1.

ideal nears possibility, the "expert and the plain man" see alike, but the expert can give reasons for his or her judgment.[2]

Criticism is the way we tell ourselves what is going on and the way we learn how to practice the art with greater insight. We are not likely to reduce speaking or any other art to science, but we still have both need and responsibility to bring to bear as much knowledge as possible when we respond to, or evaluate, discourse. To equip us for such informed responses is a general object of all liberal education and a special object of speech courses.

The broad aims of a liberal education, as we have pointed out in chapter 1, are to equip us to think sensibly in a variety of ways, to increase our abilities to judge, to enable us to choose among alternatives, and to prepare us to take responsible places in the world. We have explored theories with you, to enlarge your understanding. We have described procedures and methods, to enable you to fill your roles as speaker and as listener. As a final matter we now invite you to consider how useful, critical judgments are made about speech and speaking.

There are those who believe that students are too young and inexperienced to be critics. But criticism of live speaking is an important and necessary aspect of your study of speech. Perhaps you were not prepared to function as a critic at the beginning of your first course in speaking, but with some theories at your command you are ready and able to evaluate how well speech follows those principles at least. More importantly, critical activity of any disciplined sort will benefit you both as a speaker and as a private person.

By knowing what your audience thought of your first talks, you improved your adaptation to the group in later efforts. You learned, too, that audiences never remain the same. Having lived a day longer your classroom audience changed each time you met. Nonetheless, you found there are some criteria by which listeners rather consistently measure effective speaking—criteria that do not change from session to session. These consistent standards and recurring judgments can be used to observe and evaluate your own speech and the public speech of others.

Consider first the function of speech criticism in a speech class. Criticism in a classroom ought to be a reciprocal activity. By openly registering your responses to your peers, you can aid in their improvement immensely, just as their frank responses to your speaking provides you directions for improvement and insights into how others judge speaking.

To exercise full responsibility as a critic in your class or else-

---

2. See *De Oratore,* trans. H. Rackham (Cambridge, Mass.: Harvard University Press, 1948), vol. II, pp. 157, 159, bk. III, chap. 51.

where, your first needs are to develop your powers of discrimination and to know what methods and standards yield the most helpful, accurate, and informative criticism. We say still what Dean Everett Lee Hunt said half a century ago:

> ... we might be better satisfied with the returns from the money and energy spent on rhetorical training if we cared more about producing educated and critical audiences. ... Critical and analytical study of rhetoric and oratory should not be limited to those who expect to become professional speakers or writers, or to those who expect to teach it; it should be offered to all students who desire to understand the significance of rhetoric in modern life.[3]

Whether or not you are invited to criticize spoken or written speech in your speech course, you owe it to yourself as a part of your education to develop critical acuity toward the speeches you will hear, read, or deliver in future days or years. For this you need to have a clear idea of what it is to criticize an artistic work of any sort and a clear idea of what is unique about *speech* as an object of criticism.

THE NATURE OF SPEECH CRITICISM

Criticism of any kind is judgment and/or appreciation. Evaluation and criticism imply analysis and comparison and commendation or censure. All reactions to objects, ideas, actions, and persons are critical or noncritical. Assessments or evaluations are criticism. Descriptions, reviews, commentaries, and surveys, unless interpretive, are not. They merely report data.

Criticism is essentially a comparative activity in which we make discriminations. Whenever we make a judgment or register appreciation, we discriminate with some standards of perfection in mind. When we are subjective in our judgments, our standards are likely to be very personal. We may not even be conscious of them. When we try to become more objective, we tend to become consciously aware of the standards we apply and to identify them. Then we can tell others *why* we say what we do. Whichever cast of mind characterizes our criticism, we still apply standards, and our judgments place what we judge somewhere along a continuum of excellence. The speech we appraise is always measured by some standards and found

---

3. "Editorial: 'From Rhetoric Deliver Us,'" *The Quarterly Journal of Speech* XIV (April 1928): 266–67.

to correspond to them in some degree. It corresponds closely to our standards or it does not. This kind of discrimination is the nature of our critical judgments—of speech or anything else. Whether our judgments are useful to anyone else depends on our capacity to communicate both our standards and our judgments. This is the kind of communicated, objective criticism that is necessary if classmates are to profit. It is also the kind of criticism that makes criticism of speech —or anything else—informative to general listeners or readers.

THE CRITICAL OBJECT

A focus upon some object is the beginning of any type of criticism. The object may be tangible or intangible. It may be material or a combination of materials, an action or an ideal. In aesthetic criticism the object of criticism may be a specific painting such as Picasso's "The Lovers"; a pattern of sounds such as Beethoven's Fifth Symphony, interpreted by a great orchestra; or physical action performed by dancers, such as the *pas de deux* from *The Firebird*. Objects for literary criticism are novels, short stories, poems, or essays, usually in the tangible form of printed words on a page. Whatever the kind of criticism, there is some object that exists to be appreciated and/or evaluated and perhaps to be praised or condemned.

A critic who assesses live speaking, speaking as it is delivered, deals with a distinctive critical object. What he or she examines, appreciates, and judges consists of a combination of sounds and actions symbolizing ideas, existing in time, air, and sight. This object is in constant flight. It is not static, not arrested. It is unlike many other critical objects. It is not a statue placed on a pedestal and viewed from all sides. It is not a musical score nor a play script to be consulted again and again. It is not a painting that can be gazed at for hours. It is not print that can be pored over. Nor can live speech be taken in fully with either the eye or the ear alone. Ideally, it must be seen and heard—all in the moments of its creation. Like dance, it will not freeze for examination, and yet its verbal nature makes it seem analogous to the more stable objects of literary criticism. But speech is different; the contrasts go further. It is true that a critic viewing a painting takes in first one part, then another; and the critic of music hears sounds in sequence, in time, but a critic of live speeches faces a more exacting assignment. He must see *and* hear sequences that have never before occurred in just that way. Nor will they ever occur again. Usually he will not even have a drama critic's advantage of consulting a script before or after seeing and hearing the object, although this is possible with very formal or with recorded speeches.

A speech critic deals with a critical object that exists once and only once. Normally there will be no public preview of it, and there may even be no subsequent record. Moreover, two speeches by the same speaker may be on identical subjects and in identical words, but, still, exact duplication is impossible. At least delivery is bound to be a bit different. The components of a speech situation also constantly shift.

Take another set of cases. In public interviews the interviewee cannot foresee what he must next talk about until he receives the interviewer's question. Furthermore, in these and similar situations the bits of talk that may be regarded as small speeches—which can be parts of rap sessions, class discussions, political interchanges on television, and arbitration sessions—occur in settings that are flexible, fluid, and in constant flux. Such minispeeches can never be exactly reproduced in any future place or time. Despite all of this anyone who wants to understand and evaluate public speech must try to note and account for the ongoing adjustments speakers are or should be making.

To complicate matters further, a speech critic cannot always be present when the speech he or she needs to evaluate takes place. For example, the critic may want to get a detailed understanding of an oral utterance only after he or she finds it was of some importance to society or that it exerted some particular influence. The critic may not know a press conference was news until it is over. In such circumstances he or she is unable to experience the *real* speech; yet it may still be worthwhile to ask what happened when the speaking took place and how well the speaker or speakers lived up to their possibilities.

The most advantageous situation for criticism of past talk rarely exists. Our would-be critic with luck might obtain a video tape or sound motion picture that made all possible observations of visible and audible elements. A tape or film of this sort would come closest to reproducing the real speech, but it could not reproduce the entire speech situation because it would fail to reveal some three-dimensional aspects. Neither could it fully explain the needs and expectations of the people who were part of the situation. A video tape or film is simply not as reliable as on-the-spot observation for assessing factors such as environment, history, and audience reactions. When films are available they often contain only portions of major speeches. Ideally, a critic would make his or her own film and record useful situational information.

A second kind of critical speech object is some form of electrical transcription. This will not give you the visual aspects of the speech, but it does allow some evaluation of vocal performance, of listeners' responses, and affords a precise check on what was actually said. The last item is important since most printed texts of speeches are inaccurate in some respects.   In classrooms and outside, critics can often tape speeches and discussions while they make other kinds of observations.   They can then use the tapes to check the accuracy of impressions.   Under other circumstances, if a critic cannot make his own recording, he can sometimes obtain one through a radio or television station or buy one that has been commercially marketed.   The availability of such recordings is limited, and, of course, recordings of orators who spoke in the early days of sound recording are critical objects of dubious quality.

More often, a critic who was not present when a speech was delivered will have to content himself with some written record: a handwritten manuscript or a printed transcript of some sort.   Fortunately, he may pore over, analyze, outline, and study this kind of record.   He may be able to supplement such a transcript with other written accounts that help him reconstruct the milieu, the situation, and audience reaction.   He may be able to read the criticisms others wrote after the speech was delivered.   He may, and often does, use the methods of historical, literary, and experimental study to bolster his knowledge and objectify his analysis.   But with all these aids his critical object remains the least satisfactory of those we have thus far discussed, for he must always see and hear with the eyes and ears of others.

The critical objects for critics of spoken discourse, then, are four.   The object may be the live, pulsating, reacted-to utterance of the moment; a video tape or film; an electrical sound transcription; or a manuscript or printed text.   But the most unique thing about any of these critical objects is that they are *records*.   Therefore, they must be approached differently from the objects of other kinds of criticism because they are never real until their contexts—their situations—have been somehow understood.

The purpose of speaking also influences speech criticism. Herbert Wichelns, in his essay entitled "The Literary Criticism of Oratory," says of rhetorical criticism:

> . . . we find that its point of view is patently single.   It is not concerned with permanence, nor yet with beauty [as may be the case in the judgment of literature].   It is concerned with effect.   It regards a speech as a communication to a specific audience, and holds its business to be the analysis and appreciation of the orator's methods of imparting his ideas to his hearers.[4]

---

4. Herbert A. Wichelns, "The Literary Criticism of Oratory," in *Studies in Rhetoric and Public Speaking in Honor of James Albert Winans* (New York: Century, 1925), p. 209.   Reprinted in Donald C. Bryant, ed., *The Rhetorical Idiom* (Ithaca: Cornell University Press, 1958), pp. 1–42.   This essay may also be found in William A. Linsley, *Speech Criticism* (Dubuque, Ia.: Wm. C. Brown Co., 1968), pp. 7–38.

Wichelns was thinking mainly of criticism as a scholarly activity involving the analysis of speech texts, but what he says also applies to audiences and critics who hear and see speaking in classrooms or outside and to those who read or hear records of speaking. His elaboration of rhetorical criticism bears quotation because he concisely identifies the basic questions all speech critics need to raise in their minds.

> Rhetorical criticism is necessarily analytical. The scheme of a rhetorical study includes the element of the speaker's personality as a conditioning factor; it includes also the public character of the man—not what he was, but what he was thought to be. It requires a description of the speaker's audience, and of the leading ideas with which he plied his hearers—his topics, the motives to which he appealed, the nature of the proofs he offered. These will reveal his own judgment of human nature in his audiences, and also his judgment on the questions which he discussed. Attention must be paid, too, to the relation of the surviving texts to what was actually uttered: in case the nature of the changes is known, there may be occasion to consider adaptation to two audiences—that which heard and that which read. Nor can rhetorical criticism omit the speaker's mode of arrangement and his mode of expression, nor his habit of preparation and his manner of delivery from the platform; though the last two are perhaps less significant. "Style"—in the sense which corresponds to diction and sentence movement—must receive attention, but only as one among various means that secure for the speaker ready access to the minds of his auditors. Finally, the effect of the discourse on its immediate hearers is not to be ignored, either in the testimony of witnesses, nor in the record of events. And throughout such a study one must conceive of the public man as influencing the men of his own times by the power of his discourse.[5]

As a critic analyzes and evaluates he or she ought to keep the varied demands of the audience, the material, the situation, and the speaker uppermost in his or her mind. The assignment—the rhetorical situation—that faced the speaker should be the primary consideration as a critic describes and then sets forth what ought to have been said and how it ought to have been said under the peculiar circumstances that constituted the constraints and opportunities of that situation.

It is also of value to remember what rhetorical criticism is not. Loren D. Reid, in reflecting upon the myopia of young critics, warns:

> Rhetorical criticism is not simply a discussion of the speaker's ideas, . . . not simply a narrative of the circumstances under which a speech is

---

5. Ibid., pp. 212–13 or pp. 38–39 or p. 35.

delivered, . . . not simply a classification or tabulation of rhetorical devices, . . . [and] not primarily an excursion into other fields of learning.[6]

CRITICAL POINTS OF VIEW

If mere description is not enough to help a colleague or to provide other people with a clear estimate of the worth of speaking, we confront the question of how evaluations are made. What shall the standards be? Are some points of view about speaking more useful and practical than others?

In appendix B you will find the text of a student group's critique of a campus speech made by a university administrator. The speech concerned the administration's crackdown on the use of alcohol in students' dormitories. If you have not read that transcript, you ought to do so now, for we will use this critique as a major example in considering the different kinds of values a critic could bring to the criticism of Dr. M. Lee Upcraft's speech.

The Pragmatic Viewpoint

You could say that all that counted when Dr. Upcraft addressed the officers of the Undergraduate Student Government and other students was whether he won the support of those who listened. If you took such a viewpoint, you would say, "The *effects* are all that count." Andrew Weaver, Gladys Borchers, and Donald Smith call this applying an "empirical standard" to speaking.[7] James McBurney and Ernest Wrage label it "the results theory" of criticism.[8] We are calling it "taking a pragmatic view" of speaking. Whatever you may call it, this point of view is a critical posture that depends upon whether or not the audience approved of what the speaker said. It asks whether he "got the votes," whether he was applauded, supported, or endorsed. In Dr. Upcraft's case, the main critical question would be, "Did the students accept and endorse what he said to them?"

To ask only this kind of question about any speech would be to impose serious limitations. You may forget that failure to win an immediate, visible response does not always mean that the speaking

---

6. Loren D. Reid, "The Perils of Rhetorical Criticism," *The Quarterly Journal of Speech* XXX (December 1944): 416–22.

7. See Andrew T. Weaver, Gladys L. Borchers, and Donald K. Smith, *The Teaching of Speech* (Englewood Cliffs, N.J.: Prentice-Hall, 1952), pp. 497–98.

8. See James H. McBurney and Ernest J. Wrage, *The Art of Good Speech* (New York: Prentice-Hall, 1953), pp. 22–24.

failed. A speech may *not* elicit immediate endorsement but still have effects some time later. Who can say that public speeches proposing legalized abortion thirty years ago had no influence on those who changed the laws beginning in the 1960s? Some of the public forums, broadcast discussions, and classroom speaking of a generation ago may have readied the minds of those in the audience who later became the legislators and judges who played a part in altering the laws.

The purely pragmatic question would be inappropriate in Dr. Upcraft's case. It is obvious that he hoped for some long-range as well as immediate effects. He proposed a three-phase course for future action: (1) reconsider one of the university's regulations as written, (2) review how far the university ought to go in acting as a law-enforcement agency for the state, and (3) lobby for a lower drinking age in the state. It would not be fair to Upcraft, and it would disregard the full potentialities of the rhetorical situation Upcraft faced to judge his speech's quality only by the very positive fact that immediately after he spoke those who listened seemed more sympathetic to the administration's position than before. We ought to ask also whether he did everything possible to promote student action to get regulations and laws changed. Such action was his apparent long-range goal. Actually, he did not do everything possible to promote such ultimate response.

Of course, we should not entirely dismiss immediate effects. Yet, to consider only immediate results is to give only a partial evaluation. It is a limitation of the students' critique that they concentrated chiefly upon Dr. Upcraft's immediate accomplishment. They did not consider whether in paragraphs 11, 12, and 15 he addressed the students in the best ways possible if he genuinely wanted the constructive actions he called their best alternatives. The critique in appendix B exemplifies the major limitations of approaching any speech from a purely pragmatic view.

The Ethical Viewpoint

A second way of approaching critical tasks is to give special attention to and pass judgment on speeches as "good" or "bad," "constructive" or "destructive," and so on. A critic taking this view tends to ask, "Is the speaker honest, sincere, courageous in what he says? Is he truthful? Is he consistent? Is he on the side of the good?"

Undoubtedly these are appropriate questions to ask about speakers, if one has explainable grounds for making such judgments. You probably do not wish to uphold talk that is untrue, biased, or designed to hurt an audience. Most of us find lying, cheating, plagiarizing, and speaking with bad intent reprehensible. But taking an ethical view in all cases and taking it as an exclusive critical viewpoint makes for partial and sometimes exceedingly biased criticism.

First, talk may be filled with truth and be based on the soundest motives and still not be intelligently adapted to the exigences of its rhetorical situation. The most honest talk can be clumsy, incoherent, ill informed, badly expressed, and awkwardly presented. Should a critic who wants to understand what went on, or one who wants to be helpful, applaud the sincerity he or she perceives but neglect the artistic weaknesses of the presentation?

Still more important, perhaps, is the fact that it is not always possible to discover a speaker's motives. If you look at appendix B you will see that the students who criticized Dr. Upcraft's speech did speculate on what Upcraft's motives probably were, but they recognized that they could not be sure of them. The student critics had the good sense and humility to say only that the speech made it *appear* that Upcraft's goal was to turn the student body's irritation away from the university and toward the state's policies and laws. As it happened, Dr. Upcraft came to hear this critique, and he afterward told the critics that they had, in fact, discovered *some* of his actual intentions. Most critics do not have the advantage of directly confirming their inferences about intentions, and they would do well to emulate these student critics' caution in the face of that fact. About all any critic can say about the motives and intentions of speakers is that the *speaking* made certain motives *appear* to direct the speaker's efforts.

There is another difficulty with criticism from an ethical viewpoint. Ethical standards vary from society to society, group to group, era to era, and even from setting to setting. The first variations are obvious, but consider the last. Attorneys in courtrooms are bound by their oaths to make the strongest possible cases for their clients. Everyone in the courtroom knows or ought to know this. Some selectivity in handling evidence and some exaggeration are expected. Can we then sensibly apply to a prosecutor or a defense lawyer the same moral obligation to present *all* aspects of the evidence that we might apply to a scientist or teacher? The attorneys are supposed to present their sides. The theory of justice is that through both of these admittedly *partisan* presentations, the judge and jury will get all possibly pertinent evidence. But that is not the theory that dominates scientific research or teaching. There, each individual bears responsibility for knowing, evaluating, and fully revealing *all* pertinent evidence. Our point is simply that if one is going to try to make ethical judgments of speakers and speaking, it is as much a critic's obligation to apply only ethical criteria that are *appropriate in the rhetorical situation* as it is the obligation of a speaker to act fairly and openly toward his listeners.

So even where we can make supportable and situationally appropriate judgments on the ethical merits of speech, these cannot be our sole standards of critical judgment. If such were the case we would praise effectiveness and ineffectiveness alike. If ethical considerations are paramount in a critic's mind, there is always danger that his criticism will tell more about his private moral standards than about how speakers observe the ethical standards appropriate to their particular rhetorical situations.

The Artistic Viewpoint

We have contended throughout this book that public speaking is a liberal, practical art. We have argued that if public speech is truly artistic, it will be speech in which the full resources of human communication are appropriately applied to alter the exigences of rhetorical situations. On those premises our advice to you is that you adopt what we are calling an *artistic viewpoint*. That is, we urge you to be concerned more with the skill and knowledge of speakers than with the results of their speaking or their motives.

This artistic viewpoint has the advantage of excluding nothing that is relevant to the communicative experiences of humans. Evaluating speech from this point of view would cause you to (1) identify the particular methods and possibilities a speaker might have used in his or her rhetorical situation; (2) identify those methods the speaker *did* use and how far they exhausted the possibilities; (3) consider whether the rhetorical methods were used in the best ways the resources of the art allow; and (4) render explained judgments concerning the *fullness of achievement* that the speaking represents. When results are known, they will help you understand—but they will not, alone, explain—the speaker's art or lack of it. When ethical choices are reflected in the speaking, knowing them may provide reasons for judging the extent to which the speaking fulfilled the possibilities of artistic public communication.

We think this artistic viewpoint in criticism is more likely than any other to yield socially comprehensive and practically useful speech criticism. It is essentially the viewpoint used by the students whose critique appears in appendix B, although they drifted sometimes toward an undue amount of pragmatism. It revealed to a mature speaker some of his strengths and even the moral tone of his address. The critics might have gone farther than they did in showing Dr. Upcraft and their classroom colleagues where improvement was possible. But this is only to say they might have brought additional artistic criteria into play.

CRITICAL CRITERIA

We have said repeatedly in this chapter that all criticism begins with description. To make any informed judgment of speaking requires that you first get an accurate, fair description of precisely what the speaker or speakers did.[9] Your description need not always be detailed or intricate. This is especially true in your speech class where you will be functioning as a critic much of the time. The amount of detail in your description will depend on your intended purpose.

In your classroom, where the goal of criticism is to teach, it is essential that you know what each speaker is trying to accomplish. Data about this can come from the nature of the assignment or from what the speaker can tell you beforehand. In any case, if your criticism is to teach, you must know the speaker's intended purpose so you can compare what he or she did to achieve it with what might have been done for that purpose. Knowing the purposes of classroom speeches also tells you that what is important in one critique might not be of equal importance in another.

Changing the Emphasis in Criticism

In speech criticism the importance of criteria may change from situation to situation. This is likely to be the case when you evaluate speaking in your classroom. There you need to suit your criticism to the learning task of each speaker, and it is important to choose consciously what you will emphasize in each critique. On one occasion the organization of the speech may be at the top of your list of the aspects of the speech to be commented upon. On another occasion, structure will be far down the list. When, for example, you have been concentrating on style in classroom study, such matters as striking images and precision in choice of words are apt to take priority as you observe and evaluate.

Even outside the classroom you will need to emphasize one aspect of speaking over another in developing sound critiques. Such a change of emphasis may come about because *you* decide that ideas and arguments will be more important in a given situation than style. It is obvious that the students who evaluated Dr. Upcraft's speech decided this. For them, matters of style and structure seem to have been rather

---

9. To achieve an adequate description the students whose critique appears in appendix B went together to the meeting at which Dr. Upcraft spoke. They all took notes on the situation and the speaking. They made a tape recording of the speech and of some speaking before and after the speech. Working as a problem-solving group, they then drew up their collective description of the event to describe its details. They also made a written transcript of Upcraft's speech with this goal in mind. All of these steps were taken to create a description from which interpretation and evaluation could then be developed.

low on their hierarchy of rhetorical features to be analyzed in detail. They believed the audience was initially hostile to Dr. Upcraft because he was a representative of the university's administration. They may have been right in their decision to concentrate on ideas and arguments for the most part, but their critique would have been stronger had they told their listeners why they gave organization and style so little attention.

Our basic point here is that not every aspect of speaking is equally important in every rhetorical situation. Thus, a critic's rankings of criteria shift constantly depending upon the aims of the speaker, his or her subject matter, and the demands of the situation. You must decide upon your critical hierarchy each time you criticize speech. As you listen or read to describe and evaluate, you must separate the important from the unimportant qualities of discourse. If you do not, you may end up by concentrating on trivial matters to the neglect of items that deserved more attention.

Consideration of ideas and their reasoned structure is often neglected. You can assist your colleagues in classroom speaking by considering with special care what you and the other listeners are *required* to believe if you are to agree with what the speaker is saying. Here Professor Toulmin's concept of argument can help. Toulmin maintains the logical persuasiveness of an advocate depends especially upon whether his or her listeners can and will accept the DATA and the WARRANTS offered in support of conclusions (see pages 129–38). You can assist your colleagues greatly if you will consider why you *do* or *do not* accept the DATA and WARRANTS upon which their CLAIMS rest. Obviously, speaking cannot be persuasive unless those who hear it accept the DATA upon which CLAIMS depend. Unless "How do you get there?" (from information or DATA to conclusion or CLAIM) is answered satisfactorily for the listeners, a speaker cannot hope to convince them. So if you disagree with a colleague's CLAIMS, it will be very useful for you to explain whether it is the DATA you doubt or the WARRANTS you question. In other words, "*Why* do I believe?" and "*Why* do I doubt?" are questions you need to answer for a colleague if you are to explain your own critical reactions to his or her persuasion.

You will need to guard against developing fixations, especially about delivery. For some, voice or bodily action always occupies first place when they listen to the speech of others. These seem easiest to comment on. In your critiques of classmates a danger sign is present if you always say: "Jim doesn't make any gestures," or "John has too many breaks in fluency," or "George rattled the keys and change in his pocket—most distracting!" All you have said may be true, but you must focus on the total speech or its most important aspects for this situation, unless some special agreement within your class has determined that delivery is your only concern.

Detailing the Criteria

Once you decide which matters are most important in criticizing a specific bit of public talk, you will become concerned with more specific judgments. Usually you will start with the broader aspects of the communication and work to the details. In assessing a unit of speech giving information, for example, you will want first to ask yourself questions about the communication as a unit. Did it have an identifiable central purpose? Did it have a recognizable introduction, body, and conclusion? What was the quality of its total impact?

You will want on many occasions to ask special questions about speeches or units of speech that constitute communication calculated to give information. You might ask, "Does the audience understand the subject better now that they have heard what was said?" To answer why they do or do not, you may pose questions relating directly to expository techniques: Was there justification in the subject matter and in the audience's interest for the way this speaker used exposition, description, and narration at various points? Did this speech or unit of talk meet the special demands for good expository speaking by being accurate, clear, and interesting? Were visual aids used or needed to clarify points or were they used for their own sake?

From these kinds of questions you may turn to specific details that may or may not be exclusively applicable to informative speaking. Here, you will ask questions such as "Did the story of the male student who knitted his own socks and ate light bulbs illustrate originality or peculiarity? Were reliable statistics used to show the relationship between monetary support and the quality of higher education? Were they truly representative? Were appropriate gestures used to support the idea that public schools are bursting with students? Well coordinated? Definite enough? Isn't the word pronounced gri-*mace,* not *grim*-ace?" These and like questions of detail complete your movement: evaluating the speech or unit of communication first as a whole, then as a particular kind of speech, and finally as a communicative effort consisting of detailed strengths and weaknesses.

Criticism sheets used to assess classroom speaking will sometimes assist you in deciding which questions to ask and which questions are most important. The criticism sheet we have designed for use with formal speeches is shown in figure 11–1. It provides for both structured and unstructured comment. Aspects of speech making that need constant attention, no matter what the kind of speech, are arranged along the left side of the paper with spaces in which quick reactions can be entered while the speech is being delivered. The right half of the sheet provides space for personal notations and for revised, final reactions to the speech. The box in the lower right-hand corner encourages the user to recommend areas for improvement so the criticism will fulfill the constructive obligations of any critic's task.

NAME: _____   SPEECH NO: _____

SUBJECT: _____   DATE: _____

SUBJECT AND PURPOSE

*Subject worthwhile?*_____

*Purpose delimited?*_____

CONTENT AND ORGANIZATION

Introduction

  *Get attention?*_____

  *Needed information given?*_____

  *Purpose made clear?*_____

Development

  *Organization—soundly planned?*_____

    *—easily followed?*_____

    *—transitions effective?*_____

    *—internal summaries appropriate?*_____

  *Supporting material—clear?*_____

    *—enough of it?*_____

    *—interesting?*_____

    *—convincing?*_____

    *—visual aids effective?*_____

Conclusion

  *Provide a note of finality?*_____

  *Whole speech in focus?*_____

DELIVERY

Mental Alertness

  *Realize each idea as uttered?*_____

  *Keen sense of communication?*_____

Body

  *Eye contact adequate?*_____

  *Posture acceptable?*_____

  *Movement meaningful?*_____

  *Gestures effective?*_____

Voice

  *Distinct?*_____

  *Vocal variety adequate?*_____

    *Rate?*_____ *Pitch?*_____ *Volume?*_____

  *Fluency adequate?*_____

LANGUAGE

*Have good oral qualities?*_____

*Convey ideas clearly?*_____

*Grammar correct?*_____

*Pronunciation correct?*_____

*Increase interest and impact?*_____

OVERALL EVALUATION

*Adapted to situation and audience?*_____

*Purpose fulfilled?*_____

*Make good personal impression?*_____

*Interesting?*_____

Symbols:

  X—No

  √—Yes

Grades:

  Papers:

  Speech:

  For the round:

  Consult Instructor?

  _____

  _____

NEXT TIME work especially for:

FIGURE 11-1

We want to emphasize that this criticism sheet is not a scoring sheet. It simply contains quick-answer items that experienced teachers have to comment on and ask for comment about again and again in speech classes. If you use this or any other criticism sheet, remember what we have just said about shifting your critical criteria to suit different situations and purposes of speaking. You, not a criticism sheet, must decide the relative importance of specific criteria in each speaking situation.

THE CRITICAL ACT

In the Classroom

A good classroom critic, like a good speaker, considers the effects his or her observations will have on the audience. He or she expresses judgments that cast the most light for the largest number. In public he or she minimizes personal preferences and deals minimally with problems of concern only to a particular speaker. This critic is a student and teacher of oral discourse. Instead of using class time to comment on one speaker's peculiar vocal habit, he or she dwells on problems and strengths important to all speakers, concentrates on whatever can be useful to all and to himself or herself as a student of an art. All faults and strengths are fair game for criticism if treated constructively. In the classroom as elsewhere, matters having general application deserve public comment; basically personal matters are best criticized in private conferences or in tactful notes.

Your education as a speech critic begins in the classroom. To make the most of it, and to give others greatest benefit from your observations and judgments, we suggest you approach classroom criticism in the following ways.

1. *Ready yourself for your critical task by preparing to concentrate on what you will see and hear.* Focus, visually and aurally, upon the speaking that is going on. You must listen intently (see chapter 2, pages 25–27). Try to rid yourself of distractions from without and within. Exclude all bids for attention except those of the speaker.

2. *Locate your critical criteria consciously.* Decide what you are listening for, what aspects of speech deserve your special consideration because of their importance in *this* speaking situation. In other words, decide which achievements in speaking rank highest in importance at *this* time, for *this* speaker, in *this* situation. By attending to the facets of speech making you are currently studying in class, you

will give your criticism purpose. The more specific you can be in defining your own critical purposes, the more specific will be your description and the more useful your evaluation.

Do not try to observe every aspect of the speech at once. You cannot describe and evaluate all the phenomena of speech, so let a deliberately chosen set of critical criteria define the scope of your analysis. Register your reactions accordingly. Scattering your attention over many items will be of little service to the speaker and will impede the development of your own critical faculties. A speaker is not helped by superficial comments about a dozen things. He or she will be able to solve only a few artistic problems at a time. You will not be helped as a critic by trying to judge a host of items in haphazard fashion. Aim to substantiate and develop a few major, situationally appropriate critical judgments.

3. *Adopt a constructive attitude.* As you try to detect the choices the speaker has made, consider the alternatives. As you note merits and flaws, ask: what else might have been done in this situation given the speaker's purpose? What specific, constructive suggestions can I offer for this speaker's improvement? Negative comment, registering only personal impressions without substantiating evidence or affirmative suggestions, will be of little help. To say, "Your speech was poorly organized," or even, "Your economic argument was unsound," does not get to the heart of the matter. It does not get to the "why" of the trouble. It does not offer an analysis upon which someone else can build. "You didn't look at your audience," "Your sentences were clumsy," or "You committed several grammatical errors" may be accurate descriptions of speech, but unless they are accompanied by suggestions for correction, they are no help. Such comments are critical, but they do not teach. It is probably a good rule not to point out negative features if you cannot suggest remedies.

Starting critical remarks with positive things, with strong points, and proceeding to the less praiseworthy works well. Such an approach is simply good audience adaptation. The speaker will listen to what you say, will know you are not picking him apart for malicious reasons, and will be likely to remember to do again those things he did well and to remedy those he did poorly. It has been said, "Only those who have the heart to help have a right to criticize."

4. *Measure the speech against the criteria you are applying.* Measure what the speaker did against criteria that relate specifically to ideas, proofs, arrangement, style, and delivery. But keep the rhetorical situation uppermost in your mind as you make your educated guesses on the effectiveness, apparent intentions, and skill of what the speaker is doing.

As you listen, jot down reminders of your descriptive observations and of the criteria you are applying; then note your judgments along with the most pertinent examples and illustrations. A few notes will do. Do not become a stenographer. You and your colleagues are members of an audience, although you are also critics. You should remember that no speaker can be at his or her best when trying to address a roomful of bowed heads. Remember, too, that no critic functions effectively without giving himself or herself the opportunity to take in the visual as well as the aural elements of spoken communication.

Your job is to judge the speaking, not the person. Of course, there is never speech without a speaker, but your business is to assess that speaker's *communicated* personality as a force in the speech. Consider how his or her *ethos* contributes to the speech, not what contributes to your like or dislike for him or her as a person.

5. *Make a judgment.* This admonition may sound superfluous, but we make it because we have found it is often needed. In too many cases you will be tempted merely to describe what you see and hear. Description is, to be sure, a first step in fruitful criticism, but it is not your main business as a critic. Your ultimate function is to deliver a decision—a judgment—based upon the relationship between what you perceive and what you know. To be an effective critic you must avoid straddling the fence. Decide whether the aspect of speech you are considering is effective or ineffective, adequate or inadequate, skillfully or unskillfully handled, successful or unsuccessful, and why.

6. *Be as specific as possible in formulating your judgments.* Document your criticism with descriptive evidence. Refer directly to the speech, to specific arguments, illustrations, and wordings. Provide examples to back up both favorable and unfavorable evaluations. If you are criticizing style, strive to identify moments during which style was effective and other moments when it was less so. Refer to specific sentence structures, phrasings, and images. This will reveal that you have been both perceptive and thorough in arriving at your judgments. It will also be constructively useful to all who hear your criticism. Find segments of the speech illustrating strengths and weaknesses in clarity, liveliness, force, and the like. The more precise you can be about exactly what was done and exactly why it was effective or ineffective, the more worthy of attention your observations will be.

7. *Register your judgment.* When you present your critical assessments orally or in writing, articulate your convictions. Silence during an oral criticism period following a speech or submitting doodlings on a scrap of paper will contribute nothing to the speaker or to your own development as an intelligent, informed critic. Do not feel that you must couch your judgments in rhetorical jargon. Do feel that you must be tactful in wording and frank in your remarks. Clear, direct, precise expression of your position, the data on which it rests, and your suggestions are required.

We have emphasized that public speaking does not always take place on the platform, nor is it always a matter of *a* speaker making *a* speech that functions apart from all other talk. Public interviews draw forth units of talk that function as speeches. Debates occur in business meetings and at conference tables. The students who presented a critique of Dr. Upcraft's speech made a series of interrelated speeches that, together, formed a total communication that might be called a public speech. Segments of uninterrupted talk on broadcast talk shows affect listeners as speeches. Rap sessions involve public speeches. To understand such talks you may need to conceptualize them as *units of speeches* (the several contributions to one side of an ongoing debate or the individual speeches of the presentation in appendix B). Or perhaps you can conceptualize several separated units as comprising a *whole speech* (an interviewee's total presentation of himself or the total critique of Dr. Upcraft's speech). If you view interrupted public speech in these ways, you will often find that this kind of speaking is entirely amenable to such critical evaluation as we have discussed above.

How well someone communicates according to his or her purpose in an interview or as a contributor to a general purpose he or she shares with other speakers has as much importance as how well that person does in platform speaking. Artistic effectiveness is just as desirable off the platform as on. To see public speech as the assumption of responsibility for maintaining communicative relations on behalf of some purpose allows you to evaluate much informal speaking. For these reasons we suggest below some ways you can approach minimally formalized public speech in the same critical spirit you would apply to formal speech.

The kind of shared presentation that is represented by the students' critique in appendix B occurs very commonly—in symposiums, panel presentations, informational programs of many kinds, and as committee reports, which the critique in appendix B actually was. These kinds of presentations need to be looked at with two general questions in mind: (1) How fully did the entire group of speakers succeed in communicating a single unified message to the audience? (2) How well did each individual speaker communicate a clear message that supported or contributed to the impact of the group's total message? Approaching the material in appendix B in these ways, you could apply all of the critical procedures we have discussed to this group's public speaking.

Almost any press conference creates situations in which the interviewee can (and often should) make responses up to several minutes in length. Those responses can be understood and evaluated if you think of them as short, often one-point, speeches occasioned by a rhetorical situation and delivered under circumstances calling for artful invention, disposition, choice of language, and presentation. However impromptu, such speeches affect listeners essentially as other public speeches do. You can approach such responses in interviews, discussions, or public meetings as speech inviting criticism of the same sort as we are considering in this chapter.

Whenever and wherever you can discern a "major unit of rhetorical discourse," that talk is open to criticism as a speech, even though it may be imbedded in an interview, talk show, coverage of a space venture or, for that matter, conversation with your auto mechanic! If ideas are being developed for an audience, the criteria of speech criticism apply because artistic excellence in using rhetorical resources becomes possible. Descriptions and evaluations of purpose, applications of situationally suitable criteria, and judgments on how nearly the talk achieved its potential influence are issues whether you criticize formal or informal public communication.

Evaluating Texts of Discourse

In your public-speaking classroom you will usually evaluate speaking for which no printed text or electronic recording exists. Then you must proceed as we suggested on pp. 335–37. But sometimes you will have some record of classroom speaking you need to criticize; should you undertake to make a critique of outside speaking, the problem of how to treat the record of speech will arise. In this section we deal with aspects of that problem.

If there is some record of the speaking you want to evaluate, the first thing to remember is that it is a *record;* it is *not* public speech as the event it really was. Your critical object may be the verbatim transcript of the speaking: the one the student critics of appendix B made for themselves from their own tape recording or one that appeared in *The New York Times.* It may be an audio recording or even a video recording of the speech. In every case what you have is but a record; it is not the real thing. You have some remnants of live, oral discourse. You have to treat it rather as an archeologist would treat some pieces of a Greek vase. From the *pieces* he tries to reconstruct in his mind how the *whole* must have been. The situation is not ideal, but one can still learn a good deal. Let us suggest how and with what cautions.

In handling any record of public speech you will be taking in speech with only the eye or ear, not experiencing at first hand the total situation. Delivery cannot be described fully, if at all. Voice may be judged from a recording, but not bodily action, unless you have access to a sound film. A bit of film may have to serve as "representative." Many judgments on delivery will be far from satisfactory, since they must be based on accounts furnished by others who saw and heard what happened, on partial evidence.

Where you must work with printed texts alone, there are a number of things you must consider before you can begin the steps of criticism we have outlined in connection with criticizing "live" speeches.

1. *Determine the authenticity of your text.* Ascertaining the genuineness and completeness of the written record before you may not be easy. (See exercise 4 at the end of this chapter.) Unless you are convinced of the trustworthiness of the transcriber and editor of the text, you ought to match the text you use with others, should they be available. You will want to work with the best text obtainable. You should also be sure, insofar as possible, whether what you work with was actually composed and delivered by the speaker himself. Ghostwriters are nothing new. They have been employed since the fourth century B.C. at the very least. You ought to know, if possible, to what extent your text was prepared *for* the speaker and to what extent it was prepared *by* him.

2. *Inform yourself of the immediate speech setting.* To make judgments you must know particulars of the rhetorical situation. You must know when and where the utterance took place, to whom it was directed, and what expectations and constraints controlled the impact of the message. Getting such knowledge calls for the kind of research that will lead you to sources dealing with immediate or distant history. If possible, you ought to know who was present and who saw and heard the discourse. When you know this you ought to interview those who actually witnessed the communication if they are available and willing to talk with you. When you have exhausted these research possibilities, you will want to turn to accounts that deal specifically with the communication, treating the circumstances that determined the subject matter, the composition and the delivery, the immediate physical surroundings, and all other immediate influences that operated on the audience that heard the message.

3. *Inform yourself of the milieu.* For a full understanding of rhetorical discourse you often need to have extensive knowledge of the times as well as the immediate circumstances. It is often important to know what ideas were in the air, what philosophies prevailed, what historic events had recently occurred, and what were the day-to-day concerns of the people. No one can understand Lincoln's "Second Inaugural Address" without understanding how the Civil War was going at the time and what visions some Northerners had of reconstructing the South. Nor can one understand the speaking of Jimmy Carter as a candidate for president of the United States in 1976 without understanding what was meant by terms such as *populist, new politics,*

and *born-again Christian*.   To understand such concepts peculiar to rhetorical situations you would need to read historical and interpretive accounts of cultural, political, and religious events and ideas of the time.

It is true that understanding the milieu of public speech often entails a good deal of historical-sociological investigation, but this effort is what allows you to describe and judge speech fairly and on *its* own terms.   If it was wise rhetorical speech it was created for and influenced by listeners who were the creatures of their environment.   To know them and thereby know the speech, you must know about the environment.

4. *Inform yourself about the speaker.*   You will need to acquire information about his reputation, his place in society, his habits of mind and life, his sense of values, and his impact on other people.   To gain such insights you may need to study autobiographical and biographical materials, diaries, memoirs, photographs, and letters. Your task will be to produce a portrait of the speaker as speaker in your own mind.   To do this you ought to find whatever you can about his speech training, his methods of oral composition, his ways of thinking, and whose influence might have affected his speaking.   You will also need to look for descriptions and evaluations of him as a person.

5. *Read the criticism written by others.*   The amount of published criticism of oral utterance is usually not great, and you will sometimes find it difficult to locate.   But often there are at least some news articles, essays, headnotes, and journal articles containing criticism of speakers of the past and present.   Often the newspapers published the day after a speech will give some appraisal of what was said and of the speaker's performance.   The appraisals may be judicious or superficial, but you are not reading the criticism of others so you can imitate them.   Your purpose is to sift through all the judgments you can find and arrive at your own point of view.

Criticizing oral communication when only a record is available is more difficult than criticizing utterance you can personally witness, but it is not at all impossible or unsatisfying.   The ideal situation is, of course, that of the students who criticized Dr. Upcraft's speech.   They attended the meeting, made their own audio recording, and then made their own written text.   But another group from the same speech class evaluated a famous legal plea from the eighteenth century with equal profit and satisfaction.   By following the pattern of textual and historical-sociological research we have been describing, this group was able to produce a very well-informed judgment of why and how Lord Thomas Erskine was able to sway a jury in a British courtroom in 1794.   What is more, they could then explain to themselves and their classmates why that speech was still in print in the twentieth century.   The object of background research is simply to produce a description—a re-creation of the attendant circumstances. These attempts at re-creation will draw you into many interesting fields of knowledge—history, philosophy, literature, sociology, psychology, religion.

There are some professional educators who argue that no one is ready to criticize spoken discourse until he has passed considerably beyond a beginning course in speech. We think the critique in appendix B proves this a mistaken notion. The speaker whom this first-course group of students criticized testified both publicly and privately that he had gained from their work. They successfully and satisfyingly explained to themselves and their colleagues a major reason why, despite their university's new regulations, there were no vigorous protests against the administration itself. The students who explored Lord Erskine's legal prowess learned much about the art of legal rhetoric, much British history that interested them, and they accounted for the fact that the speech they studied has been printed and reprinted in English for nearly 200 years. These are not trivial achievements. Our own students attain as much term after term. We hope that somewhere during your education you, too, will try your hand at making a thoroughgoing criticism of some unit of public speech that occurred outside your classroom.

Evaluating Live Speech Outside the Classroom

If your assignment were the criticism of a live speech outside the classroom, how might you proceed? Suppose you were asked to do an appraisal of a sermon delivered at your church or synagogue next week or to make an evaluation of a speech by a local political candidate who is currently campaigning. Which of twelve steps discussed in the preceding two sections might you use? Which of the five for examining texts of speeches and the seven for judging classroom speaking might you pursue?

Of those dealing with the printed text, you will probably omit the first step, which concerns textual authenticity, because it is unlikely that a text of the speech will be made available to you. If it is, of course, you will want to examine it for originality of idea (perform what is called *higher textual criticism*). Chances are that a text furnished you by the speaker or his or her agent would be fairly reliable. It may be unnecessary to match it against other texts. You will, however, want to check this text against what the speaker actually says or against a recording of some sort should you have one.

Step 2 will be omitted because you will be in the immediate setting and can make your own notes about it, notice its impact and the speaker's adaptation to it.

Step 3 will also be unnecessary insofar as research is concerned, although you should take into consideration the news of the day, the philosophical, religious, and political ideas astir in society, and any other events that may affect the rhetorical situation.

Step 4 may, in the case of live outside criticism, be undertaken if you want to supplement your knowledge of the speaker. You will want to, of course, if you know very little about him or her and if there is written material on his or her life and activities. In some instances you will be able to bypass this step.

You will simply be unable to pursue step 5 unless you delay your critique until after the speech has been reported in the press, should that be the case, or unless you want to read what others have written about other speeches given by the speaker.

All of the other steps, the seven usable for classroom criticism, in the order we have given them, will then be appropriate in what some have called the "case method" of criticism—which is the sort of criticism you will be engaged in. You can follow those steps as we have given them in the foregoing pages.

The experience of completing the assignment of judging speech in a setting less laboratory-like than the classroom ought to be a rewarding one and will test and reinforce all that you have learned in class.

Criticism is judgment and/or appreciation based on informed description examined in the light of criteria. Criticism is comparative. No matter what art is investigated, criticism calls into play knowledge of the art's resources, the function of the art in the given case, and the essential features of the object being examined. When the critical object is public speech, it is necessary to understand what is possible in speaking, what are the allowances of the situation, and what are the characteristics of the speaking that is done.

The purposes that dominate in creation of most public utterances are utilitarian. Practical influence tends to control wise choices more than do considerations of permanence or beauty. But to judge rhetorical discourse by its effects alone is to forget that not all situations allow rhetorical effectiveness, and to judge by abstract ethical or moral standards alone is to forget that the same ethical standards do not apply across all rhetorical situations. We have therefore argued for speech criticism based on artistic standards, testing the degrees to which speakers exhaust the resources of their art in meeting the exigences of the rhetorical situations they enter.

In the classroom or out of it, criticism of speech requires method and wisdom. It requires (1) concentration on speech, not peripheral matters, as the critical object, (2) conscious identification of both data and criteria relevant to understanding rhetorical events in full, (3) comparison of observed performance with criteria that define the ideal, (4) formulation of judgments that are specific, cogent, and constructive, and (5) supported, documented expression of the criticism itself.

Although public speech occurs in many forms other than formal speech making, the methods of criticism as we have described them prove applicable to a vast amount of public discourse beyond individual speeches of traditional sorts. It is possible and satisfying to apply the methods of speech criticism to either immediately perceived or historic speaking. Few intellectual enterprises are more liberally educative.

EXERCISES

Written

1. Identify in advance some speech that is going to be delivered in your community. The speech should be one you can both see and hear. Prepare to criticize this speech by writing in systematic fashion all available, pertinent information concerning the speaker and his or her presumed purpose, the audience, the occasion, and the apparent exigences of the situation he or she will enter. Attend the speech. Make both descriptive and evaluative notes during the speech, using a set of criteria you have decided to make the basis of your criticism (the criteria being those you settle upon after preliminary analysis of the situation and its rhetorical potentialities, if any). Finally, develop and write a balanced evaluation of the speech as given.

2. Select a famous speech from a past era. Obtain the best record of the speech available. Collect background material on the period, including data on prevailing cultural values, living habits, and beliefs. Establish what the public's image of the speaker was as he or she entered his or her speaking situation. Once you have acquired an understanding of the total situation and of the entire speech, choose one of the following topics and write an analysis and criticism of:
   a. The speaker's rational justifications.
   b. The speaker's use of amplifying materials such as examples, narration, statistics, and definitions.
   c. The structure of the speech as it relates to the subject matter, the audience, and the occasion.
   d. The speaker's style in relation to his or her purpose and the situation.
   e. The authenticity and usefulness of the record of the speech you used.

3. Select some piece of recorded rhetoric that most people would not think open to the methods of speech criticism; for example, the lyrics of a song, a poem, a newspaper editorial, the copy in an advertisement, a dramatic scene that contains a fairly large segment of uninterrupted discourse, the copy of a flyer or pamphlet handed to you on the street.
   a. Using the pattern for criticism discussed in this chapter, write a criticism of your critical object.

b. Write several paragraphs in explaining how you had to modify your pattern of criticism (if you did) to do justice to your critical object.
4. Read Professor Robert W. Smith's "The 'Second' Inaugural Address of Lyndon Baines Johnson: A Definitive Text," *Speech Monographs* XXXIV (March 1967): 102–8; then do the following:
    a. Prepare a definitive text of any public speech. Defend its definitiveness either orally or in writing.
    b. Write an essay (or make a speech) evaluating the reliability of some speech that exists exclusively in printed form.
5. Write on (or give a speech on) the rhetorical effectiveness of one of the committee of critics whose report is in appendix B.

Oral

1. Listen closely to a classroom speech assigned to you for evaluation. Keep in mind the requirements contained in the speaker's assignment and avowed purpose. Make written notes as appropriate, and note your judgments on selected aspects of the speech. During the oral criticism period reserved for the speech assigned to you, give a one- to two-minute extemporaneous speech evaluating and advising the speaker.
2. Prepare and deliver a speech in which you discuss one of the following:
    a. The considerations essential in appraising a speaker's *invention, disposition, style, delivery, memoria* (choose one).
    b. The differences between the procedures for criticizing a live speech and those for criticizing the printed text of a speech.
    c. The distinctions between the critical object in speech criticism and the critical object in criticism of some art other than the art of public speaking.
    d. How you would arrive at a particular set of criteria to be used in judging a particular speech. (You specify the kind of speech to be considered.)
    e. The critical criteria you would apply in evaluating the rhetoric of a critical presentation such as that in appendix B.
    f. Aspects of artistic achievement you believe the panel in appendix B overlooked in evaluating Dr. Upcraft's speech.
3. With four or five of your classmates form a problem-solving committee and take as your problem question, "To what extent did X fulfill the situational requirements when speaking on the occasion of _____?" (This is the kind of question used by the committee whose presentation appears in appendix B.) As a committee, carry out the kind of critical investigation described in this chapter and form a *group* evaluation of the speaking you have studied. When you have completed your criticism, prepare a presentation for your class in which you enable your audience to reconstruct the speech in its situation and in which you explain the reasons for your collective critical judgment. Note that there are other ways than letting your audience hear or read the entire speech by which you can reconstruct the speech for your listeners: presenting only important excerpts, summarizing, presenting through dialogue the overall description on which you based your criticism, and so on.

Appendix A

Rhetorical Theory: A Heritage

The question "What makes speech effective?" has been pondered since the days of the ancient Greeks. Plato (c. 429–347 B.C.) and Aristotle (384–322 B.C.) discussed the nature of man speaking. Famous Romans such as Cicero (106–43 B.C.), a great orator, and Quintilian (c. A.D. 35–100), a great teacher, reorganized and refined what they found in Greek writings on public communication. St. Augustine (A.D. 354–430) and medieval men of learning added to and adapted their inherited bodies of rhetorical theory as they attempted to help men of their times function effectively in new kinds of speech situations. Especially in America and Europe, scholars have continued to search for new insights and fuller understandings to solve the problems of spoken discourse.

It is our purpose in this section to tell you about important thinkers and explain how some of their theories of rhetoric and speech communication have developed. We hope that knowledge of the origins of what is thought today will help you to think and to apply your thinking to the problems you face as a human being with powers of speech.

As a first step we identify some important writings that serious scholars of rhetoric and speech have used in arriving at theories of their own. Then we set forth the five major problems all communicators face. These problems were first conceptualized by Greeks and Romans sometime before the Christian era, but as creators' problems they remain with all of us. They are the problems of: *invention* (discovering communicable ideas and their logical aspects); *disposition* (organizating or structuring ideas); *style* (finding the right language); *delivery* (deciding how to present a message); and *memoria* (command of an entire speech, once planned and composed, a problem our term, memory, inadequately represents). We review ideas about these problems, pointing to those that have attained special importance in Western thought. Ours is not an ample record of how our cultural conceptions of oral communication became what they are. We offer instead a review to show that most questions you will raise as you seek to improve yourself as a speaker are questions others have raised and tried to answer ever since Western man has taken the powers of speech seriously.

LANDMARKS OF RHETORIC

Landmark works on speech and rhetoric in ancient Greece have been of towering influence to the present day. Especially important were Plato's two dialogues, *Gorgias* (c. 387 B.C.) and *Phaedrus* (c. 380 B.C.), and Aristotle's *Art of Rhetoric* (c. 330 B.C.). During the period of the Roman Republic the most influential writings published were *Rhetorica ad Herennium* (c. 82 B.C.), formerly attributed to Cicero,[1] and Cicero's *De Oratore* (55 B.C.). Quintilian's *Institutio Oratoria* (A.D. 93) and "Longinus's" *On the Sublime*[2] belong to the period of the Roman Empire.

St. Augustine's *De Doctrina Christiana* (c. 426) is a work on Christian preaching and stands as the greatest rhetorical study produced during the late Empire-medieval period. Bacon's *The Advancement of Learning* (1605) and its Latin revision, *De augmentis scientiarum* (1623), contain the most profound thought touching human communication to emerge during the Renaissance.

Fénelon's *Dialogues on Eloquence* was published in France in 1717 and was influential in France and England in the eighteenth century. This and other works of major importance in the eighteenth and nineteenth centuries can be divided into three groups.

The originators of the elocutionary movement in England had

---

1. It is now generally agreed that the work is by an unknown author. Its earlier attribution to Cicero added immeasurably to the book's reputation. For an authoritative discussion see Harry Caplan's "Introduction" to *Rhetorica ad Herennium* (Cambridge, Mass.: Harvard University Press, 1954), pp. vii, ff.

2. The author and date of this work are uncertain. Authorities place its date at either the first or third century A.D. and remain in doubt about the real author. See G. M. A. Grube's "Translator's Introduction" to *Longinus on Great Writing* (*On the Sublime*) (New York: The Liberal Arts Press, 1957), pp. vii–xxi.

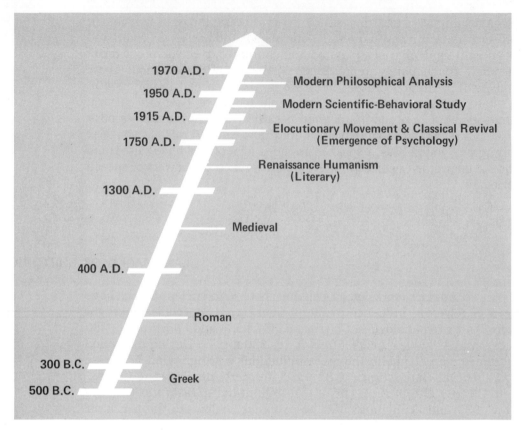

FIGURE A-1.   *Diagram Showing Major Periods in the Development of Rhetorical Theory.*

vast influence in England and America.   Representative writers in this group include: Thomas Sheridan, *A Course of Lectures on Elocution* (1756); Joshua Steele, *Prosodia Rationalis* (1775); and Gilbert Austin, *Chironomia* (1806).

In a rival tradition other writers sought to integrate classical theory and the newly emerging science of human nature.   They include British writers such as George Campbell, *Philosophy of Rhetoric* (1776) and Richard Whately, *Elements of Rhetoric* (1828).   Hugh Blair's *Lectures on Rhetoric and Belles Lettres* (1783) stands as the chief example of a third tradition reflecting classical influences filtered through writers such as Fénelon and "Longinus."   Blair also reflects a wish to intertwine the arts of rhetoric and poetic.

In the twentieth century several works have had especially wide influences on thought about speech communication.   They are James A. Winans, *Public Speaking* (1915); Charles H. Woolbert, *Fundamentals of Speech* (1920); I. A. Richards, *The Philosophy of Rhet-*

oric (1936); Kenneth Burke, *A Grammar of Motives* (1945) and *A Rhetoric of Motives* (1950); Stephen E. Toulmin, *The Uses of Argument* (1958); and Chaim Perelman and L. Olbrechts-Tyteca, *The New Rhetoric* (1969), originally published as *La nouvelle rhetorique: Traité de l'argumentation* (1958). These and other works will be briefly discussed on later pages when we sketch the development of Western thought about the five major constellations of problems in speech making. We provide at the end of this appendix a bibliography of the most easily obtainable, reliable editions of the works mentioned in the foregoing paragraphs.

RHETORICAL INVENTION

That whoever communicates rhetorically must make decisions about *what* to say is a truism that was recognized at the very beginning of Western thought about speaking. Sometime between Aristotle's day and the appearance of early Latin rhetorics, theorists' and teachers' ideas on speakers' problems of discovery came to be grouped under the general heading of *inventio*. Thus the so-called canon of *invention* came into being. The term is actually no more than a topical heading for whatever a rhetorical theorist has to say concerning problems of generating and adapting communicable ideas and whatever other forces can be directly controlled in evoking responses to speech.

Aristotle was the first to see that a speaker invents more than just ideas. He argued that there are three major kinds of force or proof by which a speaker gains his ends. These are: the intellectual content of his communication, which the Greeks called *logos*[3]—the *content;* the emotional forces in the rhetorical situation, which the Greeks called *pathos;* and the forces emanating from the speaking, which the Greeks called *ethos*. Across 2,500 years this analysis of persuasive forces has never been successfully challenged, although what is involved in the logos, pathos, and ethos of communications has been understood and misunderstood in a variety of ways. We review leading attitudes men have had about how to create and manage these forces, hoping you will gain a better understanding of these power sources in spoken communication.

---

3. All classical scholars agree that there is no single English word that expresses the meaning of this very general Greek term. Quite mistakenly, many twentieth-century rhetoricians have equated "logos" with "logic," but this is far too narrow an understanding of the Greek idea. " 'Discourse' and 'reason' are one and the same thing—in Greek they are designated by one and the same word, *logos*," says John Herman Randall, Jr., in his *Aristotle* (New York: Columbia University Press, 1960), p. 6.

Logos: *The Content*

The earliest attempts we know of to answer "How do I discover what to say?" came from two Sicilians of the fifth century B.C., Corax and Tisias. They were counsellors to citizens who had to plead their own cases in court. The chief advice Corax and Tisias gave inexperienced speakers was that the main thing to prove in court was that what you advocated was more *probably* true than your opponent's contention.[4] Allegedly these teachings on probability were carried to Athens and promulgated there.

Other views having to do with rhetorical invention included those of Gorgias of Leontini (c. 483–376 B.C.), a leading sophist.[5] He held that nothing can truly be known to exist; if anything does truly exist men cannot know it, and even if someone could know what exists he could not communicate that knowledge to others. Invention for Gorgias, then, became a matter of refining the methods of arguing the probabilities of things alleged.

Other sophists (teachers) also wrestled with the problem of how men should think and talk about the uncertain. Protagoras of Abdera (c. 480–410 B.C.) maintained that even the existence of the Gods was uncertain, that truth was relative, and that man is the measure of all things. Accordingly he taught that there are two sides to every question and that both ought to be argued. He had his pupils give speeches of praise and dispraise on human qualities such as friendship, patriotism, and cupidity because he thought the many standard themes or "commonplaces" that would then emerge were suggestive of ways to develop thoughts approving or disapproving qualities.

A very different tack was taken in the teaching of Prodicus of Ceos (c. 450 B.C.), another sophist. He taught that to face death courageously was a virtue, and he spoke in praise of the ideals of labor, hardihood, and simplicity. Clearly what and how to think were for Prodicus ethical questions as well as scientific ones. Much the same was true of Plato's view. He deplored the sophists' teachings. In *Phaedrus* (see headnote to chapter 3, page 50) he asserted that a true rhetorician must know his subject completely and also know human

---

4. Just what the relationship was between these two men and what they did teach is uncertain, but whatever the facts may have been, later rhetoricians traced their discipline back to Corax and Tisias and to these teachings. See George Kennedy, *The Art of Persuasion in Greece* (Princeton: Princeton University Press, 1963), pp. 58–61.

5. The sophists were professional traveling teachers in fields such as general culture, politics and rhetoric. Although many of them were teachers of excellence, some were so practical in their aims that they emphasized ingeniousness and speciousness more than soundness of argument. Some were early scientists and mathematicians and others preceded Plato and Aristotle in explorations of the nature of perception and logic. Sophists also evolved the basic concepts of grammar as a result of the special interest many of them had in the nature of language. See pp. 368–69.

psychology well enough to fit his own thought to the particular "soul" he addressed. Plato seems to have felt that only a true philosopher could know enough to speak the truth. The inventional problems of philosophers and orators, as speakers, thus become identical. In solution, Plato recommended the intellectual processes of defining the subject thought or spoken of and then analyzing all the details of the subject implied in its definition.

Aristotle, in dissatisfaction, stated his counterposition concisely:

> All teaching and learning that involves the use of reason proceeds from pre-existent knowledge. This is evident if we consider all the different branches of learning, because both the mathematical sciences and every other art are acquired in this way. Similarly too with logical arguments, whether syllogistic or inductive; both effect instruction by means of facts already recognized, the former making assumptions as though granted by an intelligent audience, and the latter proving the universal from the self-evident nature of the particular. The means by which rhetorical arguments carry conviction are just the same; for they use either examples, which are a kind of induction, or enthymemes, which are a kind of syllogism.[6]

This statement and its amplification in places such as Aristotle's *Rhetoric, Topics, Politics, Ethics,* and *Sophistical Refutations* constitute the Western world's most comprehensive conception of human inventional processes. Particularly important is that it recognizes the distinction between thinking and discovering in *scientific logic* (by rigorous induction and deduction) and in *rhetorical communication* (by psychologically oriented induction through *examples,* and by psychologically oriented deductions through *enthymemes*). By calling rhetorical reasoning "example" and "enthymeme" Aristotle was indicating that what an audience knows and wants and can make use of must be the chief content in all rhetorical situations. In scientific discovery and reasoning absolute self-evidence, formal logical rigor, and judgments of the best thinkers govern intellectual processes—but the knowledge and wants of audiences have no place in such thinking. Aristotle's great contribution to understanding rhetorical invention, then, was to emphasize that although its processes *resemble* those of scientific investigation, these rhetorical processes are different from the scientific because *the audience to be addressed must always guide* the speaker's search for ideas and his or her creation of chains of reasoning.[7]

---

6. Aristotle, *Posterior Analytics,* trans. Hugh Tredennick (Cambridge, Mass.: Harvard University Press, 1960), p. 25.

7. Further details of Aristotle's contributions to the theory of rhetorical invention are discussed and applied in chapter 5, Invention: General Tactics. For an especially penetrating discussion of Aristotle's *Rhetoric* in relation to other intellectual arts see Robert Price, "Some Antistrophes to the *Rhetoric,*" *Philosophy and Rhetoric* I (Summer 1968): 145–64.

The differences between logical and rhetorical invention have occupied the theorists and philosophers of rhetoric ever since.

In their love of refining and classifying earlier theory, Romans gave special attention to two questions pertaining to invention: "How does one amplify ideas and themes already discovered?" and "How does one discover which available data ought to be used in pleading a legal case?" Cicero made the contributions of most significance. He reexplored the *topoi* or topics the Greeks had referred to as places to look when searching for thoughts useful in developing a theme. In his *De Inventione* (confined to legal speaking) and *De Oratore* (his most inclusive book), he showed how lawyers and legislators ought to work their minds in preparing for speaking. He posed four inventional questions about an issue of fact: "Is it?" (Are there any facts?); "What is it?" (What are the facts?); "What is its quality?" (What does it mean?); and "Is this the forum in which to discuss it?" It would not be unfair to say that these four analytical questions were the most significant contribution the Romans made concerning the theory of rhetorical invention.

In the Roman era an unfortunate confusion of Aristotle's distinction between logical and rhetorical invention also occurred. In the centuries of the Roman Empire *all* thinking became increasingly looked upon as *rhetorical* thinking. The probable judgments of an *audience* came to control and constrain virtually every kind of thought. Science, philosophy, and literature naturally deteriorated as what-the-audience-is-*used-to* confined even men's private reflections.

During the Middle Ages and the Renaissance the confusion of rhetoric with logic, inherited from the Romans, persisted. Until the time of Francis Bacon (1561–1626) leading writers treated logic as the method that would work in a debate or disputation. With the distinction between thinking to investigate and thinking to communicate lost, there was no need for a theory of *rhetorical* invention, so rhetoric became the art of dressing logical arguments with ornaments of style and, perhaps, delivery.

There was, however, one powerful idea about the content of communication expressed by St. Augustine in the fifth century A.D. It was influential well into the sixteenth century. This was the thought that a Christian speaker's inventional problems were chiefly problems of *interpreting* sacred works. Once he had abandoned paganism for Christianity, Augustine's original mind discerned that his old rhetorical rules for amplifying a theme and analyzing a legal question were irrelevant to his new mission of expounding the Scriptures. Thus was born a new and specialized art of rhetoric called *homiletics*—literally, the art of preaching. The notion that the rhetorician's main task is to *interpret* his authority, then organize and make persuasive his interpretations, was uniquely appropriate to religious speaking. But when applied to other communication, the scheme encouraged men of the Middle Ages and the Renaissance to believe that rhetorical invention— if there was any at all—consisted merely of choosing an authority, defending the choice, and interpreting it.

In the sixteenth century two views of rhetorical invention came into open competition. The classical view that inventing for communication was a special process was espoused in England, first by Leonard Cox in *The Arte or Crafte of Rhetoryke* (1530). This was the first book on rhetoric in English, as far as we know. Thomas Wilson's *Arte of Rhetorique* (1553), a book that passed through eight editions, insisted still more strongly on the classical view of rhetorical invention. Cox and Wilson contended that rhetoricians must search the world of popular ideas for the content of their rhetoric. But in France a counter and ultimately more popular view was offered by Petrus Ramus (1515– 72). He was determined to eliminate the confusion of logic and rhetoric inherited from the Middle Ages. Thinking had two aspects, Ramus thought: discovering through reason (invention) and evaluating one's findings (judgment). He denied that the same process could exist in two "arts," assigned "invention and judgment" to logic, and thus reinforced the medieval notion that the function of rhetoric is simply to dress the products of scientific thought. Since he made no distinction between *stating* something and *discovering* something, Ramus's concept of logic was naive to the point that it was incapable of generating scientific discovery, nor was there any place in his vision for restudying the known to discover that which was adaptable to an audience. But for a century his was the dominant theory of intellectual activity taught in the schools of Western Europe, in England, and to a lesser extent in the American colonies.

A man of far greater perception than Ramus was Francis Bacon, whose primary interest was in restoring creativity to scientific thought. Threaded through *The Advancement of Learning* and *De augmentis scientiarum* were many new terms and details of an essentially Aristotelian conception of communication and rhetorical invention. Bacon deplored the exclusive stress on style and delivery in the rhetoric of his day and reexplained the distinction between investigating to discover what is true and investigating what is already known to discover what to communicate to a prospective audience.[8] Bacon defined rhetoric as applying reason to the imagination for the better moving of the will. Finding out what to do to achieve this end, he thought, required inspecting existing knowledge for its psychological appropriateness for a specific audience. For this process he recommended use of *topoi*—

---

8. Bacon's scattered observations on communication have been organized and synthesized by Karl R. Wallace in his *Francis Bacon on Communication and Rhetoric* (Chapel Hill: The University of North Carolina Press, 1943).

topics not different in kind from Aristotle's *topoi*.   Additionally he analyzed kinds of fallacies and predispositions found in popular thinking.   His famous Idols of the Tribe, Cave, Marketplace, and Theatre are identifications of the kinds of fallibility men are heir to.

Bacon's reaction against medieval logic and Ramistic rhetoric grew out of his desire to reorder all human knowledge and prepare the way for true scientific investigation.   A generation later in France, and then in England, a different reaction developed in opposition to the authoritarian interpretation of rediscovered classical works by Renaissance scholars.   A young priest, François Fénelon (1651–1715), for example, undertook to apply the then popular doctrine "follow nature" to the art of preaching.[9]   Drawing especially on St. Augustine, Plato, "Longinus," and frequently upon thoughts found in *The Art of Poetry*, written by his contemporary Nicholas Boileau-Despréaux, Fénelon emphasized the social character of rhetoric and the necessity of adapting even scriptural meanings to the differing intelligences and motivations of audiences.   He stressed "instruction" and "making men better" as the proper ends of speaking.   He insisted that a right understanding of religious and moral truth, coupled with an awareness of audiences' differences and a determination to be both "natural" and "tasteful," would lead a preacher to discover what to say and how to say it.   True knowledge was, of course, lodged in religious sources; rhetorical invention involved intuitively and psychologically adapting that truth to specific congregations.   Howell says that Fénelon's was "the earliest statement we have of what may be said to have become the dominant modern attitude toward rhetoric."[10]   The statement seems fair for "follow nature and adapt to your audience" does sum up what most modern rhetorics have advised.

From Bacon's time the naturalist-literary-religious trend in rhetorical theory paralleled attempts at scientific theory building.   In his *Philosophy of Rhetoric* George Campbell (1719–96) clearly drew upon the writings of Francis Bacon and the eighteenth-century philosopher-psychologist David Hume.   Campbell saw analysis of evidence as the persistent problem in finding truth and estimating probabilities. But once data are obtained, he thought, the object of rhetorical communication becomes to find means of arousing passions that will make listeners *want* to accept the speaker's claims.   The explanation was unorthodox in its time but not basically inconsistent with much modern psychological thinking.   Under this explanation rhetorical invention becomes much as Aristotle proposed: the discovery in the *known* of that which can by rhetorical methods be made desirable to hearers.

---

9. His *Dialogues on Eloquence* were written while he was a young man but were not published until 1717, after his death.

10. Wilbur Samuel Howell, "Introduction" in Fénelon, *Dialogues on Eloquence,* trans. W. S. Howell (Princeton: Princeton University Press, 1951), p. 46.

Hugh Blair (1718–1800), on the other hand, said almost nothing about the processes of rhetorical invention in his *Lectures on Rhetoric and Belles Lettres*. With Fénelon he believed that art or method could not help. Following nature, following standards of good taste, and thinking about "the viscera of the cause" were his only answers to how to handle content.

Richard Whately (1787–1863) extended some of George Campbell's thoughts and contracted others. Whately wrote only of argumentation in his *Elements of Rhetoric*. Other possible functions of rhetoric such as explaining, impressing, and blaming go undiscussed. Discovering the best *strategies* for supporting a proposition, given a specific audience and situation, was the main aim in Whately's view of invention. Thus, he omitted much that might have been said, but he did add several especially useful observations. He pointed out, as Aristotle had not, that arguments from example have persuasive force different from arguments by analogy. He was also first to notice that a defender of the *status quo* usually is assigned a lighter "burden of proof" by listeners and hence has a lighter inventional obligation than an arguer who contends for change in what *is*.

With Whately we come to the end of the list of older theorists who tried to cope with how rhetorical communicators invent what they communicate. From the 1820s to the mid-1900s writers have variously said, "Follow nature," or "Dress what 'logic' gives you," or "Think," or "Read what others have said." It has been assumed that rhetorical theory has nothing to tell a communicator until he has by some unfathomable means acquired all that he would say; then it can advise him on how to arrange, style, and deliver the content he has discovered and thought about.

A line of thought in philosophy began to break in upon this complacent view of rhetorical invention in the mid-1900s. A few philosophers in America and abroad pointed forcibly to the fact that formal or scientific logic does not and cannot explain how thought is communicated by people such as lawyers, judges, or even philosophers. The real, not the assumed, logos became the object of intensive philosophical speculation. For explanations of how logos actually works, some philosophers like Richard McKeon, Stephen Toulmin, Chaim Perelman, L. Olbrechts-Tyteca, Henry Johnstone, Jr., and others turned back to the classical explanation: the logos or content in a communication is the product of (1) some degree of logical investigation into what is or seems to be true, (2) a combination of that information with what is already popularly known, and (3) a further adjustment of the content to suit the knowledge and desires of whatever audience the communicator has in mind. The view has come to seem philosophically defensible. Some empirical evidence justifies it. It allows advisers on rhetoric to give speakers and writers more help than is given by telling them to "Follow nature" or "Dress your logic." It is the view we have taken in this book.   We believe that logos or content of speech has most force if it is drawn from the significant knowledge of the world and so adapted as to be meaningful to the particular audience addressed.

Pathos: The Emotive Force

From earliest recorded time in Western culture it has been recognized that the emotive force of things said has power.   Homer dwelt on leaders' powers to sway others by appealing to their feelings. Thucydides attributed a part of Pericles's ability to lead Athens to the fact that he evoked necessary feelings according to his will.   But when the Greeks began to think analytically about communication and its effects, many of them became uneasy concerning the right uses of emotion.   As with so many things, the conclusions drawn by Plato and Aristotle proved representative of kinds of judgment later preserved in Western thought.

Plato granted that a complete rhetorician must understand the nature of human feeling.   The reason was: "men of a special sort under the influence of speeches of a particular kind are readily persuaded to take action of a definite sort because of the qualitative correlation that obtains between speech and soul."[11]   But Plato was unwilling to grant that everyone should have and exercise this kind of affective power.   Accordingly, in his *Republic* he conceived an ideal system in which only philosopher-kings would have full power and only they would decide who should influence the masses intellectually and emotionally and by what means.

Aristotle was uneasy, too; but, as usual, he was pragmatic.   In his view all people act because they have desires that reflect the emotional aspects of their natures.   All but the most technical communications will thus be responded to emotionally as well as intellectually. Aristotle wished it were otherwise—that men were truly rational beings —but he was convinced that human nature encompassed more than intellect.   Somewhat sadly, perhaps, he concluded that pathos was bound to be a persuasive force in all rhetoric and that speakers must understand the different kinds of human emotions, what causes them, toward whom they are likely to be directed, and how to arouse them and allay them.   This knowledge was an integral part of a speaker's necessary equipment, Aristotle thought, and he devoted most of Book II of his *Rhetoric* to a discussion of these topics.   The section is a veritable social psychology of Athenian audiences.

The Romans were no less sensitive to the inevitability of emo-

---

11. Plato, *Phaedrus,* trans. W. C. Helmbold and W. G. Rabinowitz (New York: The Liberal Arts Press, 1956), p. 63.

tional power in communication, but their responses to that fact differed from those of the Greeks.   In *Rhetorica ad Herennium,* for example, the author undertakes to tell his pupils exact ways to put emotional qualities into their speaking.   Among other things, he tells them how to sound indignant, accusing, and calm.   He cautions against being emotional in introductions but calls for emotionality in conclusions. Many Roman teachers of rhetoric followed this lead, treating emotion as something to be *put into* the content of a speech or its delivery. They treated the emotive power of speech as something a speaker added or subtracted as he composed and delivered his ideas.   The Greek idea that feelings occur not in language but in people, and are to be regulated by speech, was drastically narrowed.

Even Cicero and Quintilian failed to see the full difference between advising speakers how to put *in* emotional appeals and advising them how to *understand* the emotions of audiences and how to *adjust* to that reality as purpose required.   However, Cicero, as a statesman, had a further concern with the acknowledged emotional power of content, style, and delivery, and Quintilian followed Cicero's lead.   To Cicero it was important that emotions displayed and emotions aroused be properly Roman, with due gravity, dignity, and decorum always maintained.   Both attitudes toward emotional force in communication, as revealed in Cicero's writings and the *Rhetorica ad Herennium,* had the severe limitation of emphasizing study of the speaker's emotionality and minimizing study of the emotional readinesses of listeners.   Ultimately, in the later days of the Roman Empire, it became difficult to distinguish speakers from actors, so strong was concern with how emotions could be portrayed.

St. Augustine, once converted to Christianity, had to rethink the implications of emotions' roles in speaking and in the responses of listeners.   His conclusion was perhaps simplistic, but it was more functional than the conventional Roman views.   One must give information (Christian teaching) *pleasingly,* he said, else it would not be attended to.   Once understanding was achieved, the speaker must arouse strong feelings or there would be no change in the listeners' actual behavior.   It was aroused emotion that caused the will to change. Augustine's analysis was more lasting than any previous thinker's.   Its main weakness was that it saw teaching, pleasing, and moving emotively as separated functions, but it restored to Western thinking the conception that emotions are present or absent in people, not in messages per se.

Logic, grammar, and disputation preoccupied the attention of most commentators in the Middle Ages.   Men like Ramus tended to ignore audiences, and men like Bacon were suspicious of the feeling states of human beings.   It was therefore not until Fénelon that another major rhetorician gave serious attention to the role of emotion in the proofs of rhetorical speech. This was natural, for he depended heavily on the writings of St. Augustine and was caught up in the thought of literary men eager to free themselves from the tyranny of neoclassical rules of communication. As we have already suggested, Fénelon saw the preacher's function as providing first the "bread" of reasoning to generate understanding, then the "spice"—"everything capable of arousing your [the listener's] sentiments, of making you love demonstrated truth. This is what is called persuasion."[12] Fénelon clung to Augustine's conception that emotion was not involved in understanding but was a different force that moved people to accede to the content of messages. The philosopher, he said, acts only to conceive, but the orator must go beyond, using every resource capable of arousing sentiments. Only so will he secure willful adherence to the demonstrated truth.

Here, the Western world's ideas on the role of emotion in rhetorical response stood for more than a century. In the eighteenth century, the scientific spirit in England led David Hume and then George Campbell to reexamine these dimensions of communication. Campbell came to a conclusion that would have troubled Plato, Aristotle, Augustine, and Fénelon:

> If the orator would prove successful, it is necessary that he engage in his service all these different powers of the mind, the imagination, the memory, and the passions. These are not the supplanters of reason, or even rivals in her sway; they are her handmaids, by whose ministry she is enabled to usher truth into the heart and procure it there a favourable reception. As handmaids they are liable to be seduced by sophistry in the garb of reason, and sometimes are made ignorantly to lend their aid in the introduction of falsehood. But their service is not on this account to be dispensed with; there is even a necessity of employing it, founded on our nature. . . . Nor are those mental powers, of which eloquence so much avails herself . . . perfectly indifferent to good and evil, and only beneficial as they are rightly employed. On the contrary, they are by nature . . . more friendly to truth than to falsehood, and more easily retained in the cause of virtue, than in that of vice.[13]

The modern, psychological age appears to have arrived prematurely in Campbell's analysis of the inseparable, inevitable, emotional and logical forces that rhetorical communication expresses and governs. He saw reason and feeling as "handmaids" existing outside the message, in the audience. He saw the complex response capabilities of humans as challenges to speakers' intelligent, purposeful art. Aristotle might have agreed sadly; Augustine and Fénelon would have found the

---

12. *Dialogues,* trans. W. S. Howell, "Second Dialogue," p. 89.
13. George Campbell, *Philosophy of Rhetoric,* ed. Lloyd F. Bitzer (Carbondale: Southern Illinois University Press, 1963), p. 72, bk, I, chap. 7.

"handmaid" concept hard to understand; but with Campbell the interrelatedness of the thinking-feeling forces of communication were at last recognized.

The "handmaid" notion remained difficult for those who could not see men as unitary beings. Although he was Hume's personal friend, Hugh Blair never recognized the new psychology's challenge to the old reason-emotion dichotomy, and Whately avoided the issue in a way that was generally followed for the next century. Using different terms, he readopted Augustine's formula. Part I of his *Elements of Rhetoric* was labeled, "Of the Address to the Understanding, with a View to Produce Conviction (Including Instruction)." Part II reasserted (without reference to them) Augustine's and Fénelon's conceptions of instructing and moving as two separate steps in communication. Whately entitled his second section "Of the Address to the Will, or Persuasion." It was here that he treated "address to the feelings generally" and "of the favourable or unfavourable disposition of the hearers or readers toward the speaker or writer, and his opponent."

In nineteenth- and twentieth-century books on speaking and writing the "conviction-persuasion" dichotomy persisted almost without challenge until Charles Henry Woolbert (1877–1929) attacked it in a series of essays published in the *Quarterly Journal of Speech*, beginning in 1917.[14] Although many would quarrel with Woolbert's purely behavioristic premises, few psychologically sophisticated persons today would dispute his basic contention against the rhetorical tradition that conceived the emotive power of speech as separable from its intellectual power. Wrote Woolbert:

> . . . the error of the conviction-persuasion, emotion-intellect, thought-action duality is found in the fact that we discuss this issue not in terms of what the responder actually does, but in terms of what the observer perceives him doing. . . . *It is a difference, not between acting and thinking, but between one kind of action that happens also to be perceivable movement* [emotional response] *and another kind of action in which the movement is invisible and unperceivable* [intellectual response].[15]

14. From premises of behavioristic psychology Woolbert attacked the notion that respondents to communication experience reasoned and emotive responses as separable processes. His essays included, "Conviction and Persuasion: Some Considerations of Theory," *Quarterly Journal of Speech* III (July 1917): 249–64; "The Place of Logic in a System of Persuasion," ibid., IV (January 1918): 19–39; "Persuasion: Principles and Methods," ibid., V (January 1919): 12–25; "Persuasion: Principles and Methods," V (March 1919): 101–19; "Persuasion: Principles and Methods," ibid., V (May 1919): 212–38. (The journal referred to was published under varying titles but is indexed under the title given here.)

15. "Conviction and Persuasion: Some Considerations of Theory," ibid., III (July 1917): 258. Italics in the original.

In the same essay Woolbert concluded:

> The whole theory of argumentation, conviction, persuasion, the rhetoric of public address, must be rewritten to fit the facts of mind as accepted today; which will be tantamount to restating them in terms of stimulus-response, object-subject, and environment-attitude.[16]

Speech scholars continue to investigate the functioning of emotive power in human communication. They have arrived at no final explanation. But it seems psychologically clear that: (1) the emotional power of a communication is not in the communication or its delivery but in the readiness of listeners to respond both feelingly and reasoningly to particular features of logos and to the credibility of the messenger; (2) speech can modulate but it cannot create feelings that are not at least latent in listeners; (3) people do not feel *or* reason, they reason because they feel and feel because they think they have reason for it; (4) human experience in response to speech or any other stimulus is *unitary*—there is always some blend of what the world has come to call, probably mistakenly, "reason and feeling."

In our earlier discussions of invention, disposition, style, delivery, and speech criticism, we have tried to hold to this modern understanding that the emotive power of speech is not devoid of reasonableness nor reasons devoid of appeal to human desire.

Ethos: Credibility of the Source

What creates or diminishes the credibility of a speaker and how perceptions of credibility prove or disprove in the minds of listeners fascinated the Greeks and Romans and has received more attention than any other single aspect of rhetoric in the twentieth century. These questions seem first to have been raised in connection with the teaching and speaking of the Greek sophists. To some, these men seemed less credible because they took money for teaching and speaking. Some of them insisted rhetoric was an amoral art, and this made all they said seem less believable to their critics. If we can rely on Plato's and Aristotle's pictures of him, Gorgias of Leontini claimed not to care what means he used as long as he achieved his rhetorical ends. In his *Gorgias* Plato condemns both Gorgias and the entire art of rhetoric as dishonest, deploring rhetoric as a mere art of flattery.

Aristotle explored the sources of credibility in rhetoric more deeply than any other of the ancients. He conceptualized all speakers as communicating an ethos—a complicated quality of believability or unbelievability comprised of their *seeming* intelligence, personal integrity, and goodwill toward their listeners. Interestingly, modern

---

16. Ibid., p. 264.

empirical researchers have identified "expertness" and "trustworthiness" as clear constituents of any communicator's "credibility." Aristotle's idea that good motives are searched for by listeners has not been confirmed to date, nor is it certain that "dynamism," a quality some experimenters suggest is an aspect of credibility, is responded to by hearers.

We are left to believe, therefore, that there is such a persuasive force as *credibility* or ethos in all speaking, that this force either reinforces or undermines what a speaker's content says, and that intelligence-expertness and integrity-trustworthiness are qualities listeners constantly measure in their minds as they determine whether to accept what they hear.

Cicero's conception of the force of ethos in speaking was naturally that of an orator, not that of an analyst such as Aristotle. What *ought* a speaker to *be* as well as seem? was the question that interested him. His answer was deeply colored by his love of the Roman Republic and his personal philosophy concerning the duties of men to each other and to the state. Perhaps the clearest statement of what he thought could produce a *proper* identification between speaker and listener is in his philosophical essay, *On Duties:*

> . . . of all the ties that cement us together, there is none stronger or more admirable than that which unites in genuine intimacy good men of like tastes and character; for if we behold even in another that goodness to which I refer so frequently, we are attracted by it and seek the friendship of him who seems to us to possess it. And though every virtue attracts us and makes us love those in whom it appears to us to dwell, yet justice and charitableness exert the most powerful attraction of all. Besides, nothing draws men more closely and affectionately together than the mutual appeal of good character; for when both have the same interests and inclinations, it follows . . . that each loves the other as himself, and . . . many have become one.[17]

It is clear that possessing substantially the virtues Aristotle isolated, plus "like tastes and character," was the source of ethos in Cicero's view.

Quintilian attempted to establish the "oughts" of credibility also; however, his method was not descriptive, as was Cicero's, but definitional. In the twelfth book of his *Institutes* Quintilian makes his argument on behalf of Cato's definition: an orator is "a good man, skilled in speaking." The argument is circular and ends with Quintilian contending no more than that if he cannot call a speaker "good" he will deny him the name "orator." Quintilian's difficulty exemplifies how easily one can confuse answers to two quite different questions about a speaker: Do *I* endorse him? Is he credible *to those he addresses?*

---

17. Cicero, *On Duties,* trans. Hubert M. Poteat, in *Brutus, On the Nature of the Gods, On Divination, On Duties* (Chicago: The University of Chicago Press, 1950), p. 485.

Like a good many commentators before and after his time, Quintilian gave his answer to the first question and then treated that answer as though it were a statement about the *actual* credibility or ethos of the speaker in a specific rhetorical situation.   Aristotle's and Cicero's insistence that it is *seeming* qualities that affect response in rhetorical and personal relationships furnishes the classical era's clearest analysis of how the force of ethos works in actual speaking.

In *On the Sublime* the author sought the *source* of that credibility that critics said was present in great oratorical works.   Ultimately, Longinus thought, there must be evidence of "nobility of soul" or "largeness of conception."   Boldness in thinking and feeling, and enthusiasm, seemed to him also discernible in works admired over generations.   The uniqueness of Longinus's observations lies in the fact that his is the first great effort to infer critically, from works themselves, what human qualities contributed to their popularity.

St. Augustine was, of course, concerned chiefly with the credibility of preachers.   Their humbleness before God, their love of others, and their knowledge of sacred works were the qualities he most wanted speakers to reveal.   He insisted that *display* of art was likely to invite either distrust or ignorant applause from listeners.   Either effect would demolish the true function of preaching: teaching, reminding listeners of the truths that were within them.   On the whole Augustine's view of ethos as a force was like Cicero's, with Christian virtues and duties substituted for virtues Cicero associated with the Roman Republic.   For Augustine as for Cicero, if the speaker possessed virtue, it would show through and become a part of his proof; if he lacked virtue, this too would show and operate in listeners' minds against even good content.

Fénelon's was the next major discussion of ethos.   On the whole Fénelon's *Dialogues* restated St. Augustine's position, applying that view to seventeenth-century French preaching.   But, perhaps reflecting literary theory of the time, Fénelon also contended that things cannot be truly beautiful unless they are true, and he made this idea the basis for severe criticism of showy French preachers who sought to be impressive not for their truth and devotion but for their artistry.   Their choices showed shallowness and self-centeredness, Fénelon insisted, and these qualities must detract even from truths they might utter.

Bacon gave little direct attention to the role of ethos.   Campbell, Blair, and Whately were all Christian preachers who tended to presuppose the moral integrity of the rhetors for whom they wrote.   Campbell, ahead of his time as usual, also thought a speaker's reference groups, as we would now put it, significantly modified this ethos.   Blair followed Cicero and Quintilian and treated the subject unoriginally. He reflected the times in which he lived by emphasizing the importance of good taste and acquaintance with all the liberal arts as qualities speakers must show to influence the educated.   Blair followed Augustine in insisting that preachers, in particular, must be known to live impeccable lives, else their reputations would undercut their religious messages.

In most respects Whately, too, treated ethos traditionally, but he made the important point that having a reputation for eloquence can damage a persuader's ethos.   Such speakers are apt to be suspected of trying to succeed by art rather than by substance.   Whately made Cicero's and Blair's comments on "good taste" more practical by pointing out that tastes vary among audiences.   If speakers are to enhance their ethos, they must adjust marks of taste to specific audiences, said Whately.

As we have hinted, the functioning of ethos or credibility has been a major topic of interest in the twentieth century.   Rhetoricians, advertisers, image makers, journalists, and social psychologists have discussed, studied, and speculated about this force.   The literature is too large to summarize here,[18] but on the whole Aristotle's analysis has been confirmed.   Practical speakers may operate confidently on his counsels: that ethos—listeners' impressions of the speaker himself—is a powerful force in determining the effects of any oral message; that it is important for speakers to *improve on* their reputations for intelligence and trustworthiness *during* speaking; and that they need to give evidence of good motives toward listeners or dynamic identification with them.

DISPOSITION

Ideas about structuring oral presentations seem to have appeared in the very earliest writings on rhetoric.   A lost work attributed to Corax and Tisias apparently taught that a speech ought to have at least three parts: a proem or introduction to win the favor of listening judges, a narration or proof of one's case, and an epilogue or conclusion.   In his *Phaedrus* Plato also argued that discourse ought to have three parts, comparable, he said, to the parts of the human body.   Introduction, body, and conclusion are to a composition as head, torso, and feet are to a human being.

Aristotle took issue with the older three-part concept.   He opened the final section of Book III of his *Rhetoric* by saying earlier

---

18. The 1975 cumulative index to speech journals lists 105 published papers on the subject not including the many studies reported in journals of other academic fields.   See chapter 5, pp. 138–47 for further discussion of basic findings and their implications.

speculations on the divisions of speeches had been absurd. A speech has only two *essential* parts, he said: (a) you state your point or case and (b) you prove it. In certain kinds of speaking there would be room to narrate a relevant set of circumstances, but these adjustments of the essentials were seen as *special* responses to special speech situations. They were not always needed in effective, satisfying communications.

Some of what Aristotle had to say about rhetorical structure was specifically related to the *types* of speeches commonly composed in his day: the epideictic (or ceremonial), the deliberative (or legislative), and the forensic (or speech for the court). He also gave scattered bits of advice concerning ways claims to ethos and variations in style might be necessary to fulfill the functions of divisions of speeches.

Cicero, Quintilian, and the authors of most Roman school manuals discussed the organization of speeches (especially legal speeches) with great enthusiasm. They detected six divisions in normal speeches: introduction, statement of facts or the narration, division or preview of proofs to be offered, proof, refutation, and conclusion. As is plain from this list, it was in what we would call the *body* of a speech that the Romans thought they found additional, special functions regularly carried out. The list reflects their special concern with legal speaking. There are, of course, facts of a case to be given or events and conditions to be described as a normal part of presenting the case. Arguments to be developed are often previewed as the pleader asserts what he will and will not try to prove. Once the arguments have been supported, it is also common in courts to refute and try to remove objects before concluding. Roman theory about organization was, then, largely a theory for forensic speaking. Thinking was highly formalistic in contrast to Aristotle's functionalism, and in most later periods the formal, Roman views about building speeches overshadowed the Greek in Western thought.

Between Roman times and the Renaissance there were few fresh thoughts about rhetorical organization. When the humanists of the Renaissance rediscovered their ancient heritage, they tended to collapse rhetoric, poetry, and history into a single art of eloquence. Style was seen as the interesting common property of all verbal art and adaptive structural differences received little attention in theory and criticism.[19]

Fénelon understandably rejected the rigid, artificial rules of organization inherited from Rome and medieval homiletics. In his *Dialogues* he contends that the organic unity of a communication is destroyed by imposing complicated divisions on subject matter.

---

19. For a full treatment of these developments see Jerrold E. Seigel, *Rhetoric and Philosophy in Renaissance Humanism* (Princeton: Princeton University Press, 1968), especially pp. 260–62.

Fénelon's arguments forecast those of some modern teachers who also feel that speech ought to follow natural forms allegedly inherent in subjects. Fénelon made milder claims for another idea sometimes contended for today: that the order in which ideas reach the threshold of a creator's consciousness is a natural order for presentation. A problem with both views is that if carried to their logical conclusions they justify purely expressive, stream-of-consciousness communication lacking adaptations to the requirements of specific rhetorical situations.

If we except psychological writers like Bacon and George Campbell, it is fair to say that from Fénelon's time to the twentieth century most commentators on rhetoric have taken refuge either in rigid classical (Roman) rules or in the doctrines of natural order we have mentioned in referring to Fénelon. Twentieth-century experiments to discover the effects of formal structures on listeners have produced conflicting results and yielded little reliable advice. One contemporary, empirical scholar accurately says: "Indeed, the original question asked . . . [Should the most important point be presented first or last?] is still unsolved."[20]

We suggest that at least two misunderstandings contribute to the confusion and contradictions in past and present thought about disposition of ideas in oral communication. First, the full subtlety of the best ancient thinking about disposition has been missed by many. As Russell H. Wagner pointed out some years ago:

> The service which will be rendered by a return to "disposition" in rendering *dispositio* and in referring to its classical doctrines, will be nugatory indeed, if we do not restore the full meaning behind the term. . . . It is concerned with the principles of disposing (in the sense of using) the materials invented for a speech, in the best possible manner, for the purpose of effecting the end intended by the speaker in any given situation. The discussion of disposition usually begins by describing the typical form of the speech—the parts or divisions—or it may be altogether organized under those conventional heads. But always, in the best writers, the principle of adaptation to need is uppermost, and the distinction between conventional organization and functional use of material is insistently made. It is this meaning—the functional selection and use of materials for a particular purpose—which must supplant "arrangement" and which, as "disposition," may well be added to our rhetorical terminology in English.[21]

Experience makes it plain, as you will find, that how you manage or dispose or marshal what you say is a problem you cannot solve apart from *what* you choose to say—the products of your rhe-

---

20. Ernest C. Thompson, "Some Effects of Message Structure on Listeners' Comprehension," *Speech Monographs XXXIV* (March 1967): 50.

21. Russell H. Wagner, "The Meaning of *Dispositio*," in *Studies in Speech and Drama in Honor of Alexander M. Drummond* (Ithaca, N.Y.: Cornell University Press, 1944), pp. 292–93.

torical invention. As we have shown in chapter 7, there is the further fact that ideas are not maneuverable entirely at your will. To some extent they will impose their own constraints on your organizational choices. This is a fact to which the natural-order theorists responded rightly if too exclusively. Second, the experience and expectations of listeners determine to some degree how communicated ideas must be structured. One will err at least sometimes if one tries to structure every communication in the same way—strictly according to rule. Introductions, bodies, and conclusions are normally necessary, but not invariably, as Aristotle was first to point out. Certain units do appear in the bodies of legal speeches, but not all audiences are like courtroom audiences. So there is no reason to suppose statement-division-proof-refutation is a universally desirable sequence of ideas for the body of a talk. Sometimes what hearers receive *first* will impress them most, but in other circumstances and on other subjects what they hear *last* will be best remembered. Efforts to make rules about the parts of a speech or the importance of first and last positions are based on the assumption that what is being said, who is listening, and where have no influence on how we are to dispose ideas for presentation. As you have seen in chapters 7 and 8, our advice is that you adopt a middle position between the natural-order and the rule-seeking theorists, organizing your communications with an eye to standard organizational strategies that work *most* of the time but are not rules, while remaining alert to the *special* organizational demands that subject matter, a specific audience, and a specific rhetorical situation impose upon you.

STYLE

Referring to what we call *style*, a Roman or medieval writer or speaker would have said *elocutio.* Yet *we* associate derivatives from elocutio (eloquent, elocution, etc.) with aspects of delivery. This semantic shift needs explanation before we discuss theories of style and then theories of delivery.

Our word *style* derives from Old French, which in turn derived its term from the Latin *stilus,* the name of the instrument used in writing. Between 1650 and 1750 the word *style* replaced the Latin word *elocutio* as the name for problems associated with language and its use in composition. As elocutio and its derivatives ceased to mean style, the Latin word *pronuntiatio* and its derivatives came into use to designate the peculiarly oral aspects of using language, hence the modern term *pronunciation.* The shifts are of some significance to students of oral rhetoric because they reflect the modern tendency to associate style with the written word and to emphasize the delivery aspects of the spoken word. We have shown in this book that there is place for more serious thought about *oral* style than is often given.

Problems of language were among the earliest concerns of Westerners who studied human speech. Among the early sophists, Protagoras of Abdera observed and classified grammatical parts of speech, verb tenses, and moods, founding the concepts of grammar. Gorgias of Leontini is often called the founder of the *art* of prose because he experimented with ways of giving beauty to prose. Prodicus of Ceos was a kind of early semanticist, exploring meanings and the workings of synonyms. Isocrates (436–338 B.C.) rejected Gorgias's excesses, seeking to conceal his verbal art while creating speech that was at once striking but unified. These and others among the early Greeks may be said to have *founded* the study of language as a resource open to conscious use in communication. Even among them, the perennial issues about choice of language arose: What is *correct?* What is *beautiful?* What *works?* As we will see, it is about the relative importance of these three questions and their answers that theorists of rhetorical style have chiefly differed over the centuries.

Plato was a brilliant, inventive writer; yet he makes Socrates say in the *Phaedrus* that *correct* diction is the leading standard to be applied to style and that writing is of *doubtful* value because it produces forgetfulness. Plato's art rather than his theory has exerted influence on the development of style in the West. Predictably, Aristotle was more direct.

He began Book III of his *Rhetoric* by asserting that however important argument might be, *how* things are said must be seriously weighed. Clarity and liveliness were the two qualities of speech Aristotle insisted on most strongly, provided appropriateness to the situation was observed. Metaphors, similes, antitheses, realism, and varied rhythms were the speaker's major resources for achieving clarity and liveliness, he thought. Aristotle's answers to what speakers ought to seek through style were relatively simple and decidedly pragmatic. *What works?* and *Why?* were the questions he chose to try to answer.

As they had in exploring the structural patterns of rhetoric, the Romans who studied rhetorical style seemed more interested in identifying possible maneuvers than in finding out what those maneuvers did and why. Probably the trend had been set by post-Aristotelian Greeks; at any rate, the oldest existing Latin treatise on rhetoric defined and illustrated more than sixty figures of speech. Having finished his lengthy list of verbal forms exemplified, the unknown author concluded:

> I have here carefully collected all the principles of embellishing style. If, Herennius, you exercise yourself diligently in these, your speaking will possess impressiveness, distinction, and charm. As a result you will speak like a true orator, and the product of your invention will

not be bare and inelegant, nor will it be expressed in commonplace language.[22]

Knowing and inserting known and approved verbal devices would produce the impressive, distinctive, and charming speaker!

Cicero, the orator, was likewise fascinated by the options offered by known, approved forms of verbal manipulation. He discussed at length the characteristics and uses of "plain," "middle," and "grand" style. His emphatic belief that there were clearly distinguishable *levels* of style was derived from rhetoricians before him, but he seems to have been oblivious of the fact that plain-middle-grand express impressions *people* have of language, not *data about* that language. The goals to which he urged speakers to aspire were correctness (presumably as *he* defined it), clearness (presumably an absolute quality), appropriateness (to the speech of a "proper" Roman citizen), and ornateness (achieved by full use of verbal resources).

The great Roman teacher of rhetoric Quintilian was most concerned with the question: What is *correct*? "Style," he said, "has three kinds of excellence, correctness, lucidity and elegance. . . . Its faults are likewise three-fold, namely the opposites of these excellences."[23] Much of Quintilian's advice on style is scattered through his work, but he concentrates on this subject in Books VII and IX. On balance, he is an apostle of formal correctness, although he does not wholly disregard the pragmatic question, "What works and how?" Where he deals with this latter question, however, his eye is almost exclusively on the courtroom.

"Longinus" is a perplexing Roman figure. Whenever he may have written and whoever he was, no extant ancient work on rhetoric draws up his thoughts concerning the relation of language to effect in communication. Parts of his book are lost—several important bits of thought developments are missing—but some of his observations read like direct challenges to the traditional formalism of Roman doctrine on style. For example:

> What, then, is this puerility? Clearly, a pedant's thoughts, which begin in learned trifling and end in frigidity. Men slip into this kind of error because, while they aim at the uncommon and elaborate and most of all at the attractive, they drift unawares into the tawdry and affected.[24]

But Longinus's complaints of classical formalism appear to have influenced no one until the French literary critic Boileau discovered and translated his work in 1674!

---

22. *Rhetorica ad Herennium*, trans. Caplan, p. 409, bk. IV, sec. 69.
23. *Institutio Oratoria*, ed. and trans. H. E. Butler (Cambridge, Mass.: Harvard University Press, 1920), I, 79, bk. I, sec. 1.
24. Longinus, "On the Sublime," trans. W. Rhys Roberts, in J. H. Smith and E. W. Parks, *The Great Critics*, (New York: W. W. Norton, 1951), pp. 67–68.

As far as the record shows, then, the classical interest in how language works in practical communication moved from an era of exploration by the sophists through a period of practical experimentation and theorizing, of which Isocrates and Aristotle were part, into a long period in which artifice was increasingly admired. "What is beautiful?" became the primary question. "What is correct?" meant much the same thing.

This view of rhetorical style predominated for centuries. Through the Middle Ages and the Renaissance rhetorical and poetic styles were badly confused. As late as the sixteenth century beauty was lauded as an end of rhetorical style. In about 1510 the Englishman John Lydgate published his *Court of Sapyence*, in which he asserted that the chief purpose of rhetorical language was to give pleasure to the ear. Stephen Hawes had in 1506 written a work with a similar theme: *The Pastime of Pleasure*. Hawes's book contained an allegorical treatment of the liberal arts in which rhetoric was called the "honied speech" of poets.

Fénelon had nothing to say in his *Dialogues* about the figures of speech that had made up so much of the centuries' lore on style. Instead, he reflected a new perception of what spoken or written words can do for people: words can *portray*. "Prose has its paintings, albeit more moderated [than poetry]. Without them one cannot heat the imagination of a listener or arouse his passions," Fénelon wrote.[25] A theory was emerging that language achieves its effects through visual qualities and should therefore be concrete to stimulate the passions of hearers and readers, and Fénelon was one of the first to reflect the development.[26]

George Campbell and Hugh Blair both drew on the conception that a major power of language lies in its power to *portray*—to generate experience that approximates sensory experience, but Campbell's development of the idea was the most interesting. Lloyd F. Bitzer says of Campbell that, "Vivacity, or the lively idea, is without doubt the key concept of Campbell's theory of rhetoric—the concept which fixes the character of his theory."[27] Aristotle's idea that liveliness is essential to effective style became the cornerstone of Campbell's theory of communication, now based on the new science of human nature and the view that the main function of language is to generate experience as near as possible to experiencing through the senses. Vivacity together with *perspicuity* (clarity) and nationally reputable grammar and vocabulary were, in Campbell's view, primary forces in effecting

---

25. *Dialogues on Eloquece*, trans. Howell, p. 93 (Second Dialogue).
26. Gerard A. Hauser discusses these seventeenth- and eighteenth-century developments in his "Empiricism, Description, and the New Rhetoric," *Philosophy and Rhetoric* V (Winter 1972): 24–44.
27. "Editor's Introduction" to Campbell, *The Philosophy of Rhetoric*, p. xxv.

rhetoric's ends of enlightening, understanding, pleasing the imagination, moving the passions, and influencing the will. Expressing indebtedness to Bacon and to David Hume, Campbell brought functionalism back to the theory of how and why language serves the purposes of rhetoric. But Campbell did not hold the field.

Blair's cast was, of course, literary, and he dealt with style at length. Fifteen of his forty-seven lectures were devoted to discussion of the subject and, if we count the four lectures on taste and the four on language, just under half of his famous *Lectures* was devoted directly or indirectly to style. His touchstones for excellence in choice of language were "taste" and "beauty." His definition of style had wide influence in England and America:

> [Style] is the peculiar manner in which a man expresses his conceptions, by means of language. . . . Style has always some reference to an author's manner of thinking. It is a picture of the ideas which rise in his mind, and of the manner in which they arise there. . . . Style is nothing else, than that sort of expression which our thoughts most readily assume.[28]

Blair's pronouncements did not yield much insight into *how* language works, but his widely circulated lectures spread the concepts that beauty, good taste, and correctness were the ideal avenues to effective portrayal through words.

Richard Whately's nineteenth-century treatment of style in his *Elements of Rhetoric* was, according to one of his editor's, "a dreary rehearsal of time-worn advice about the selection and arrangement of words."[29] It is true there was nothing very new in what Whately had to say about oral style, for he undertook to blend Campbell's and Blair's observations. In doing so, he tended to blunt Campbell's pragmatic view of the rhetorical functions of language by appending to them Blair's and others' traditional injunctions that speakers should seek elegance or beauty in utterance.

Whately's mixture of formalism and pragmatism forecast most of what would be said in the nineteenth century about style. A few, but not many, additional thoughts emerged to affect us today. Samuel Taylor Coleridge emphasized in his essay "On Style" (1818) that major stylistic qualities are not translatable from language to language. Alexander Bain's *Manual of English Composition and Rhetoric* (1866, rev. ed. 1872) expanded Blair's laws of the sentence and put into formal circulation what we now hear of as "laws of the paragraph."

---

28. Hugh Blair, *Lectures on Rhetoric and Belles Lettres,* ed. Harold F. Harding (Carbondale, Ill.: Southern Illinois University Press, 1965), I, 183–84.

29. "Editor's Introduction" to Richard Whately, *Elements of Rhetoric,* ed. Douglas Ehninger (Carbondale, Ill.: Southern Illinois University Press, 1963), p. xxi.

On the whole American teaching of composition, oral and written, followed Bain's insistence that the study of rhetoric (meaning *style*) is the study of managing the words and the structures of language and has little or nothing to do with content or oral presentation *per se*. Nineteenth-century rhetorics in England and America were chiefly rhetorics of style, chiefly of written style, and chiefly of style detached from content.   They were what Douglas Ehninger has called *managerial rhetorics*, and by the late 1800s virtually all of Aristotle's, Bacon's, and Campbell's pragmatic inquiries about language had been lost.

In reaction, perhaps, twentieth-century treatments of literary and rhetorical style have often returned to the pragmatic question: "What *works* and *how?*"   How words work psychologically and how we arrive at their meanings have been the main focuses of I. A. Richards's studies.[30]   Richards's theory that all language is metaphorically symbolic and that to understand language the emotive and referential functions of words must be differentiated constitutes a theory of semantic analysis that has much influence in literary and rhetorical studies today.   Word-by-word analysis of literary works and audience-centered criticism reflect "The New Criticism's" indebtedness to Richards.   So, too, does the emphasis on metaphor and image found in a good deal of speech criticism.

Kenneth Burke's studies of rhetorical style have also had major influence on rhetorical and literary criticism.   *A Grammar of Motives* and *A Rhetoric of Motives* have been especially influential.   "Identification" is Burke's key concept.   He sees use of language as a search for interpersonal identification—a search motivated by the divisiveness that seems part of the human condition.   Because there is division that separates human beings, they seek to remove it by using language as a public and collective instrument for reducing division.   Burke thus provides a fresh interpretation of the rhetorical function of language.   He emphasizes the importance and value of man's power to symbolize and sees study of rhetoric as the method of studying symbolic behavior.

Two other theorist-critics who suggest expansions of critical methods by starting from traditional premises about the nature of rhetorical style are Wayne C. Booth and Ross W. Winterowd.   In *The Rhetoric of Fiction* (1961) Booth suggested that even in fiction authors *address* their readers to control attention and belief in rhetorical ways, and he analyzed the rhetorical strategies they use for these purposes. Winterowd's *Rhetoric: A Synthesis* (1968) and other of his writings draw upon the thoughts of Kenneth Burke and upon those of grammarians who have developed the theory of *generative grammar*.   From

---

30. For example, I. A. Richards, *The Meaning of Meaning,* written with C. K. Ogden (1923), and his *The Philosophy of Rhetoric* (1936).

these, from classical sources, and from the findings of psycholinguistics, Winterowd hopes to evolve better principles of both composition and criticism.

Special concern with the social significance of meanings motivated Alfred Korzybski to write his *Science and Sanity,* published in 1933, and to found a branch of study called General Semantics. His work was the basis for a popular version of the theories of General Semantics, S. I. Hayakawa's *Language in Action* (1941), later revised as *Language in Thought and Action.* Levels of abstraction are illustrated by General Semanticists with an abstraction ladder representing the levels of meaning beyond the denotative. General Semanticists make the special point that people develop problems when they react to words as though the words *were* the things they name. That our language maps of the world are *not* the territories of the world is a central lesson taught by this group of students of style.

A still different way of looking at rhetorical style has come from a group of philosophers interested in the branch of philosophy called *theory of argument.* Especially important to practical rhetoricians is *The New Rhetoric* by Chaim Perelman and L. Olbrechts-Tyteca. Working from both classical and modern theories of language, these authors demonstrate that in rhetoric words and word forms *argue* as surely as traditional argumentative forms such as inductions, deductions, analogies, and arguments from cause. Reflections of this line of thought will be found in our treatment of figures of speech in chapter 9, pages 269–78.

Thought about the role of language in rhetoric, including oral rhetoric, has completed something of a circle. "What works and how?" was the question most interesting to some Greek sophists and to Aristotle, and it is the question increasingly asked today in Western Europe, England, and the United States. The nineteenth century's oratory of beauty and impressiveness is little heard, and the standards that bred it seem little valued. The practical student of practical speaking can, we think, congratulate himself that his is an age in which study of the pragmatic uses of languages is in vogue. Doing business, not observing forms for their own sakes, is the thrust in the modern speech classroom—as it was in Aristotle's and Isocrates's schools!

DELIVERY

We have seen how Western thinking about disposition and style vacillated between practical, communicative considerations and the search for formal rules, doctrines of correctness, principles of aesthetic beauty. The same vacillation characterized thought about presentation of public speech.   During many periods our ancestors seem even to have thought about delivery more than was good for practical communication.

  We do not know just when students of speech began to analyze the manners of delivery they thought effective, but it must have been very early.   From the time of Theophrastus (c. 370–285 B.C.) we have evidence of writers' analyses of vocal and gestural patterns.   In *De-Oratore* Cicero repeats a story that goes back at least to Theophrastus,[31] that Demosthenes was once asked what was most important in speaking.   He replied, "Delivery."   When asked what was next in importance, he answered the same, and to the question of what came third, he repeated, "Delivery."   This story, like the legend telling how Demosthenes improved his articulation by speaking with pebbles in his mouth, indicates that at least practitioners were preoccupied with delivery from the earliest part of the classical period.   It was not so with the earliest theorists we know of.

  Plato did not mention delivery specifically, although he did say practice would add to a speaker's natural capacities.   Aristotle discussed the subject almost grudgingly in a brief passage at the beginning of Book III of his *Rhetoric*.   There he said delivery must be attended to as "something we are bound to do."   He granted that it was not enough to know what to say; one must know *how* to say it.   But he said these things reluctantly, apparently feeling that such matters fell in the province of actors and were therefore vulgar—at least for a theorist to discuss.   Similarly, a book by an unknown author who probably wrote in the generation after Aristotle's omitted mention of problems of oral presentation.   The work's Latin title is *Rhetorica ad Alexandrum*.

  Although concepts about presenting speeches were slighted by the Greek theorists we know, the subject later received detailed attention at Rome.   The unknown author of *Rhetorica ad Herennium* showed his penchant for classification, and that he had some fairly detailed works to draw on, when he classified and described vocal qualities under three headings: volume, stability, and flexibility.   He endorsed what he called *conversational tone* and identified four variations of it: the dignified, the explicative, the narrative, and the facetious.   He then discussed how these tones should be used in the various parts of speech. He gave little attention to gestures and facial expressions beyond mentioning their importance, and he concluded by confessing he was not sure it was possible to explain delivery in writing.   His confession may be a hint that delivery was still the concern of more practitioners and pedagogues than theorists.

  Cicero wrote of delivery as a practitioner, naturally enough, although in what he had to say he offered some interesting speculations

---

31. Kennedy, *The Art of Persuasion in Greece*, p. 283.

on the relative importance of various aspects of presentation. His most significant observations appear in *De Oratore,* some being confirmed in his later book, *Orator,* a discussion of the "perfect" speaker. Cicero seems to have accepted the emphasis on delivery reflected in the story of Demosthenes to which we have referred. In Cicero's view, dignity and grace were so important in speaking that those with highest mental capacity would lose esteem without these qualities and speakers of only moderate intellect but great skill in delivery would surpass their intellectual betters. He went beyond the author of *Rhetorica ad Herennium* by discussing both vocal and gestural activity, and he followed the earlier author in stressing that qualities of delivery express speakers' emotions and must, therefore, be precisely suited to thoughts being uttered. Words, Cicero said, can move only those who share your language, but all mankind—illiterates and even barbarians—can see and understand physical behavior.

Aristotle's notion that rhetorical presentation and the presentations of actors are alike did not satisfy Cicero. He insisted that gestural patterns in public speaking were markedly different from the patterns appropriate to acting. Accordingly he paused over the place in rhetorical speech for gestures of the hands and arms, for stamping one's foot, and, especially, the emotional expressiveness of the eyes. He thought that of all the facial features, the eyes best expressed a speaker's emotion.

Quintilian's *Institutio* contained a good many descriptions of vocal and gestural behaviors without differing much from what the author of *Rhetorica ad Herennium* and Cicero had said. But Quintilian did make two points worth mentioning here. He insisted that the ideal speech—in court or elsewhere—was one that had been fully written beforehand. He revealed that at least some Roman teachers thought speaking and singing required the same kinds of vocal resources and management. Not so, said Quintilian, as he pointed out that speakers need "strong and enduring" voices, not "soft and sweet" ones and that singers must strive for perfection in pitch although speakers need worry little about that problem. In general, Quintilian's third chapter of Book XI of the *Institutio* shows that he and presumably other Romans had studied the speech production system of humans with considerable care and were at least beginning analyses of the human voice not unlike those that reemerged as delivery began to receive scientific attention in the eighteenth century.

On the whole the Romans *described* vocal and gestural behavior and then tried to *prescribe* specific behaviors for specific emotions, parts of speeches, and rhetorical situations. From fuller understanding of the phenomena of presentation, they moved toward more and more rules. This tendency to formulate rules was inherited by men of the Middle Ages and the Renaissance as they rediscovered learning through classical works. The special interest in *style,* which marked the resurgence of literary interest during the Renaissance, discouraged thought about oral delivery. Insofar as the subject was important, the issue was: how shall one read aloud? That question was, of course, quite different from the one the Romans had, at least at first, tried to ask: How shall one speak to be understood as thought and feeling demand?

Fénelon gave much more attention to aspects of delivery than others of the Renaissance. In his *Dialogues* he seemed to be trying to fill out, for delivery, Augustine's themes of devotional directness and pastoral adaptation. These St. Augustine had developed at length relative to style, but he had said little about the preacher's delivery. Fénelon addressed the issues directly, condemning the rigid, artificial rules he found too much followed by his contemporaries. The goal in delivery ought to be artlessness rather than mechanical control, said Fénelon. In the spirit of Augustine and in the spirit of emerging literary theories, Fénelon urged all speakers to put their reliance on cultivated, earnest feeling toward listeners; right feeling would naturally yield appropriate, reinforcing, vocal and gestural behaviors.

In contrast with Fénelon's doctrines of naturalness there grew up less than a century later a new-old body of theory called *elocution.* Its concepts were the antitheses of Fénelon's. To a degree the new concepts were scientific extensions of the Romans' ambition to *describe,* then *prescribe;* but there was also new driving force in this movement. Frederick W. Haberman writes:

> Elocution was an offshoot of rhetorical study. It was an exhaustive and systematic analysis of delivery. The elocutionary movement, which began about 1750, was a response to the demands of the age. This widespread and intense study of delivery was an answer to the eighteenth-century denunciations of oratorical frigidity, to the pressure for professional and educational training in speech, to the new consciousness of the need for standardization of spoken language, to the desire of the people to obtain facility in speaking a language of which they were becoming proud, and to demands of those who dealt with democratic movements. The elocutionary movement, however, was more than a simple renaissance of a particular canon of rhetoric. It was rather, a new ordering of an old subject.
>
> This new ordering resulted from the application of the tenets of science and of rationalism to the physiological phenomena of spoken discourse. The new study of delivery was affected by the impact of science and of rationalism in precisely the same way that the study of history, of economics, of politics, of poetry, and of prose style was affected.[32]

---

32. Frederick W. Haberman, "John Thelwall: His Life, His School, and His Theory of Elocution," *The Quarterly Journal of Speech* XXXIII (October 1947): 294.

Three kinds of textbooks came out of the elocutionary movement: thorough, often research-based, works treating voice, rhythm, and gesture; elementary rule books; and collections of useful and elegant extracts for practice. The elocutionists developed systems for observing voice, gesture, and language and means of recording these observations. In these efforts their work resembled that of modern-day students of nonverbal behavior.

As Haberman indicates, the elocutionists worked from scientific-rationalistic premises. They presupposed that man is ruled by natural laws. Nature is a compelling force. It has immutable laws in the physical universe and immutable codes in the social universe. These laws and codes are systematic and can be disregarded only at one's peril. These theorists thought speech and all worldly matters were capable of scientific systematization. So they embarked upon their mission to reduce speaking to system.

The outpouring of elocutionary books and magazines during the last half of the eighteenth and throughout the nineteenth centuries was much too vast to review here, but Haberman has identified four founders of the movement and a note on each will suggest the directions of research and exposition that characterized this movement.[33] Thomas Sheridan (1719–88) published *Lectures on Elocution* in 1756. In it he examined the individual sounds of speech and the gestural behaviors associated with familiar emotions. Among other things, he was seeking a scientific phonetics with which to describe pronunciation and a kind of grammar of gesture by which to teach appropriate and natural physical action. Joshua Steele (1700–91) devised a system of musical notations by which to describe the management of the voice. His *Prosodia Rationalis* treated patterns of melody, rhythm, and pitch in speech and music. John Walker (1732–1807) was an actor turned elocutionist. He invented a system by which to describe the natural interrelations between vocal inflections and grammatical forms. His chief publication was *Elements of Elocution* (1781). Finally, James Burgh (1714–75) expressed the article of faith Cicero had expressed that gave the elocutionists much of their driving energy. In *The Art of Speaking* (1761) Burgh said "nature had given every emotion of mind its proper expression." The task for the elocutionists, as for some Romans, seemed to be to catalogue those nonverbal, emotional expressions, the better to *teach* them "naturally"!

The elocutionary movement, with its research impulse, its enthusiasm for detailed description, and its determination to *prescribe* natural behavior in speaking and acting, dominated English and American thought about speech delivery until the beginning of the

---

33. Frederick W. Haberman, "The Elocutionary Movement in England, 1750–1850," unpublished Ph.D. thesis (Cornell University, 1947).

twentieth century.   In their desire to apply the laws of nature to man's speaking behavior, the elocutionists often produced artificial rules and systems more complex than any Roman had had the tools to produce, but in a number of cases their research efforts became the foundations for modern sciences such as phonetics, vocal acoustics, and some branches of linguistics.   Indeed, a good deal of current research on nonverbal behavior covers ground on which the elocutionists were pioneers.

The classical revivalists who wrote on communication during the period in which elocution burgeoned and flourished insisted on a different way of thinking about speech behavior.   Both Hugh Blair and Richard Whately differed from the elocutionists, but they also differed from one another, and the viewpoint of each has its knowing or unknowing followers today.

Blair's conception of delivery and the aspects he considered important are discussed chiefly in Lecture XXXIII of his *Lectures on Rhetoric and Belles Lettres*.   The lecture is titled "Pronunciation, or Delivery." Blair saw delivery as vocal and gestural behavior that operates within natural languages understood by all.   Words, he said, are arbitrary symbols of ideas and therefore are not universally understood. The natural symbolizations of voice and gesture are not so confined in meaning.

There are hints that Blair thought what he called "pitches of voice" were naturally and uniquely associated with specific kinds of speaking. Also, other remarks scattered through his lectures indicate that he thought different styles of delivery were peculiarly suited to different kinds of speech.   In most other respects Blair's comments on delivery were traditional, but his advice to speakers contained subtle, internal contradictions one can also see in discussions of speech making today.

Like most writers, Blair urged speakers to let delivery reflect their actual feelings. "Follow nature," he says in effect.   On the other hand, he suggested that the secret of effective delivery is thinking one's thought clearly while uttering it.   Further, he counseled study of proper models and practice "for many persons are naturally ungraceful."   But then: "Whatever is native, even though accompanied with several defects, yet is likely to please; because it shows us a man; because it has the appearance of coming from the heart."[34]   Blair seems not to have considered these pieces of advice incompatible, and in this he resembled many moderns who advise speakers to "be natural" but then criticize those speakers' grace and taste.

Richard Whately was more vigorous in reaction against the

---

34. Lecture XXXIII.   *Lectures on Rhetoric and Belles Lettres*, ed. H. F. Harding, II, pp. 223, 224.

elocutionists than Blair, but he did not, as some have believed, counsel "following nature" in impulsive, undisciplined ways. What he said of naturalness echoed Blair but was more clearly thought out. Whately was strongly critical of all mechanical guides to natural or effective presentation, but it is evident that he did not advocate impulsive response to feelings. He did say:

> The practical rule then to be adopted, in conformity with the principles here maintained, is, not only to pay no studied attention to the Voice, but studiously to *withdraw* the thoughts from it, and to dwell as intently as possible on the Sense; trusting to nature to suggest spontaneously the proper emphases and tones.[35]

At an earlier point Whately had added this qualification:

> When however I protest against all artificial systems of Elocution, and all *direct* attention to Delivery, *at the time*, it must not be supposed that a *general* inattention to that point is recommended; or that the most perfect Elocution is to be attained by never thinking at all on the subject; though it may safely be affirmed that even this negative plan would succeed far better than a studied modulation.[36]

It is clear that Whately was recommending that speakers occupy their minds with ideas rather than prescribed behaviors, and in this he was injecting a new thought into Western lore on how people can best express what they mean, vocally and physically. The notion was radical and it required modification, but in the mind of the American James A. Winans, Whately's thought evolved into a balanced, cogent view of what is required mentally for the most natural delivery possible in public speech.

Winans's (1872–1956) influence on contemporary theories about practical delivery has been immeasurable since 1915. Contending that Whately's "think-the-thought" doctrine could as easily produce soliloquy as direct, effective, public speech, Winans altered the formula by adding to it. He wrote:

> . . . your delivery will have the desired conversational quality when you retain upon the platform these elements of the mental state of live conversation:
> 1. Full realization of the content of your words as you utter them, and
> 2. A lively sense of communication.[37]

---

35. Richard Whately, *Elements of Rhetoric*, ed. Douglas Ehninger, p. 352.
36. Ibid., pp. 346–47.
37. James A. Winans, *Public Speaking* (New York: The Century Co., 1917), p. 31.

Winans's first point was Whately's; his second the corrective.   Winans was convinced that effective delivery depends on *both* awareness of one's thought *and* a strong wish to convey the thought to someone else.

Refining another familiar notion—that effective delivery is somehow related to the conversational—Winans also argued for a distinction between *conversational quality* and *conversational style*. Public speech ought to have the *quality* of conversation, Winans insisted, but if it *imitated* the style of ordinary, informal conversation it would belie the publicness of the speaker's situation.

To us, at least, Winans seems to have resolved the paradox of centuries: speakers have to *mean* what they say, both vocally and physically; yet they speak with special responsibilities in public settings, and these responsibilities are *not* natural for them.   Greek rhetorical theory, as we know it, virtually ignored the problem. Romans and elocutionists counselled *learning* proper behaviors of nature.   Fénelon and others trusted nature and feelings completely, but candor forced the eclectic Blair to admit that some who want to speak are naturally clumsy until they *learn* otherwise.   Whately saw the *thought* as the generator of meaningful behavior, but it remained for Winans to emphasize the importance of being *dually* aware—of thought and of the communicative relationship with others.   Our treatment of delivery in chapter 10 developed from the Whately-Winans premises.

MEMORIA

Memoria has been called the "lost canon" of rhetoric, presumably meaning that no one pays attention to it any more.   The term *memoria* refers to that body of theory and advice that concerns managing and controlling utterance, according to plan, when speaking occurs.[38]   The English term *memory* connotes considerably less than the full range of rhetorical problems that confront a speaker who has prepared a speech and now must present it.   More than memorizing or recall of a plan is involved.   It is for this reason we are using the Latin term, there being no sound equivalent in English.

Speakers face problems involving *memoria* from the outset of speech preparation.   They must choose subjects they will be *able to command;* they must set purposes they *will still understand* when they

---

38. For a thorough discussion of memoria emphasizing its role among the ancients, see Harry Caplan, *Of Eloquence: Studies in Ancient and Mediaeval Rhetoric* (Ithaca, N.Y.: Cornell University Press, 1970), Essay IX, "Memoria: Treasure-House of Eloquence," pp. 196–246.

are speaking; they must build structures and frame outlines and notes they, themselves, *will be able to follow;* they must choose language natural enough to them so they *will be able to command it under pressure;* they must make plans for delivery they *will be able to execute;* and, of course, they must keep their wits and all their plans about them as they speak. Much more than *memory* is involved, but this has not always been recognized in Western thought about *memoria.*

For much of the classical era *memoria* meant little more than *memory* of one's speech. The earliest writers seem to have felt that the best service they could render speakers was to pass on instructions on memory systems. Thus the story of Simonides of Ceos is repeated in several books on rhetoric. Simonides was a poet. After reading a long, lyric poem at a banquet, he was called from the hall. Moments later the roof fell in, killing the remaining guests and disfiguring them beyond recognition. But Simonides was able to match the bodies and the names by mentally picturing the former seating arrangement. His alleged success dramatized for others the usefulness of associating ideas with spaces. One could then call up the spatial image and, by association, remember the ideas "put there."

The Simonides story came from Greece, but the Greek theorists we know of did not deal with those problems the Romans called the problems of *memoria.* The first extended treatment of the subject now known appears in the *Rhetorica ad Herennium.* There *memoria* is called "the guardian of all the parts of rhetoric," but the author seems not to have had a conception of a speech as a *plan* of internally grouped ideas. The story of Simonides is told to illustrate how an *artificial* memory system can help the *natural* memory. In short, this early Roman author seems to have been mainly interested in supplying his pupils with mnemonic devices for jogging their memories, whether the task was to recall words, related ideas, or situations.[39]

Cicero treated memoria briefly in *De Oratore,* and he emphasized the point that it is possible to store proofs in the mind in *interrelated ways* so they can be recalled as pertinent to specific lines of argument useful in building legal cases and legislative arguments. For him, the problem was to file away data and ideas in ways that would allow a speaker to recall and use those ideas *adaptively.* The problems of memoria were more complex for Cicero than the mere problem of memorizing, although he also gave advice on memorizing.

Quintilian's was the most extensive treatment of memoria among the existing ancient writings, but he generally followed Cicero's

---

39. Today people still use mnemonic systems such as those found in: Harry Lorayne and Jerry Lucas, *The Memory Book* (New York: Stern and Day, 1974); Donald A. Laird and Eleanor C. Laird, *Techniques for Efficient Remembering* (New York: McGraw-Hill Book Co., 1960); David M. Roth, *Roth Memory Course* (Cleveland, Ohio: Ralston Publishing Co., 1959); and Bruno Furst, *How to Remember* (New York: Greenburg, 1944).

topics of discussion.   Quintilian seems to have seen new dimensions of the subject, however, for he touched upon at least two new points. He observed—and was the first known writer to do so clearly—that paying attention to the (logical?) principles of rhetorical division and composition could be of great value to a speaker trying to command his speech in anticipation of delivering it.   "If our composition be what it should, the artistic sequence will serve to guide the memory."[40]   Here the connection between a speaker's *planning* and his *capacity to command* the whole discourse seems recognized.   A second new consideration recognized by Quintilian was that the psychological problems of commanding ideas and language during extemporaneous speaking are different from those faced when a speaker memorizes and delivers a *set* speech.   Once more, Quintilian seems to have been the ancient writer who saw most clearly that Simonides's mnemonic devices could not answer all of an active speaker's problems of self-command.

Except as treated in tracts on preaching, which stressed *division* (preview) as helpful to determining and remembering systems of arrangement, little was said in rhetorical treatises on rhetoric written during the Middle Ages.   True, Alcuin (c. 735–804) did advise the emperor Charlemagne that a speaker ought to avoid drunkenness if he expected his memory to function effectively![41]   In the main, however, it was not until the appearance of Thomas Wilson's *Arte of Rhetorique* that memoria was again discussed even at the level of Roman sophistication.   Since succeeding rhetorics tended to deal with both speaking and writing, the special problems of speakers' memoria received limited attention until the twentieth century.[42]

It is in textbooks on speaking published in the twentieth century that speakers' memoria problems have been faced with greater penetration than Quintilian's.   James Winans's and Charles Woolbert's early textbooks explained the contributions of the new discipline of psychology to solving speakers' problems of command during speaking. Borrowing from pragmatic psychology, Winans pointed to the importance of outlines as mental guides and assurances that speeches would be presented with their planned, "due proportion, emphasis, unity, and coherence."   Said Winans, outlines serve as visual images of the soundness and the "logic" of interconnections among ideas; once seen, these interconnections allow speakers to sense their observations as *wholes*, not as series of points.   Woolbert was devoted to a different psychology, behaviorism, so he stressed a different aspect of the theory of memoria. Let speakers *condition* themselves properly, was his major counsel.

---

40. *Institutio Oratoria*, trans. Butler, IV, p. 235, bk. IV, sec. 39.
41. Wilbur S. Howell, *The Rhetoric of Alcuin and Charlemagne* (Princeton: Princeton University Press, 1941), pp. 137, 139.
42. A more detailed discussion of memoria as treated in works we are passing over is Wayne E. Hoogestraat's "Memory: The Lost Canon?" *Quarterly Journal of Speech* XLVI (April 1960): 141–47.

Accordingly, he urged that speakers (and readers) first formulate the perspective of their material, then concentrate on details, doing both *orally*—so as to involve their sense of hearing in the acquisition of material—and performing all these functions in imagined or real circumstances as nearly approximating the actual circumstances of speaking as possible.

The psychologies on which Winans and Woolbert depended are partially outmoded today, but as each advance is made in understanding how human beings *learn*, advances can be made in solving the perennial problems of memoria that *public* speakers, especially, face. How we can best command the whole of our plans during the moments of speaking and adjusting to rhetorical situations is still not fully known; there is much mystery still.[43] But one idea held by both ancients and moderns seems especially valuable: commanding a *visual* plan of ideas and their interconnections—in outline or other form—establishes content and plan in the mind but with sufficient flexibility to allow the adaptive restructuring that public speech so often demands.

We have been concerned with command of material and action throughout this book—with mental and physical command. As we have treated invention, disposition, style, and delivery and the special problems of audience adaptation, we also have treated ways of solving the problems of command through consciousness of what one is doing in preparation and through bringing plans into visual, practiced form, the better to assure true memoria in the moments of speaking.

The matter of commanding the entire speech means that you must prepare carefully, both on paper and in oral rehearsal, to be wholly familiar with your material. What you intend to say must be at your beck and call to the degree that (1) you can return to your train of thought should there be some unforeseen interruption; (2) you can recover from a lapse of memory involving the omission of material you intended to include; (3) you can answer questions your audience may have when you have finished speaking; and (4) you can conceal your thoroughness of preparation by appearing to summon your thoughts freshly at the moment you utter them.

The degree of a speaker's command is revealed most in the moments of delivery. Evidences that the speaker is not in complete control include: slips of tongue, mispronunciations, forgetting ideas and connections, breaks in fluency (the "ers" and "uhs" we hear), awkward silences, poor transitions or none at all, staring into space as he or she tries to recapture his or her thoughts. (See pp. 42–45; 288–92.)

---

43. See, for example, Will Bradbury, "The Mystery of Memory," *Life* LXXI (November 12, 1971): 66–76, and Mark R. Rosenzweig, "Biologists Try to Learn Exactly How We Learn," *The New York Times*, January 12, 1970, p. 72C.

These are the reasons we have been concerned with command of material and action.

In the history of Western thought about oral rhetoric only disposition and memoria of the five great constellations of communicative problems have missed their hour in the limelight. Neither has ever dominated thought about public speech; invention, style, and delivery have so dominated, not without unfortunate results for balanced, forceful speaking.

The ancient Greeks laid a foundation for the art of public speech, importantly stressing the necessity of transforming thoughts into *communicable* thoughts. Romans refined and amplified, ultimately stultifying the art by excessive formalization in the period of the Roman Empire. Augustine christianized the Roman lore, but for preaching only. His achievement could not prevent later confusion of rhetoric with poetic or the ultimate absorption of rhetoric into logic. When the residual rhetoric was style, there were some who clung to the classical tradition in which invention was the key process in speech communication—an emphasis ultimately restored in the twentieth century despite the tempting distractions of naturalism and elocution. To the new classical revival, modern psychological and philosophical investigation has added and continues to add to the ways speakers can learn to meet those invariably present problems of speaking: deciding what to say, how to give it form, what language to use, how to present it, and how to keep plans under command.

If there is a practical lesson to be learned from this historical review, it seems to be that to neglect *any* or to overvalue *one* or *two* of these sets of problems has proved mistaken wherever it has occurred, across more than 2,500 years. But when men and women have thought as hard as they knew how about *all* of these problems, they have produced thought of historic significance and public speech of great practical and artistic merit.

BIBLIOGRAPHY OF LANDMARK WORKS IN RHETORIC[44]

Plato, *Gorgias.* Translated by W. R. Lamb. Cambridge, Mass.: Harvard University Press, 1925.*

——, *Phaedrus.* Translated by H. N. Fowler. Cambridge, Mass.: Harvard University Press, 1914.*

---

44. We have listed here the most reliable and, where contemporary editions are available, most readily obtainable editions. The works are listed in chronological order. Works identified by * are in the Loeb Classical Library series.

Aristotle, *The Rhetoric of Aristotle.* Translated and edited by Lane Cooper. New York: Appleton-Century-Crofts, 1932.

Rhetorica ad Herennium. Translated by Harry Caplan. Cambridge, Mass.: Harvard University Press, 1954.*

Cicero, *De Oratore.* Translated by E. W. Sutton and H. Rackham. 2 vols. Cambridge, Mass.: Harvard University Press, 1942.*

Quintilian, *The Institutio Oratoria of Quintilian.* Translated by H. E. Butler. Cambridge, Mass.: Harvard University Press, 1953.*

Longinus, "On the Sublime." Translated by W. Rhys Roberts. In J. H. Smith and E. W. Parks, *The Great Critics,* 3rd ed. New York: W. W. Norton, 1951.

Saint Augustine, *On Christian Doctrine.* Translated by D. W. Robertson, Jr. Indianapolis: The Bobbs-Merrill Co., Inc., 1958.

Bacon, Francis—See Wallace, Karl R., *Francis Bacon on Communication and Rhetoric.* Chapel Hill: The University of North Carolina Press, 1943. (This is a masterful synthesis of Bacon's ideas on rhetoric as found in the works mentioned in this chapter.)

Fénelon, *Dialogues on Eloquence.* Translated by Wilbur S. Howell. Princeton: Princeton University Press, 1951.

Sheridan, Thomas, *A Course of Lectures on Elocution.* London, 1762.

Steele, Joshua, *Prosodia Rationalis.* London, 1779.

Austin, Gilbert, *Chironomia or a Treatise on Rhetorical Delivery.* Edited by Mary Margaret Robb and Lester Thonssen. Carbondale, Ill.: Southern Illinois University Press, 1966.

Campbell, George, *The Philosophy of Rhetoric.* Edited by Lloyd Bitzer. Carbondale, Ill.: Southern Illinois University Press, 1963.

Blair, Hugh, *Lectures on Rhetoric and Belles Lettres.* Edited by Harold F. Harding. Carbondale, Ill.: Southern Illinois University Press, 1965.

Whately, Richard, *Elements of Rhetoric.* Edited by Douglas Ehninger. Carbondale, Ill.: Southern Illinois University Press, 1963.

Winans, James A., *Public Speaking.* New York: Century Company, 1917.

Woolbert, Charles H., *The Fundamentals of Speech: A Behavioristic Study of the Underlying Principles of Speaking and Reading.* New York: Harper & Brothers Publishers, 1920.

Richards, I. A., *The Philosophy of Rhetoric.* New York: Oxford University Press, 1965.

Burke, Kenneth, *A Grammar of Motives and A Rhetoric of Motives.* Berkeley. The University of California Press, 1969.

Toulmin, Stephen E., *The Uses of Argument.* New York: The Cambridge University Press, 1958.

Perelman, Chaim, and Olbrechts-Tyteca, L., *The New Rhetoric: A Treatise on Argument.* Translated by John Wilkinson and Purcell Weaver. Notre Dame, Ind.: University of Notre Dame Press, 1969.

EXERCISES

Written

1. Write a book review (1,500–2,000 words) treating the whole or a part of one of the works on rhetorical theory mentioned in this chapter.

2. Write an essay comparing the treatments of one of the rhetorical canons (invention, disposition, style, delivery, or memoria) in two of the books cited in this chapter. For example, compare Aristotle's theory of oral style with Blair's, or Cicero's theory of delivery with Whately's.
3. Explore some contemporary psychological research on communicative credibility and write a report comparing those findings with Aristotle's speculations (or Cicero's or Quintilian's).

Oral

1. Prepare and deliver a two- to three-minute speech introducing a person whose name is mentioned in this chapter. Assume that he is about to deliver a lecture to your class on an aspect of rhetorical theory.
2. After reading in one of the works mentioned in this chapter, make a short report on some aspect of theory that you feel is applicable to speech making today.
3. With four or five classmates engage in a discussion on the question, "What is it to be 'natural' in speaking publicly?" When your group has come to a conclusion or unresolvable disagreement, report the results to your class.

Appendix B

Speech Criticism

INTRODUCTION

What follows is the text of a classroom presentation of a critique developed by a group of students enrolled in a first course in effective speaking. The course stressed processes of group problem solving as well as problems in public speaking. The first assignment or problem to be solved by each of several groups of students was this: "To what extent, if at all, did _____ fulfill the exigences or requirements of the rhetorical situation he or she faced?" Each group of students chose some example of public speech, studied the situation and the speech for approximately two and one-half weeks, outlined the group's critical conclusions about the rhetoric involved, and organized and presented its findings to the entire class.

The group whose presentation is printed here chose to attend a mass meeting of students, presided over by a student panel, which assembled to consider and, probably, to protest a new university policy regulating the consumption of alcohol on university premises. Having tape recorded a considerable portion of the meeting, the group of speech students decided to focus their criticism on a talk given at the mass meeting by Dr. M. Lee Upcraft, director of residential life at the University Park campus of The Pennsylvania State University.

While developing their criticism, the students studied and discussed the contents of chapters 1, 5, portions of chapter 9, and chapter 11 of *Public Speaking as a Liberal Art*. Since the group presentation was the student's first formal speaking in this class, they had also read and discussed portions of chapter 2.

On the evening before the presentation printed here, one of the students in the group telephoned Dr. Upcraft to tell him of the presentation and to invite him to attend the class if he found it convenient. He attended.   Neither the instructor nor most of the speakers realized until moments before the presentation that Dr. Upcraft would be present to hear and respond to the critique.

The presentation took place on October 4, 1976.   It illustrates what is commonly called a *panel* or *symposium* format in which several speakers participate in presentation of a public message.   It also exemplifies the everyday fact that problem-solving groups are very often responsible for presenting their informal findings to audiences.

Joe: We're going to analyze for you a speech by Dr. Lee Upcraft, and the reason we picked the Upcraft speech was that it's a contemporary speech, a relevant speech to all the people that were involved, and it was something that the rest of you students in the class could relate to.

First I want to give you a little more background on the overall problem that the speech was concerned with.   Are you all familiar with the incident this summer, in which a student consumed too much alcohol and nearly died?   [Indications that the audience knew of the incident.]   Ok.   The result of this incident and what followed was much student unrest.   There were massive demonstrations planned, and everyone was hating the university and hating Dr. Upcraft for the change in the policy [concerning the presence and consumption of alcohol in university housing].

So this was the reason a meeting was called, so that all the people that were concerned could testify at this hearing—give their opinions.   And all the information could be brought out, so that a decision could be reached [by the Student Government Panel].

Now, the goals of our project are to show (1) how Dr. Upcraft made clear to the students the position that the university was in, and (2) how he defused the meeting and redirected the students' anger away from the university and the Office of Residential Life onto the State of Pennsylvania.

Now, the way we have our presentation set up is, first, you all have mimeographed sheets of that speech.   Second, we're going to play the tape of the speech so that you can get a little bit of the atmosphere and know how the speech was presented.   Afterwards we're going to analyze the speech section by section, as we have it set up on the mimeographed sheets.

Now we'll play the speech; after that Kathy will be first and she will analyze the introduction of the speech.   Ok, now we'll play the speech.

DR. M. LEE UPCRAFT: TO A MASS MEETING OF STUDENTS
[1] *I appreciate the opportunity to make a few remarks about this.   I think it's important to talk a little bit about the context under which this policy was developed.   For those of you who weren't around*

in 1972. Before 1972, there were no alcoholic beverages permitted on campus, anyplace. In '72, the committee that was revising the discipline system suggested that, as a part of the code of conduct, students who were twenty-one would be allowed to drink in their individual residence-hall rooms. As a result of that committee's recommendations, the president and the board accepted Article J of the current code of conduct, which, to paraphrase it, says something like: Use and possession of alcohol are prohibited on campus, except in individual residence hall rooms.

[2] I think, for a while, the consumption of alcohol was contained in individual resident hall rooms; so it didn't present a problem for us. But I think over the last four years, the consumption of alcohol in the residence halls has increased. It's increased not only in terms of individual consumption in rooms, but it's also increased in the number of larger gatherings where people who were of age, and who were not of age, were consuming alcohol in the residence halls.

[3] I think the Collegian *is probably quite correct, in a sense, that the university probably did adopt a policy of what they called "benign neglect." That is, unless the alcohol consumption created a problem for us in terms of a disturbance or some control problem, unless it was directly brought to our attention, we were ignoring it.*

[4] Then the infamous incident this summer in which a student nearly lost his life as a result of overconsuming alcohol. And I think that probably brought to my attention, and to the attention of the university, the potential dangers and the potential liabilities involved in continuing to tolerate underage drinking in the residence halls.

[5] I think the reason why we have gone in the direction we have is that, historically, the university has and does assume the responsibility for enforcing the university rules and regulations. Once you accept that responsibility, then, if you're negligent in the performance of that responsibility, I think you can be held legally liable. Our attorneys tell us that that is a definite possibility; and if we directly observe it, we have to do something about it. If we don't do something about it, then we can be held accountable in the courts.

[6] I'm not going to comment on the specific incident of this summer, or the action that was taken as a result of it, because it is a personal matter. But let's suppose there was a student at some hypothetical university, at some hypothetical time, who did consume too much alcohol, and nearly died, or something serious happened to him. If one of our staff members directly observed the alcohol going into that room, and if one of our staff knew that there were underaged people in the room or were planning to be there, and if the staff member directly observed people drinking and did nothing about it, then if something happened at that party which resulted in physical or psychological damage to someone, it's fairly clear that the university could be held liable and could be held responsible.

[7] As the director of residential life, I am not going to put my staff in a position where, through "benign neglect," they're going to get

themselves into legal trouble, and in some way be held accountable for
something that some student does that's dumb.

[8] *I think, probably, if there is any one reason why we decided*
to pursue this policy, it was precisely that—that we could no longer
continue to skate on thin ice; we could no longer continue to put the
university, and my position, and the position of the RA's [resident
assistant's] in such jeopardy.

[9] *I think as a state institution, we have assumed the responsi-*
bility of enforcing state laws. And so long as that responsibility stays
with the institution, I don't see how we can back away from doing
something about underage drinking in the residence halls, when we
observe it, and when we know about it.

[10] *I think it's a very difficult position that I'm in. It's a very*
difficult position the RA is in, and a very difficult position the university
is in. I think—my own personal opinion is that the state drinking age
should be lowered to eighteen and the privilege should be extended to
include all of the people in Pennsylvania. When they're eighteen they
can own a bar, but they can't drink in it. That doesn't make much
sense to me. I'm surprised that it hasn't been constitutionally chal-
lenged. I'm not on a moral crusade. I grew up in New York. I went
to school in New York. I was able to drink when I was eighteen, and
I don't think the problems of alcohol and alcohol abuse among students
in New York is any greater or any less than they have with students
in Pennsylvania.

[11] *As far as courses of action are concerned, I think there are*
several things that I hope the panel will look at. First of all, probably
Article J of the code of conduct ought to be reconsidered. From a very
practical standpoint, this article, if strictly interpreted, and strictly
enforced, would mean that no one could drink in the residence hall
rooms. Because it would be illegal to transport alcohol from the source
of supply to the room. It's also not consistent with practice in that the
Nittany Lion Inn has a liquor license. The Faculty Club would like to
get one, and the Kern graduate building, under certain circumstances,
allows alcohol to be served. But I think, at a basic level, we have to
look at Article J and at least bring it into line with current practice. I
think a second issue that the people here tonight ought to consider and
the panel ought to consider in its recommendations, is whether or not
the university should continue in loco parentis, that is, continue to act
on behalf of the state in enforcing underage drinking laws in the residence
halls. I personally think that issue ought to be thought through very
carefully. Apparently what happens is, if your RA catches you drink-
ing, he writes a referral. If you're twenty-one, and caught drinking in
the wrong place, chances are you'll get a warning letter from the Office
of Public Standards, with no disciplinary action, merely a warning
letter. If underage drinking is involved, and it's proven that that was
the case, chances are you'll get a disciplinary warning. That's the
lowest of the disciplinary actions taken. It's on your transcript for the
length of the time of the action, and it's removed from your transcript—

your permanent transcript—once that's over. The advantages of this system are that, in no way does your university record—rather, there is no criminal record kept.

[12] If the university absolves itself of its responsibility for liquor enforcement, then the alternative, if a student wanted to do something about somebody, underage, drinking, would be to call the police. In that instance you would involve civil authorities, you would involve the possibility of establishing in your record a fact which might influence such things as getting into law school, graduate school, and medical school, and so forth. So I think when you're considering whether or not the university should absolve itself of that responsibility, what you are in effect doing is transferring the consequences for the student from the university to society. Frankly, society is much more strict, and keeps records around a lot longer than the university does. But I think that's a legitimate question to raise and talk about.

[13] I think probably the other thing I'd like to comment on, which I spoke to you of briefly before, is the fact that I think it's probably going to be very difficult to deal with this situation unless the state of Pennsylvania does something about its drinking age. As an administrator, I don't like to say that to a student, "OK if you don't like what's going on here, write to your congressman." I think in some ways that's a put-off. On the other hand, I do in this instance feel that part of the problem is the fact that the state has an unrealistic drinking age, and I think steps should be taken to encourage the legislature to lower the drinking age, or to challenge the constitutionality of that law. These are some things you should give consideration to.

[14] I don't particularly like the position I'm in, but I don't feel as if I have any other choice. And I think until something changes in regard to the circumstances I am presented with, I really don't feel as though any other stance can be taken by the university at this point.

[15] I'd like to say something else about strategy, particularly if you're concerned about lowering the drinking age. A lot of outraged students, and I think justifiably outraged students, have suggested some sort of massive action, some demonstration of that outrage. I think you have to very carefully consider what the impact of that is going to be. There are people in the legislature who, for one reason or another, think that eighteen-year-olds shouldn't drink. Whether they think you're too immature to handle it, or whether they think that traffic accident fatalities will increase, or whatever. But I don't think that the prospect of 2,000 roaring drunk students in the quad of East Halls is going to convince the legislature of your maturity. I furthermore don't think it's going to convince the university to change its policy. I think the most constructive forms of action are the three things I've suggested: consider Article J, consider whether or not the university should continue its enforcement stance for this location, and consider taking some constructive steps to lower the drinking age. As I said in the Collegian, if any of those things change, I'll be the first one to stand in some public place in the university, and personally burn this policy.

[16] *I will be here for the rest of the evening. I want to listen carefully to what the students have to say, and I'd be glad to respond to any questions of the panel.*

Kathy: A thing any speaker has to do in introducing what he has to say is get and keep the audience's attention.   And he has to somehow let the audience know what he is talking about.   Dr. Upcraft did this by presenting the history of the policy.   He brought the audience up to date about how the policy came to be and how the situation had worsened.   He points out, in fact, that although the university didn't corral anyone, it was the rule that students under twenty-one were not to drink.

It's important to notice that he implies that students over twenty-one *were* allowed to drink, so long as no disturbances resulted.   In other words the university was giving a privilege to students. One student took advantage of that privilege, and in so doing he forced the university to change and adopt the new system.

Dr. Upcraft argues that as long as Article J is there to be enforced, the university is going to have to more stringently enforce it and the state laws.

Dr. Upcraft redirects the students' hostility from the university to the state by saying that the university was allowing the students to enjoy themselves until one student, as you'll recall, forced the university to completely change its policy in order to enforce the laws of the state, or face a stiff lawsuit, or be held otherwise accountable in the courts.

Now, Ron will show you more about this redirection of attitudes.

Ron: I have two points to make about how Dr. Upcraft redirected the hostility of the students in his audience, and the university Student Government in general.

The first point is that he used special examples to sway the hostility of the students to the state.   Without such examples, it would be hard to change a hostile person's opinion.   Just as, if as I talk to you, I *tell* you to change opinion, that says nothing.   I need to use examples, too.   Now here is my example of Dr. Upcraft's use of examples.   It will show you what I mean.   It's on your first page, fifth paragraph.   Dr. Upcraft says, "I think the reason why. . . . [Reads the entire paragraph.]

Now here, Upcraft has used a good example, because he doesn't try to snow his audience, but he tells them what can happen in the state courts.   This shows they are *forced* to be responsible.

The second point I would like to make is in reference to a sentence in which Dr. Upcraft says it is the state laws which make the university adopt the antidrinking policy.   Therefore it is the state, and not the university, at which the students should be hostile.   This sentence is on the second page, paragraph 9.   Here Upcraft says, "I think as a state institution, we have assumed the responsibility of enforcing state laws."   In other words, as long as the university stands as a part of the bureaucracy, it must enforce the laws of the bureaucracy. Just so long as, he says, the university is a part of that system, "responsibility stays with the institution." So, the university must do what it does because it is a state institution.

We believe these examples of the university's position work not so much to admit that the university *chooses* to enforce its policy as to assert that it is the state laws that *compel* the university to be responsible, not just to students. We think this is another way Dr. Upcraft diverts students' irritation. You can almost hear them say, "If it wasn't for those blankety-blank state laws, and if the university wasn't a blankety-blank state institution, there'd be no problem with the university at all." Dr. Upcraft might have said this himself and gotten applause, but, of course, this wasn't possible for *him*, in this rhetorical situation, without repercussions.

Now Patti, and a little later Greg, will point out how Dr. Upcraft uses himself as a proof in this speech.

Patti: Dr. Upcraft also tried to persuade the students to see *his* side of the issue. This happens, for example, on the second page of the text at paragraph 10. There, he asks the audience to consider the difficulty of the position he is in. Immediately he gives his own personal opinion that the drinking age ought to be lowered, and with this he identifies with the audience's probable views. By these processes he establishes his own status as a persuader, apart from the state and its rules. This is another turning point at which he switches blame from the university, *and himself,* to the state; he absolves himself and the university of blame by this process.

Another example of how he develops his own image as a source of proof appears in this same paragraph 10. Here Dr. Upcraft is saying the university is in a very difficult position because of the law. And he criticizes the law, first with irony: an eighteen-year-old can own a bar but can't drink in it. He gets some humor here, but he makes a point and makes himself believable. Then he goes on to a personal testimony: "I grew up in New York, I went to school in New York. . . ." [reads entire sentence]. We think he not only uses himself as an experienced authority here but that he probably made students think additional things like, "And I can drive at eighteen and be drafted at eighteen," and so on.

From this he goes on to use his built-up authority with the audience to propose revision of Article J and other steps. We think he's in a position to do this, now, just because he has established himself as a person not responsible for what he had to do, and as one whose opinions are very much like the students'. You'll also notice that in paragraph 11 he is shifting the responsibility for future action. In other words, the university personnel can't do anything except what they are doing until *someone else* changes the rules.

Now, Greg is going to continue with this analysis.

Greg: You'll notice that Upcraft points out that the penalties imposed by the university are a lot less severe than those that would be imposed by civil authorities. This is especially true with regard to records of any infraction. As Upcraft pointed out in his speech, your academic record won't carry anything that will stand against you if you're trying to get into med school or law school or something like that. University records of infractions are expunged when the time of a penalty is over.

Now, you'll have to admit that it's doubtful that Dr. Upcraft convinced his audience that the university acts out of the bigness of its heart in protecting students against a police record. But he has made progress toward his goal, which seems to be to make the state, rather than the university, the villain here. And he gives some reasons for hanging on to Article J. In paragraph 12 he's arguing that for the university itself to accept responsibility is really a good thing. This puts Dr. Upcraft, the university, and the students—even on this drinking policy—all on the same side, against state policies regarding drinking and enforcement on a campus.

It's in paragraph 13 that Dr. Upcraft really throws the blame on Harrisburg for the whole situation. He calls the Pennsylvania state law on the drinking age unrealistic, and he continues with recommendations for positive action by the students. He encourages students to try to convince the legislature to change the law, and even to challenge the constitutionality of the law.

Now, probably, none of these solutions is really practical. It's unlikely that students could make them work. However, just the fact that he gives them supports the belief that Dr. Upcraft is really on the students' side and that he and the university have been forced into this situation by an unrealistic and possibly unconstitutional law about the drinking age. Dr. Upcraft again establishes himself as a support for his own position because he declares his support for students' efforts to get these changes.

Now, Stephanie will show you how Dr. Upcraft closed his speech.

Stephanie: The conclusion of this speech fulfills the important functions of any conclusion. It shows that Dr. Upcraft was there to help the students find some action that would do some good. He repeats that he doesn't like the position he's in, but that until outside policies change he'll continue to be in this awkward position. But instead of just saying, "This is your problem. You take care of it," he goes on to offer three cautions about what the students can do and how to do it. This again shows that he's not against the students. It's very important that he doesn't condone any outrageous behavior by the students—like a demonstration at East Halls. Here, he gets at the students' reason and practical sense. He makes the students see how much of a drawback it would be to their real goals. Then he turns to a new strategy and, in what I think is a key point in the speech, he repeats a pledge he made earlier in the *Collegian:* "If any of those things [policies] change, I'll be the first one to stand in some public place in the university and personally burn this policy." Thus, at the end, he clarifies one last time that he is for and not against the general principle for which the students came together at this meeting. He implies, as he has throughout, that he's also willing to work *with* the students.

He ends by saying he's going to stay with the students, *here.* He will listen, and he implies he will do so sympathetically. And he'll respond to any questions. All in all, the speech ends on precisely the right note to put aside anger at him or at the university. The last part of the speech adds up to saying, "If you help me, I'll help you. So, let's work together on *our* problem."

Now, Joe is going to sum up our analysis of Dr. Upcraft's address to the students and officers of the university Student Government. Joe.

Joe: I'd like to conclude our presentation by giving you a brief summation of what actually happened as a result of this rhetorical effort.

In regard to Dr. Upcraft's goal, which was to, we believe, redirect the students' anger away from Penn State onto the state of Pennsylvania, the committee that heard him sent out a report on the alcohol policy. The main points of this report were to reconsider Article J, as Dr. Upcraft advised, and, second, to initiate a statewide lobby and letter-writing campaign in order to lower the state drinking age to eighteen, which Dr. Upcraft also mentioned.

As far as the students were concerned, there was no mass action resulting from this meeting, so our group has concluded that the speech was very effective in actual fact. We think he attained his goals by means of the rhetorical processes we have outlined in our report today.

That's our presentation, and we'll be glad to answer any questions. As an added factor on this particular occasion, Dr. Upcraft is sitting in the back of the room, so we can also get his opinions on our opinions about his speech.

Dr. Upcraft: I wish the people who attended the hearing that night had been as open minded as these six panelists were. It wasn't an entirely open-minded audience; let's put it that way. I went into that situation mainly to state my position and do the things you've suggested. My main goal was to get students to understand why we did what we did. I wasn't, I think, in a persuasive mood quite so much as you tend to suggest. When you use words like "strategy" and so forth, I want to say that I knew the audience and I wasn't foolish enough to think I was going to *persuade* very many people one way or the other. For that reason I tried to focus my attention on the members of the panel that was to lead discussion that night, because I knew they were reasonable students. I was there more to persuade the panel [at the meeting] than to testify before all the audience of students. The whole audience, I felt, was pretty much a lost cause.

I think you're right. I was trying to redirect students' concern to the liquor laws of the state and away from Penn State. I was trying to get them to *understand* why we did what we did, rather than trying to persuade them that what we did was *right*.

I wish I had your optimism about how successful my speech was. I don't think the issue is quite as dead as, perhaps, you think it is.

I gave a completely extemporaneous speech. I was not operating from any notes. I just did a lot of thinking about what I wanted to say, before I went there. It's a strange feeling to hear yourself again, and to read yourself in print. I also want to say to the class that I didn't know anything about this whole business until last night when Joe called to invite me here. I appreciate that.

Now, the only criticism I would have of your critique of my speech is that I think you're giving me too much credit. At least, I didn't set about, consciously, to accomplish all the things that you said I did. I was just hoping to get out of there alive.

Special Index for the Study of Types of Speeches

This index is designed as an aid to students and teachers who want to structure the study or preparation of speeches around purposes for which speeches are made. The general section of the index identifies treatments of topics pertinent to all or to several purposes. Subsequent sections indicate the portions of this book that relate directly or have special relevance to a specific type of speech.

Index

r